T0280228

RATIONALITY AND THE
GENETIC CHALLENGE

Should we make people healthier, smarter, and longer-lived if genetic and medical advances enable us to do so? Matti Häyry asks this question in the context of genetic testing and selection, cloning and stem cell research, gene therapies and enhancements. The ethical questions explored include parental responsibility, the use of people as means, the role of hope and fear in risk assessment, and the dignity and meaning of life.

Taking as a starting point the arguments presented by Jonathan Glover, John Harris, Ronald M. Green, Jürgen Habermas, Michael J. Sandel, and Leon R. Kass, who defend a particular normative view as the only rational or moral answer, Matti Häyry argues that many coherent rationalities and moralities exist in the field, and that to claim otherwise is a mistake.

MATTI HÄYRY is Professor of Bioethics and Philosophy of Law at the University of Manchester and Professorial Fellow at the University of Helsinki Collegium for Advanced Studies, Finland.

CAMBRIDGE LAW, MEDICINE AND ETHICS

This series of books was founded by Cambridge University Press with Alexander McCall Smith as its first editor in 2003. It focuses on the law's complex and troubled relationship with medicine across both the developed and the developing world. In the past twenty years, we have seen in many countries increasing resort to the courts by dissatisfied patients and a growing use of the courts to attempt to resolve intractable ethical dilemmas. At the same time, legislatures across the world have struggled to address the questions posed by both the successes and the failures of modern medicine, while international organisations such as the WHO and UNESCO now regularly address issues of medical law.

It follows that we would expect ethical and policy questions to be integral to the analysis of the legal issues discussed in this series. The series responds to the high profile of medical law in universities, in legal and medical practice, as well as in public and political affairs. We seek to reflect the evidence that many major health-related policy debates in the UK, Europe and the international community over the past two decades have involved a strong medical law dimension. Organ retention, embryonic stem cell research, physician-assisted suicide and the allocation of resources to fund health care are but a few examples among many. The emphasis of this series is thus on matters of public concern and/or practical significance. We look for books that could make a difference to the development of medical law and enhance the role of medico-legal debate in policy circles. That is not to say that we lack interest in the important theoretical dimensions of the subject, but we aim to ensure that theoretical debate is grounded in the realities of how the law does and should interact with medicine and health care.

General Editors
Professor Margaret Brazier, *University of Manchester*
Professor Graeme Laurie, *University of Edinburgh*

Editorial Advisory Board
Professor Richard Ashcroft, *Queen Mary, University of London*
Professor Martin Bobrow, *University of Cambridge*
Dr. Alexander Morgan Capron, *Director, Ethics and Health, World Health Organization, Geneva*
Professor Jim Childress, *University of Virginia*
Professor Ruth Chadwick, *Cardiff Law School*
Dame Ruth Deech, *University of Oxford*
Professor John Keown, *Georgetown University, Washington, D.C.*
Dr. Kathy Liddell, *University of Cambridge*
Professor Alexander McCall Smith, *University of Edinburgh*
Professor Dr. Mónica Navarro-Michel, *University of Barcelona*

Marcus Radetzki, Marian Radetzki, Niklas Juth
Genes and Insurance: Ethical, Legal and Economic Issues
Ruth Macklin
Double Standards in Medical Research in Developing Countries
Donna Dickenson
Property in the Body: Feminist Perspectives
Matti Häyry, Ruth Chadwick, Vilhjálmur Árnason, Gardar Árnason
*The Ethics and Governance of Human Genetic Databases: European
Perspectives*
Ken Mason
The Troubled Pregnancy: Legal Wrongs and Rights in Reproduction
Daniel Sperling
Posthumous Interests: Legal and Ethical Perspectives
Keith Syrett
Law, Legitimacy and the Rationing of Healthcare
Alastair Maclean
Autonomy, Informed Consent and the Law: A Relational Change
Heather Widdows, Caroline Mullen
The Governance of Genetic Information: Who Decides?
David Price
Human Tissue in Transplantation and Research
Matti Häyry
Rationality and the Genetic Challenge: Making People Better?

RATIONALITY AND THE GENETIC CHALLENGE

Making People Better?

MATTI HÄYRY

CAMBRIDGE
UNIVERSITY PRESS

CAMBRIDGE UNIVERSITY PRESS
Cambridge, New York, Melbourne, Madrid, Cape Town, Singapore,
São Paulo, Delhi, Dubai, Tokyo, Mexico City

Cambridge University Press
The Edinburgh Building, Cambridge CB2 8RU, UK

Published in the United States of America by Cambridge University Press, New York

www.cambridge.org
Information on this title: www.cambridge.org/9780521763363

First published by Cambridge University Press 2010

A catalogue record for this publication is available from the British Library

ISBN 978-0-521-76336-3 Hardback
ISBN 978-0-521-75713-3 Paperback

CONTENTS

Preface   *page* xi

1   Seven ways of making people better   1
 1.1 The genetic challenge   1
 1.2 The best babies   3
 1.3 Deaf embryos   6
 1.4 Saviour siblings   9
 1.5 Reproductive cloning   11
 1.6 Embryonic stem cells   14
 1.7 Gene therapies   16
 1.8 Considerable life extension   19
 1.9 The questions   22

2   Rational approaches to the genetic challenge   24
 2.1 Six authors, three approaches   24
 2.2 Rational tangibility: Glover and Harris   28
 2.3 Moral transcendence: Kass and Sandel   31
 2.4 Everybody's acceptance: Habermas and Green   35
 2.5 Why none of the approaches is *the* one   40
 2.6 A nonconfrontational notion of rationality   43
 2.7 Equilibria, equipoises, and polite bystanders   48
 2.8 Plan for the rest of the book   50

3   The best babies and parental responsibility   52
 3.1 From infanticide to embryo selection and beyond   52
 3.2 Parental responsibility as seen by Plato, Aristotle,
     Kant, and Mill   55
 3.3 Disregard and givenness   58
 3.4 Knowledge and moderation   61
 3.5 Procreative beneficence as a duty   64
 3.6 Arithmetical rationality   67
 3.7 Assumed parental roles   70

3.8 Moral limits   72
3.9 Parental rationalities   75

4   Deaf embryos, morality, and the law   78
4.1 Deafness as a test case   78
4.2 Techniques and their uses   79
4.3 Case, options, and stands   80
4.4 Moral case for the 'medical view'   81
4.5 Moral case for the 'social view'   84
4.6 Case for legal permissiveness   86
4.7 The instability of the situation   87
4.8 Moral case for the 'medical view' reconsidered   88
4.9 Moral case for the 'social view' reconsidered   90
4.10 Towards a nondirective compromise   92
4.11 The nondirective compromise   94
4.12 Contested rationalities   95

5   Saviour siblings and treating people as a means   99
5.1 Facts and regulations   99
5.2 The logic of the case   101
5.3 What could justify invasive procedures?   103
5.4 Why would noninvasive procedures be a problem?   106
5.5 Rational consent and genetic privacy   108
5.6 Means, mere means, and outcomes   109
5.7 Means, individuals, and values   113
5.8 Green's three readings of Kant   116
5.9 Ends *and* means: two different principles?   119
5.10 Saving rationalities   122

6   Reproductive cloning and designing human beings   124
6.1 An almost universal condemnation   124
6.2 Distinctions and politics   125
6.3 The case for cautious progress   127
6.4 Arguments for an absolute prohibition   130
6.5 Lack of limits and defective individuals   131
6.6 Asexual reproduction and distorted families   134
6.7 Project of mastery and misshapen communities   136
6.8 Loss of mystery and perverted societies   138
6.9 Forsaken self-understanding and a confused species   140
6.10 Design for a transhuman world   142
6.11 Cloning rationalities   144

7   Embryonic stem cells, vulnerability, and sanctity   146
    7.1 What, why, and how regulated?   146
    7.2 Alternatives and conjectures   148
    7.3 Connections with ethical challenges   152
    7.4 Would women be unnecessarily used?   153
    7.5 Would women be unfairly used?   156
    7.6 Would women be wrongfully used?   160
    7.7 The destruction of embryos is always wrong   164
    7.8 The destruction of embryos is never wrong   167
    7.9 The destruction of embryos is sometimes wrong   169
    7.10 Embryonic rationalities   172

8   Gene therapies, hopes, and fears   174
    8.1 Trials and errors   174
    8.2 Somatic and germ-line interventions   177
    8.3 Therapies and enhancements   180
    8.4 Construing benefits and harms   182
    8.5 Defining values   184
    8.6 Technological optimism and pessimism   187
    8.7 Technological determinism and voluntarism   189
    8.8 Precaution, fear, and hope   190
    8.9 Therapeutic rationalities   193

9   Considerable life extension and the meaning of life   195
    9.1 Mortality and ageing   195
    9.2 Towards considerable longevity   197
    9.3 Identity beyond considerable longevity   200
    9.4 How mortality benefits individuals   204
    9.5 How freedom to choose benefits individuals   206
    9.6 From individual immortality to social transcendence   211
    9.7 Natural morality and the meaning of life   212
    9.8 Immortal rationalities   215

10 Taking the genetic challenge rationally   220
    10.1 From challenges to solutions   220
    10.2 Basic tenets and their interpretations   220
    10.3 Arguments that cut both ways   223
    10.4 Arguments for and against   226
    10.5 What is required of a complete case?   227
    10.6 Measuring the challenge   229
    10.7 Sensing the challenge   232

10.8 Negotiating the challenge   234
10.9 The methods of genethics   236
10.10 Taking the genetic challenge nonconfrontationally   237

Bibliography   241
Index   261

Would you like your child to be healthy, strong, and clever? Would you like your child to be similar to you? If you have a seriously sick child, would you like to have another child who could provide a cure? Many parents have answered 'Yes' to these questions, and a growing number of scientists are trying to accommodate their wishes by perfecting technologies for prenatal selection.

What about yourself? Would you like to have a cure for ailments that threaten your life and health? Would you like to live longer? Would you like to live forever? Many people have answered 'Yes' to these questions, too, and an equally growing number of scientists are trying to accommodate *their* wishes by developing stem cell treatments, gene therapies, and other new remedies.

Other people, including many parents-to-be, have objected to these developments. Some have claimed that choosing your child is an uncaring thing to do, because children should be accepted as they are. Others have stated that it is wrong to use infants or embryos as medicine. And some have argued that genetic alterations will change human life beyond recognition.

This is a book about genetic selection and therapies and their impact on our lives. It is also a book about the moral and political concerns that parents, scientists, public decision makers, and academic ethicists have regarding attempts to make better future people and to make existing people better. But most of all, this is a book about bioethical rationalities – on distinct and self-contained ways of thinking about emerging technologies and their applications to medicine and healthcare.

Meaningful ethical discussion on genetic selection and novel treatments is often hampered by deep disagreements concerning the nature of rationality and morality. People tend to think that only one rationality or one morality exists; that those who disagree with them are unreasonable or evil; and that all ethical issues can be solved once and for all by employing their own point of view. The point of this book is to show that rationalities vary, that disagreement is not necessarily an indication of stupidity or wickedness, and that although ethical issues have solutions within individual rationalities, they cannot be universally solved by intellectual arguments. People should listen to each other more and try to understand each other's ways of thinking. This would not automatically give us the right answers to our questions. But it could help us to get rid of some of the currently popular wrong answers, and possibly pave the way to finding better ones in the future.

This book has had a long gestation period. In a sense, I made preparations for it for a quarter of a century, since my graduation in philosophy in 1984. My first two topics in bioethics were beginning-of-life and end-of-life issues, which still loom large in selective and therapeutic choices. A few years later I turned my attention to genetics and participated in the debates on prenatal selection and the use of modified organisms, on cloning and stem cell research, and eventually on designer babies and impending immortality. During the past decade, I entertained half a dozen different ideas about a monograph on these developments and their ethical dimensions; but none of these survived the rapid scientific and political changes in the field.

My first serious attempt to put my thoughts together in the order in which they appear in this book was in spring 2006, when I taught a course on applied moral philosophy to postgraduate students at the University of Manchester. Thanks are due to them for many insightful comments. Encouraged by the experience, I then applied for funding to investigate things further and to have sufficient time for writing. As a result, my Manchester colleagues at the Centre for Social Ethics and Policy, the Institute for Science, Ethics and Innovation, and the School of Law granted me research leave for seven months in 2008. This was followed in 2009 by a fellowship at the Helsinki Collegium for Advanced Studies, which enabled me to complete my research and finalise the book. My thanks are due to these institutions for their support.

I have also received institutional and financial support from the Department of Social and Moral Philosophy at the University of Helsinki, the Academy of Finland (projects 38996, 50040, and 105139), and the Wellcome Strategic Programme 'The Human Body, Its Scope and Limits' at the Institute for Science, Ethics and Innovation. I acknowledge all these instances of support with gratitude.

Peter Herissone-Kelly read the manuscript with a critical eye and provided invaluable comments. Lotika Singha copyedited the manuscript with admirable skill, thoroughness, and forbearance.

My biggest thanks go to Tuija Takala, who has patiently read and commented on all the chapters and prevented me from saying things that I did not want to say.

1

Seven ways of making people better

In this chapter, I introduce the practical themes examined in the book. After some preliminary remarks concerning the challenges that nature and scientific developments produce, I describe the topics of the subsequent chapters and identify, one by one, the main ethical questions to which they give rise.[1]

1.1 The genetic challenge

Humankind is challenged in its pursuit of happiness and wellbeing by three intertwined forces. The first is nonhuman nature. The natural environment sets limits and conditions to our actions, and we have for millennia created strategies to adapt to and to overcome these. On many occasions, our attempts to control nature have resulted in further problems, which have had to be dealt with separately. The second force is human nature in its psychological and social forms. We live, of necessity, in communities and wider societies, and to ensure their smooth operation we have devised a variety of political rules and arrangements. The systems produced have often generated unwanted friction and strife, which have had to be settled with new or additional procedures. The third force to be reckoned with is human nature in its biological sense. We are vulnerable to illness, injury, and death, and to counteract and postpone these we have established many kinds of healing and caring professions. Since their practices have sometimes been seen as futile or detrimental, ways have had to be found to regulate and reorganise them.

---

[1] Note: the page referencing system followed in the footnotes is designed to indicate whether I am referring to a whole chapter from a book or a journal article or to specific page(s) within a book or journal article. In references related to books, when I am referring to a whole chapter, the page range is preceded by a colon and when I am referring to specific page(s), the page range is preceded by 'pp.' (or 'p.'). In the case of journal articles, when I refer to specific page(s), the full page range is followed by the specific page numbers (e.g. 99–100, p. 97). All the websites referred to in this book were accessed on 15 May 2009.

1

The *genetic challenge*, as I understand the notion in this book, is a set of questions raised by the engineering, political, and medical solutions to the original threats posed by nonhuman and human nature. By 'engineering' solutions I mean our responses to natural obstacles; and by 'political' and 'medical' I refer to our attempts to control our own psychological, social, and physical shortcomings. The genetic challenge, like many other tests to humanity, arises when we cannot readily agree on what our reactions should be and on what grounds.

Our search for therapeutic and preventive measures against morbidity and mortality, combined with scientific knowledge and political aspirations, have led many to believe that a radical upgrade can and should be made to the human constitution to improve the lot of the race. Philosophers and scientists have throughout Western history argued that humanity could be made better by careful procreative planning and selection.[2] The birth of modern genetics in the 1950s and subsequent advances in molecular biology, reproductive medicine, and related subjects have taken this idea to new levels. Children's inborn characteristics can be detected by prenatal and preimplantation tests; the molecular processes of the human body can be studied and modified; and changes can be introduced to our inherited and heritable features either individually or collectively. Some of these developments are not, strictly speaking, genetic. They have, however, been initiated and shaped by the scientific evolution which started with the discovery of the double helix structure of deoxyribonucleic acid (DNA).[3] As DNA is the basic element of genetics, it is fitting to group the questions under the common heading 'genetic challenge'.

The subtitle of this book, *Making People Better?*, has many different meanings. We can make individuals healthier by preventing their illnesses and injuries, and by curing, treating, and caring for them when such maladies occur. These are tasks assumed by medicine, nursing, and healthcare, including public health activities. We can try to improve the health of nations by population-level reproductive programmes. Eugenic movements, past and present, have attempted to do this by selecting either who

---

[2] I have traced the development of this idea from Plato and Aristotle through the philosophical movements of the eighteenth and nineteenth centuries to the eugenic programmes of the turn of the twentieth century in my article: Matti Häyry, 2008, 'The historical idea of a better race', *Studies in Ethics, Law, and Technology* 2, Article 11 – www.bepress.com/selt/vol2/iss1/art11.

[3] See, e.g. *The Francis Crick Papers* – http://profiles.nlm.nih.gov/SC/Views/Exhibit/narrative/doublehelix.html. The original finding was reported in James Watson and Francis Crick, 1953, 'Molecular structure of nucleic acids – a structure for deoxyribose nucleic acid', *Nature* 171: 737–8.

should or who should not have children, or both.[4] We can help parents in their attempts to have healthier babies by allowing genetic tests, embryo selection, and abortions by choice. This alternative has been made possible by advances in the life sciences. And we can make people's lives better by increasing their material wellbeing or promoting compassion and justice in our dealings with each other. Communities and societies can take on this mission by education and political endeavours.

This book deals with seven ways of making people better. These do not include education, population-wide eugenics, or political undertakings; rather, they are all related to genetics and medicine at a more individual level. The headings under which the topics will be treated, first briefly in Sections 1.2, 1.3, 1.4, 1.5, 1.6, 1.7, and 1.8 below and then more fully in Chapters 3, 4, 5, 6, 7, 8, and 9, are:

- the best babies;
- deaf embryos;
- saviour siblings;
- reproductive cloning;
- embryonic stem cell research;
- gene therapies; and
- considerable life extension.

I will explain, in this chapter, the practices I see falling under these seven headings; how I think that they are linked to making people better; and what philosophical questions I can see arising from them for my closer analysis in Chapters 3, 4, 5, 6, 7, 8, and 9.

1.2 The best babies

Under the first heading, the question of making people better is approached from the angle of 'making better *people*', or more accurately, of letting only individuals who are considered good come into existence. The science behind this is that genetic testing allows us to find out many things about potential individuals before they are conceived, born, or implanted. Tests on prospective parents can indicate certain or probable health conditions; prenatal tests during pregnancy are used to reveal undesired mutations; and in the context of in vitro fertilisation (IVF), preimplantation embryos

---

[4] Good descriptions of these can be found in Allen Buchanan, Dan W. Brock, Norman Daniels, and Daniel Wikler, 2000, *From Chance to Choice: Genetics and Justice* (Cambridge: Cambridge University Press).

can be tested for many inherited and congenital qualities. Public health services offer some of these tests routinely, whereas many more are gradually becoming available through commercial channels. Parents can determine or preclude certain qualities and conditions, and increase or decrease the probability of others, by selecting their offspring on the basis of the test results. But should they, and if they should, in which cases and to what extent? And should we, as a society, permit, and even encourage, them to do so?[5]

The arguments *for* the option of reproductive testing are easy to state. Scientists should, in the name of free thought and speech, be allowed to develop the techniques and to publicise them. Laboratories and clinics should, in the name of free enterprise, be permitted to market the tests. Parental autonomy demands that potential mothers and fathers can purchase or otherwise acquire information about the essential physical qualities of their children, if this is pragmatically possible. Parental responsibility may even require that they ought to have this information to ensure their children the best possible lives. The condoned existence of reproductive tests will satisfy our scientific curiosity, uphold market freedom, support procreative self-determination, and, in due course, serve the children's best interests and provide societies with healthy, efficient citizens.

The duties of parents towards their children have been intensely debated in recent bioethical and related discussions. One view is that when people contemplate having offspring, they should try their best to have the healthiest, strongest, and most intelligent progeny they can. If this can be achieved by picking the right reproductive partner or by making lifestyle adjustments, these options should presumably be pursued. More to the point here, however, is the obligation to genetically test one's potential children at their embryonic or fetal stages and to select for subsequent existence only those who can be expected to have the best lives. According to this notion, reproducers fail to honour their parental responsibilities if they do not make full use of the knowledge provided by genetic testing.[6] Another view is that people should aim at a reasonable

---

[5] An additional question here is *who* forms the society making these judgements? I have presented some preliminary remarks on this in Matti Häyry, 2009c, 'Is transferred parental responsibility legitimately enforceable?', in Frida Simonstein (ed.), *Reprogen-Ethics and the Future of Gender* (Dordrecht: Springer): 135–49.

[6] Julian Savulescu, 2001, 'Procreative beneficence: why we should select the best children', *Bioethics* 15: 413–16; cf. Matti Häyry, 2004a, 'If you must make babies, then at least make the best babies you can?', *Human Fertility* 7: 105–12.

prospect of a good life for future individuals. This means that embryos and fetuses must not be chosen if their test results predict excruciating diseases or severely incapacitating disabilities. Parents should not, however, be prevented from or pressurised against having children with adverse but more manageable conditions. They may have society's permission to avoid this, too, but they do not have an obligation to do so.[7] Yet another view states that people should not pay any attention to genetic tests. Once aspiring parents have made clear their commitment to having offspring, they should simply take what nature gives them and love their children unconditionally, whatever their physical qualities or health conditions.[8]

Arguments *against* reproductive testing are based on moral principles and psychological concerns. The existence of the technology and the availability of the services confront parents with the initial question, which is whether to test or not to test. Positive results, that is, results showing that the condition or mutation scanned for is present, pose the further challenge of a decision between forsaking a life and accepting a different and possibly difficult parenthood. Critics of genetic tests argue that neither choice is free or uncoerced. If attitudes towards acquiring the information are favourable, social pressures make it almost impossible to take the path of ignorance. An example is provided by the test for Down's syndrome, which is routinely available in many countries, socially accepted, and seldom rejected in the cases in which it is medically indicated. Likewise, if popular opinion favours a particular image of health and normality, positive test results for deviations from this during pregnancy tend to lead to abortions.

Selective abortions and the selective destruction of embryos can be seen as morally problematic from the complementary viewpoints of dignity, solidarity, and precaution.[9] *Dignity*, or life's sanctity, is violated when human lives are ended for whatever reason. Justified punishment, warfare, and self-defence are possible exceptions, but they have nothing

---

[7] Laura Purdy, 1995, 'Loving future people', Joan Callahan (ed.), *Reproduction, Ethics and the Law* (Bloomington, IN: Indiana University Press): 300–27; Michael Freeman, 1997, *The Moral Status of Children: Essays on the Rights of Children* (The Hague: Kluwer Law International); Peter Herissone-Kelly, 2006a, 'Procreative beneficence and the prospective parent', *Journal of Medical Ethics* 32: 166–9.

[8] Simo Vehmas, 2002, 'Is it wrong to deliberately conceive or give birth to a child with mental retardation?', *Journal of Medicine and Philosophy* 27: 47–63; Michael J. Sandel, 2007, *The Case Against Perfection: Ethics in the Age of Genetic Engineering* (Cambridge, MA: The Belknap Press of Harvard University Press), pp. 45, 86.

[9] Matti Häyry, 2003a, 'European values in bioethics: why, what, and how to be used?', *Theoretical Medicine and Bioethics* 24: 199–214.

to do with prenatal decisions. *Solidarity* is questioned when some people are treated differently from others, based on their physical characteristics. Selection means that individuals with undesired conditions and qualities are not allowed to be born. While this may not have an effect on them, since they do not and will not exist, it will influence others who currently live with the same conditions and qualities. They will feel unwanted to the extent determined by their own self-image and by other people's attitudes and actions. *Precaution*, in its turn, requires us to be alert to future risks that are caused by our present actions and policies. Even if selection could be, in theory, condoned in some mutually recognised cases, it is not wise to open, in practice, the door for similar-looking but more sinister activities. Testing for intolerable diseases can lead, indirectly and inconspicuously, to testing for eye colour or something equally frivolous.[10] According to these lines of argument, the best babies are the babies people have and care for, as they should as responsible parents.

In Chapter 3, I will study these and related views in more detail, trying to identify their shared and conflicting premises and the implications of this mix to moral judgements and legislative decisions.

1.3   Deaf embryos

In discussions on reproductive genetic testing, the default value has been that its purpose is to prevent the birth of individuals who would be physically or mentally ill or disabled. Many philosophers and ethicists have argued that any children who are brought into existence should have at least a decent chance of living a fulfilling and relatively independent life, without major bodily or intellectual impediments that could jeopardise the achievement of this goal. The argument is reasonable in the light of current ethical theories and also in line with most established population policies and healthcare practices. Recently, however, the tests have been put to another use which seems to contradict the original aim. Parents who themselves have a particular condition, most notably individuals who are congenitally deaf, have used genetic selection or preimplantation tests in attempts to produce

---

[10] The objection based on precaution takes here the form of a 'slippery slope' argument, where initially good things are suspected to lead to atrocities in other fields or in the future. This is frequent in the genetic context, because the primary intention of interventions is in most cases to do good, although the ensuing practices can raise new questions.

children who would be similar to them.[11] Is this a case of making people better or worse? Should these attempts be somehow regulated or discouraged?

Traditional moral doctrines can be easily geared towards banning or discouraging practices like the selection of gamete donors or embryos to create a deaf baby. Virtue theories evoke an imagery of human flourishing which, if given an individual-oriented slant, advocates health, independence, and ability to function in society without special aids or arrangements. Deontological theories emphasise unhampered reason as the basis of morality, and seem to be fundamentally opposed to choices that could deprive a future individual of a good instrument of intellectual communication and growth. Consequentialist views stress happiness and wellbeing, as well as the absence of suffering and woe, so if deafness is the source of any unpleasantness, there seems to be a case against it. Alternative interpretations can be given to the three theories, and the assessments can then be different, but these are the surface readings that are reflected in, or reflect, contemporary policies on selecting against impending deafness.

A natural defence for selecting donors and embryos to have deaf babies is offered by the ideas of free choice and parental autonomy, already used in the justification of more widely approved types of genetic testing. Scientists should be allowed to develop the tests, laboratories ought to be permitted to make them commercially available, and people planning to reproduce cannot be denied the benefits of the technology just because their intentions are not shared by all others. After all, the aims of the currently condoned tests are not universally approved either, but the inviolability of family life is seen as a sufficient justification for them. Advocates of tests against disease and disability may want to claim that their goals are better and more ethical, but this can be, and has been, contested.

Disability scholars and parents of children with impairments often contend that physical conditions which can be regarded as adverse do not necessarily hinder individual flourishing.[12] It is true, they say, that painful ailments hurt; that mental retardation curbs cognitive

---

[11] Liza Mundy, 2002, 'A world of their own', *Washington Post*, 31 March, p. W22; Merle Spriggs, 2002, 'Lesbian couple create a child who is deaf like them', *Journal of Medical Ethics* 28: 283; S. Baruch, D. Kaufman, and K. L. Hudson, 2008, 'Genetic testing of embryos: practices and perspectives of US in vitro fertilization clinics', *Fertility and Sterility* 89: 1053–8.

[12] A divergent view is stated by Jonathan Glover, 2006, in his *Choosing Children: Genes, Disability, and Design* (Oxford: Clarendon Press), pp. 6 ff., 25.

functions; that restricted mobility slows down movement; that the blind cannot see; and that the deaf cannot hear. None of these prevents, however, individuals from enjoying their lives and making a contribution, especially with proper medical services and social support. This is a particularly understandable and credible line of argument in the case of deafness. In an environment where many people are deaf and sign language is a universal method of communication, deafness can be seen as a culture instead of a disability. Like all minority cultures, it can have difficulties in its dealings with the majority's rules and attitudes, but sensitivity, nondiscrimination, and mutual respect make the personal and interpersonal flourishing of its members every bit as probable as anybody else's.

As for deontological and consequentialist objections, they seem to be mostly inapplicable here. Deafness as such cannot be associated with reduced intelligence,[13] so there are no grounds for believing that the condition would make people less capable of formulating moral judgements in the light of their reason. And although a 'deaf child will not hear the car coming',[14] congenital deafness is not an inherent source of harm and suffering, nor does it lead to less subjectively experienced happiness in life unless its effects are amplified by discriminatory attitudes or behaviour.

An interesting question, and one that I will examine in Chapter 4, is the relationship between morality and the law in the regulation of genetic testing for deafness. Some theorists hold that attempts to create deaf babies are immoral, whereas others maintain that they are understandable and acceptable. Despite the moral disagreement, most of them agree, however, that parents should legislatively be left free to make up their own minds.[15] As I will show, this is an uneasy compromise, because the ethical convictions underlying the opposite views, as can be expected, also draw their advocates into different directions when legal solutions are considered.

---

[13] McCay Vernon, 2005, 'Fifty years of research on the intelligence of deaf and hard-of-hearing children: A review of literature and discussion of implications', *Journal of Deaf Studies and Deaf Education* 10: 225–31.

[14] Glover, 2006, p. 23.

[15] E.g. John Harris, 2000, 'Is there a coherent social conception of disability?', *Journal of Medical Ethics* 26: 95–100; John Harris, 2001, 'One principle and three fallacies of disability studies', *Journal of Medical Ethics* 27: 383–7; Tom Koch, 2001, 'Disability and difference: balancing social and physical constructions', *Journal of Medical Ethics* 27: 370–6; Tom Koch, 2005, 'The ideology of normalcy – the ethics of difference', *Journal of Disability Policy Studies* 16: 123–9; Peter Singer, 2005, 'Ethics and disability: A response to Koch', *Journal of Disability Policy Studies* 16: 130–3.

1.4   Saviour siblings

In attempts to produce the 'best babies' and in decisions to select 'deaf embryos' preimplantation genetic tests are used to make better *people*, at least in the eyes of their parents. Similar tests can also be utilised to make people *better* in the medical sense. Some children have conditions that can be treated effectively only by tissue or stem cell transplants. Matching donors cannot always be found among the living and when this is the case, parents can try to produce another child who could fulfil the role. A number of embryos are produced by IVF, they are tested for their suitability, and good ones are implanted to initiate a pregnancy. If all goes well, a child with the planned qualities is born and its umbilical cord blood or tissue can be collected to help the ailing sibling. A new human being, a 'saviour sibling', is designed and created to restore the health of an existing individual.

The obvious rationale of the practice is medical. Someone whose life could not be saved or whose illness could not be cured otherwise will have a chance to live a longer and better life. The parents will probably be happier and society can benefit from the contribution of the citizen rescued from the brink of death or permanent injury. Apart from this, further reasons are provided by the principle of procreative autonomy. If people are allowed to set limits and conditions to the kinds of offspring that they want to have in other respects, then why draw the line here? The survival and health of an older sibling is surely as important a concern as the physical condition of the future child.

Objections to creating saviour siblings range from appeals to the sanctity of life through the consideration of probable and possible harm to the condemnation of designing lives and using people as a means.[16] As in all preimplantation genetic testing, some embryos are discarded in the selection of the donor candidates, and this can be seen as a violation of the sanctity-of-life principle. I will discuss this criticism in the context of stem cell research (Section 1.6 below and Chapter 7). And as in all reproductive testing, parents and geneticists are in these cases planning the qualities of children and by doing this, it can be argued, assuming a role that is not rightfully theirs. I will return to this view, and

---

[16] The major arguments for and against the practice can be found, e.g. in Sally Sheldon and Stephen Wilkinson, 2004, 'Should selecting saviour siblings be banned?', *Journal of Medical Ethics* 30: 533–7; Caroline Berry and Jacky Engel, 2005, 'Saviour siblings', *Christian Medical Fellowship Files* 28 – www.cmf.org.uk/literature/content.asp?context=article&id=1317.

other variants of the 'design' objection, in the discussion on reproductive cloning (Section 1.5 and Chapter 6). In the meantime, what about the other arguments against saviour siblings?

The children created to provide a donor for their siblings can be physically harmed in the process. This is not necessary or inevitable, but it is a possibility. If the tissue needed can be taken from the umbilical cord, no bodily harm is inflicted. But if the initial treatment fails and a bone marrow transplant is required, a relatively painful and possibly dangerous procedure will be imposed on a child without its consent. It is commonplace in the literature to assert that this is not harmful, since no permanent damage usually occurs. This view conflates two separate things. The pain and the risk can be deemed trivial in comparison with the agony of the older sibling.[17] They are, nonetheless, real, and this can be counted as harm, whatever the reasonable attitude towards the practice in its entirety.

Saviour siblings can also be psychologically harmed by their parents' expectations, especially but not only if the older child cannot be helped by their tissue. Again, this is not necessary or inevitable, but it is a genuine possibility. Since the number of cases so far is very small and since it is probably unsafe to draw analogies from other types of situation, we have no real knowledge about the severity of the issue. The parents who have gone through the experience have asserted that they would have had another child anyway and that they would have loved the planned baby regardless of its medical performance. But disappointment can show in many ways, and the mere awareness that one has been produced for an external purpose may influence the self-esteem of the individual earlier or later in life.

Another objection based on the impacts of the practice is that the creation of saviour siblings, while acceptable in and by itself, would be a step on a genetic slippery slope. We could, so the argument goes, condone in principle attempts to produce a donor for a sick child. By doing this we would, however, also authorise parental choices in less significant cases, or at least send a message saying that it could be done. As a result, the number of genetic tests for less significant reasons would increase, until everybody would be choosing their children by eye colour, gender, height, intelligence, and jocularity. Critics of this popular idea have countered it with two observations. The link between kinds of

---

[17] I would like to see everyone who claims this immediately register as bone marrow donors, though, to put their flesh where their mouths are.

selection can probably be broken by laws and regulations. And it would not necessarily be so terrible if parents could decide the qualities of their children.

The most interesting ethical issue here, and the one that I will focus on in Chapter 5, is the problem of exploitation, or instrumentalisation. Are 'saviour siblings' primarily used as a means to the wellbeing of others?[18] If they are, is this wrong and why? These questions are, if not unique, at least central to making babies in order to help their sisters and brothers. Concerns related to the sanctity of life, the immorality of reproductive planning, unnecessary harm, and slippery slopes can be extended to most forms of 'making people better'. The argument that it is wrong to use individuals as a means finds its most plausible application right here.

1.5   Reproductive cloning

Reproductive cloning, like the cases of the best babies, deaf embryos, and saviour siblings, is a topic that gives a pivotal role to the production of new individuals. Unlike the sibling discussion, it is also about making better *people* (rather than people *better*). The initially distinctive feature of the cloning debate, however, is that it has, with advances in the relevant know-how, rapidly proceeded from abstract reflection to concrete legislative action.

Before 1997, cloning was mostly seen as a transcendental threat – it was used in ethical arguments as an ultimate worst-case scenario: the bottom of the pit into which the slippery slope of genetics leads us. Images in the media made allusions to science fiction, most notably Aldous Huxley's *Brave New World* and George Orwell's *Nineteen Eighty-Four*.[19] The fact that cloning is not particularly central to the plots of either novel did not seem to matter: the technology was seamlessly associated with their main themes of totalitarian control, loss of individuality, and mindless collectivism. Cloning was seen as an epitome of the evils of designing people and societies.

Since the genetic duplication of adult individuals looked like a distant and improbable peril, the news about Dolly, the first mammal cloned by somatic-cell nuclear transfer, took most ethicists by surprise in February

---

[18] See, e.g. Ronald M. Green, 2001a, 'What does it mean to treat someone "as a means only": Rereading Kant', *Kennedy Institute of Ethics Journal* 11: 247–61.

[19] Aldous Huxley, 1932, *Brave New World* (London: Chatto & Windus); George Orwell, 1949, *Nineteen Eighty-Four* (London: Secker and Warburg).

1997.[20] Since then, the scientific progress in the field has been rapid and many other mammals, including cows, mice, rats, goats, pigs, rabbits, cats, horses, and dogs, have been produced by this method.

Politicians and lawgivers were quick to react to the new situation. Governments competed to ban human reproductive cloning and research into it. Laws and regulations were enacted to halt the development. In November 1997, the technique was unequivocally condemned in UNESCO's *Universal Declaration on the Human Genome and Human Rights*, which decreed that 'Practices which are contrary to human dignity, such as reproductive cloning of human beings, shall not be permitted.'[21] In a way, this sums up the nature of the responses. A research group clones a sheep. Although this could be basically acceptable, it could lead to cloning people. This cannot be permitted, because it would go against people's ethical intuitions. As these intuitions are difficult to articulate, a link is made to the popular principle of 'human dignity', despite the unclarity of the concept.[22] The charges are very general, and some unpacking is needed before the components of this appeal become visible.

The many alleged wrongs of human reproductive cloning include loss of life, instrumentalisation, inadequate justification of the costs, safety issues, and loss of uniqueness.[23] Loss of life, as noted above, is a concern in all invasive and potentially lethal dealings with human embryos and fetuses, albeit that the apprehension is limited to ethicists with particular views on life and its meaning. These views will be examined below (Section 1.6 and Chapter 7). Instrumental use, in its turn, can be a problem both in research, where many embryos will perish, and in the ensuing reproductive applications, where it is unrealistic to expect that one embryo fashioned by nuclear transfer will always be enough to start a

[20] I. Wilmut, A. E. Schnieke, J. McWhir, A. J. Kind, and K. H. S. Campbell, 1997, 'Viable offspring derived from fetal and adult mammalian cells', *Nature* 385: 810–13.

[21] *Universal Declaration on the Human Genome and Human Rights*, 1997, adopted by the General Conference of UNESCO at its 29th session on 11 November 1997, § 11.

[22] I have studied the ambiguities involved in Matti Häyry and Tuija Takala, 2001, 'Cloning, naturalness and personhood', D. C. Thomasma, D. N. Weisstub, and C. Hervé (eds), *Personhood and Health Care* (Dordrecht: Kluwer Academic Publishers): 281–98; Matti Häyry, 2003b, 'Deeply felt disgust – a Devlinian objection to cloning humans', B. Almond and M. Parker (eds), *Ethical Issues in the New Genetics: Are Genes Us?* (Aldershot: Ashgate): 55–67; Matti Häyry, 2003c, 'Philosophical arguments for and against human reproductive cloning', *Bioethics* 17: 447–59; Matti Häyry, 2004b, 'Another look at dignity', *Cambridge Quarterly of Healthcare Ethics* 13: 7–14.

[23] Tuija Takala, 2005, 'The many wrongs of human reproductive cloning', Matti Häyry, Tuija Takala, and Peter Herissone-Kelly (eds), *Bioethics and Social Reality* (Amsterdam: Rodopi): 53–66.

successful pregnancy. These, too, are objections that are best studied in the context of sanctity-of-life doctrines. A residual worry is that parents could wish the new individual to be similar to someone else, perhaps a respected member of the family whose somatic cell has been used in the procedure. Admittedly, this does not sound entirely healthy. It is not clear, however, that this is an issue specifically for cloning. People produce offspring for many interrelated reasons and parental expectations can put a burden on children, whichever method has been used in their creation.

Since human reproductive cloning, to become reality, requires expensive research and high-tech implementation, it can only be justified in a cost-benefit analysis if its applications can be expected to be very useful to many people. This is not obviously the case. The scientific work could possibly be sanctioned as basic biological research, but if the practical purpose is to help a few hundred or a few thousand people to have genetically related children, I believe that the money could be better spent on other purposes. This is especially true, because the unsafety of the procedure presents an indirect problem. An argument for human reproductive cloning is that while it is too dangerous to be liberated now, it could be condoned once the risks have been cleared. But how could this happen? Experiments on animals may not be enough and human beings cannot within modern research governance frameworks be subjected to the type of hazard that being the first cloned human being would pose. This seems to indicate that the technique can never be ethically perfected.[24]

Loss of uniqueness in its different forms is *the* distinctive theme in the ethics of cloning. Do we have a right to a genetic makeup that is not shared with anyone else? Identical twins do not have this privilege, but perhaps their 'natural' way of being is different from the 'designed' existence of clones. Would the awareness of being a genetic duplication cast a shadow on an individual's life?[25] Are we entitled not to know what hereditary diseases probably await us?[26] Is life a mystery which should not be exposed by excessive design?[27] These are the types of questions that will occupy me in Chapter 6.

[24] Takala, 2005, pp. 58–9.
[25] Søren Holm, 1998, 'A life in the shadow: One reason why we should not clone humans', *Cambridge Quarterly of Healthcare Ethics* 7: 160–2.
[26] Takala, 2005, pp. 61–2.
[27] David Gurnham, 2005, 'The mysteries of human dignity and the brave new world of human cloning', *Social and Legal Studies* 14: 197–214.

1.6   Embryonic stem cells

Stem cells are totipotent, pluripotent, multipotent, or unipotent cells, which have the capacity to either multiply as they are or become differentiated. If they are totipotent they can develop into the whole organism or into any of its parts or tissues. If they are pluripotent, they can turn into any of the organism's parts or tissues but not into the organism as a whole. If they are multipotent, they can develop into cells belonging to their own general type, but not into others (haemopoietic stem cells that can specialise as different blood cells are an example of this). If they are unipotent, they can renew cells of their own specific kind (for instance, muscle cells). Stem cells are present in the human body at all stages in our existence, including fetal and embryonic life.

Human stem cells can be acquired by a variety of means: by collecting them from the umbilical cord blood; by isolating them from living (postembryonic) individuals; by nuclear transfer (the Dolly method); and by harvesting the inner cells of embryos. Umbilical cord blood, bone marrow, and other tissues donated by adults and children provide a relatively uncontroversial source of stem cells for treating diseases. The use of nuclear transfer is more awkward because of its connection with reproductive cloning. But the most heated debate surrounds the retrieval and cultivation of embryonic stem cells, which has been technologically possible since 1998.[28]

Medical and biological human embryonic stem cell research enables us to understand better the mechanisms and systems that keep us alive and well. It makes possible the reintroduction of vital tissues into the human body, which is essential for the successful treatment of certain hitherto incurable diseases. It may also, in the future, make possible the creation of entire organs and rejuvenating treatments. On the other hand, the development of drugs and therapies is a slow process, so promises of a quick turnover sometimes reported in the popular media are in most cases exaggerated. What is more, the creation of human stem cell lines seems to be inexorably linked with the destruction of embryos, and this is deeply problematic from the sanctity-of-life point of view.

---

[28] James A. Thomson, Joseph Itskovitz-Eldor, Sander S. Shapiro, Michelle A. Waknitz, Jennifer J. Swiergiel, Vivienne S. Marshall, and Jeffrey M. Jones, 1998, 'Embryonic stem cell lines derived from human blastocysts', *Science* 282: 1145–7. On the early debate, see Søren Holm, 2002, 'Going to the roots of the stem cell controversy', *Bioethics* 16: 493–507; Søren Holm, 2003a, 'The ethical case against stem cell research', *Cambridge Quarterly of Healthcare Ethics* 12: 372–83.

Many research groups have tried to find a way to create useful and viable human stem cell lines without the destruction of embryos. Some have preferred the use of adult stem cells[29] and others have used somatic cells to produce material closely resembling embryonic stem cells.[30] The difficulties of these attempts include the facts that adult stem cells do not necessarily have all the specialisation powers desired and that the somatic-to-almost-embryonic cells derived from ordinary tissue remain, for now, unsafe. The most intriguing development for some seems to be the removal of the inner cells of embryos without destroying the originals and the creation of embryonic stem cell lines by using the extracted material.[31] This method can help researchers bypass legislative obstacles in countries where the creation of new lines is banned, but it does *not* provide a solution to the underlying ethical dilemma. The 'extracted material' itself could develop into a new human being, which means that *it* can, and logically should, be seen as an embryo doomed to destruction in the process.

Embryonic stem cell research and possible future therapies raise serious questions about dignity, solidarity, and vulnerability. The starting point of the activities can arguably be a solidaristic concern for the health and worth of the individuals whose incurable illnesses have rendered them frail and defenceless. But these considerations can also be turned against the development and use of the technology. The claim can be made that the ill effects of permissive policies will primarily be felt by unborn human beings and exploitable women. Embryos are destroyed in the process and, as a consequence, sensitivity in related matters such as abortion can decrease – both grave concerns for those who believe in the sanctity and inviolability of early human life. Women, again, will be needed for the acquisition of embryos; and this is alarming since the procedure is

[29] David A. Prentice and Gene Tarne 2007, 'Treating diseases with adult stem cells', *Science* 315: 328.

[30] K. Takahashi, K. Tanabe, M. Ohnuki, M. Narita, T. Ichisaka, K. Tomoda, and S. Yamanaka, 2007, 'Induction of pluripotent stem cells from adult human fibroblasts by defined factors', *Cell* 131: 861–72; Junying Yu, Maxim A. Vodyanik, Kim Smuga-Otto, Jessica Antosiewicz-Bourget, Jennifer L. Frane, Shulan Tian, Jeff Nie, Gudrun A. Jonsdottir, Victor Ruotti, Ron Stewart, Igor I. Slukvin, and James A. Thomson, 2007, 'Induced pluripotent stem cell lines derived from human somatic cells', *Science* 318: 1917–20; Søren Holm, 2008, 'Time to reconsider stem cell ethics – the importance of induced pluripotent cells', *Journal of Medical Ethics* 34: 63–4.

[31] Young Chung, Irina Klimanskaya, Sandy Becker, Tong Li, Marc Maserati, Shi-Jiang Lu, Tamara Zdravkovic, Dusko Ilic, Olga Genbacev, Susan Fisher, Ana Krtolica, and Robert Lanza, 2008, 'Human embryonic stem cell lines generated without embryo destruction', *Cell Stem Cell* 2: 113–17.

invasive and not likely to be consented to without deception, coercion, or financial inducements.[32]

Whether or not adult stem cells or other alternatives can be used instead of embryonic material is a question that belongs to the wider scientific discussion on stem cell research and therapies. The two aspects that merit special examination in the human embryonic stem cell debate are the moral status of embryos and the role of women in their acquisition. Some believe that life is sacred and that any interference with the early human being is wrong. Others contend that the few cells of the blastocyst possess no intrinsic worth, and that their use cannot raise any reasonable objections. Yet others think that embryos have some value, and that some uses and applications can be more easily justified than others. An important consideration for those who hold one of the more permissive views is what else, apart from the status of the embryo, needs to be accounted for in a full ethical analysis. The costs and benefits are important but can be dealt with in more general dialogue between the interested parties. The remaining issue is, would women be exploited in the acquisition of the required embryos and would this be a sufficient reason for banning the practice? These questions concerning embryos and women will be studied more closely in Chapter 7.

1.7   Gene therapies

Gene therapies, like stem cell research, are primarily about making people better in the sense of curing illnesses and making existent individuals physically stronger. They also contain the aspect of making better people in that some of their effects will be seen in the descendants of the originally treated people. All gene therapies are currently at their experimental stages and despite their promise they are still, after two decades of concentrated efforts, far from becoming routine medical treatments. Advocates argue, however, that once the ongoing trials have been completed, rapid breakthroughs can be reasonably expected.[33]

---

[32] See, e.g. Holm, 2002, p. 499.

[33] See, e.g. Adam M. Hedgecoe, 1998, 'Gene therapy', Ruth Chadwick (ed.), *Encyclopedia of Applied Ethics* Volume II (San Diego, CA: Academic Press): 383–90; Eric T. Juengst and Hannah Grankvist, 2007, 'Ethical issues in human gene transfer: A historical overview', Richard E. Ashcroft, Angus Dawson, Heather Draper, and John R. McMillan (eds), *Principles of Health Care Ethics*, second edition (Chichester: John Wiley & Sons): 789–96.

A line has been drawn between somatic and germ-line gene therapies. Somatic therapies are only designed to work on the individuals who are actually treated. The children of people who receive this type of care will be unaffected and they will probably have the same genetic defects that were corrected in their parents. Germ-line therapies have an effect on gametes or on the cells that produce them either before or after conception. The alteration caused by the treatment will be present in the off-spring of the patients unless reverse measures are taken in their case. The line is not impermeable, though, as genes inserted to other parts of the body can travel to reproductive tissues.[34] This is potentially embarrassing for legislators, because many governments have allowed trials on somatic cells while making a point of banning germ-line therapies as unethical.

The ethical distinction is often based on two intertwined ideas. The first is that knowledge concerning the long-term consequences of inheritable genetic modifications is very limited and that it would be wrong to expose new human generations to them. The second is that recipients of somatic gene therapy can themselves decide to participate in the trial, while only proxy or hypothetical consent is available in the case of future people. Both ideas are appealing, but they can both be challenged. Our knowledge may be limited now, but science advances and this obstacle can be overcome. If and when it is overcome, the expected-outcome argument against germ-line treatments evaporates. As regards consent, many contemporary trials involve small children whose parents have accepted the procedures on behalf of their young. If the alleged distinction is based solely on consent, then either all gene therapies on children are wrong (there is no actual consent) or germ-line therapies can be condoned, after all (there can be parental consent).[35]

These observations do not make the distinction void; they just show that it cannot be justified by lack of knowledge or assent. The reasons for condemning deliberate hereditary changes by gene technology must be found elsewhere: perhaps in appeals to the dignity and rights of prospective individuals; in the 'unnaturalness' of moulding people; or in the wrongness of 'playing God'.[36] Such ideas will be explored in Chapter 6

---

[34] Nell Boyce, 2001, 'Trial halted after gene shows up in semen', *Nature* 414: 677.

[35] Since the changes will be permanent over generations, 'parental consent' should in the case of germ-line therapies be understood to include grand-parental consent, great-grand-parental consent, and so on.

[36] I have studied these in Matti Häyry, 1994a, 'Categorical objections to genetic engineering – A critique', Anthony Dyson and John Harris (eds), *Ethics and Biotechnology* (London and New York, NY: Routledge): 202–15; Matti Häyry and Heta Häyry, 1998,

in the context of reproductive cloning and the immorality of designing people. In Chapter 8, I will return to this theme and inspect the variation introduced into it by germ-line gene therapies.

A line has also been customarily drawn between genetic therapies and enhancements. Therapies are aimed at *restoring* and *maintaining* the normal functioning of those treated, while enhancements are aimed at *improving* their functioning over and above normality. The former are often deemed more natural and morally worthier than the latter. But caution is needed in the use of the separation in ethical judgements.

Consider the case of the 'bubble boys' – boys who have X-linked severe combined immunodeficiency (X-SCID). They have virtually no resistance mechanisms so every infection, however innocuous to others, is a serious threat to their life and health. Without treatment they have died very young, which is why some of them have been subjected by their parents to the gene therapy trials that started in 1998. The trials themselves have their ethical problems, but the point here is to elucidate the role of normal and improved functions in our thinking.[37]

If 'function' is seen as a biological concept, normal functioning is what the organism naturally does. In the bubble boys, the immune system does not offer any resistance against infections but it is, for them, natural and part of their genetic constitution. Attempts to change this for the better would be enhancements, not therapies. If, on the other hand, 'function' is seen as a normative concept, the criteria can be borrowed from other human beings. Statistically speaking, it is normal *species* functioning for us to be able to live in unsterile environments. Since this is the aim of the X-SCID gene treatments, they are therapies, not enhancements.

There are other details that need to be clarified if the normative route is taken. Is it average human species functioning to see things clearly? If it is, then spectacles are therapy. But is it not also a regular feature that people lose this ability when they get older? If it is, then spectacles are enhancements. The use of the concept of 'normal species functioning' seems to draw, in this case, an ethical line between spectacles for children on one hand and adults on the other, and this does not look very promising. Intuitively, we could probably use a three-layer classification: *therapies*

'Genetic engineering', Ruth Chadwick (ed.), *Encyclopedia of Applied Ethics* Volume II (San Diego, CA: Academic Press): 407–17.

[37] See, e.g. Erika Check, 2003, 'Second cancer case halts gene-therapy trials', *Nature* 421: 305; Erika Check, 2005a, 'Gene therapy put on hold as third child develops cancer', *Nature* 433: 561; Erika Check, 2005b, 'Gene-therapy trials to restart following cancer risk review', *Nature* 434: 127.

restore and maintain normal species functioning (glasses for the young); an unnamed category, say *aids*, improve abilities within the range of species functioning (glasses for the older); and *enhancements* add abilities beyond current species functioning (a treatment that gives us infrared vision). But it would still not be clear what the ethical implications are. Why should we not make additions to our good abilities, if they can be made without risking harm to ourselves or others?

It seems that, apart from the 'design' objections, gene therapies should be assessed in the light of the benefits that they can supply and the harms that they threaten to cause, in other words, according to their consequences. But what are the consequences? Reliable information is difficult to obtain, and this is why the results of the analyses often turn on the attitudes that people already have for or against the technology.[38] Some oppose them due to fears, others defend them due to hopes, and yet others remain cautiously sceptical. In Chapter 8, I will study further this phenomenon and its implications to the debate on gene therapies.

1.8   Considerable life extension

The last of my seven themes deals with both making (existent) people better and making better (future) people. The topic is considerable life extension, sometimes also discussed in the literature under the title 'immortality'.[39] Depending on the methods proposed for prolonging human life, this may or may not involve gene therapies, but it is definitely a part of the genetic challenge, as defined in Section 1.1.

Efforts towards helping people live longer lives can be categorised as: case-by-case postponement of death; moderate life extension; considerable life extension; and indefinite life extension. The first two are already a part of our everyday lives, while the last two are more controversial.

---

[38] E.g. Heta Häyry, 1994, 'How to assess the consequences of genetic engineering?', Anthony Dyson and John Harris (eds), *Ethics and Biotechnology* (London: Routledge): 144–56; Matti Häyry, 2007a, 'Utilitarianism and bioethics', Richard E. Ashcroft, Angus Dawson, Heather Draper, and John R. McMillan (eds), *Principles of Health Care Ethics*, second edition (Chichester: John Wiley & Sons): 57–64.

[39] See, e.g. Leon R. Kass, 2002, *Life, Liberty, and the Defense of Dignity: The Challenge for Bioethics* (San Francisco: Encounter Books); John Harris, 2003a, 'Intimations of immortality: The ethics and justice of life-extending therapies', M. D. A. Freeman (ed.), *Current Legal Problems 2002* (Oxford: Oxford University Press): 65–95; John Harris and Daniela Cutas, 2007, 'The ethics of ageing, immortality and genetics', Richard E. Ashcroft, Angus Dawson, Heather Draper, and John R. McMillan (eds), *Principles of Health Care Ethics*, second edition (Chichester: John Wiley & Sons): 797–801.

Case-by-case postponement of death occurs when life is extended by life-saving and life-prolonging interventions. Emergency operations are an obvious example, but many other medical treatments and acts of self-preservation also belong to this category. By *moderate life extension* I mean the avoidance of accidents and other potentially fatal hazards (bar fights and foreign travel could be examples); healthy dietary and lifestyle choices; and the use of supposed anti-ageing products (vitamins and nutrition supplements). Calorie restriction, which has been shown to prolong the lives of rats, mice, fish, flies, worms, and yeast,[40] can also be counted under this heading. All these have more to do with regular medicine, public health measures, and common sense than with recent advances in the life sciences.

Considerable life extension strategies challenge the basic biological processes that lead to ageing and death. Most organisms are mortal, but it remains unclear why exactly this is the case. One possibility is that complex systems are simply born to fail sooner or later. Another explanation is that the body accumulates chemical damage that cannot be reversed. Or perhaps the continued life of the species once depended on genetic diversity, and evolutionary processes favoured individuals who remained healthy until they had reproduced and raised their young but then quickly died away. If this is the case, the biological cause of mortality could be found in the shortening of telomeres – a feature which may protect us from cancer earlier in our life and then expose us to it when we are not needed for breeding any more. Whatever the exact mechanism is, some biogerontologists question the inevitability of ageing and argue that it should be treated like a lethal disease.[41] This, they say, could lead to considerable longevity, threatened only by accidents and acts of violence. People could expect average lifespans of a thousand years instead of the current under a hundred years, and if the genetics of the system could be revealed and controlled, germ-line changes could make considerable longevity an inherited human quality for future generations.

---

[40] Leonie K. Heilbronn and Eric Ravussin, 2003, 'Calorie restriction and aging: review of the literature and implications for studies in humans', *The American Journal of Clinical Nutrition* 78: 361–9.

[41] Aubrey D. N. J. de Grey, Bruce N. Ames, Julie K. Andersen, Andrzej Bartke, Judith Campisi, Christopher B. Heward, Roger J. M. Mccarter, and Gregory Stock, 2002, 'Time to talk SENS: Critiquing the immutability of human aging', *Annals of the New York Academy of Sciences* 959: 452–62. For an informative and accessible account of the work of Aubrey de Grey, the best known 'interventive biogerontologist', see Thomas Bartlett, 2005, 'The man who would murder death: A rogue researcher challenges scientists to reverse human aging', *The Chronicle of Higher Education* 52, Issue 10 (28 October): A14.

Indefinite life extension requires going beyond the promise of biogerontology. Human beings should somehow be made indestructible to allow lives that have no foreseeable end point. An indirect and temporary measure could be offered by cryonics. If individuals cannot be fixed by the means that are available at the time of their impending demise, cryopreservation could be used as an 'ambulance to the future', to a time when medicine has advanced enough for them to be thawed and repaired. More direct methods could involve cyborg techniques mixing human and artificial components, or mind uploads, storing and continuing our mental lives cocooned by computers. These ideas, favoured by advocates of 'transhumanism',[42] belong to a new generation of notions that deserve their own scrutiny but fall outside the scope of this book.

Champions of 'immortality' – that is, considerable to indefinite longevity – argue simply that more life is better than less, as evidenced by our own chronic reluctance to die just yet. The question for them is not 'Do I wish to live forever?', but 'Do I want to die now?' If the answer to the latter query is negative every time it is made, this shows that our will to live knows no limits and longer lifespans are always superior to shorter ones. To the stock criticisms the champions respond matter-of-factly. Would it not be terrible or boring to live forever? 'Well, life extension should be seen as an opportunity, not as a threat. If your life is intolerably horrid, feel free to end it in your own time.' Where do we put all the extra people, when no one dies any more? 'Well, overpopulation is mostly about too many people being born. Surely we cannot start killing old people or letting them die to make room for new generations.' Is this not awfully expensive? 'Well, it saves lives at a cost. Unless you want to suggest that we start pricing human life, this is money well spent.' And so on.[43]

Opponents of the idea of extending human lives argue, in their turn, that the issues of safety, efficiency, and justice are far from being solved;[44] that finitude is a blessing; and that the quest for immortality by genetic

---

[42] E.g. Nick Bostrom, 2005, 'In defence of posthuman dignity', *Bioethics* 19: 202–14.

[43] See, e.g. John Harris, 2007, *Enhancing Evolution: The Ethical Case for Making Better People* (Princeton: Princeton University Press), pp. 59–71; Aubrey de Grey, 2007, 'Life span extension research and public debate: societal considerations', *Studies in Ethics, Law, and Technology* 1 – www.bepress.com/selt/vol1/iss1/art5; cf. Matti Häyry, 2007b, 'Generous funding for interventive aging research now?', *Studies in Ethics, Law, and Technology* 1 – www.bepress.com/selt/vol1/iss1/art13.

[44] Walter Glannon, 2002a, 'Extending the human life span', *Journal of Medicine and Philosophy* 27: 339–54; Walter Glannon, 2002b, 'Identity, prudential concern, and extended lives', *Bioethics* 16: 266–83; Walter Glannon, 2002c, 'Reply to Harris', *Bioethics* 16: 292–7.

and medical technologies defies its own purpose.[45] I will examine all these arguments in more detail in Chapter 9. The last point is worth a comment already at this stage. It is definitely true that technology does not, as far as we can tell, bring humankind immortality in the sense of individuals living forever. All biological and technological systems are, in the end, vulnerable, and in time life in the solar system and in the universe will become impossible. This being the case, the real task could be to lull people into believing in some kind of an eternal life. Medicine might have a role to play even in this scheme, but better alternatives could be offered by religious teachings or by the already thriving rejuvenation industry. Many faiths promise an everlasting existence after earthly death, and cosmetics, cosmetic surgery, lifestyle choices, and miracle potions can make people look and feel young regardless of their years. Reflections on the wish to keep alive and young will, in Chapter 9, take us close to pondering the meaning of life itself.

1.9   The questions

The preceding sections have enabled me to do two things. First, I have introduced the practical themes of the book. These include the technological advances that define seven aspects of the 'genetic challenge', or the seven ways of making people better. And they include the most important moral arguments for and against the advances. Secondly, I have also identified the more precise philosophical and ethical questions that will occupy me in the following chapters. To recapitulate, they are:

- What is the nature and role of parental responsibility in the face of genetic testing opportunities and in the light of moral principles?
- What is the relationship between morality and the law in the context of selecting for deafness?
- What are the moral limits of using people as a means and are they reached in the creation of saviour siblings?
- In what sense can people be designed and what, if anything, is wrong with it in practices such as human reproductive cloning?
- What is the moral role of vulnerable groups such as embryos and exploitable women in the acquisition and use of material for human embryonic stem cell research?
- How can pre-existing attitudes influence our assessment of consequences and what significance does this have in debates on gene therapies?

---

[45] Kass, 2002.

- What is the aim and meaning of extending human life, and how can different views on this affect discussions concerning immortality?

All these issues have been considered in bioethical controversies during the last few decades, yet they all remain open for comments and disagreement. In Chapter 2 I will first outline the main approaches that have been chosen for ethical studies in this area to date, and then go on to describe the method that I propose to use in Chapters 3, 4, 5, 6, 7, 8, and 9 of this book.

2

Rational approaches to the genetic challenge

In this chapter, I present the main normative approaches to the ethics of genetics. I describe the views of six prominent authors in the field and contrast their prescriptive positions with my own nonconfrontational notion of rationality.

2.1   Six authors, three approaches

The dimensions of the 'genetic challenge' have been intensively studied in recent literature on philosophical bioethics.[1] The conclusions drawn by different authors vary considerably. Some say that all scientific and

---

[1] John Harris, 1998, *Clones, Genes, and Immortality: Ethics and the Genetic Revolution* (Oxford: Oxford University Press); Jonathan Glover, 1999, *Humanity: A Moral History of the Twentieth Century* (London: Jonathan Cape); Allen Buchanan, Dan W. Brock, Norman Daniels, and Daniel Wikler, 2000, *From Chance to Choice: Genetics and Justice* (Cambridge: Cambridge University Press); Deryck Beyleveld and Roger Brownsword, 2001, *Human Dignity and Biolaw* (Oxford: Oxford University Press); Matti Häyry, 2001a, *Playing God: Essays on Bioethics* (Helsinki: Helsinki University Press); Leon R. Kass, 2002, *Life, Liberty, and the Defense of Dignity: The Challenge for Bioethics* (San Francisco, CA: Encounter Books); Onora O'Neill, 2002, *Autonomy and Trust in Bioethics* (Cambridge: Cambridge University Press); Mary Warnock, 2002, *Making Babies: Is There a Right to Have Children?* (Oxford: Oxford University Press); Jürgen Habermas, 2003, *The Future of Human Nature*, translated by William Rehg, Max Pensky, and Hella Beister (Cambridge: Polity Press); Nicholas Agar, 2004, *Liberal Eugenics: In Defence of Human Enhancement* (Oxford: Blackwell); John Harris, 2004, *On Cloning* (London: Routledge); Richard Weikart, 2004, *From Darwin to Hitler: Evolutionary Ethics, Eugenics, and Racism in Germany* (New York, NY: Palgrave Macmillan); Jonathan Glover, 2006, *Choosing Children: Genes, Disability, and Design* (Oxford: Clarendon Press); Andrew Stark, 2006, *The Limits of Medicine: Cure or Enhancement* (Cambridge: Cambridge University Press); Jonathan Baron, 2007, *Against Bioethics* (Cambridge MA: MIT Press); Ronald M. Green, 2007, *Babies by Design: The Ethics of Genetic Choice* (New Haven, CT: Yale University Press); John Harris, 2007, *Enhancing Evolution: The Ethical Case for Making Better People* (Princeton, NJ: Princeton University Press); Matti Häyry, 2007c, *Cloning, Selection, and Values: Essays on Bioethical Intuitions* (Helsinki: Societas Philosophica Fennica); Michael J. Sandel, 2007, *The Case Against Perfection: Ethics in the Age of Genetic Engineering* (Cambridge, MA: The Belknap Press of Harvard University Press).

clinical advances in the field should be embraced and that regulation must in all cases be kept to a minimum. Others contend that the development and application of the new interventions devised by life scientists ought to be viewed with suspicion and in many cases halted or banned. More middle-of-the-road authors have suggested that since the promises are attractive and the threats alarming, sensitive regulation is needed to achieve a balance between the prospects and risks of the process.

In this chapter, I am more interested in the methods by which authors have reached their conclusions than in the conclusions themselves. I have chosen for closer scrutiny the approaches of six prominent scholars in bioethics: Jonathan Glover, John Harris, Leon Kass, Michael Sandel, Jürgen Habermas, and Ronald Green. By this choice I do not mean to imply that the work of others is any less significant – I will return to their arguments and views in the following chapters. Rather, I have made this particular selection because the three most interesting approaches to contemporary applied ethics are admirably represented, if not always thoroughly explicated, in the contributions of these six seminal authors.

The first approach stresses that the arguments presented for or against normative ethical views should always be transparent, clear, and rationally comprehensible. To realise this ideal, the proponents of the view analyse phenomena closely and try to reduce descriptions of them into sentences about concrete, tangible, easily understandable elements. In the case of reproductive cloning, for instance, they could argue that the procedure cannot be condoned now, because it is unsafe and the individuals created by it would probably be forced to suffer without their consent. Instead of introducing lofty moral doctrines or engaging in discussions on popular opinions, this approach brings the matter down to questions such as, 'Does it hurt?' and 'Did they give you permission to do that?' Of the authors that I have named, Glover and Harris come closest to this kind of thinking. I will describe their views in Section 2.2.[2]

---

[2] Jonathan Glover, 1977, *Causing Death and Saving Lives* (Harmondsworth: Penguin Books); Jonathan Glover, 1984, *What Sort of People Should There Be? Genetic Engineering, Brain Control, and Their Impact on Our Future World* (New York, NY: Penguin Books); Glover, 1999; Glover, 2006; John Harris, 1980, *Violence and Responsibility* (London: Routledge & Kegan Paul); John Harris, 1985, *The Value of Life: An Introduction to Medical Ethics* (London: Routledge); John Harris, 1992, *Wonderwoman and Superman: The Ethics of Human Biotechnology* (Oxford: Oxford University Press); Harris, 1998; Harris, 2004; Harris, 2007.

The second approach proceeds from the opposite end of the continuum. Its central tenet is that transparency, clarity, and comprehensibility in the sense understood by liberal individualists are fetishes of a historically distinctive, and mistaken, school of thought, namely analytical philosophy. Moral problems should not be dissected to death but taken holistically. They should be confronted in their complexity and with their emotional, social, and spiritual connections, acknowledging that they can contain mysteries which cannot be grasped by reason alone. Within this type of thinking, bans on cloning can be justified by appeals to emotional responses or to the secret of life that the practice would upset. Of my chosen ethicists, Kass and Sandel represent versions of this view which will be explained in more detail in Section 2.3.[3]

The third approach is, in a way, an attempt to strike a balance between the two extremes. It does aim at clarity and transparency in ethical assessments, but it can also settle for acceptance which is widely shared without necessarily insisting on an explanation for it. According to this approach, moral decisions should be made quasi-publicly. When we try to determine what is right or wrong, we must consider everyone's interests and opinions and promote rules that could be agreed to by all reasonable people. An argument against cloning within this outlook would be that its authorisation could not be rationally approved by everyone in society. Habermas and Green fall into this methodological category, although they tend to lean towards the opposite ends of the debate – Habermas towards complexity and Green towards simplicity.[4] Their stances will be explicated in Section 2.4.

[3] Leon R. Kass, 1985, *Toward a More Natural Science: Biology and Human Affairs* (New York, NY: The Free Press); Leon R. Kass, 1994, *The Hungry Soul: Eating and the Perfecting of Our Nature* (New York, NY: The Free Press); Leon R. Kass and James Q. Wilson, 1998, *The Ethics of Human Cloning* (Washington, DC: The American Enterprise Institute); Leon R. Kass and Amy A. Kass, 2000, *Wing to Wing, Oar to Oar: Readings on Courting and Marrying* (Notre Dame, IN: University of Notre Dame Press); Kass, 2002; Leon R. Kass, 2003, *The Beginning of Wisdom: Reading Genesis* (New York, NY: Free Press); Michael J. Sandel, 1982, *Liberalism and the Limits of Justice* (Cambridge: Cambridge University Press); Michael J. Sandel, 1996, *Democracy's Discontent: America in Search of a Public Philosophy* (Cambridge, MA: Harvard University Press); Michael J. Sandel, 2005a, *Public Philosophy: Essays on Morality in Politics* (Cambridge, MA: Harvard University Press); Sandel, 2007.
[4] Jürgen Habermas, 1984–87, *The Theory of Communicative Action* Volumes I-II, translated by Thomas McCarthy (Cambridge: Polity Press); Jürgen Habermas, 1990, *Moral Consciousness and Communicative Action*, translated by Christian Lenhardt and Shierry Weber Nicholsen (Cambridge, MA: MIT Press); Jürgen Habermas, 1993, *Justification and Application: Remarks on Discourse Ethics*, translated by Ciaran Cronin (Cambridge: Polity Press); Habermas, 2003; Ronald M. Green, 2001b, *The Human Embryo Research Debates: Bioethics in the Vortex of Controversy* (New York, NY: Oxford University Press); Green, 2007.

One way of describing the three approaches is to say that they represent the three normative doctrines of Western moral philosophy: consequentialism (outcome- and utility-directed ethics), teleology (purpose- and virtue-oriented ethics), and deontology (rule- and duty-based ethics). It is true that the first style is superbly exemplified by the writings of Jeremy Bentham, the founder of modern utilitarianism and the classical author whose work bears the closest resemblance to Glover and Harris.[5] It is also true that the traditional and communitarian ways of thinking adopted by Kass and Sandel have been associated with the work of Aristotle, the paragon of teleological ethics.[6] And it is true that Habermas and Green work quite consciously within the framework set up by Immanuel Kant, the archetype of duty-based moral philosophy.[7] But this is not the whole picture: Glover and Harris do not always restrict their arguments to mere consequences;[8] Kass and Sandel add two millennia of theology and philosophy to Aristotle's thinking; and Habermas and Green shun the solipsistic intellectualism of Kant. The prefix 'neo' could be added to the three traditional headings to mark the variation (neo-consequentialism and so on), but the headings should still not be used as more than a heuristic device in the context of the six named authors, whose ideas elude ready-made classifications.

In this chapter, I will first portray the three ways of tackling the 'genetic challenge' by the six scholars (Sections 2.2, 2.3, and 2.4) and state my reasons for not regarding any of them as *the* solution to the choice of methodology in this context (Section 2.5). I will then go on to state my own ideas about rationality and morality (Section 2.6) and the 'polite bystander's' point of view (Sections 2.7 and 2.8), which will then be assumed in the chapters dealing with the seven ways of making people better.

---

[5] E.g. Jeremy Bentham, 1982, J. H. Burns and H. L. A. Hart (eds), *An Introduction to the Principles of Morals and Legislation* [1789] (London: Methuen).

[6] Aristotle, 1982, *Nichomachean Ethics* (Cambridge, MA: Harvard University Press).

[7] E.g. Immanuel Kant, 1994, *Ethical Philosophy* [*Grundlegung zur Metaphysik der Sitten* 1785a and *Metaphysische Anfangsgründe der Tugendlehre* 1797a], translated by J. W. Ellington, second edition (Indianapolis, IN: Hackett Publishing Company); Immanuel Kant, 1999, *Metaphysical Elements of Justice* [*Metaphysische Anfangsgründe der Rechtslehre* 1797b], translated by J. Ladd, second edition (Indianapolis, IN: Hackett Publishing Company).

[8] Tuija Takala, 2003, 'Utilitarianism shot down by its own men?', *Cambridge Quarterly of Healthcare Ethics* 12: 447–54; Matti Häyry, 2007a, 'Utilitarianism and bioethics', Richard E. Ashcroft, Angus Dawson, Heather Draper, and John R. McMillan (eds), *Principles of Health Care Ethics*, second edition (Chichester: John Wiley & Sons): 57–64.

2.2   Rational tangibility: Glover and Harris

Glover, Harris, and other advocates of the 'rational tangibility' approach find the foundation of their search for morality in a startling question, namely, 'Why is it wrong to kill people – if and when it is?'[9] Just asking the question has stirred an array of objections. Opponents of the view have thought that 'if' and 'when' are not appropriate words in this context. Killing people is wrong, it is always wrong, and even to raise the question is dangerous and a sign of moral corruption. Human life has absolute value, which cannot and should not be discussed or weighed. Philosophers who even have to ask the question do not, by rights, deserve to lecture on ethics to unsuspecting audiences.[10]

The point of the query for Glover and Harris, however, is this. Some killing of human beings is accepted, anyway. People all around the world approve just warfare, capital punishment, self-defence, and terminations of pregnancy. Most of us condone at least some of these forms of killing. In addition, many human beings die before their time because their

[9] The other advocates of this type of approach, with variations, include at least J. J. C. Smart, R. M. Hare, Peter Singer, and Julian Savulescu. Some of my own writings link me to this school, too, although I have in my more recent work emphasised a different fundamental question, which is, 'Why can't I do what I want – if and when I can't?' The contributions of Joel Feinberg and Robert Nozick have provided me with important insights in this development. See, e.g. J. J. C. Smart, 1973, 'An outline of a system of utilitarian ethics' [1961], reprinted in J. J. C. Smart and Bernard Williams (eds), *Utilitarianism: For and Against* (Cambridge: Cambridge University Press); R. M. Hare, 1975, 'Abortion and the Golden Rule', *Philosophy & Public Affairs* 4: 201–22; R. M. Hare, 1981, *Moral Thinking: Its Levels, Method and Point* (Oxford: Clarendon Press); Peter Singer, 1979, *Practical Ethics* (Cambridge: Cambridge University Press); Julian Savulescu, 1998a, 'Consequentialism, reasons, value and justice', *Bioethics* 12: 212–35; Joel Feinberg, 1967, 'The forms and limits of utilitarianism', *Philosophical Review* 76: 368–81; Joel Feinberg, 1984–88, *The Moral Limits of the Criminal Law* Volumes I-IV (Oxford: Oxford University Press); Robert Nozick, 1974, *Anarchy, State, and Utopia* (Oxford: Blackwell).

[10] The opponents of the 'rational tangibility' view in ethics in general have included, among others, Elizabeth Anscombe, Bernard Williams, Philippa Foot, Anne Maclean, Onora O'Neill, and Jennifer Jackson. See, e.g. Elizabeth Anscombe, 1970, 'War and murder', Richard A. Wasserstrom (ed.), *War and Morality* (Belmont, CA: Wadsworth Publishing): 42–53; Bernard Williams, 1973a, 'A critique of utilitarianism', J. J. C. Smart and Bernard Williams (eds), *Utilitarianism: For and Against* (Cambridge: Cambridge University Press); Philippa Foot, 1978, *Virtues and Vices and Other Essays in Moral Philosophy* (Berkeley, CA: University of California Press); Philippa Foot, 2001, *Natural Goodness* (Oxford: Clarendon Press); Philippa Foot, 2002, *Moral Dilemmas: And Other Topics in Moral Philosophy* (Oxford: Clarendon Press); Anne Maclean, 1993, *The Elimination of Morality: Reflections on Utilitarianism and Bioethics* (London: Routledge); Onora O'Neill, 2002, *Autonomy and Trust in Bioethics* (Cambridge: Cambridge University Press); Jennifer Jackson, 2006, *Ethics in Medicine* (Cambridge: Polity Press).

lives are not saved. We could in many cases save those lives, for instance, by donating money to charitable organisations that run vaccination programmes in developing countries. By not doing this, we make ourselves almost as responsible for the deaths of unvaccinated children as we would be if we travelled to their countries and killed them. So killing people and knowingly letting them die is already going on, and the remaining questions – the ones that Glover and Harris ask – are, why and when is this right and why and when is it wrong?[11]

Where can the answer to the questions be found? According to Glover and Harris, it *cannot* be found in God, nature,[12] religious tradition, deontological arguments, or moral sentiments.[13] These yield answers that are false or unintelligible,[14] conceptually incoherent or logically inadequate;[15] and generate consequences that cannot be accepted.[16] The only reliable guide in moral enquiries is rational argumentation,[17] and this will in most cases lead to the consideration of the concrete, tangible impacts of our choices on people who are affected by them.[18]

The view that Glover and Harris develop by using rational argumentation states the following.[19] It would be wrong to kill someone who has a life worth living[20] or a life of value.[21] It would also be wrong to kill individuals who want to go on living, for two reasons. Their willingness to live can, for all we know, prove that their lives are worth living or have value.[22] And, apart from this, it is important that people's autonomy is respected, especially in irreversible decisions such as hastening their death.[23] Furthermore, since there is no intrinsic moral difference between killing people and failing to save their lives, it would be wrong not to save individuals whose lives are worth living or have value, or who want to go on living.[24]

According to Glover and Harris, then, one fundamental reason against killing people and failing to save their lives is that these choices would eliminate the worthwhile future existence of a currently existing

---

[11] Glover, 1977; Harris, 1992. Both Glover (2006) and Harris (2007) have published more recent books on aspects of the genetic challenge, but their theoretical stances (which in the new contributions remain unchanged) are presented best in the cited (older) works.

[12] Glover, 1977, p. 84.   [13] Harris, 1992, pp. 35, 40–3, 46, 146.

[14] Glover, 1977, p. 84.   [15] Glover, 1977, p. 25.   [16] Glover, 1977, pp. 25–6.

[17] Harris, 1992, p. 5.   [18] See, e.g. Häyry, 2001a, pp. 64–78.

[19] This formulation is mostly based on Glover, 1977. Judging by Glover's own later books his view remains the same. Harris's view differs from this only so slightly that it makes no difference in a general description such as this.

[20] Glover, 1977, p. 52.   [21] Harris, 1985, pp. 15–19.   [22] Glover, 1977, pp. 53–4.

[23] Glover, 1977, pp. 78–83.   [24] Glover, 1977, p. 116.

person. Similar reasons can be extended to reproductive choices. Failure to conceive and a decision to terminate a pregnancy would also eliminate the future existence of a person, albeit a currently nonexistent one. Therefore the view stipulates that it would be wrong not to bring about a life worth living or of value, provided that the life is qualitatively so good that it does not lower the average goodness of the lives of the population as a whole.[25] Slightly surprisingly, this does not seem to imply that people actually must have children or shy away from abortions. One reason cited for this is the need to respect people's reproductive autonomy;[26] another is that unwanted children can have lives qualitatively below the average.[27]

Put in terms of worth, Glover and Harris postulate three categories of lives: those *more* worth living; those *less* worth living; and those *not* worth living. This postulation produces several normative judgements that have relevance in the discussion on making people better. The first is that if some people's lives can be made longer and more worth living without making other people's lives shorter or less worth living, it would be wrong not to do so.[28] This has obvious implications on the development of new drugs and treatments, including saviour sibling, stem cell, gene, and life-extending therapies. The second is that if we can choose between two future individuals, one who would have a good life and another who would have a so-so or a bad life, it would be wrong not to select the one with the good life.[29] This sanctions preimplantation genetic selection; and abortions on genetic grounds *when* this gives way to a new pregnancy through which an individual with a better life replaces the individual with the worse life. The third is that if we have to choose between creating a life less worth living and no life at all, it would *not* be wrong to choose the life less worth living. If parents can have only disabled children, having them can be better than remaining childless.[30] The fourth and final normative judgement is that it would be wrong to bring about lives which are not worth living. The criteria are difficult to specify, but prenatally predicted or diagnosed severe disabilities in a future child entail, according to this view, a moral duty not to conceive the child, or to terminate the pregnancy if it is already on the way.[31]

Critics of Glover and Harris tend to classify them as individualists and consequentialists. This is not unreasonable given some of their views.

---

[25] Glover, 1977, pp. 69–70, 140; cf. Harris, 1992, pp. 176–7.   [26] Harris, 1992, p. 71.
[27] Glover, 1977, pp. 140–2.   [28] Glover, 1977, pp. 54–7.   [29] Glover, 1977, p. 140
[30] Glover, 1977, p. 147; Harris, 1992, pp. 71–2.   [31] Glover, 1977, pp. 145–8.

They believe that it is always justified 'to want more of a good thing than less of it',[32] and the good things they have in mind are eventually experienced or lived by particular human beings. But the classification can, on closer scrutiny, be challenged on both accounts.

The principle of replaceability, needed in the defence of selective abortions, makes the role of individuals virtually void in the model. It does not matter which of two embryos or fetuses is allowed to continue its development as long as the resulting worth or value of life is maximised. Glover and Harris would not kill existing people against their will, presumably because they would have sufficient respect for the *subjective* worth or value of their lives. But they would, in the light of their theory, prefer a world with human lives which are more rather than less worthwhile. If I could be easily replaced by a better copy, Glover and Harris would have no problem with *me* being lost, because they have no respect for me as an *objectively* separate entity. And this is exactly the logic by which they also ignore the individuality of embryos and fetuses.

The division of lives into the three rather vague categories, in its turn, makes the consequentialism of the view questionable. The standard idea of the doctrine is that the impacts of actions and inactions can be assessed and compared with each other by using commensurable units of value. The question concerning expected outcomes is genuine and empirically testable: we ask which one of our action alternatives produces the best results, in the light of the knowledge we have about the world. But with the division introduced by Glover and assumed by Harris, the conclusion can be manipulated to match our predetermined views. If we do not want to condone the birth of individuals with a specific congenital ailment, we simply define this ailment as making their lives not worth living, and no further calculations are needed. This, I would like to argue, is not consequentialism in its purest form.[33]

2.3   Moral transcendence: Kass and Sandel

Kass and Sandel's search for the basis of morality also centres on a startling question, in their case, 'What is the meaning of life?' or 'What gives human life its meaning?' This is the kind of enquiry that is made more frequently in religious contexts (and Woody Allen movies) than in contemporary philosophical ethics, which is why many scholars tend to dismiss their efforts as theological metaphysics smuggled into secular

[32] Glover, 1977, p. 56.   [33] Cf. Häyry, 2007a.

discussion.[34] But, despite the heavy use of biblical language, both Kass and Sandel assure their readers that their arguments can be understood without any reference to particular religions.[35] Kass has in fact been criticised for *not* taking his views to their theological conclusion.[36]

The answer to the questions cannot, according to Kass, be found in modern philosophical analyses, because these are hyperrational and void of ethical significance. Clarity, consistency, and coherence are overrated, and the pride of place given to them is primarily responsible for the sorry state of current bioethics.[37] Utilitarian and other consequentialist ways of thinking, with their emphasis on rationalisation over reason, inclination over duty, and pleasure over goodness, are particularly detrimental to any moral pursuit.[38] And although Kass thinks that Kantian opposition to these degradations is admirable, the emphasis given within this school of thought on the pure *willing* of and *thinking* about the good and the right is not sufficient for him, either.[39] Since humans are also *begetting* and *belonging* beings, excessive concentration on the mind disembodies us and makes us less than human.[40] Instead of making intellect our starting point, Kass believes, physical and moral repugnance could be our best initial guide towards the right direction – to moral wisdom.[41]

The core of moral wisdom, Kass argues, can be found in biology, and in the close connection between sex and mortality. We are naturally (although not always consciously) drawn between two aspirations: *self-preservation* and the *urge to reproduce*. Self-preservation aims at personal permanence and satisfaction. But reproduction has a different goal altogether. Unlike and even against the first drive, it is self-denial for the sake of transcending our finite individual existence.[42] Man and woman come together to produce a child that will eventually survive them both. The flesh, name, ways, and hopes of the parents will live on in the child, thus providing them a 'future beyond the grave'.[43] Having this aim in mind is what elevates love above lust and gives human life the meaning and

---

[34] E.g. Leon Eisenberg, 2003, 'Life, liberty, and the defense of dignity: The challenge for bioethics' (book review), *The New England Journal of Medicine* 348: 766–8; Carson Strong, 2005, 'Lost in translation: Religious arguments made secular', *American Journal of Bioethics* 5: 29–31.

[35] Kass, 2002, pp. 86, 114; Sandel, 2007, pp. 92–5.

[36] Marc D. Guerra, 2003, 'Life, liberty, and the defense of human dignity: The challenge for bioethics' (book review), *First Things*, February – www.firstthings.com/article.php3?id_article=429.

[37] Kass, 2002, pp. 57–65.   [38] Kass, 2002, p. 16.   [39] Kass, 2002, pp. 16–17.

[40] Kass, 2002, p. 17.   [41] Kass, 2002, pp. 149–53. Cf. Häyry, 2007c, pp. 57–73.

[42] Kass, 2002, pp. 19, 155–7.   [43] Kass, 2002, p. 157.

dignity that it has.[44] Apart from the figurative immortality of individuals, it makes possible moral growth through the uninterrupted existence of 'families and communities of worship, where cultural practices enable the deepest insights of the mind to become embodied in the finest habits of the heart'.[45] Cultural continuity by procreation, not personal satisfaction, is the distinctively *human* and *dignified* element of our lives.

The view Kass puts forward has important implications for the technological ways of making people better. He readily admits that many of these, perhaps all, promote liberty, equality, health, longevity, freedom, prosperity, and happiness. But the problem is that they also threaten human dignity.[46] If sex is taken out of reproduction, the meaning of life – its erotic and social continuation – will be gradually lost. And taking sex out of reproduction is exactly what is happening with assisted insemination, in vitro fertilisation, and especially cloning, which does not even allow the union of two separate genomes.[47] The search for considerable life extension, again, challenges procreation indirectly by trying to make existing individuals so long-lived that few new individuals, if any, are eventually needed.[48] Based on these considerations, Kass thinks that if we let the specifically human part of our existence – again, erotic and social continuation – erode, we cease to be what we have been for millennia and slowly but surely turn into inhuman or posthuman beings.[49]

Sandel, like Kass, believes that analytic ethics is unable to solve the problems created by the new genetics. When we are troubled by enhancements and other technological developments we are not fundamentally concerned about violations of autonomy, fairness, or individual rights, which are the bread and butter of the purely cerebral philosophers of our time.[50] Most ways of making people better actually promote freedom, justice, and rights, so there is no cause for complaint on this front. But

---

[44] Kass, 2002, p. 156. This, at least, is what I think Kass is saying. Here is a passage from the same page that I did not fully understand, though: 'Whether we know it or not, when we are sexually active we are voting with our genitalia for our own demise. The salmon swimming upstream to spawn and die tell the universal story: sex is bound up with death, to which it holds a partial answer in procreation.' I can understand that sex leads to procreation and procreation leads to an immortality of sorts, so that accounts for the 'partial answer' bit. But 'voting with our genitalia for our own demise'? Is there a causal connection between sex and death? Do people who do not have sex live longer? Am I missing something really obvious here?

[45] Kass, 2002, p. 53.   [46] Kass, 2002, p. 22.

[47] Kass, 2002, pp. 159–61.   [48] Kass, 2002, pp. 19–20.

[49] Kass, 2002, pp. 21–2. See also Francis Fukuyama, 2002, *Our Posthuman Future: Consequences of the Biotechnology Revolution* (London: Profile Books).

[50] Sandel, 2007, pp. 6–9.

we *are* troubled, says Sandel, and to understand why we are 'we need to confront questions ... about the moral status of nature, and about the proper moral stance of human beings toward the given world.'[51] If these questions sound unfamiliar or theological, this cannot be helped because they have already been raised by science and technology.[52] Human dignity is under threat by enhancements, cloning, and genetic engineering, and the task now is to find out '*how* these practices diminish our humanity' and what 'aspect of human freedom or human flourishing ... they threaten'.[53] Since the answer cannot be found in liberal principles, a more helpful vocabulary has to be assumed.

Sandel argues that the part of humanity biotechnology endangers is our ability to see and value the role of 'giftedness' in our lives.[54] By giftedness he means that human life is always partly beyond our control, and by the ability to see and value its role he means that this should be accepted and held in awe, not fought against or cursed. Sports, according to Sandel, provide a platform for the recognition of giftedness over human effort. The admiration we feel for a naturally talented top athlete will never be extended to mediocre sportspeople, even if they trained every bit as hard as the champion.[55] Parenthood, however, is the area of life where people understand the notion of giftedness best. Children come as they are, and good parents take this for granted and love their young unconditionally in their given state.[56] But the genetic challenge threatens to change this. If children are planned and designed, parents will have expectations concerning them and their love will become conditional. Aspirations of wilfulness, dominion, and moulding replace the traditional ideas of giftedness, reverence, and beholding in our attitudes toward the world as we see it.[57]

The wrong Sandel sees in all this is that the genetic revolution can lead us to the assumption of a 'project of mastery', the abandonment of good habits of mind and ways of being, and the loss of 'human goods embodied in important social practices'.[58] The goods that will be lost, with the sense of giftedness, are humility, a limited sense of responsibility, and solidarity.[59] Humility and reasonable accountability for what we do will be replaced by excessive pride in our achievements and a crushing liability for what we are as a result of our own manipulations. If we succeed, it is all our doing. But if we fail, we are also the only ones to blame. This, Sandel

---

[51] Sandel, 2007, p. 9.   [52] Sandel, 2007, pp. 9–10.   [53] Sandel, 2007, p. 24.
[54] Sandel, 2007, p. 29.   [55] Sandel, 2007, pp. 26–9.   [56] Sandel, 2007, pp. 45, 86.
[57] Sandel, 2007, p. 85.   [58] Sandel, 2007, pp. 96, 97–100.   [59] Sandel, 2007, p. 86.

argues, will undermine our sense of solidarity – the sensitivity to the role of chance in human life that makes us share risks and pool resources in the form of social insurance.[60] So, in the end, whatever the promises of new genetic technologies may be in terms of freedom, happiness, and fairness, we should be wary of them lest we lose the central human value of solidarity.

Although different in detail, the accounts of Kass and Sandel share a common core. What is at stake in the introduction of cloning, enhancements, and the like is not personal freedom or individual wellbeing but humanity as we know and cherish it. The answer to the question, 'What gives human life its meaning?' is essentially the same for both. We and our actions can contribute to realising value in our lives, but the ultimate answer transcends our limitations. The meaning of life must come from something beyond our desire, will, and manipulative power; be that God, nature, or just an inexplicable reverence for our biological, moral, and social existence.

2.4   Everybody's acceptance: Habermas and Green

As seen so far, Glover, Harris, Kass, and Sandel are all interested in defining the kind of human life that is worth protecting and promoting. Glover and Harris find the answer in the quality of individual lives, while Kass and Sandel focus on the good life of the species as a whole. Habermas and Green initially deviate from this starting point. The basic question in their theories is, 'How can a decision be acceptable to all?' or 'Which decisions take everyone's interests fully into account?' Interestingly, though, their own responses to the queries lead them to mutually conflicting normative conclusions when it comes to making people better.

Habermas requires that moral rules can be universalised. By this he means that a norm must meet the following requirement: 'All affected can accept the consequences and the side effects its *general* observance can be anticipated to have for the satisfaction of *everyone's* interests (and these consequences are preferred to those of known alternative possibilities for regulation)'.[61] As a justification for this, Habermas presents observations concerning human nature. It is important for us, as human beings, to create an identity and to preserve it during our lives. Since we are fundamentally social beings, our identities can only be formed and protected in interactions with other people. The web of these interactions constitutes

---

[60] Sandel, 2007, pp. 89–92.   [61] Habermas, 1990, p. 65.

our form of life, and due to our social nature we can only have a universal morality in the context of a form of life. In that context we can negotiate, through argumentative discourse between equal participants, the particular norms and actions that can be accepted by all and are in everyone's interest.[62]

In the negotiation, Habermas wants to keep the language used as neutral and generally accepted as possible. Many people have claimed, for instance, that bans on abortion, embryology, and genetic tests can be based solely on the intrinsic dignity of the early human being.[63] Habermas disagrees, although he believes that the practices in question are 'reifying', 'disgusting', and 'obscene'.[64] There is, he argues, reasonable variance in views concerning the moral status of embryos and fetuses, and while a value judgement in favour of the bans can be coherently made, it would be wrong to conflate values (everybody *agrees* that embryos have human value) and rights (everybody *does not agree* that embryos have human rights); the latter also being required for the establishment of a universal norm in this matter.[65]

According to Habermas, an alternative way to approach the issue is to focus on *the ethical self-understanding of the human species*, which is a necessary condition of our individual and social development. If we do not have a clear and solid view of what makes us human, we cannot see and respect, as we should, ourselves and others as autonomous persons with our own life histories.[66] The clear and solid view that we currently have of ourselves includes at least three important elements: an awareness that there is a part of us that is naturally grown and not self-made (or otherwise human-made); a conviction that in the realm of the self-made we are capable of self-determined and responsible action; and a recognition of the equality of all human beings in our dealings with each other.[67] These elements are intertwined. If the distinction between the grown and the made is demolished, this will blur the idea of responsible self-determination and undermine our sense of and respect for equality.

Habermas believes that the ethical self-understanding of the species provides grounds for rejecting reproductive selection in all its forms, cloning, and gene therapies that are not aimed at restoring the health of the treated individuals.[68] In all these cases, the moral logic is the same. If individuals are the result, even partially, of parental choices or technological

[62] Habermas, 1990, pp. 130, 207; Habermas, 1993, pp. 31, 37, 83–4.
[63] Habermas, 2003, pp. 29–37.   [64] Habermas, 2003, pp. 20, 39.
[65] Habermas, 2003, pp. 31–2, 36.   [66] Habermas, 2003, p. 25.
[67] Habermas, 2003, pp. 29, 42, 56–8.   [68] Habermas, 2003, pp. 43–4, 52, 57–8, 63–4, 73–4.

manipulation, they will lose their actual and perceived 'ownness'. They can still understand themselves as social beings in communicative inter-action with others. But they will not be able to claim a natural core self, untouched by others, which could be used as their own perspective to controversial matters. This part of them has been taken over by other people's choices, and the selected and manipulated individuals have been left without a sense of self-madeness, identity, or freedom.[69]

Habermas does not maintain that people who have been screened, cloned, or enhanced would be or feel any less human or possess less human dignity. The argument is not in that sense metaphysical or psycho-logical. The crux of the matter is what we do to our self-understanding as a species if we even try to choose people or interfere with them without their consent.[70] By doing this we would neither be listening to them nor giving them a chance to say 'Yes' or 'No' based on their own interests and reasons. Yet everybody's opportunity to agree or to disagree is a necessary condition for the formulation of universally acceptable norms – which define our humanity. If some individuals are denied their say in our com-municative interaction, as is suggested by genetic engineering, we cannot see ourselves as equal, autonomous, responsible agents any more.[71] The 'moral indignation proper' that accompanies this revelation differs dras-tically from the less serious 'disgust at something obscene' that we feel, for instance, in debates over the use of embryos in research. As Habermas puts it, 'It is the feeling of vertigo that seizes us when the ground beneath our feet, which we believed to be solid, begins to slip'.[72] Gene technologies destroy, conceptually speaking, the foundation of our moral life.

Green agrees with Habermas that moral norms should be accept-able to all. His formulation of this is: 'The right thing to do is that which omnipartial, rational persons would accept as a public rule of conduct (norm): that is, as a form of conduct known by everyone and applicable to everyone'.[73] An interesting difference, and probably the one that accounts for the disagreement in the ensuing normative conclusions, is that Green restricts the scope of moral decision makers to *rational* persons. Habermas requires in his universalisation thesis that *everyone* affected by a norm's general observance should have a say in its approval.[74] This leads him to examine how selection, cloning, and enhancements influence everyone's

---

[69] Habermas, 2003, pp. 56–8.   [70] Habermas, 2003, p. 60.
[71] Habermas, 2003, pp. 54–7.   [72] Habermas, 2003, p. 39.
[73] Ronald M. Green, 2005, 'New challenges of genetics and ethics' – www.dartmouth. edu/~ethics/resources/elsi2005.html.
[74] Habermas, 1990, p. 65.

prospects to participate equally, freely, and responsibly in genetic decision making; and to conclude that genetic advances challenge the very root of our prevailing morality by cancelling out this type of participation by all. For Green, it seems to be sufficient that a group of rational persons accept the norm, provided that they take everybody's interests into account in the process.

Green himself accounts for interests by first giving meticulous descriptions of scientific achievements and people's reactions to them, and then examining critically arguments against the use of genetics.[75] The results of his analysis can be summarised in three main points. The first is that worries about children and families in the age of genetics are exaggerated. The second is that people's fear of change is often the only (irrational) reason for their objections. The third is that all risks and challenges posed by genetics can be dealt with by regulations rather than prohibitions. Let me explain these one by one.

The first point allays all concerns about psychological damage potentially caused to children and families by selection, cloning, and gene therapies. It is possible that parents will expect specific traits or qualities to manifest in their chosen or enhanced offspring, and it is possible that their young will feel the pressure of these expectations. But Green argues that this should not prevent us from using these techniques. As a reason for this, he offers a 'psychological principle', namely, the generalisation that 'Parental Love Almost Always Prevails.'[76] By this Green means that parents nearly without fail 'bond to children *as they are*' and 'love the children they get no matter what qualities they possess'.[77] He gives as an illustration his daughter who wanted to have a girl, had a boy, and five years later 'could not imagine this wonderful child to be other than what he is'.[78] He also cites disability activists who argue that 'parents love their disabled children, often regard them as the highlight of their lives, and usually adjust their various family responsibilities to meet the extra needs of their "special" child'.[79] So it does not pay to agonise over the impact of genetics on children: parents will connect with them anyway.

The second point is designed to cover residual anxieties about the ill-effects of change. Even given that parental love almost always prevails, society, morality, and humanity may become different as a result of genetic selection and enhancements. Against those who use this as an argument for prohibitions (like Kass, Sandel, and Habermas do), Green

---

[75] Green, 2007.   [76] Green, 2007, p. 114.   [77] Green, 2007, p. 116.
[78] Green, 2007, p. 114.   [79] Green, 2007, p. 115.

evokes the 'reversal test' introduced by Nick Bostrom and Toby Ord.[80] The idea is that if changes to one direction are seen as dangerous, the situation is reversed and people are asked to judge corresponding changes to the opposite direction. For instance, if people oppose genetic attempts to raise the intelligence quotient (IQ) of a population by 10 points, they are invited to think whether *lowering* the IQ of the same population by 10 points would be a better idea. If both proposals are met with suspicion and only the prevailing situation is deemed acceptable, the evaluators could 'suffer from *status quo bias*'.[81] And if this is the only reason for opposing changes, it can be ignored as irrational.

The third point is that the more concrete physical, moral, and social risks related to genetic advances can be controlled best by regulation. Green offers four guidelines for this: 'Genetic interventions should always be aimed at what is reasonably in the child's best interests';[82] 'Genetic interventions should be almost as safe as natural reproduction';[83] 'We should avoid and discourage interventions that confer only positional advantage';[84] and 'Genetic interventions should not reinforce or increase unjust inequality and discrimination, economic inequality, or racism'.[85] It is notable that these norms are geared towards accommodating almost all forms of selection, reproduction, therapy, and enhancement, provided that they are 'reasonably' or 'almost' safe. The only prohibitions that Green seems to condone are against clones bred for organ donation (glaringly exploitative but also science fiction);[86] height modification with an increased risk of heart disease (a question of physical harm and safety);[87] reducing children's cognitive abilities to make them more obedient to the elders of a religious cult (here again Green's basic concern is future vulnerability to harm);[88] and elevated red blood cell function with an increased risk of heart disease (bodily harm yet again).[89]

It seems, then, that the general requirement of universal acceptance, shared by Habermas and Green, can produce very different norms depending on the details of the chosen moral theory. Habermas starts from everybody's consent and ends up condemning selection, cloning, and enhancements in their entirety, while Green settles for the consent of

---

[80] Green, 2007, pp. 104–6; Nick Bostrom and Toby Ord, 2006, 'The reversal test: Eliminating status quo bias in applied ethics', *Ethics* 116: 656–79.
[81] Green, 2007, p. 104; quoting Bostrom and Ord, 2006 (italics added).
[82] Green, 2007, p. 216 (italics removed).   [83] Green, 2007, p. 218 (italics removed).
[84] Green, 2007, p. 223 (italics removed).   [85] Green, 2007, p. 225 (italics removed).
[86] Green, 2007, p. 216.   [87] Green, 2007, p. 217.
[88] Green, 2007, p. 218.   [89] Green, 2007, p. 224.

rational people and finishes off by approving all the debated practices in monitored and regulated forms.

2.5   Why none of the approaches is *the* one

I do *not* aim in this book to criticise other ethicists' views at a normative level. To claim that any of the six scholars whom I have introduced is wrong in any absolute sense forms no part of my philosophical conclusions. But for the sake of clarity and fairness, it is probably best that I express my own personal opinions concerning the six views before moving on to point out their limited applicability and troubled relationships with each other. While inadmissible as theoretical evidence, these opinions undoubtedly set the background against which the rest of my argument should be viewed. Let me re-emphasise, however, that I do *not* see the following scattered musings, for reasons that will become apparent in the next sections, as conclusive enforcements or criticisms of the ideas of Glover, Harris, Kass, Sandel, Habermas, and Green.

To begin with, I have a lot of sympathy for the commonsense and dedication of Glover and Harris. Their prescriptions are always designed to reduce suffering and to promote the physical and psychological good of humanity in an impartial and equitable manner. If traditional rules or prevailing opinions seem to intervene, they are brushed aside with arguments that show their intellectual weaknesses. Metaphysical assumptions are kept to a minimum and religion is kept apart from moral judgements. Responsibility is assigned to deliberate omissions as well as actions, which is a good way of making the prevailing situation just one of the options open to us when we make our choices.

I see two main question marks in the model advocated by Glover and Harris. The first is their division of life's worth or value into the three levels of 'more', 'less', and 'none'. Many qualities can, of course, be divided like this – intended insults are more offensive or less offensive or not offensive at all, and so on. But in this case it seems that definitions follow evaluations rather than precede them. In prenatal choices Glover and Harris tend to decide first that, say, parents should not have blind children if they can have seeing children instead. To justify this choice, they then decree that the lives of blind people have less worth or value than the lives of seeing people. This seems to apply across the board. We do not have a primary criterion of worth or value which could then be predictably applied to particular cases; we have a list of cases that Glover and Harris have reacted to intuitively and rationalisations of these reactions in terms of worth and value. My second problem with the model is its tendency to see opposing views as irrational. All appeals to prevailing norms and values, be they grounded on religion, local custom, or people's actual beliefs, are dismissed as going against reason – unless they happen to support the ideas championed by Glover and Harris, in which case they go unquestioned. So while I personally agree with their general ethos, I see difficulties both in their positive case for this ethos and in their defence of it against challenges.

Kass and Sandel's particular strength lies in their allegiance to humanity's and community's accumulated wisdom. People have lived together in groups for millennia and their organically developed ways of thinking can well indicate our best responses to social and natural threats. When our ways of thinking are deeply ingrained, it is also possible that immediate reactions of indignation and repugnance mark the boundaries of morality more reliably than analytical efforts by philosophers and ethicists. As to the ideals we should aim at, Kass and Sandel are not afraid to use metaphors that can be considered old-fashioned but are understood by most people. A prominent example of this is the notion of 'giftedness' which is set against our will to control matters in our environment.

My personal difficulties with the views of Kass and Sandel are twofold. Their reliance on concepts that have deep cultural meaning makes, in my eyes, their philosophy shallow. Erotic and social continuation through sex and reproduction has so far been a feature of human life, and children have often been seen as gifts. But these are just isolated observations. It is also true, and culturally meaningful, that sex gives pleasure whether or not it is linked with reproduction. Why is *this* not seen as the cornerstone of ethics? Their failure to compare and examine things further gives me the impression that the authors are just hanging on to the first words they can find in justifying their preset views on gene technologies. This is linked to my other concern, as well. Kass and Sandel admit that genetic advances could, and probably would, promote autonomy, rights, fairness, liberty, equality, justice, health, longevity, prosperity, and happiness – but argue that progress would still be wrong because it would threaten the meaning of life. What exactly can this mean? Would it not be good to endorse the listed values? It seems to me that Kass and Sandel turn their backs on all these modern ideals rather too casually. It is one thing to have a traditional sense of what is right and what is wrong, but quite another to completely disregard the principles on which our current liberal and democratic societies are founded.

Habermas and Green definitely have a point when they say that universal consensus is a prerequisite of universal morality. Habermas moves cleverly from this position to the idea that we would be wrong to make decisions for future generations without their permission. Once the argument has proceeded to this stage, nothing seems to be able to save genetic selection, cloning, and enhancements. Green takes a different route and postulates rational persons who will make the decisions hypothetically for themselves and others. The shift from all to 'only' rational individuals seems acceptable, because we would probably dislike being captive to the opinions of irrational people. And the way rationality pans out in Green's view, his permissive conclusions seem to be difficult to escape if we have already gotten so far as to approve the original limitation.

I do not want to engage in involved arguments with either Habermas or Green at this stage, and I will simply state the main worries I have with their approaches. I do not understand how Habermas can dodge the fact that by deciding *not* to enhance their offspring parents already make a choice for which consent would be needed. The only way to respect future generations would seem to be not to produce them at all (a respectable solution, I believe, but probably not one that he is after). In Green's thinking, I do not fully grasp his notion of 'rationality'. If we are trying to determine what people could rationally condone *and* we know that apparently rational people like Habermas do not condone human cloning, how can we legitimately and without argument ignore the variation in opinions?

I will return to the more specific views of Glover, Harris, Kass, Sandel, Habermas, and Green in Chapters 3, 4, 5, 6, 7, 8, and 9. Going any deeper into their general theories at this stage would be futile, because there is no Archimedean point from which I could judge them in a universally gratifying way. I may personally think that some or all of these authors are mad as hatters, but then again, they have all attracted at some point in their career, reviews stating that they are the best thing since sliced bread. This enthusiastic support for conflicting views is, in fact, my main justification for saying that none of these views is *the* one that should be endorsed by everyone in all places and at all times. Glover and Harris will never be accepted by the proponents of Kass and Sandel; Kass and Sandel will never be accepted by the defenders of Glover and Harris. Habermas and Green come from the same approximate school of thought, but they cannot even be accepted by each other. Are some of them right and some of them wrong? This is a distinct possibility, but who is and on what criteria?

I believe that it is more constructive to try to find points and methods of comparison on a different level.[90]

2.6   A nonconfrontational notion of rationality

Ethical debates on the genetic challenge are often sharply polarised. Some authors hail all developments in the field, while others see them as a peril. Could this mark an unavoidable clash between *rationality* and *morality*? I do not think so, but the language used by many proponents and opponents of new technologies certainly encourages the idea. Glover and Harris do not see much value in traditional moral norms when these cannot be upheld by rational arguments.[91] And Kass and Sandel reject excessive rationality because it tends to erode the foundation of our shared morality.[92] This, however, does not necessarily reveal a gap between rationality and morality. Most work is done in these descriptions by attributes such as 'traditional' and 'excessive'. If the concepts are adequately defined, very few philosophical ethicists would like to be labelled as either 'irrational' or 'immoral'.

Let me propose and explicate, for the purposes of this book, the following *nonconfrontational notion of rationality*:

> A decision is rational insofar as it is based on beliefs that form a coherent whole and are consistent with how things are in the world; and it is aimed at optimising the immediate or long-term impacts on entities that matter.

This definition is not intended to be complete or exclusive. Rationality can, for all I know, have many additional dimensions and aspects. But it

---

[90] What I take to be a similar point in a closely related field is succinctly expressed by Margaret Brazier and Emma Cave in the context of legislating on what is permissible in genetics, biotechnology, and reproduction: 'But above all, each side of the moral debate is convinced that they are right and the other irretrievably wrong. What tends to be overlooked is that, in many ethical debates today, there is no answer that will be accepted as unchallengeably right. The question for legislators is not to find a right answer, to achieve a moral consensus, but to determine how in a liberal, democratic society legislation can be formulated in the absence of such consensus. To evade that task is to give the scientists free rein to do as they see fit. To criticise them with hindsight is unfair and unproductive. Theologians, ethicists, lawyers, and (indeed) all citizens must be prepared to grapple with these awkward moral dilemmas and, probably, be ready to compromise.' Margaret Brazier and Emma Cave, 2007, *Medicine, Patients and the Law*, fourth edition (London: Penguin Books), p. 68. On the possibility of pluralism from a philosophical angle, see David Archard (ed.), 1996, *Philosophy and Pluralism* (Cambridge: Cambridge University Press).

[91] Glover, 1977, pp. 25, 84; Harris, 1992, pp. 35, 40–3, 46, 146.

[92] Kass, 2002, pp. 57–65; Sandel, 2007, p. 9.

seems to me that none of the features listed here can be easily repudiated. And it seems to me that these features are all useful when it comes to identifying and classifying philosophical views in bioethical debates. Some explanations are needed, though.

Decision. The definition is limited to the rationality of decisions, but it is also important to discuss the rationality of persons, views, and arguments. I believe that the connection can be made in each case without straining the idea too much. Persons are rational insofar as their decisions tend to be rational; and views and arguments are rational insofar as they tend to support rational decisions. Similar links can be built to any area in which the concept is required.

Insofar as. The definition does not give clear-cut criteria for rationality. It does not include expressions such as 'only if' or 'if', which would imply that necessary or sufficient conditions were given. The more (or less) a decision complies with the defining features, the more (or less) rational it is. Objects of assessment are not in this model black or white, but different shades of grey.

Based on beliefs. Decisions must be based on beliefs in order to be evaluated for their rationality. It is possible that human actions or behaviours are sometimes instinctive or automatic and that no cognitive mental states or processes are then consciously involved. In these cases, rationality does not enter the discussion; or if it does, it does so indirectly. It is neither rational nor irrational that I involuntarily and without thought straighten my leg as a response to the physician's reflex hammer. And if I do something mechanically, say, based on intensive training, it is the decision to give or take the training that can be indirectly assessed.

Beliefs that form a coherent whole. A decision is not fully rational if it is based on a set of beliefs that can yield different results in relevantly similar cases. The recognition of this principle has given rise to a variety of 'parity of reasoning' arguments in bioethics.[93] Champions of embryo research, for instance, point out that people who protect blastocysts in the scientific context should also be extremely worried about the loss of unborn human life in early miscarriages. Opponents of late abortions, in contrast, note that the criterion of moral worth implied by third-trimester terminations can also be used in defence of infanticide. The logic in both cases is to show that the views launched by the opposition

---

[93] See Søren Holm, 2003b, '"Parity of reasoning" argument in bioethics – some methodological considerations', Matti Häyry and Tuija Takala (eds), *Scratching the Surface of Bioethics* (Amsterdam: Rodopi): 47–56.

are either wrong because they lead to ridiculous or intolerable norms *or* incoherent because they cannot be followed to their logical conclusions. My impression is that all current views in bioethics, and quite possibly all ethical stances, have shortcomings of this type. Sometimes these can be explained away, but even if they cannot, they merely show that no position is *fully* rational *and* completely free of funny or repulsive entailments, especially in the eyes of its adversaries.

Beliefs that are consistent with how things are in the world. If decisions are based on beliefs that have *no regard to how things are* in the world around us, they can legitimately be called irrational. But this is very rarely the case in bioethical disputes. Mostly, parties just disagree because their world views are in conflict. Some believe that the universe consists exclusively of matter, events, and people's individual experiences and actions. Others hold that the world also contains social, cultural, or spiritual elements. For the former, only analytic and secular considerations are feasible; for the latter, traditional and religious ideas can also have their place. Insofar as people's world views are coherent and beliefs consistent with these views, their decisions are, according to my nonconfrontational account, rational.[94]

Aimed at optimising. Notions of rationality differ radically in their preferred approaches to optimising the effects of decisions. Some aim at maximising good impacts; others at minimising bad ones. Some dictate that risk-taking is a true sign of rationality; others that precaution is the preferable choice. Yet others specify more complex mixtures of strategies, sometimes guided by external responses to the original moves made by the agent. Choices made between these views can influence considerably the resulting rationalities.

Optimising the immediate or long-term impacts. Many general theories of rationality can only accommodate decisions and doctrines that concentrate on physical, psychological, and economic consequences.[95] This is not true of my nonconfrontational account. The question will be further clarified below in my description of entities that matter, but

---

[94] This analysis equates the way the world *is* and the way it *is seen to be*. Some people argue, and they can be right in arguing, that at least the physical world is what it is regardless of what we think. The definition that I am offering here is, however, a definition of rationality in the context of *morality*. And morality cannot, as far as I can see, be helpfully reduced to physics. Its intricacies can, therefore, be handled better by assuming the relative validity of spiritual (etc.) as well as physical explanations and justifications.

[95] See, e.g. John Rawls, 1972, *A Theory of Justice* (Oxford: Oxford University Press); John C. Harsanyi, 1978, 'Bayesian decision theory and utilitarian ethics', *The American Economic Review* 68: 223–8.

the gist of the affair is this. Some analyses of what is rational restrict, legitimately from their own point of view, their attention to the actual, probable, hoped-for, or dreaded material outcomes of choices and actions now and in the future. But others can with equal justification focus on the immediate, and possibly immaterial, impacts that our decisions have on ourselves and on other significant beings: violations of rights, disrespect for dignity, threats to communal integrity, corruption of the character, and the like. Ways of optimising these can differ drastically from the arithmetical calculation of hedonistic or monetary gains.

Optimising impacts on entities that matter. The definition of entities that matter tends to bring moral overtones to the discussion. Consider, for instance, the following list of possibilities: God, man, woman, human being, sentient being, living being, nature, and culture. Almost regardless of other dimensions, rationalities identifying these as significant entities turn into corresponding ethical doctrines: theological, patriarchal, feministic, humanistic, hedonistic, vitalistic, ecological, and communitarian.

The three approaches that I have studied here suggest a different classification. Glover and Harris focus on persons as beings who can value their own lives, and attach importance to the degree to which their lives are worth living. Kass and Sandel place value on tradition; on the dignity of human life; and on solidarity between members of communities and societies. Habermas and Green concentrate on principles and their acceptability, arguing that negotiations between discerning individuals produce norms that ultimately matter. To put these positions in a nutshell, they define *persons, traditions,* or *principles* as the entities that matter. Morality comes into play in different ways in these accounts. The 'person' model usually recognises a distinction between prudential decisions that concern only agents themselves and moral ones that also involve others. The 'tradition' perspective normally sees all individual-related calculations as merely prudential and requires that morality should go beyond these. And the 'principles' approach is prone to drawing a line between genuinely moral considerations and the contingencies of mere personal happiness and prevailing ways.

The rationalities of Glover, Harris, Kass, Sandel, Habermas, and Green have been summarised in the light of these considerations in Table 2.1.

The 'high' level of coherence required by every author shows that the core of rationality for them all is in the resolve not to tolerate illogical,

Table 2.1 *Six rationalities*

	What level of coherence is required?	How are things in the world?	How should impacts be optimised?	What entities matter?	What makes decisions moral?
Glover	High	Scientific	By maximising and minimising	Persons and their lives worth living	Regard for others
Harris	High	Scientific			
Kass	High	Spiritual	By respecting humanity's continuity	Traditions and their preservation	Disregard for individual concerns
Sandel	High	Traditional			
Habermas	High	Scientific and moral	By communication and negotiation	Principles and their acceptability	Disregard for contingent concerns
Green	High	Scientific			

self-contradictory views. The variation in all other respects, in turn, reflects the width and depth of disagreement between ethicists. This disagreement is not always made visible, though. On the contrary, in current bioethical debates participants often *avoid* revealing their views on the major variants listed here: how they believe things are in the world; how they think impacts should be optimised; and what entities matter to them.[96] The role of faith, ideology, and values in arguments is hidden and disputes are dressed up as purely logical exercises in coherence. This gives conflicting claims an air of universality that is not always conducive to respectful dialogue. If one view is universally right, then all others are universally wrong; and since this can seldom be proven by logic alone, the judgement depends ultimately on the choice of worldviews, attitudes, and ideas about the foundation of moral worth. More often than not, the result is a heated doctrinal shouting match camouflaged as a dispute over what makes sense and what is reasonable.

If my nonconfrontational account can be relied on, there are many divergent rationalities, all of which can be simultaneously valid. There

---

[96] One author who makes this avoidance explicit is Harris, 1992, p. 5. But it is also quite a chore to tease out the theoretical presuppositions of Glover, 2006, Kass, 2002, Sandel, 2007, and Green, 2007. Habermas, 2003, is the only one of my six chosen authors who makes his fundamental ethical views explicitly known in his treatise on the ethics of genetics.

are also, as a consequence of this, many rational moralities. Views that are grossly incoherent can be deemed irrational, and ethical doctrines that are based on such views can be put in the same category and dismissed. But the remaining moralities are all more or less rational. Their 'shades of grey' can be assessed both internally and externally. The internal evaluation must be conducted in terms of coherence only: any variety in the other factors produces a different type of rationality, to be judged by its own criteria. The external evaluation can include all the aspects, and there are potentially as many verdicts as there are competing rationalities.

2.7   Equilibria, equipoises, and polite bystanders

The possibility of measuring rationalities can lead to a temptation to compare them and to elevate one of them above the others. I believe that this temptation should be resisted. But an examination of how the method of 'reflective equilibrium' could be used in the assessment illustrates nicely some of the features of my own 'polite bystander's point of view'.

Philosophers have used the notion of a *reflective equilibrium* in attempts to choose the best principles of induction[97] and justice.[98] The idea in ethics is to seek a balance between our particular judgements about morality and the general principles that can explain or justify these in the best possible way. We can, for instance, make a considered judgement that racial minorities should have special protections, and also hold the principle that race should not influence our policies.[99] If the view on protections is strong, the principle of racial neutrality cannot in its strictest form be our final theoretical stand. According to the doctrine of reflective equilibrium, we must revise the general rule – and possibly also our opinions on more specific norms – until the situation is stable. This is the method that John Rawls utilised to prove that his theory of justice as fairness is better than any of the competing doctrines.[100] Could it also be evoked to show how one rationality is superior to all others?

The answer is 'No and yes and no'. The method of reflective equilibrium cannot support the view that one rationality should be assumed by

---

[97] Nelson Goodman, 1955, *Fact, Fiction, and Forecast* (Cambridge, MA: Harvard University Press), pp. 65–8.

[98] Rawls, 1972, pp. 20, 48–51, 120, 432.

[99] Ronald Dworkin, 1989, 'The original position', Norman Daniels (ed.), *Reading Rawls: Critical Studies on Rawls' 'A Theory of Justice'* [1975] (Stanford, CA: Stanford University Press), pp. 16–53, 29.

[100] Rawls, 1972.

all the authors whose notions I have outlined in the preceding sections. The problem is that the model presupposes relatively similar judgements on particular normative issues to begin with. Rawls, in introducing the approach to ethics, postulated that human beings have a sense of justice that guides them roughly into the same direction.[101] This may or may not be true in the context of political justice, but in debates on genetic advances it is clearly a questionable assumption. People's views on selection, cloning, and enhancements differ so markedly that it seems impossible that one rationality or rational morality could satisfy them all.

The method could be used in more limited settings. When ethicists by and large agree on the opportunities (Glover, Harris, and Green) or threats (Kass, Sandel, and Habermas) of making people better but disagree on the level of theory, it should be possible to commence balancing exercises that would ideally lead to some doctrinal convergence. In the end, this could lead to fewer and more comprehensive normative views on rationality and rational morality. But it is not obvious what the advantages of such an undertaking would be. There would still be separate doctrines for the proponents and opponents of genetic advances, and some of the clarity and variety offered by the competition between approaches yielding parallel conclusions would be lost.

In Chapters 3, 4, 5, 6, 7, 8, and 9 I will *not* be trying to find a reflective equilibrium between 'our' particular judgements and 'our' preferred rationality or morality. There is no 'we' that would support this line of enquiry. Instead, I will tacitly assume that the six rationalities described so far – and other rationalities that will emerge in the course of the analysis – represent, more or less, the balance that their authors have had in mind in expressing their views.

If any comparison is involved, it will be in the spirit of *reflective equipoise*. In clinical trials, the principle of equipoise states that experiments are morally acceptable if medical experts genuinely disagree on the value of alternative treatments.[102] Researchers themselves are not required to be drawn between options; it is sufficient for them to ascertain that some of their colleagues would prefer each alternative.

Ethical analyses are not controlled trials that would confirm moral judgements like medical experiments confirm clinical decisions. But I like the idea of philosophers studying practical issues fully recognising that for each normative view examined there is a reputable school of

---

[101] Rawls, 1972, pp. 567–77; cf. Dworkin, 1989, pp. 22–3.
[102] B. Freedman, 1987, 'Equipoise and the ethics of clinical research', *The New England Journal of Medicine* 317: 141–5.

thought which believes in its accuracy. I do not need to be drawn between the options myself; it is enough for me to acknowledge that the philosophical community is.

This leads to the definition of my *polite bystander's point of view*. In what follows, I will constantly assume that all the scrutinised principles and judgements have respectable support among philosophical, bioethical, or other relevant scholars (reflective equipoise) *and* that the combination of principles and judgements is in each case in a stable balance (reflective equilibrium) seen from their author's angle. I will not intentionally take sides in the issues that I analyse, *except* in cases in which I think that a solution could be accepted by all parties. Instead, I will politely and from a distance describe views, study their interpretations, and formulate possible evaluations of them from different perspectives.

2.8   Plan for the rest of the book

I have now presented the main ethical themes surrounding the 'genetic challenge' and the methodological styles that can be assumed in investigating them. It is time to make a note of the findings so far and to lay down a plan for the rest of the book.

In Chapter 1, I described the background and primary issues of 'making people better'. Seven practices were identified: selection for the best babies, selection for deaf embryos, selection for saviour siblings, human reproductive cloning, stem cell research, gene therapies, and considerable life extension. In Section 1.9, I went on to list the related ethical issues to be studied in more detail: parental responsibility; the relationship between law and morality; the instrumental use of people; our licence to design the lives of others; human vulnerability; the effect of optimistic and pessimistic attitudes on ethics; and the meaning of life.

In the first part of Chapter 2, I sketched six notable approaches to the genetic challenge, those of Jonathan Glover, John Harris, Leon Kass, Michael Sandel, Jürgen Habermas, and Ronald Green. In the latter part of the chapter, I have explored my own methodological preferences. These are based on my 'nonconfrontational notion of rationality', which denies the supremacy of any particular theory of rational morality. Ethical doctrines can be examined by assuming a reflective equipoise among them, but attempts to reduce them into one by using devices such as the reflective equilibrium are bound to be biased.

In Chapters 3, 4, 5, 6, 7, 8, and 9, I aim to create a comprehensive account of the main ethical arguments and approaches that can be used in the assessment of the genetic challenge and the seven ways of making people better. I will do this by assuming the 'polite bystander's point of view' – by analysing impartially judgements, principles, rationalities, and rational moralities as applied to my chosen themes and questions.

What will emerge from these analyses, I hope, is a sharper picture of the multimodal distribution of normative convictions regarding advances in genetics; and clusters of judgements, principles, beliefs, attitudes, and ideals that explain the variance and define distinct rationalities and moralities. By 'multimodal distribution' I mean the phenomenon we have already encountered with the ethical views presented in this chapter. The views of the six philosophers do not follow the 'bell curve' (unimodal) normal distribution model. There is no convergence on moderate, middle-of-the-road positions; instead, opinions are polarised into two extreme positions. I hope that this image becomes more focused in the next seven chapters.

In Chapter 10, I will summarise the rationalities employed in the ethics of genetics in terms of philosophical assumptions, ethical intuitions, and normative commitments, as they have been unveiled in Chapters 3, 4, 5, 6, 7, 8, and 9. My analysis of the rationalities will bear a resemblance to Henry Sidgwick's nineteenth-century definition and assessment of the three main approaches to moral philosophy in *The Methods of Ethics*.[103] Accordingly, one of my aims in this book will be to outline the main contemporary 'methods of genethics' for further examination.

[103] Henry Sidgwick, 1907, *The Methods of Ethics* [1874], seventh edition (London: Macmillan). See also Matti Häyry, 1994b, *Liberal Utilitarianism and Applied Ethics* (London: Routledge), pp. 50–3.

3

The best babies and parental responsibility

In this chapter, I examine three views on parental responsibility in reproductive selection. The first says that all selection is wrong; the second allows some selection at the discretion of the parents; and the third makes choices in the light of genetic and medical information a moral duty.

3.1 From infanticide to embryo selection and beyond

Most people want to have children and most societies support them in this endeavour. But many people have specific views about the kind of children they want to have and many societies support, officially or unofficially, their views. Newborn infants with disabilities have historically been excluded from the category of desired offspring. Health and normal physical and mental development have often been seen as reasonable parental expectations; and hopes of beauty, strength, and intelligence have not always been frowned on, either.[1] A variety of methods have been suggested to achieve the coveted results, ranging from killing babies of the wrong type or letting them die, through terminations of pregnancy and the selection of embryos before implantation, to choosing reproductive partners and changing the qualities of unborn human beings by therapies or enhancements.

Philosophers of all schools of normative ethics have from time to time condoned infanticide, the disposal of unwanted babies, for one reason or another. Plato and Aristotle held up the idea of getting rid of defective newborns for eugenic purposes.[2] Immanuel Kant maintained that a child born out of wedlock presents such a threat to the mother's honour as a woman that she has a moral duty to terminate its existence.[3]

---

[1] By 'normal' I mean here 'average' or 'like all others' as seen by the parents. No value implications are intended.

[2] Plato, 2007, *The Republic*, translated by Desmond Lee (Harmondsworth: Penguin Books), V 457d–466d; Aristotle, 1981, *The Politics*, translated by T. A. Sinclair (Harmondsworth: Penguin Books), VII 16 1335.

[3] Immanuel Kant, 1999, *Metaphysical Elements of Justice* [1797b], translated by John Ladd (Indianapolis, IN: Hackett Publishing Company), p. 143.

Jeremy Bentham argued that humanitarian concern for women should force lawgivers to assume a lenient attitude towards infanticide.[4] These views reflect, to a degree, the social realities and perceptions of their times. More recently questions of honour have not been regarded as decisive in the affluent West, and some non-Western cultures are criticised for their ongoing practices of sex-selective infanticide. But severe disabilities are still used as a reason for not keeping neonates alive in hospitals – and this policy has considerable ethical and philosophical support.[5]

Since letting infants die, let alone killing them, sounds like a callous and uncaring thing to do, earlier decisions are generally preferred to these late solutions. Prenatal diagnostic techniques like ultrasound scans, maternal serum screening, and amniocentesis are now routinely used for detecting fetal abnormalities. If these are found, pregnancies can in many jurisdictions be terminated at their later stages – during which abortions would not be allowed on personal or social criteria any more. Philosophical responses to this vary,[6] but the practice is widespread.

Abortion is a contested issue and its use in prenatal selection is particularly problematic when late choices need to be made. As a broad rule, the sooner the predictions of congenital defects are available the better. This is why preimplantation genetic diagnosis (PGD) has been hailed as a method that renders obsolete many questions surrounding selective abortion.[7] Embryos produced by combining sperm and egg in vitro are allowed to develop until they have divided into six- to eight-cell blastocysts. One of the cells is carefully removed and tested for genetic mutations. If the result is satisfactory, the remaining embryo is transferred in to the woman's

---

[4] Jeremy Bentham, 1931, *The Theory of Legislation*, C. K. Ogden (ed.) (London: Kegan Paul), pp. 437, 479.

[5] See, e.g. Nuffield Council on Bioethics, *Critical Care Decisions in Fetal and Neonatal Medicine: Ethical Issues* – www.nuffieldbioethics.org/go/ourwork/neonatal/publication_406.html; Michael Tooley, 1985, *Abortion and Infanticide* (New York, NY: Oxford University Press); Helga Kuhse and Peter Singer, 1985, *Should the Baby Live? The Problem of Handicapped Infants* (Oxford: Oxford University Press); John Harris, 1985, *The Value of Life: An Introduction to Medical Ethics* (London: Routledge and Kegan Paul).

[6] E.g. Rosamond Rhodes, 1999, 'Abortion and assent', *Cambridge Quarterly of Healthcare Ethics* 8: 416–27; Matti Häyry, 2001b, 'Abortion, disability, assent and consent', *Cambridge Quarterly of Healthcare Ethics* 10: 79–87; Simo Vehmas, 2001, 'Assent and selective abortion: A response to Rhodes and Hayry', *Cambridge Quarterly of Healthcare Ethics* 10: 433–40.

[7] E.g. Christian Munthe, 1999, *Pure Selection: The Ethics of Preimplantation Genetic Diagnosis and Choosing Children without Abortion* (Gothenburgh: Acta Universitatis Gothoburgensis).

uterus in the hope of starting a pregnancy. Technically, abortion does not take place, as no pregnancy exists before the implantation (which may or may not follow the transferral).

However, PGD is ethically suspect for those who identify conception as the beginning of a new human life in need of protection. This is because the embryos that are *not* chosen for implantation are usually discarded. To focus distinctly on procreative choices, then, even less invasive instruments of selection need to be considered. Such instruments can be found in the screening of reproductive partners and in embryonic or fetal alterations. The idea of finding suitable propagation mates has been around for quite a while. Plato suggested that only the best citizens should be encouraged to have children, and the eugenic movements of the nineteenth and twentieth centuries advocated a similar rule.[8] On an individual level, many people try to find clever and good-looking spouses to have bright and beautiful children. Cyprus runs a premarital genetic testing programme to decrease the incidence of thalassaemia.[9] The dilemma confronting these policies is that while individual choices are relatively ineffective, more successful collective measures in their turn are prone to jeopardise people's freedom.

The remaining alternatives belong more to science fiction than to current science, but they would, if technically safe and feasible, confine the discussion exclusively to choosing the qualities of our prospective offspring. In principle, potential parents could be genetically profiled or their gametes could be tested to give them information about the probable features of the children they can have. Gene treatments, again, could be used to cure diseases or to alter nondisease traits either before embryos are implanted or during pregnancy. None of these methods would involve the loss of early human life, which is one of the key ethical obstacles to infanticide, abortion, and PGD. Profiling and fetal surgery would, of course, have to operate on a strictly voluntary basis to avoid violations of people's physical integrity, but on that condition choices to use these means would be as close to 'pure selection' as we can get.

In this chapter's discussion on parental responsibility and the best babies, I will primarily have in mind the pure selection of offspring; without side effects such as loss of life, violations of privacy, restrictions

---

[8] See, e.g. Matti Häyry, 2008, 'The historical idea of a better race', *Studies in Ethics, Law, and Technology* 2, Article 11 – www.bepress.com/selt/vol2/iss1/art11.

[9] See, e.g. Antonio Cao, Maria Cristina Rosatelli, Giovanni Monni, and Renzo Galanello, 2002, 'Screening for thalassemia: A model of success', *Obstetrics and Gynecology Clinics of North America* 29: 305–28.

on procreative autonomy, or cultural or social pressures. All these are important issues, but when they are bracketed for the time being, the issue of parental choice becomes more clearly visible. I will begin (in Section 3.2) by reviewing what four classical philosophers – Plato, Aristotle, Immanuel Kant, and John Stuart Mill – have had to say about the responsibility of parents for their offspring. I will then go on to present three normative views on parental duties in reproduction (Sections 3.3, 3.4, and 3.5) and the rationalities that underlie these views (Sections 3.6, 3.7, and 3.8). I will close the chapter by offering some comments on the views and rationalities portrayed in the debate (Section 3.9).

3.2   Parental responsibility as seen by Plato, Aristotle, Kant, and Mill

Western philosophical thought has, as a rule, supported the production of good individuals when this is possible.[10] The responsibilities assigned to parents in this respect, however, have varied from one school to the other.

In Plato's vision of an ideal republic, the children of the ruling classes are brought up by the state. Leaders of the state monitor citizens to find the best reproductive matches and then encourage, by ritual arrangements, the right people to engage in procreative activities with each other. When children are born, they are taken from their mothers and state officials decide their fate. If they are healthy, they will be brought up collectively by the republic, and parents will not know who their children are. If the babies are deformed, they will be put away in a mysterious, unknown place. The latter procedure also applies to the unplanned children of inferior rulers who are not seen fit to continue the race. The main duty of parents in this model is to abide by the rules and regulations set and enforced by the leaders of the state.[11] Echoes of this can be seen in later eugenic policies, including current attempts to reduce major diseases by premarital genetic testing.[12]

Aristotle did not believe that ignorance about family relations would be beneficial either to individuals or to the state, and his population programme made parents and officials more equally responsible for

---

[10] See Häyry, 2008.   [11] Plato, 2007, V 457d–466d.

[12] E.g. Cao *et al.*, 2002; cf. Rogeer Hoedemaekers and Henk ten Have, 1998, 'Geneticization: The Cyprus paradigm', *The Journal of Medicine and Philosophy* 23: 274–87; Barbara Prainsack and Gil Seagal, 2006, 'The rise of genetic couplehood? A comparative view of premarital genetic testing', *BioSocieties* 1: 17–36.

the health of the race. On the basis of his biological observations, he recommended that children should be produced by men between the ages of 37 and 55 and by women between the ages of 18 and 36. In case of pregnancies that deviated from the rules, his remedy was abortion before sentience and animation take place – up to 40 days after conception for male fetuses and up to 80 days for female fetuses.[13] During pregnancy, Aristotle believed in the importance of moderate exercise, which is why he thought that authorities should encourage or require women to take daily walks to the temples of gods of fertility and childbearing. Defective offspring are in this model, like in Plato's, destined for immediate death.[14] As many of these lines of thought have in one form or another survived to this day, we can deduce either that Aristotle had uncanny powers of foresight or that our thinking has not developed much in the past two and a half millennia.

With Kant, the outlook on reproduction becomes qualified by Christian credos and Enlightenment ideals.[15] The religious influence is at its strongest in Kant's views on sex, marriage, and honour,[16] while the rational implications of voluntary choices seem to dominate his ideas concerning parental and filial obligations.[17] Since sex should be confined to marriage, the first duty of potential parents is to abstain from producing illegitimate children. According to Kant, a 'child born ... outside marriage is outside the law ... and consequently it is also outside the protection of the law ... so that its existence as well as its destruction can be ignored'.[18] This seems to imply that a woman safeguarding herself against the disgrace of becoming known as an illegitimate mother cannot be punished for killing her baby like ordinary murderers can.[19] For children born in wedlock, however, parental duties are clear and stringent. Being the result of free acts of the will, they have a strong moral entitlement to be nurtured by their parents until they can take care of themselves. Since

[13] Aristotle, 1991, *History of Animals* Volumes VII–X, translated by D. M. Balme (Cambridge: Loeb Classical Library), VII 3 583b.

[14] Aristotle, 1981, VII 16 1335.

[15] This mix is not always easy to untangle. See, e.g. Matti Häyry, 2005a, 'The tension between self-governance and absolute inner worth in Kant's moral philosophy', *Journal of Medical Ethics* 31: 645–7.

[16] Kant, 1999, pp. 87–91, 143.

[17] Kant, 1999, pp. 91–3; Immanuel Kant, 1887, *The Philosophy of Law: An Exposition of the Fundamental Principles of Jurisprudence as the Science of Right* [1796], translated by W. Hastie (Edinburgh: T. and T. Clark) – htttp://oll.libertyfund.org/?option=com_staticxt&staticfile=show.php%3Ftitle=359&chapter=55777&layout=html&Itemid=27.

[18] Kant, 1999, p. 143.   [19] Kant, 1999, pp. 143–4.

children come to existence without their own consent, their filial duties are, according to Kant, limited.[20] But parents have an obligation 'to make their children – as far as their power goes – contented with the condition' into which they have been brought.[21] Here traditional matriarchal and patriarchal values are questioned in the name of moral reason and self-chosen responsibility.

Mill added to Kant's after-the-fact parental duties the aspect of deliberation before producing brood. If people know that they would not be able to take care of children, they should not have them. In Mill's words, 'to bring a child into existence without a fair prospect of being able … to provide food for its body [and] instruction and training for its mind, is a moral crime, both against the unfortunate offspring and against society'.[22] In addition to the forward-looking aspect, another notable detail here is the introduction of the 'unfortunate offspring' into the picture. Mill, like Plato, Aristotle, and a string of philosophers after them, evaluated the creation of offspring mainly as a public practice, criticising the burden that unwanted and unattended children place on society. But here we can also detect concern for the possible new individuals themselves. What would life be like for the would-be child if it were brought into existence? There is probably a path from this early individualistic insight to the current significance of 'the best interest of the child' in legal and ethical debates.[23]

Plato, Aristotle, Kant, and Mill diverge in their notions of rationality, and this corresponds with their main normative differences. Put very crudely, Plato aspired towards a rational autocratic state with healthy and obedient citizens; Aristotle was attracted to an organically developed community with reasonable human beings leading naturally good lives; Kant wanted an enlightened government to coincide with the rational morality of virtuous individuals; and Mill wanted people's own light of reason to guide them as long as they did not endanger others in living their life freely. Flowing from these premises we can see

[20] Kant, 1999, p. 93.   [21] Kant, 1999.
[22] John Stuart Mill, 1869, *On Liberty* [1859], fourth edition (London: Longman, Roberts & Green) – www.bartleby.com/130/5.html.
[23] On the best interest of children in English law, see, e.g. Margaret Brazier and Emma Cave, 2007, *Medicine, Patients and the Law*, fourth edition (London: Penguin Books), pp. 375–407. Mill's ideas concerning responsible parenthood find support, perhaps unexpectedly (because of doctrinal differences: Mill's philosophy is utilitarian and O'Neill's Kantian), in Onora O'Neill, 2002, *Autonomy and Trust in Bioethics* (Cambridge: Cambridge University Press), pp. 62 ff.

practical solutions as varied as Plato's totalitarian eugenics; Aristotle's more moderate lifestyle regulation; Kant's rigorous views on responsibility; and Mill's irritation in the face of reckless propagation. All these strands of thought are still alive in contemporary debates, and there is wide agreement that parents are in one way or another accountable for their offspring.[24]

In what follows, I will focus on one specific kind of answerability created by advances in genetics and reproductive medicine. When people plan to have children, they can now in many cases choose some of the qualities that their eventual offspring will have. With progress in gene therapies and prenatal surgery, they may in the future be able to fine-tune actual individuals (embryos or fetuses) who are already destined for existence. For the time being, though, the choice occurs mostly *between individuals*. Tests reveal traits in potential children and parents can make choices based on the acquired information. Individuals with undesired qualities can be rejected and those with desired traits can be picked. The questions then are: What should responsible parents do? Should they seek the information? And if so, what should they do with it?

3.3   Disregard and givenness

A traditional response is that parents should *not*, as a rule, seek the information. Genetic and other prenatal tests can only be useful if they indicate a curable condition or if their purpose is to prepare parents for the needs of the child. Selection, be it embryonic or fetal, is not right and should not be condoned. Children should be taken as they come and accepted without conditions.[25]

The ideas of children as a gift and parental love as an unconditional commitment belong to the teachings of most world religions; and

---

[24] I have studied the extent of this responsibility in Matti Häyry, 2009c, 'Is transferred parental responsibility legitimately enforceable?', in Frida Simonstein (ed.), *Reprogen-Ethics and the Future of Gender* (Dordrecht: Springer): 135–49.

[25] This view is supported, in one form or another, by Leon R. Kass, 2002, *Life, Liberty, and the Defense of Dignity: The Challenge for Bioethics* (San Francisco, CA: Encounter Books); Jürgen Habermas, 2003, *The Future of Human Nature*, translated by William Rehg, Max Pensky, and Hella Beister (Cambridge: Polity Press); and Michael J. Sandel, 2007, *The Case Against Perfection: Ethics in the Age of Genetic Engineering* (Cambridge, MA: The Belknap Press of Harvard University Press). My way of presenting it deviates from theirs in that I involve more consciously the systematic combination of the principles (or values) of 'dignity', 'solidarity', and 'precaution'.

many interpretations of them have been given in the related doctrines. My main concern here, however, is secular ethics, and in this context a natural justification can be based on the values of dignity, solidarity, and precaution.[26] All these notions have been used in the debate, albeit primarily as reactions to more liberal views. In what follows, I will reconstruct an independent moral case against reproductive choices by using the lines of thought that seem to underlie these reactions.

Selection based on genetic and medical data is a violation against the *dignity* of human beings in several intertwined ways. It is an affront to the 'defective' individuals who are rejected in the process and to their living peers. The insult can be more or less concrete depending on the method of choice: late abortions involve the physical termination of a viable human life (very concrete); PGD leads to the demise of embryos that could have developed into people (less tangible); and genetic matching can only be construed as a symbolic threat to existing individuals with undesired traits (quite abstract). The symbolism is, however, clear in all cases. If a quality makes human beings unwanted before conception or birth, there is a sense in which the same quality *must* make them unwanted after birth, as well. Parental love may almost always prevail,[27] but the more general judgement of society will still be: 'It would have been better if these people had not been born.'[28]

Selection can also be seen as an affront to the individuals actually chosen and to those who do the choosing. It is degrading to the selected ones, because we should not be forced to pass a quality control test before we are accepted by our own parents. They are not allowed to disown us if our grades at school are bad, so why should they be permitted to make a similar decision earlier? Besides, potential parents debase themselves by

---

[26] On these values as an alternative (or as a supplement) to the more familiar bioethical principles of 'autonomy', 'nonmaleficence', 'beneficence', and 'justice' see, e.g. Matti Häyry, 2003a, 'European values in bioethics: why, what, and how to be used?', *Theoretical Medicine and Bioethics* 24: 199–214; 2007c, *Cloning, Selection, and Values: Essays on Bioethical Intuitions* (Helsinki: Societas Philosophica Fennica), pp. 153–77; and (with Tuija Takala), 2007, 'American principles, European values, and the mezzanine rules of ethical genetic data banking', Matti Häyry, Ruth Chadwick, Vilhjálmur Árnason, and Gardar Árnason (eds), *The Ethics and Governance of Human Genetic Databases: European Perspectives* (Cambridge: Cambridge University Press), pp. 14–36.

[27] Ronald M. Green, 2007, *Babies by Design: The Ethics of Genetic Choice* (New Haven, CT: Yale University Press), pp. 114–16.

[28] Or, as one bioethicist puts it, 'it is bad that blind and deaf children are born when sighted and hearing children could have been born in their place'. Julian Savulescu, 2001, 'Procreative beneficence: why we should select the best children', *Bioethics* 15: 413–26, p. 423.

discriminative reproductive choices. Even if they do not actually kill or threaten anyone, they make a call that denies the equality of all human beings. The denial takes place in principle, not in practice, but the realm of principles is precisely where our personally experienced morality resides. By making biased choices we defile our own dignity as ethical decision makers.

Selection based on genetic and medical data undermines *solidarity* both directly and indirectly. The mere fact that some possible human beings are excluded from the human community because of their physical or mental qualities gives sufficient grounds for this claim. Solidarity, like its affiliated principles of *justice* and *fairness*, requires that people should be treated equally despite their attributes and features. Reproductive choices of offspring go, symbolically but unmistakably, against this requirement. Furthermore, as in the case of dignity, the exclusion of individuals based on their genetic and medical conditions poses an indirect threat to people living with these conditions. If prenatal discrimination is allowed, what prevents the same rule from being applied to postnatal attitudes and actions?

The argument presented by Michael Sandel (Section 2.3) adds an explicitly political dimension to this line of thought.[29] In his view, our lives as communal beings are crucially facilitated and humanised by our mutual solidarity, which is founded on an experienced uncertainty concerning the future and which prompts us to create systems of social insurance. The perception of uncertainty arises from our lack of control concerning our qualities and fates. As far as we can see, blind chance influences heavily what we are and what happens to us. But prenatal selection, Sandel argues, is an attempt to remove the role of chance from procreation, and as such it marks a change in our outlook on life and its associated responsibilities. Parents become accountable for the characteristics of their offspring, and this has the potential of making them excessively proud of their children's achievements and crushingly humiliated by their failures.[30] In either case, the (mistaken) sense of control alienates reproducers from the chance-based fellow feeling that forms the foundation of essential solidaristic institutions.

Finally, selection based on genetic and medical data is at odds with the principle of *precaution*. New technologies, including those that enable the

---

[29] Sandel, 2007, pp. 26–9, 45, 85–6, 89–92, 96–100.

[30] In Sandel's formulation, children seem to share this hubris and liability, but I believe that the argument proceeds more smoothly if only parents are involved. Children can, of course, themselves become parents, in which case they are once again included.

choice of offspring, can have frightening repercussions, especially when scientific advances are accompanied with an inadequately regulated market economy.[31] These repercussions are perhaps most commonly thought of in terms of future harm and injustice: if we abort fetuses with adverse physical conditions now, we will eventually slide down a slippery slope to state-controlled eugenics and genocide.[32] But they can also be conceptualised in a deeper anthropological way, as Habermas does in his theory (Section 2.4).[33] According to him, our ethical self-understanding as a species depends on the distinction that we currently see between what we are 'naturally' and what we can 'make of ourselves'. This self-understanding, Habermas maintains, is the cornerstone of our personal identity and moral autonomy, and it would be rash and foolish to test its strength by allowing the unfettered, market-driven development of reproductive technologies.

Precaution does not necessarily dictate that scientific activities should be banned indiscriminately or forever. We may lose our present sense of ourselves as human beings, but if a 'post-human' future population can produce a better morality, such a possibility does not need to be rejected outright. The proper role of precaution is perhaps to slow the process down until we comprehend better the new ways of thought that are emerging. The important thing, however, is to protect our current, tolerable ways of life – unless we know that something at least as palatable as that awaits us in the future.

The arguments from dignity, solidarity, and precaution are focused on the responsibility of prospective reproducers to moral values and social stability rather than to their possible children. This feature is also present in the view that advocates total reproductive freedom, as will be seen in Section 3.5 below.

3.4   Knowledge and moderation

A more modern and probably more popular account of parental responsibility calls for a balancing exercise between the needs of parents, children, and society as a whole. It acknowledges, although at times cautiously, the

---

[31] E.g. Hans Jonas, 1984, *The Imperative of Responsibility: In Search of Ethics for the Technological Age* [1979] (Chicago, IL: University of Chicago Press).

[32] On how this is a cornerstone of bioethical thinking in Germany, see, e.g. Eric Brown, 2004, 'The dilemmas of German bioethics', *The New Atlantis* Nr 5, Spring, pp. 37–53 – www.thenewatlantis.com/publications/the-dilemmas-of-german-bioethics.

[33] Habermas, 2003, pp. 25, 29, 42–4, 52, 56–8, 63–4, 73–4.

developments in contraception, prenatal testing, abortion policies, and new technologies in liberal democracies that hold the individual freedom of their citizens in high esteem. The basic tenets of this view include the desirability of knowledge and the necessity of moderate regulation.[34]

Rosamond Rhodes finds a justification for the moderate account in voluntary parental choices and the responsibilities rational individuals assume by making them.[35] She starts with the premise that reproductive obligations result from the *assent* of pregnant women to bring their pregnancies to term.[36] This assent can be pronounced explicitly at any point after (or indeed before) conception, but even if it is not, Rhodes believes that by the third trimester assent for continuing an unproblematic pregnancy has been implicitly given. Two closely related obligations flow from the agreement. These are *caring* for the new individual 'until it can be independent and able to assume obligations as a moral agent'[37] and *nurturing* it 'to develop and train the child to be a responsible moral agent'.[38] Both obligations have the same goal, but the first concentrates on physical and emotional wellbeing whereas the second centres on ethical education. Since being alive is a prerequisite of becoming a moral agent, the prospective individual also acquires its right to life by the act of parental assent.

Rhodes argues, however, that the acquired right to life is conditional on the ability of the potential child to reach the goals set for its upbringing. If physical or mental disabilities would make it impossible for the offspring to develop into an independent moral agent, the deal is off and parents can withdraw from it. Even third-trimester abortions are permissible, when prenatal tests show serious abnormalities. Rhodes sees a justification for this in the principle that parental agreements remain valid only as long as the project of parenthood is reasonably acceptable; and this is true only as long as the project has a limited time span. It is not obligatory for rational reproducers to commit themselves to a lifelong caring relationship when the original point of having children – which is the creation of new self-sustained and responsible citizens – has already been lost.[39]

As reasonable people can, if they so choose, also opt for a lifelong commitment to dependent offspring, Rhodes does not assign prospective parents a duty to terminate pregnancies on genetic or medical grounds. The permission to do so gives them, however, full licence to use technologies to

---

[34] A version of this view is defended by Green, 2007.   [35] Rhodes, 1999.
[36] Rhodes talks about women, but much of the analysis can, of course, also be extended to men who plan to have children.
[37] Rhodes, 1999, p. 418.   [38] Rhodes, 1999, p. 426 n. 20.
[39] Rhodes, 1999; cf. Häyry, 2001b; Vehmas, 2001.

select the children they want to have. If her analysis of parental obligations is accepted in the case of late abortions, it stands to reason that it should also be accepted in the contexts of earlier prenatal choices and embryo selection based on PGD.

Another justification for a moderate account is presented by Peter Herissone-Kelly.[40] Unlike Rhodes, he does not see the parental–filial relationship in terms of agreements and assent; instead, he argues that people should in their procreative decisions assume an *attitude* that is compatible with their role as prospective parents. Genetic and medical tests generate knowledge that predicts to a degree the quality of life that potential children could have, and this confronts reproducers with choices. Herissone-Kelly considers the case of two embryos produced by in vitro fertilisation (IVF) and tested by PGD. When the results become known, prospective parents face a choice between a 'better life embryo' and a 'worse life embryo'.[41] How should they assess the situation?

According to Herissone-Kelly, the only fitting and appropriate parental response in these circumstances is to adopt an 'internal' rather than an 'external' perspective for the assessment.[42] Adopting an external perspective would mean comparing the potential quality of life of one future child with the potential quality of life of the other; and this would probably result in an obligation to choose the better life embryo. Herissone-Kelly concedes that this line of thought is often obligatory to public decision makers who have to keep an eye on the wellbeing of the entire population.[43] It is not, however, obligatory or even suitable for prospective parents, who are better advised to assume the internal perspective. This means that they need to 'imaginatively inhabit both possible future lives' and try to figure out what life would be like for each separate individual.[44]

The assumption of the internal viewpoint cancels out the default preference for better life embryos, established by the external perspective. Imagining what life would be like for someone with or without a desired or undesired trait or condition yields remarkably similar results in each case. Every life is the best life for the one living it, and it is not made any worse by the fact that someone else could have arguably lived a better one.[45] Parents have no decisive moral reasons to choose either 'better' or 'worse' embryos.[46] In Herissone-Kelly's view, the only limitation to this

---

[40] Peter Herissone-Kelly, 2006a, 'Procreative beneficence and the prospective parent', *Journal of Medical Ethics* 32: 166–9.
[41] Herissone-Kelly, 2006a, p. 167.   [42] Herissone-Kelly, 2006a, p. 168.
[43] Herissone-Kelly, 2006a, pp. 167–8.   [44] Herissone-Kelly, 2006a, p. 168.
[45] Herissone-Kelly, 2006a, p. 167.   [46] Herissone-Kelly, 2006a, p. 168.

is unacceptable suffering. If there would be too much pain and anguish in the existence of future children, parents would behave properly in not letting this happen. This 'principle of acceptable outlook' condones the exclusion of both individuals whose lives would not be worth living at all and individuals whose lives would be worth living but contain more misery than their parents are willing to allow.[47]

The ideas presented by Rhodes and Herissone-Kelly defend the moderate view against different opponents. The contractual case offered by Rhodes wrestles with the traditional assumption that human life must always be protected. By introducing her assentist doctrine on rights and responsibilities, she carves a niche for exceptions to this rule in the case of offspring who cannot be expected to reach autonomous moral agency. The view proposed by Herissone-Kelly, on the other hand, tackles the modern liberal eugenic notion that we should always produce the best children we can. By distinguishing between the external and internal viewpoints, he finds a place for parental deliberations that concentrate on individual children instead of the general wellbeing of the population.[48]

3.5   Procreative beneficence as a duty

The most technologically oriented view on parental responsibility dictates that people should know all they can about the qualities of their potential children and make their reproductive decisions accordingly. This view has found one of its strongest defences in the contributions of Julian Savulescu.[49]

---

[47] Herissone-Kelly, 2006a, p. 169.

[48] An interesting question here is what the interplay between public and private decision makers will look like if authorities have (at least almost) a duty to encourage the selection of better life embryos and parents have (almost a) duty to ignore them. Will the eugenic influence of the 'externally oriented' state make parental choices difficult or even impossible? On the differences and similarities of eugenics and genetics, see, e.g. Merryn Ekberg, 2007, 'The old eugenics and the new genetics compared', *Social History of Medicine* 20: 581–93.

[49] Savulescu, 2001. See also Julian Savulescu, 2005, 'New breeds of humans: the moral obligation to enhance', *Ethics, Law and Moral Philosophy of Reproductive Biomedicine* 1: 36–9. By and large, the same view is supported by Jonathan Glover, 2006, *Choosing Children: Genes, Disability, and Design* (Oxford: Clarendon Press); and John Harris, 2007, *Enhancing Evolution: The Ethical Case for Making Better People* (Princeton, NJ: Princeton University Press). On the normative similarities and dissimilarities of the ethical views of Savulescu and Harris, see, e.g. Julian Savulescu, 1998a, 'Consequentialism, reasons, value and justice', *Bioethics* 12: 212–35; John Harris, 1999a, 'Justice and equal opportunities in health care', *Bioethics* 13: 392–404; Julian Savulescu, 1999, 'Desire-based and value-based normative reasons', *Bioethics* 13: 405–13.

Information that is significant to procreative choices can involve 'disease genes', 'non-disease genes', 'behavioural genes', and 'other genes'.[50] Relevant diseases in Savulescu's account include cystic fibrosis, cancer, asthma, and Down's syndrome, while notable nondiseases comprise height, intelligence, character, gender, and 'Mozartness'.[51] When it comes to modes of behaviour that can have genetic foundations, Savulescu presents an entire catalogue: aggression and criminal behaviour; alcoholism; anxiety and anxiety disorders; attention deficit hyperactivity disorder; bipolar disorder; homosexuality; maternal behaviour; memory and intelligence; neuroticism; novelty seeking; schizophrenia; and substance addiction.[52] Other possibly optional traits and conditions include hair colour, eye colour, blindness, deafness, and dwarfism.[53]

Potential parents have, according to Savulescu, a moral obligation to 'select the child, of the possible children they could have, who is expected to have the best life, or at least as good a life as the others, based on the relevant, available information'.[54] After IVF and PGD, embryos with a prospect of cystic fibrosis, cancer, asthma, or Down's syndrome and embryos with undesired behavioural, nondisease, or other traits should in this view be rejected. The children chosen by their parents should be as healthy as possible and have as many good qualities as possible. If bad genetic traits are unavoidable (present in all the embryos that individuals or couples can produce), parents are allowed, and possibly required, to have children who have these traits. If would-be parents can have a baby with a manageable disability but not one without it, they should probably have the child with the condition.[55] But otherwise all traits that can reduce health and decrease wellbeing should be avoided.

This philosophy of 'procreative beneficence' can, Savulescu argues, be justified by an appeal to rationality, as follows. Imagine we can choose between two boxes, A and B, each containing a random amount of money ranging from zero to a million dollars. If we choose box A, we will automatically get all the money in it. If we choose box B and someone throws a dice, if the number on the top is 6, we will lose a hundred dollars from the amount found in the box, that is, we can end up paying a hundred dollars

---

[50] This list is not meant to be precise or exclusive; it is just intended to present the variety of factors that can, according to Savulescu (2001), be taken into account in parental choices.

[51] 'Mozartness' is implied in Savulescu, 2001, p. 418.   [52] Savulescu, 2001, p. 417.

[53] Savulescu, 2001, pp. 423–4.   [54] Savulescu, 2001, p. 415.

[55] The requirement is not stated clearly by Savulescu. I am here extrapolating (and hoping that this is a justified extrapolation) from the views presented by Savulescu's fellow consequentialists Glover and Harris, see Section 2.2 above.

if the box is empty. Or if we hit the jackpot instead, we can still receive 999 900 dollars instead of the million in the box.[56]

Savulescu asserts that the rational move in the game is to choose box A; *and* that 'choosing genes for non-disease states' (and presumably against disease states) 'is like playing' the game.[57] When the amount of money in the boxes is not known, option A is always better – it is only slightly better if the amounts involved are large but more so if the amounts are on the lower side. In situations of complete uncertainty, rational decision makers give all available alternatives the same initial probability of being the winner. In this case, the balance of uncertainty is tipped by the one to six chance of losing a hundred dollars with the choice of box B. This leaves box A in front with the highest expected utility overall.

The same logic can, Savulescu maintains, be applied to choosing good genetic traits and avoiding bad ones. Whatever combination of things constitutes the worth of an individual's life as a whole, it is always better to start one's existence *without* traits that can cause problems *and with* traits that can turn out to be helpful. Genetically diagnosed embryos are like boxes A and B – where embryo A has more good and fewer bad traits than embryo B. We cannot know what the lives of A or B would be like in their entirety, and it is perfectly possible that embryo B would in the end have the best life if brought to existence. This corresponds with the amounts of money that we can eventually take home from Savulescu's game. (Sum B can, even after the deduction, be larger than sum A.) But in the light of 'the relevant, available information' we have no grounds to believe so. On the contrary, taking into account that information, we have (minor but solid) reason to believe that embryo A would end up having the better life. And this is why we should choose it.

When Savulescu states that prospective parents 'should choose the best child', the 'should' in his statement 'implies that persuasion is justified, but not coercion'.[58] Parents are, according to him, morally responsible *for* producing the best babies they can, although *to whom* they owe this responsibility is not entirely clear. They could themselves be happy to have children of lower genetic quality, so the duty is not necessarily self-directed. Parents do not seem to be answerable to the 'B' embryos that are not chosen, because they can deny them existence (which is, in Savulescu's view, as a rule a worthwhile experience). They could be accountable to the 'A' babies in the sense that had the 'B' babies (if born) had better lives than the 'A' babies (which is feasible), the latter could

[56] Savulescu, 2001, p. 414.   [57] Savulescu, 2001, p. 414.   [58] Savulescu, 2001, p. 415.

complain about not being the best possible children their parents could have had. But this complaint would be based on the child's existence, which is reminiscent of 'wrongful life' charges and conceptually complicated.[59] The only remaining possibilities, then, seem to be moral reason and society as a whole.

This means that the 'recipients' of parental responsibility are basically the same in the two more extreme accounts. Both Savulescu and the proponents of the traditional view (Section 3.3) believe that people with the right ethical attitudes (these are, of course, different in the two positions) can legitimately push others into accepting their outlook. This may or may not be accompanied by state coercion, but it will certainly be supplemented by state pressure if either one of these parties has sufficient influence on reproductive policy making. Prospective parents will be responsible to moral leaders and their adjacent public authorities for abiding by either the 'unconditional acceptance' or the 'procreative beneficence' policy.

3.6 Arithmetical rationality

Savulescu's notion of rationality is based on the maximisation of net wellbeing resulting from people's reproductive choices. This account leaves, as such, little or no room for other personal or traditional values. But these values can be accommodated on ethical and political levels as good reasons for individual action, or as good reasons for collective noninterference.[60]

Savulescu believes that *rationality* requires us to 'treat like cases alike'[61] and to aim to maximise human wellbeing.[62] If I can save either one child or two children from drowning, I should rationally opt for two. Even if the one child was mine and the two children were someone else's, I would, in a detached analysis and other things being equal, have most reason to save the latter rather than the former.[63] And as Savulescu thinks that *morality* obliges 'us to do what we have most reason to do',[64] it could, according to him, be morally right for me to

[59] An interesting case against bringing anyone into existence is presented by David Benatar, 2006, *Better Never to Have Been: The Harm of Coming into Existence* (Oxford: Clarendon Press).

[60] Savulescu, 1998a; Julian Savulescu, 1998b, 'The present-aim theory: a submaximizing theory of reasons', *Australasian Journal of Philosophy* 76: 229–43; Savulescu, 1999; Savulescu, 2001.

[61] Savulescu, 1998b, p. 239.   [62] Savulescu, 1998b, p. 231; Savulescu, 2001, p. 417.

[63] Savulescu, 1998b, p. 240.   [64] Savulescu, 2001, p. 415.

abandon my own child to rescue two strangers.[65] This is not, however, the whole story.

Savulescu also recognises that parents can have special bonds with their children, and that this can constitute the relevant difference needed for treating dissimilar cases dissimilarly.[66] Reasons for action are relative to agents, and parents can have most reason to decide in favour of their own children.[67] Although Savulescu is 'not sure if any meaningful, non-normative definition of "relevant difference" can be given', he is convinced that in such difficult cases, 'a person should be free to choose, unconstrained by the demands of rationality'.[68] I take this to mean that the initial obligation to maximise value evaporates when something close to the decision makers themselves comes into play. Irrational choices can sometimes be moral.

Translated into reproductive choices, this logic seems to imply the following. Procreative decisions are rational if they are likely to produce as much wellbeing as possible. Potential parents should rationally acquire all the significant information that they can have, and they should, in the light of this information, aim to have the child who is expected to have the greatest amount of wellbeing – *even if they have to abandon their own inferior children in the process.* And as morality obliges us to do what we have most reason to do, we could have an obligation to opt for the best child.

Savulescu does not systematically explicate the caveat concerning 'their own inferior children',[69] but it is an implicit part of his view in two different ways. The first is that if the prospective child has already developed into its fetal stages, parents may have grown attached to it. As Savulescu notes, 'selection by abortion has greater psychological harms than selection by PGD'.[70] The second is that if individuals with specific disabling traits (Savulescu's example is dwarfism) want to use IVF and PGD to have children like themselves, it would go against their commitment to equality, personal interests, and procreative autonomy to discard their preferred embryos in order to have a child with a better life.[71] This is why

[65] For a view that makes this an unequivocal moral duty, see William Godwin, 1985, *Enquiry Concerning Political Justice and its Influence on Modern Morals and Happiness* [1793], I. Kramnick (ed.) (Harmondsworth: Penguin Books), p. 170.
[66] Savulescu, 1998b, p. 240.
[67] For a similar view, see John Harris, 1992, *Wonderwoman and Superman: The Ethics of Human Biotechnology* (Oxford: Oxford University Press), p. 116.
[68] Savulescu, 1998b, p. 242.   [69] It is not even a part of his original vocabulary.
[70] Savulescu, 2001, p. 421.   [71] Savulescu, 2001, p. 424–5.

'those with disabilities should be allowed to select a child with disability, if they have a good reason.'[72]

It seems that Savulescu operates on two separate levels here. In the *dwarfism* issue, his point is that in liberal democracies people should be allowed to make what others see as suboptimal reproductive choices. This is true even if people do not have particular reasons for their irrationality (because procreative autonomy is still on their side) although in these cases medical professionals are entitled 'to persuade them to have the best child they can'.[73] It is particularly true if additional principles such as self interest or equality can be cited, and 'then there may be no overall reason to attempt to dissuade the couple'.[74] The distinction in all these cases is between morality and public intervention. People have a moral duty to have the best children, but they should not be coerced (or sometimes even persuaded) to fulfil this duty.

In the *abortion* issue, Savulescu's point could be different. If the bond parents can have with a fetus is anything like the bond they can have with their born child, then this could provide grounds for treating similar cases similarly. It would be irrational but not immoral to continue a pregnancy which cannot be expected to produce the best child. Applied to PGD, this could exonerate parents who would like to have a suboptimal child. Diagnostics can show that all the embryos produced so far by a couple have disease traits that could be avoided by further attempts. But they could argue that these are already 'their children' and insist that they be implanted, for personal moral reasons. Savulescu does not raise this argument or discuss its validity, but a nod in its direction is made by his remark that the selection of gametes rather than embryos would 'have the lowest psychological cost'.[75]

Savulescu defends an arithmetical account of rationality, but he does not extend its requirements automatically to morality or the law. Procreative beneficence is, according to him, always a rational obligation, and in cases of 'pure selection' a moral duty, as well. Psychological attachment to one's potential offspring can, however, cancel out the moral dimension; interests and principles can negate the benefits of

[72] Savulescu, 2001, p. 425.   [73] Savulescu, 2001, p. 425.   [74] Savulescu, 2001, p. 425.
[75] Savulescu, 2001, p. 421. The 'their children' point can only work on a concrete level if embryos or fetuses are counted as *something*. This is not necessarily true in the consequentialist theories of Savulescu and others who make consciousness or at least brain function a sine qua non of morally significant personhood. See Julian Savulescu, 2002a, 'Abortion, embryo destruction and the future of value argument', *Journal of Medical Ethics* 28: 133–5, p. 134.

persuasion; and simple disagreement is a sufficient defence against legal coercion.

3.7   Assumed parental roles

Defenders of moderate views pay less attention to technical rationality than Savulescu. They do not identify ideal morality with the maximisation of wellbeing. Instead, Herissone-Kelly concentrates on perspectives that are suitable for social roles, and Rhodes focuses on what others can reasonably expect of parents.

Herissone-Kelly argues that future lives can be assessed from two mutually exclusive viewpoints: the external and the internal.[76] The external perspective centres on maximising wellbeing and making the best babies, and it is prima facie obligatory for public authorities.[77] The internal perspective requires that we imaginatively inhabit the lives of our potential children, and this is appropriate for prospective parents. It would also be appropriate for them to make sure that their children do not suffer unacceptably.

Interestingly, the two perspectives have natural counterparts in Savulescu's model. His notion of rationality is almost inseparable from Herissone-Kelly's external perspective; and the concessions he makes to parental decision making when one's own child is in jeopardy seem to converge with Herissone-Kelly's internal considerations.[78] The difference appears to be in the different standings given to rationality and parental attitudes in view of morality. Savulescu sees rational decision making as the paragon of morality and parental qualms as flaws that have to be accommodated for compassionate reasons. Procreative beneficence represents excellence from which people, sentimental creatures that they

---

[76] Herissone-Kelly, 2006a, pp. 167–8. See also Matti Häyry, 2006, 'Three questions about the Principle of Acceptable Outlook', *Journal of Medical Ethics Online*, 8 March; Peter Herissone-Kelly, 2006b, 'Häyry's three questions', *Journal of Medical Ethics Online*, 23 March – both at: www.jme.bmj.com/cgi/eletters/32/3/166.

[77] On the prima facie qualification, see Herissone-Kelly, 2006b.

[78] This is not true if what Herissone-Kelly has in mind is a deeper connection with the thoughts and feelings of individuals who do not exist yet. But if this is what he has in mind, he should be prepared to answer some probing questions about the similarities and dissimilarities between his 'imaginative inhabitation' and corresponding notions such as 'empathetic understanding' (Dilthey), 're-enactment' (Collingwood), 'radical translation' (Quine), and 'radical interpretation' (Davidson). These, too, are contested methods of understanding what others might think (or might have thought). The question would be, how exactly does Herissone-Kelly think that prospective parents would know how possible future individuals would see their as yet nonexistent lives?

are, must sometimes be allowed to stray. Herissone-Kelly, on the other hand, sees parental feelings and attitudes as the hard core of family-level reproductive ethics. Rationality is in most cases good in public policies, but moral excellence comes through the proper recognition of one's own role as a prospective parent.

The paramount role of parental mind-sets in Herissone-Kelly's view comes into sharp focus with his ideas on the suffering that children can be made to endure. His 'principle of acceptable outlook' decrees that it would be proper for parents to hold attitudes such as 'I do not want any child of mine to suffer unacceptably'. He then goes on to observe that 'what counts as unacceptable suffering, or precisely where the level of accept-able outlook ought to be fixed, are not questions to which any very def-inite answers can be supplied'.[79] It would, of course, be possible to fix the level at zero avoidable suffering and say, 'I do not want any child of mine to suffer if it can be prevented.'[80] But this, according to Herissone-Kelly, would mean either collapsing into the improper external perspective or setting the standard 'curiously high'.[81] Parents can allow foreseeable suf-fering in their progeny as long as they have the right way of looking at their own role and responsibilities.[82]

Herissone-Kelly asks potential parents to think what life would be like for their possible children. Rhodes, in her turn, asks society to think what life would be like for the *parents* of children who cannot be expected to develop into responsible moral agents.[83] Parenting, she believes, should be seen as a practice with a goal, and this goal is to produce a new gener-ation of human beings capable of good decision making and right action. Parenting, she also believes, should not be an indefinite project: when chil-dren come of age, the initial commitment to their wellbeing and education expires, although their moral tutelage can continue on more equal terms.

Reasonable people understand these conditions when they plan to produce offspring. When pregnancies are started deliberately, repro-ducers assume an obligation to continue them to term *in the normal course of events*. But the course of events is not normal in the sense

---

[79] Herissone-Kelly, 2006a, p. 169.   [80] Häyry, 2006 (not a direct quotation).
[81] Herissone-Kelly 2006b.
[82] An alternative to the view that children *can* be allowed to suffer is that they can*not* be allowed to suffer. Herissone-Kelly is probably aware that this could lead to the total ban of human reproduction and wants to avoid this conclusion. See Matti Häyry, 2004c, 'A rational cure for pre-reproductive stress syndrome', *Journal of Medical Ethics* 30: 377–8.
[83] Rhodes, 1999.

intended by Rhodes if the potential child is disabled so that it would be unlikely to become a moral agent *or* likely to become a lifelong burden to its genitors. Prenatal selection is in these cases a reasonable choice and it should be respected as such by lawgivers and healthcare professionals.

The views on rationality and rational morality held by the defenders of the moderate view can be described as 'reasonable', 'sensible', 'restrained', and 'modest'. The main point is that extremes in any direction are avoided. It is unfitting to seek perfection; possibly because it cannot be attained and its pursuit leads to disappointments. It is also improper to require absolute commitments; possibly because they cannot be honoured and their assumption leads to unnecessary blame and regrets. To the extent to which rationality is a matter of maximising wellbeing and morality is a matter of protecting all unborn life, the moderate view denounces these in the name of judicious compromises.

3.8   Moral limits

The key to understanding the position based on dignity, solidarity, and precaution is in the realisation that mathematical calculations do *not* form any part of it. The logic underlying the restrictive view, promoting the disregard of information and the givenness of the next generation's features, has nothing to do with adding, subtracting, multiplying, or dividing good or bad things. Computations like this are at the core of almost all more technical notions of rationality, but different explanations are needed in this case.

In certain senses, human dignity can sometimes be reduced and even completely eliminated. Chronic illness, mental confusion, physical decay, and loss of independence can produce conditions in which people themselves feel that their poise and composure has been irretrievably lost. Individuals who are subjected to prolonged inhumane treatment can also come to believe that their integrity and worth have been incorrigibly compromised. Others can think that those who treat their fellow beings cruelly renounce their humanity by doing so. In these scenarios, there would seem to be room for at least simple arithmetic: it would surely be better to retain some dignity (or indeed as much of it as possible) if the alternative is to lose it altogether.

Within this interpretation, reproductive selection does not necessarily produce insuperable violations of dignity. Embryos and fetuses cannot experience the kind of loss attributed to ailing adults, because they are incapable of experiencing any physical or mental pain to begin with.[84] People already living with disabilities do not actually feel the ill effects of prenatal discrimination, inhumane as it may be, provided that they themselves are treated in the same way that others are treated. And parents do not inevitably abandon their humanity by refusing to conceive or bear to term offspring with qualities that they do not want their eventual children to have.[85]

This is not, however, the interpretation that the restrictive position calls for. It calls for the more challenging view that while dignity in and by itself can never be lessened or misplaced, it can well be battered and corrupted. The variations in one's dignity are, according to this reading, qualitative rather than quantitative. Thus the integrity of individuals with disabilities undergoes no numerical change when embryos or fetuses with similar conditions are discarded, but it is assaulted and possibly dented. An analogy may be helpful here. A physically violated person remains the same person but is still worse off for the attack; likewise, an individual whose qualities are symbolically insulted are rendered worse off although their dignity as a person remains the same. As for the parents who reject their potential children, their integrity as moral agents is still theirs but it is tainted. Just as criminals retain their human rights and ethical obligations, so do these parents. But the dignity of moral agents can be of better or worse quality, and theirs has, at least momentarily, lost some of its excellence and glow. These are the types of deterioration of poise and character that the restrictive position draws attention to in its appeals to dignity.[86]

[84] This depends on what kinds of entities are seen as morally significant. If embryos are moral persons in the same sense as all other human beings, this remark becomes void, sentience or no sentience. I will return to the question of the moral status of embryos in Chapter 7.

[85] If embryos or fetuses have moral significance, this is more accurate in the case of conceiving than it is in the case of bearing to term – then the extermination of early human life can be seen as wrong. But if parents can avoid an illness in their eventual offspring by abstaining from reproductive sex for a short time, most people would probably allow, if not recommend, the delay. For the paradoxes involved in the ethics of such a decision, however, see, e.g. Derek Parfit, 1984, *Reasons and Persons* (Oxford: Clarendon Press), pp. 351–79; Derek Parfit, 1986, 'Comments', *Ethics* 96: 832–72, pp. 857–61.

[86] The imagery here is difficult to catch. Perhaps it should be seen from an aesthetic angle: the value of dignity is a function of its size, shape, and colour; and deteriorations in any aspect leave the person worse off in some way. The 'size' would then stand for the effects of our condition and treatment by others on our dignified-ness; 'shape' for the results of symbolic respect and disrespect for our equality as persons; and 'colour' for the outcomes of our own actions on our character. Illness and ill-treatment can reduce my dignity; perceived insults can batter it; and my disrespect for others can taint it.

Solidarity follows a comparable logic and it can also be read in two ways. The cohesion and integrity of societies and communities can be measured in many ways, and if solidarity is defined in terms of these quantifiable features, there can obviously be more or less of it. Relevant objects of assessment could then include reported feelings of togetherness, frequency of spontaneous acts of altruism, and assumed systems of social insurance.

This is not, however, the meaning that all defenders of solidarity have in mind. Sandel, for one, keeps his distance from this interpretation, stating that his 'point is not that genetic engineering is objectionable simply because the social costs are likely to outweigh the benefits'.[87] His idea seems to be that we should preserve our good ways of thinking ('norms of unconditional love and an openness to the unbidden')[88] and revise our social institutions to correspond to them, instead of letting our morality decay and 'changing our nature to fit the world'.[89] This preservation, according to him, has intrinsic value quite apart from its impacts on the rights, liberty, and wellbeing of individuals.

In sociological terms defined by Émile Durkheim,[20] Sandel appears to prefer something like the 'mechanical solidarity' associated with premodern communities to the 'organic solidarity' of modern societies. The former is characterised by small populations, repressive sanctions, collective authority, religion, and transcendental thought; whereas the latter is linked with larger populations, contracts and negotiations, individual reflection, secularity, and this-worldliness.[91] Since current Western societies are quite probably better *described* by the 'organic' list, Sandel's goal is at the same time *prescriptive* and *conservative*. People should retain their old ways of thinking because they are better, although not in the sense of producing more happiness or wellbeing.

Precaution, as proponents of the restrictive position understand it, is closely related to the notion of conservative solidarity.[92] Habermas illustrates this partly with his considerations on the ethical self-understanding of the species.[93] According to him, if we allow the genetic selection of

---

[87] Sandel, 2007, pp. 95–6.   [88] Sandel, 2007, p. 96.   [89] Sandel, 2007, p. 97.

[90] Émile Durkheim, 1997, *The Division of Labor in Society* [1893], translated by George Simpson (New York, NY: The Free Press).

[91] Steven Lukes, 1973, *Émile Durkheim: His Life and Work – A Historical and Critical Study* (London: Allen Lane/The Penguin Press).

[92] See, e.g. Matti Häyry, 2005b, 'Precaution and solidarity', *Cambridge Quarterly of Healthcare Ethics* 14: 199–206.

[93] Habermas, 2003, pp. 25, 29, 42–4, 52, 56–8, 63–4, 73–4.

future human beings, we lose the distinction between what is given and what is made in our lives. If we lose this distinction, we lose our ethical self-understanding. If we lose our ethical self-understanding, we lose our personal and moral identity; and with it ourselves, both individually as dignified persons and collectively as solidaristic societies. Precaution does not, in this view, mean that we should calculate the risks and benefits of particular reproductive policies and make our decisions separately in each case. Rather, it means that we should be wary of embracing new technologies, since by doing so we would be losing our way of life as we know it.

3.9   Parental rationalities

I have, in this chapter, shown how different views on parental responsibility in reproductive choices are based on different rationalities. The 'permissive' view that identifies the best reasons with the maximisation of future wellbeing and the minimisation of future suffering produces an obligation to have children with as few undesirable disease and non-disease traits and as many desirable nondisease traits as possible.[94] The 'moderate' stance that focuses on what is reasonable allows parents to use their own judgement when untoward genetic mutations are detected prenatally; the alternative 'moderate' outlook that emphasises what is fitting for progenitors encourages parents to prepare for their role by rejecting the rationality of maximisation. Finally, the 'restrictive' position that denies calculations altogether entails a responsibility to welcome and accept babies as they come, resisting the temptation to screen them for their inborn qualities.

The remaining terminological question is, why call the third alternative *rational* at all? Its own proponents denounce excessive rationality;[95] and its opponents see its core as irrational.[96] Rational decision making is usually seen as an exercise in measuring and computing risks and benefits, but these are rebuffed by this option. And the question is made even more pertinent by the debate over the moral status of human embryos, in which 'rationalists' appeal to analytic scientific facts and 'moralists' to

---

[94] Whether this guarantees maximum wellbeing or not is another question: disease does not necessarily involve suffering and desirable nondisease traits do not necessarily result in wellbeing. I have studied the 'social' versus 'medical' ways of ensuring that children will have the best lives in Matti Häyry, 2004a, 'If you must make babies, then at least make the best babies you can?', *Human Fertility* 7: 105–12.

[95] E.g. Kass, 2002, pp. 61–5.   [96] E.g. Harris, 1992, pp. 35, 40–3, 46, 146.

traditional human values. So why not return to the suggestion already presented in Chapter 2 and concede that the main conflict here is between rationality on one hand and morality on the other?[97]

My reason for not doing this is that the matter is not as simple as it appears to be. It is true that the restrictive stance on selection is based on factors that cannot be calculated – but so are some moderate and permissive views. Herissone-Kelly makes this explicit by distinguishing between the external and internal perspectives; the former involving measurements and the latter not; the former being appropriate for public authorities, the latter being fit for parents. Arithmetical rationality is in this model recognised but it does not dictate the reproductive ethics of prospective mothers and fathers. Savulescu comes to similar conclusions in discussing selective abortions and parents with disabilities, although he tends to present the distinction as a moral–legal rather than rational–moral one. It is clear, however, that he is in certain circumstances ready to allow reproductive decisions that do not maximise children's good traits and minimise their bad qualities.

It transpires, then, that although the degree to which calculations matter varies, there is room in all outlooks for factors that go beyond wellbeing and suffering. Restrictive positions see respect for tradition as obligatory; moderate stances see proper parental attitudes as fitting; and permissive views can see combinations of these as tolerable. These facts can be interpreted in two ways. The first is to say that rationality depends on measurements; that none of the outlooks is fully rational; and that the restrictive attitude is completely irrational. This would support the suggestion that the conflict is between rationality and morality. The second option, however, is to say that rationality extends beyond mathematics and that all the views are rational, albeit differently. This is the line of thought that I have advocated in Chapter 2.[98]

Rationalities in the sense that I understand them come close to Max Weber's motivators of social action: instrumental rationality, value-oriented rationality, emotion, and tradition.[99] While the last two categories, emotion and tradition, can in many cases be seen as opposites of logic and deliberation,[100] there is no natural way to exclude ethical and philosophical reflections on values from the sphere of reason. If this could be

---

[97] In the beginning of Section 2.6.   [98] Sections 2.6, 2.7, and 2.8.
[99] Max Weber, 1978, *Economy and Society* [1921], Guenther Roth and Claus Wittich (eds) (Berkeley, CA: University of California Press).
[100] Cf., however, Martha C. Nussbaum, 2001, *Upheavals of Thought: The Intelligence of Emotions* (Cambridge: Cambridge University Press).

done, only an arithmetic of means to achieve preset ends would count as rational. An example would be congenital health combined with potential for strength and intelligence. If these were the only reasonable ends of our action, Savulescu would be right and prospective parents would be responsible for making the best babies that they can. But ends can be debated and this allows the discussion to move on to value-oriented, and quite possibly also emotion- and tradition-based, rationalities and motivations. And these, in their turn, yield completely different, yet arguably rational, normative conclusions.

4

Deaf embryos, morality, and the law

In this chapter, I explore arguments for and against selecting offspring who would probably be deaf. I suggest that reasonable parties could agree to disagree morally on the issue to achieve the nonrestrictive legal solution they prefer, before noting that conflicting rationalities can present obstacles to this.

4.1   Deafness as a test case

In the general discussion on prenatal selection in Chapter 3, it became clear that many ethical theorists draw a line between moral and legal norms. Moral duties cannot be automatically translated into legal obligations; and legal permissions do not always imply moral acceptance. This is clearly visible in the case of 'deaf embryos' – in the attempt of parents to create children who would be deaf like them.

This chapter studies the ethics of selecting 'deaf embryos' and argues that the deep moral disagreement visible in contemporary bioethical debate on the possibility of choosing deafness should probably be recognised and accepted, not drowned in feuds. I will first describe, in Sections 4.2 and 4.3, the background of the practice in emerging reproductive technologies and sketch the main moral and legal stands in its assessment and regulation. I will then go on to examine, in Sections 4.4 and 4.5, the moral justifications that have been given to the two competing views on the issue: the 'medical view' and the 'social view'. The first of these states that selecting 'deaf embryos' is morally dubious although it should, as far as the law is concerned, be left to the discretion of the parents. The second contends that the practice is morally unproblematic or even commendable but agrees that the law should not interfere with parental choice. Following the ethical analyses, the permissive legal stance, potentially shared by the two views, is outlined in Section 4.6, and stock is taken of the argumentation so far in Section 4.7. Problems identified in the moral cases for the medical and social views are considered in

Sections 4.8 and 4.9. My suggestion in Sections 4.10 and 4.11 is that to avoid directive pressure on potential parents, it could be wise for both parties to admit that the choice to select 'deaf embryos' is not obviously right or wrong, but genuinely morally contested.

It should be noted that the polarisation of this particular debate occurs in the 'middle ground' of the normative spectrum. The main rivals agree on the value of legal neutrality, and this provides the starting point of my analysis and eventual suggestion. This does not, of course, mean that the more extreme views are silent on the moral issue. Those who believe that all traits classified as disabilities must be avoided and those who think that this belief is blatantly wrong can disagree with my conclusions. The rationalities underlying such positions are presented in Section 4.12.

4.2   Techniques and their uses

The reproductive and diagnostic techniques needed for selecting 'deaf embryos' are in vitro fertilisation (IVF), preimplantation genetic diagnosis (PGD), embryo selection (ES), and embryo transfer (ET).

In IVF, separately retrieved eggs and sperm are incubated together in a Petri dish until, in successful cases, fertilisation occurs. In PGD, one cell of the six- to eight-cell embryo is usually removed on day three after fertilisation, and genetic analyses are performed by one or more methods. The preferred embryos are then selected and transferred into the uterus of the potential mother for implantation. IVF has been used since 1978 and currently over 1% of all pregnancies in the United Kingdom and the United States are conceived by it; in Denmark this figure is over 4%. The first PGD births were produced in 1990, and although the exact numbers are not known the practice seems to be gaining popularity.

Both IVF and ET are primarily used in clinical settings as an infertility treatment for people who cannot have children by other means. PGD and ES can also be used in this context: the chances of a successful pregnancy can be improved by screening embryos to be transferred for their survival and implantation qualities. Additionally, PGD and ES have been developed to rule out genetic conditions in individuals to be born. If genetic mutations can be detected in time, terminations and selection can be used to eliminate monogenic diseases (conditions believed to be caused by a single gene) and the probability of polygenic and multifactorial diseases (conditions caused by a combination of hereditary and environmental factors). This has been seen as an opportunity to increase parental choice and, where PGD is used, as a way to reduce abortions. The ultimate aims include the prevention of harm and suffering and the production of healthier members of society.

The focus of this chapter is on a different practice, though – the attempt to use these techniques to create deaf offspring. In a famous case in 2001, a deaf lesbian couple wanted to have deaf babies, arguing that their condition is not a medical affliction but a culture that they wanted to share with their children. Their way of pursuing this was to use a sperm donor with five generations of deafness in his family.[1] With appropriate advances in science, the chosen methods could conceivably have been PGD and ES.[2] Although the possibility of success is currently unclear, a review conducted in the United States in 2006 revealed that 3% of the PGDs provided by 137 IVF clinics were to 'select for a disability'.[3]

4.3   Case, options, and stands

The hypothetical case to be considered in my analysis involves six embryos that have been produced by IVF. PGD reveals that three of them are 'deaf' and three are 'hearing'. Three embryos can be implanted, and the question facing the decision makers is, which ones? One option would be to select all the 'deaf' embryos. Another would be to select all the 'hearing' embryos. Yet another option would be to 'let nature take its course', either by ignoring the information or by deliberately implanting a mixture of 'deaf' and 'hearing' embryos. (The attributes 'deaf' and 'hearing' are placed in scare quotes here and throughout the chapter as predicates of embryos, because embryos do not have the proper organs and capacities for hearing. The expression refers to an increased probability of the ensuing individual being deaf or hearing.)

The rightness and wrongness of decisions made in cases such as this can be assessed both morally and legally. It can be said that a decision to choose a specified course of action is *morally wrong*, in which case the moral reasons for making it are outweighed by the moral reasons against making it; *morally contested*, in which case the moral reasons for and

[1] Merle Spriggs, 2002, 'Lesbian couple create a child who is deaf like them', *Journal of Medical Ethics* 28: 283.

[2] For some of the earlier ethical discussion on this, see John A. Robertson, 2003, 'Extending preimplantation genetic diagnosis: the ethical debate', *Human Reproduction* 18: 465–71, p. 470.

[3] Susannah Baruch, David Kaufman, and Kathy L. Hudson, 2008, 'Genetic testing of embryos: practices and perspectives of US in vitro fertilization clinics', *Fertility and Sterility* 89: 1053–8.

Table 4.1 *The medical and social views*

Selecting 'deaf embryos' is/should be			
↓/→	Legally prohibited	Legally permitted	Legally required
Morally wrong	*Medical view*		
Morally contested			
Morally right		*Social view*	

against it have approximately equal weight; or *morally right*, in which case the moral reasons against making it are outweighed by the moral reasons for making it. In a similar vein, it can be argued that a specified course of action should be *legally prohibited*, *legally permitted*, or *legally required*.

The relationship between moral and legal judgements can be seen in many ways. Briefly, natural law theorists believe that the law should reflect morality at least to the degree that serious moral wrongs are legally prohibited regardless of their consequences; legal positivists think that law should be kept completely separate from moral considerations; and liberals standardly hold that morality should not be enforced by law unless immoral actions can be expected to inflict harm on innocent bystanders. The definition assumed here is, more concretely, that legal prohibitions and requirements can justifiably be backed up with state-enforced financial or physical sanctions (fines, imprisonment, and the like), whereas moral condemnations and obligations cannot.

Two main stands have been taken in recent literature regarding the morality and legality of selecting 'deaf embryos'. These are presented schematically in Table 4.1.

The 'medical view' proceeds from the dual idea that deafness is a disability and that disabilities are conditions that individuals have and are harmed by. The 'social view', in contrast, starts from the assumption that disabilities are human-made constructs predicated to individuals and groups on the basis of cultural perceptions.[4] The moral bases of these notions will be examined in Sections 4.4, 4.5, and 4.6.

---

[4] See, e.g. Simo Vehmas and Pekka Mäkelä, 2008, 'A realist account of the ontology of impairment', *Journal of Medical Ethics* 34: 93–5. The possibly counterintuitive idea that the latter view legally requires the selection of deaf embryos will be explained in Section 4.10.

4.4   Moral case for the 'medical view'

One of the first principles of traditional medical ethics is to 'do no harm'.[5] Medical interventions should benefit individual patients by removing or relieving ailments or by preventing them from occurring or getting worse. If an intervention is also expected to harm a patient, the harm should be outweighed by the anticipated benefit. For instance, although the loss of a limb is generally seen as a harm, amputation can in certain cases be justified, if it probably saves the life of the patient.

The application of this principle to reproductive choices has always been controversial, because these choices involve comparisons between people. Abortions, for instance, have sometimes been defended on the grounds that they would prevent harm to pregnant women. But if the potential child is taken into account, and if denying it life is seen as harm, the comparison of the two types of harm (now inflicted on two different beings) falls outside the original, more individual-oriented, scope of the 'do no harm' rule. Another kind of balancing exercise seems to be needed.

The tool for the balancing exercise across individuals can be found in consequentialist ethics. According to this type of thinking, an action is morally right when it is aimed at producing more net good than any other action alternative open to the decision maker at the time of the choice.[6] The model has been extended to reproductive choices between prospective children (embryos or fetuses) by two stipulations. The first states that individuals, especially unborn ones, are 'replaceable'. It does not intrinsically matter which one of two possible human beings will actually come into existence: a potential life can be replaced by another potential life without violating any rights or absolute moral rules.[7] The second asserts that when a choice between future people is made, we should exercise 'procreative beneficence' and seek to create the best individuals we can. The idea is that, with the number of persons remaining the same, better human beings would make up a better world than worse human

[5] Raanan Gillon, 1985, *Philosophical Medical Ethics* (Chichester: John Wiley & Sons): 80–85.

[6] Matti Häyry, 1994b, *Liberal Utilitarianism and Applied Ethics* (London: Routledge); Matti Häyry, 2007a, 'Utilitarianism and bioethics', Richard E. Ashcroft, Angus Dawson, Heather Draper, and John R. McMillan (eds), *Principles of Health Care Ethics*, second edition (Chichester: John Wiley & Sons): 57–64.

[7] Richard M. Hare, 1976, 'Survival of the weakest', Samuel Gorovitz (ed.), *Moral Problems in Medicine* (Englewood Cliffs, NJ: Prentice-Hall): 364–9.

beings.[8] (The distinction between 'better' and 'worse' human beings will be questioned in due course below.) The most vocal defence of the medical view in the context of selecting 'deaf embryos' has come from John Harris, and it combines features of the traditional medical ethos and the more specifically consequentialist approach.[9] The mixture is not entirely unproblematic, since the 'do no harm' rule is compatible with a variety of other principles, including the non-outcome-oriented versions of the principles of autonomy, justice, and dignity, while consequentialism sees outcomes as the only criterion of rightness and wrongness. It is therefore best to examine the two strands of justification separately.

Harris presents his 'medical ethics' argument in the form of four scenarios which he sees as morally similar: deafening a hearing child; not curing an illness that would make a hearing child deaf; not making a deaf newborn hearing when there is a chance; and selecting a 'deaf embryo'. Two claims need to be made, and have been made by Harris, to turn this list into an argument. The first is that deafening a hearing child is always clearly wrong, and something that a doctor should never do. The second is that the items on the list resemble each other so closely as to be equivalent or at least almost equivalent in moral terms. Since deafening a hearing child would be wrong and since selecting a 'deaf embryo' is morally on a par with it, it is also wrong.[10] Both choices would violate the 'do no harm' rule.

The consequentialist case for the medical view is based on the assumptions that deafness is a disability and disabilities are harms. Disability, according to Harris, is 'a condition that someone has a strong rational preference not to be in and one that is in some sense a harmed condition'.[11] As a test, Harris suggests that 'a harmed condition is one which if a patient was brought unconscious into the accident or emergency department of a hospital in such a condition and it could be reversed or removed the

---

[8] Julian Savulescu, 2001, 'Procreative beneficence: why we should select the best children', *Bioethics* 15: 413–26; cf. Matti Häyry, 2004a, 'If you must make babies, then at least make the best babies you can?', *Human Fertility* 7: 105–12; Michael Parker, 2007, 'The best possible child', *Journal of Medical Ethics* 33: 279–83.

[9] John Harris, 2000, 'Is there a coherent social conception of disability?', *Journal of Medical Ethics* 26: 95–100; John Harris, 2001, 'One principle and three fallacies of disability studies', *Journal of Medical Ethics* 27: 383–7; John Harris, 2007, *Enhancing Evolution: The Ethical Case for Making Better People* (Princeton: Princeton University Press), pp. 102–3. On Harris and consequentialism, see Matti Häyry, 1999, 'What the fox would have said, had he been a hedgehog: On the methodology and normative approach of John Harris's Wonderwoman and Superman', Veikko Launis, Juhani Pietarinen, and Juha Räikkä (eds), *Genes and Morality: New Essays* (Amsterdam: Rodopi): 11–19; but cf. Tuija Takala, 2003, 'Utilitarianism shot down by its own men?', *Cambridge Quarterly of Healthcare Ethics* 12: 447–54.

[10] Harris, 2000, p. 97; Harris, 2007, pp. 102–3.   [11] Harris, 2001, p. 384.

medical staff would be negligent if they failed to reverse or remove it'.[12] As examples he gives deafness and the 'loss of the bottom joint of the little finger.'[13] When it comes to choosing among the six embryos, he argues that the potential mother 'has a reason to do what she can to ensure that the individual she chooses is as good an individual as she can make it' and 'therefore [she has a reason] to choose the embryo that is not already harmed in any particular way [...]'.[14] To prevent future disability and harm, and thereby to produce the best possible individual, the potential mother has a moral duty *not* to choose the 'deaf embryos'.

Both lines of argument for the medical view will be critically reconsidered in Section 4.8.

4.5   Moral case for the 'social view'

The moral justification of the social view needs two elements. The first is to challenge the idea that deafness in particular and conditions associated with disabilities in general can be counted as harms. The second is to build a positive case for selecting 'deaf' as opposed to 'hearing' embryos. Success on both fronts would imply that the moral reasons for selecting 'deaf embryos' can outweigh the moral reasons against it, which is the criterion of rightness assumed above (in Section 4.3). An additional aspect, often emphasised by disability scholars, is an explanation of the disadvantages of 'being different' in terms of social reactions and constructs rather than medically definable impairments.

Defenders of the social view have countered the 'harmed condition' argument by drawing attention to the experiences people actually have, as opposed to the 'rational preferences' they ought to have (according to consequentialist thinkers like Harris). The lesbian women who wanted to have deaf babies, Sharon Duchesneau and Candace McCullough, for instance, stated in the media that deafness for them is an identity, culture, and community, not a medical problem or a harmful condition.[15] Others in the deaf community have argued to the same effect that 'a congenital

---

[12] Harris, 2001, p. 384.   [13] Harris, 2001, p. 384.

[14] Harris, 2001, p. 385. In the passage marked with [...] Harris continues that the chosen individual should 'have the best possible chance of a long and healthy life and the best possible chance of contributing positively to the world it will inhabit'. I have omitted this rhetorical addition because deafness and missing fingertips do not, as far as I know, have any direct or inevitable impact on longevity, general health, or contribution to society.

[15] Liza Mundy, 2002, 'A world of their own', *Washington Post*, 31 March, p. W22. On deafness as a culture, see also Robert Sparrow, 2005, 'Defending Deaf culture – the case of cochlear implants', *The Journal of Political Philosophy* 13: 135–52.

lack of hearing is not necessarily a harm' and that 'their lives are equally full'.[16] People conduct their lives as they physically are, and this shapes their aspirations and social interactions so that in the end questions concerning the harmfulness or beneficialness of particular inborn conditions becomes virtually meaningless.[17] Being deaf or lacking the tip of one's little finger is an integral part of who one is, not an emergency in need of medical attention.[18]

Going beyond the question of harm, many people have argued that their physical conditions, described by others as disabilities, have actually been a positive force in their lives, individually and socially. Physicist Stephen Hawking has amyotrophic lateral sclerosis, which has gradually led to near-complete paralysis, but his contention is that this has actually been helpful for his academic career by making his style of writing economic and concise.[19] Many others have reported that their physical dependencies have been more than compensated by 'an increased richness in interpersonal relations.'[20] And where an actual community of physically distinctive individuals exists, its culture and values should command the same respect as the culture and values of other majority and minority groups. This seems to be exemplified by the environment in which Sharon Duchesneau and Candace McCullough work and live with their children – Gallaudet University in Washington DC, with most of the staff deaf and the majority of staff and students living in the vicinity, forming a genuine deaf community.[21]

The social view does not deny that disabilities (as defined by the advocates of the view) can be, and often are, harmful. The harm is not, however, caused directly or necessarily by the difference or impairment individuals live with. It is caused by the attitudes of people without the difference or impairment and by the ensuing poor recognition of the needs of those with particular conditions. Although differences are inevitable and morally neutral, disabilities are social constructs which harm

---

[16] Tom Koch, 2005, 'The ideology of normalcy – the ethics of difference', *Journal of Disability Policy Studies* 16: 123–9, p. 124.

[17] Tom Koch, 2001, 'Disability and difference: balancing social and physical constructions', *Journal of Medical Ethics* 27: 370–6, p. 373.

[18] Being deaf and lacking the tip of one's little finger are, of course, two different things. They are mentioned here together simply because they are Harris's examples (see Section 4.4) of harmed conditions which should be avoided.

[19] Stephen Hawking, 1993, *Black Holes and Baby Universes* (New York, NY: Bantam Books), p. 167.

[20] Koch, 2001, p. 373; Tom Koch, 2000, 'Life quality vs the "quality of life": assumptions underlying prospective quality of life instruments in health care planning', *Social Science & Medicine* 51: 419–28.

[21] Mundy, 2002; Parker, 2007, p. 279.

individuals and groups to whom they are assigned.[22] The way to alleviate the situation is to focus on societal reactions and support systems, not on medically defined variations in individuals. Not hearing can be simply a condition, but deafness can be a culture if allowed to be one or a disability if forced to be one.

The strength of the moral case for the social view will be revisited in Section 4.9.

4.6   Case for legal permissiveness

Despite the disagreement at the moral level, defenders of the opposing models of disability potentially agree on the value of legal neutrality when it comes to selecting 'deaf embryos'. The agreement is an uneasy one, as I will further elaborate in Section 4.10, but it is conceptually defensible.

The consequentialist advocates of the medical view state strongly and repeatedly that what they say about the morality of selecting 'deaf embryos' should not be transformed into legal prohibitions or regulations. Harris, while insisting that it is wrong to bring avoidable suffering into the world, is also adamant in declaring that parental choices should be respected as long as the resulting children can be expected to have at least a minimally decent life ahead of them. Unless the lives of individuals are so miserable that they would not by any account be worth living, the individuals themselves are not harmed by being brought into existence.[23] According to Harris, 'most disabilities fall far short of the high standard of awfulness required to judge a life to be not worth living', which is why he professes to have 'consistently distinguished reasons for avoiding producing new disabled individuals from enforcement, regulation or prevention'[24] and 'always stoutly upheld the principle of reproductive freedom or reproductive autonomy'.[25]

Another consequentialist champion of the medical view, Julian Savulescu, explores the matter in some detail and supports reproductive freedom by means of the nineteenth-century liberal utilitarianism of John Stuart Mill.[26] In his theory,[27] Mill argued that people should be allowed to

[22] Simo Vehmas, 2004, 'Ethical analysis of the concept of disability', *Mental Retardation* 42: 209–22.
[23] Harris, 2000, pp. 96, 100.   [24] Harris, 2000, p. 100.   [25] Harris, 2000, p. 96.
[26] Julian Savulescu, 2002b, 'Deaf lesbians, "designer disability"', and the future of medicine', *British Medical Journal* 325: 771–3, pp. 772–3.
[27] John Stuart Mill, 1869, *On Liberty* [1859], fourth edition (London: Longman, Roberts & Green) – www.bartleby.com/130/5.html.

experiment with different, even conflicting, practices and ideas, because this is the only way to prevent state oppression and eventually to find reasonable and mutually acceptable modes of living. If views that could turn out to be right are suppressed, they may never be discovered by society as a whole. And if views that could turn out to be wrong are suppressed, the right views could be accepted for the wrong reasons, and consequently applied incorrectly to changing situations in the future. This is why freedom of thought and action should prevail unless harm is inflicted on nonconsenting others, individually or socially. Savulescu sees this as a sufficient foundation for parental autonomy in the context of most disabilities. Like Harris, he contends that individuals born with disabilities are not usually harmed by those who have produced them. And although he recognises the possibility that society could be economically hurt by an over-abundance of people with special needs, he is confident that this is not a serious concern, as 'it is unlikely that many people would make a selection for disability'.[28] In all, although he believes that 'deafness ... is bad', he also believes that his 'value judgment should not be imposed on couples who must bear and rear the child.'[29]

Those who hold the social view may have difficulties with the general idea of reproductive autonomy, and I will return to these in Section 4.10. But in the specific case of deaf parents trying to have deaf offspring, the option of being legally required to do as others see fit should not seem too attractive. After describing his own minor physical limitations, Tom Koch, for instance, goes on to say that were '[his] partner currently pregnant and given the choice of a fetus with [his] genetic pattern or one that was "normal", [he] would likely choose the former.'[30] And Sharon Duchesneau and Candace McCullough certainly 'wanted to increase [their] chances of having a baby who is deaf' seriously enough not to take an institutional 'no' for an answer: before they solicited the help of their deaf friend, they had been turned down by their local sperm bank, which had a policy of excluding congenitally deaf donors.[31] Choices like these can only be accommodated by legal permission to select 'deaf embryos'.

4.7   The instability of the situation

The academic debate described in the preceding sections shows that ethical opinion in the field is divided. Some insist that selecting 'deaf embryos'

---

[28] Savulescu, 2002b, p. 773.   [29] Savulescu, 2002b, p. 772.
[30] Koch, 2001, p. 373.   [31] Mundy, 2002.

would be the moral equivalent of deliberately harming an innocent child;[32] others counter that preventing the choice is the mark of an uncaring and discriminatory society. Attempts to reconcile the conflict have failed so far, and there is no reason to assume that similar endeavours would be more successful in the future.[33]

Differences of opinion are, of course, common in real-life ethical discussions, and there are at least two ways of dealing with them. The first is to show that one of the competing views is self-evidently superior to all the others. I will demonstrate in the next two sections that this is not feasible in the current context, because both main views can be comprehensively challenged, even without using the premises employed by the competing camps. The second is to admit the disagreement and try to find practical compromises to the issue. In Sections 4.10 and 4.11, I will explain why and how I would favour this route, and why the main parties of the debate should agree with me.

4.8   Moral case for the 'medical view' reconsidered

The defences given to the medical view by John Harris are by no means unassailable. On closer examination, his 'medical ethics' view collapses into the consequentialist approach, and this, in its turn, logically implies a judgement that Harris consistently and vehemently denies.

The medical ethics, or 'do no harm', line assumes that a variety of different practices are morally on par. These include the deafening of a hearing child, letting a child lose her hearing, not curing a deaf child, and selecting a 'deaf embryo'. The problem is that these practices are different in many respects that ethicists have seen as important. Some of them involve acts while others involve omissions.[34] The intention of deafening the hearing child is presumably to harm the child, whereas selection of

[32] I will return to the flip side of the coin – whether or not they should argue for similar equivalence in law, with some potentially embarrassing entailments – in Section 4.12.

[33] Solveig Magnus Reindal, 2000, 'Disability, gene therapy and eugenics – a challenge to John Harris', Journal of Medical Ethics 26: 89–94; Harris, 2000; Koch, 2001; Harris, 2001; Savulescu, 2002b; N. Levy, 2002, 'Deafness, culture, and choice', Journal of Medical Ethics 28: 284–5; Kyle W. Anstey, 2002, 'Are attempts to have impaired children justifiable?', Journal of Medical Ethics 28: 286–8; Häyry, 2004a; Matti Häyry, 2004d, 'There is a difference between selecting a deaf embryo and deafening a hearing child', Journal of Medical Ethics 30: 510–512; Koch, 2005; Peter Singer, 2005, 'Ethics and disability: A response to Koch', Journal of Disability Policy Studies 16: 130–3; Parker, 2007.

[34] Tuija Takala, 2007, 'Acts and omissions', R. E. Ashcroft, A. Dawson, H. Draper, and J. R. McMillan (eds), Principles of Health Care Ethics, second edition (Chichester: John Wiley & Sons): 273–6.

a 'deaf embryo' is meant to benefit the future individual.[35] In the first cases a child already exists when the choice is made, but in the PGD case this is not true.[36] Some of these distinctions may be morally insignificant, but their presence suffices to cast doubt on the purely intuitive reaction expressed by Harris. Apart from his personal view, however, the only similarity between the four scenarios seems to be that they all result in someone being deaf. This is probably a relevant consideration, but it is markedly outcome based, which means that the 'do no harm' appeal turns out to be just a variant of the more general consequentialist case.

This interim conclusion can be fatal to Harris's justification of the medical view. If our moral duty, and our only moral duty, is to make the world as good as possible *and* if we have a moral duty not to have deaf children, then, by logical implication, deaf individuals make the world worse than hearing individuals. The world would be a better place without them. It would be better if they did not exist. We have a duty to see to it that they do not exist in the future. Whichever way the sentence is twisted, it sounds discriminatory and callous. This is presumably why consequentialists are at pains to disown the view expressed by it. Harris, for instance, argues that although he would not like to lose one of his hands, he would not by losing a hand 'become less morally important, less valuable in ... the "existential sense", more dispensable or more disposable'. According to him, 'to have a rational preference not to be disabled is not the same as having a rational preference for the non-disabled as persons.'[37]

Other defenders of outcome-based ethics have made similar points and claimed that they see individuals with disabilities as equal persons with full rights.[38] But it is not clear how they can escape the callous judgement. 'Hearing embryos' ought to be selected, because the resulting state of affairs would be better than if 'deaf embryos' are selected. This is because deafness is a harmed condition which detracts value from a normal (hearing) life. Hence a hearing life is better and a deaf life is worse. And if this judgement cannot be eluded in the consequentialist analysis provided by Harris, his defence of the medical view seems to be self-contradictory.

In Section 4.12, I try to reconstruct a model that would elude the judgement while remaining as close as possible to Harris's view.

---

[35] Mundy, 2002.   [36] Häyry, 2004d.

[37] Harris, 2001, p. 386; John Harris, 1992, *Wonderwoman and Superman: The Ethics of Human Biotechnology* (Oxford: Oxford University Press), pp. 72–3.

[38] Singer, 2005, p. 133.

4.9   Moral case for the 'social view' reconsidered

The social view does not have the internal logical problems that the medical view suffers from, but it, too, can be challenged on at least three different grounds. Two of these have to do with the social and individual welfare of the eventual child, and the third is a plea for fairness and efficiency in providing for unavoidable as opposed to optional special needs. (A number of other concerns have been aired by the consequentialist defenders of the medical view, but I have forgone these here because their credibility depends on the view's already contested moral justification.)

The first objection questions, on a factual level, the idea of a deaf culture as the primary basis for personal identity. Defenders of the social view argue that the children of deaf parents will have the best possible lives when they are members of a community which consists mainly of deaf people and in which the primary means of communication is sign language. Hearing would be an obstacle for their development, and it should not be favoured or pursued. While this can be true in principle and while the idea may just be workable in relatively established deaf environments such as Gallaudet University and its neighbourhood, it is probably not practicable in many other contexts. Deaf communities are enveloped by homogenising wider societies, and their continued existence, like the continued existence of any minority or majority culture, is always under potential threat. But if communities are not stable over time, they cannot be expected to guarantee their young the identity-building packages that are, according to the social view itself, required for the best life as a deaf person. This leaves room for at least practical doubts about selecting 'deaf embryos' as a way to secure optimal lives for the children of deaf parents.

The second objection concentrates on the welfare of the individual regardless of the attitudes and actions of the surrounding community. Deafness in and by itself does not make a person generally unhealthy or less likely to contribute positively to the endeavours of the wider society. Recognition and support can substitute the lack of hearing in dealings and communication with those who are not deaf. However, if intelligible contact with others is important for human flourishing, there is a catch here. It is that similar comments can be extended, separately, to sight and touch – the two other main channels through which we interact with each other and with the world. We can, no doubt, live good lives without one or even two of these. But if for any reason we lose all three, we are, in the absence of telepathy or fantastic new technology, well and truly isolated. Parents who do not want to gamble on the wellbeing of their children might want to consider even such improbable turns of events when they make their reproductive choices. Making a child begin her life without one of the three instruments of communication increases inevitably the (marginal but existing) chance that they might, later in life, become totally separated from others.[39]

The third objection raises questions about fairness and efficiency in the allocation of scarce resources. As one author comments, 'people might find it hard to accept that ... deaf people might prefer to have deaf children and then request society's support in order to be able to meet their children's special needs.'[40] One reason for this possible reaction is that the people in question themselves and their loved ones have needs, 'special' and not, and they are worried that these will be ignored in order to meet purely optional and superfluous claims created by parents who try to make copies of themselves. The last part of this concern, the accusation of copy-making, does not seem to be justified in the case of Sharon Duchesneau and Candace McCullough, for whom, reportedly, the future child's welfare as a part of their family was paramount.[41] But this still leaves intact the comparison of optional and inevitable needs. If there is a limited amount of resources for 'special needs', then producing a child who is less likely to have them liberates resources for catering for already extant needs. And, other things being equal, a deaf child's likelihood to require societal adjustments is greater than a hearing child's probability of needing them. My logic in claiming this is the following: as long as lack of hearing requires adjustments from society, the deaf child's likelihood to have deafness-related special needs is 100%, but if there are no other differences in health conditions or family circumstances, a hearing child's likelihood to have these special needs is less than 100%, although it is not zero because the child can become deaf later. Whatever other needs individuals may have, these are in this calculation, by hypothesis, equally likely and equally extensive. I have also

---

[39] This can be countered by saying that reproduction would become impossible if very small risks like these were taken into account in decisions to have children. For a discussion of whether or not they should, and what the implications would be, see Matti Häyry, 2004c, 'A rational cure for pre-reproductive stress syndrome', *Journal of Medical Ethics* 30: 377–8; and Matti Häyry, 2005c, 'The rational cure for prereproductive stress syndrome revisited', *Journal of Medical Ethics* 31: 606–7.

[40] Christian Munthe, 1999, *Pure Selection: The Ethics of Preimplantation Genetic Diagnosis and Choosing Children without Abortion* (Gothenburgh: Acta Universitatis Gothoburgensis), p. 239. This citation does not, by the way, necessarily reflect the views of the author – Munthe is simply reporting what people in general could think about parents who do not want to use genetic testing to exclude the possibility of congenital deafness.

[41] Mundy, 2002.

Table 4.2 *The nondirective compromise*

Selecting the 'deaf embryos' is/should be:			
$\downarrow/\rightarrow$	Legally prohibited	Legally permitted	Legally required
Morally wrong	*Medical view*		
Morally contested		*Nondirective compromise*	
Morally right			*Social view*

assumed that the potential contributions to society of deaf and hearing individuals are equal. Is it justifiable, then, to jeopardise the need satisfaction of people who do or will exist anyway for the sake of reproductive or communitarian wish-fulfilment?

4.10   Towards a nondirective compromise

Since the moral cases for the medical and social views are both convincing to their supporters, and since both can be plausibly challenged by third parties, it is improbable that the question of selecting 'deaf embryos' can be satisfactorily solved by claiming that one or the other case is universally valid and should therefore be accepted. This is why I believe that the solution might be to admit that the practice is genuinely morally contested and to proceed to find other grounds for a palatable deal. The location of my suggested 'nondirective compromise' is presented schematically in Table 4.2.

My case for the nondirective compromise can be outlined as follows. As I have shown in Section 4.6, even scholars who disagree on the moral status of selecting 'deaf embryos' can potentially agree on the permissive legal stand that should be taken in the matter. This is a welcome agreement, if nondirectiveness is valued in parental counselling – as many people think it should. Neither the medical view nor the social view can, however, unequivocally support the permissive line, because in both models the underlying moral convictions create strong tensions towards a more rigid legislative stance. A full recognition of the moral contestedness of the practice can best lead to the desired and desirable leniency in legal terms.

The issue of the proper role of nondirectiveness in genetic counselling is an unresolved one, mainly because definitions abound; many different types of genetic information are discussed all at once; and several authors reasonably doubt the ability of clinicians to provide neutral advice in matters in which their own minds are already made up.[42] My notion here is that parental counselling is nondirective if and only if the healthcare practitioner does not intentionally or unintentionally persuade potential parents into making choices favoured by the practitioner. The emphasis in this kind of interaction is on the 'wisdom of the process', and not on the 'wisdom of the decision' as seen by health professionals or authorities.[43]

One way to illustrate the value of nondirectiveness in selecting 'deaf' or 'hearing' embryos is to consider it pragmatically in the context of political uncertainty. While advocates of the medical and social views could prefer a situation in which their own kind of directiveness rules in genetic counselling, they cannot be sure that this is realistically achievable. To avoid the worst outcome, which is directiveness as defined by the opposition, it might be prudent for both parties to forgo attempts at supremacy and to settle for the 'second best' alternative, which is nondirectiveness.[44] If it is too much to ask that individual practitioners could be value-neutral or present the cases for both sides, teams of counsellors should perhaps be set up to explain to would-be parents the conflicting views on the matter. Whichever way the practicalities should be arranged, unquestioned neutrality and permissiveness would be required at the level of law. But this is a requirement that neither of the warring parties can confidently be trusted to meet. As presented in Table 4.2, the medical view has an intrinsic tendency to slide towards the restrictive direction. The main defence of legal permissiveness within the model's consequentialist variant is that social experiments should be allowed as long as they do not harm nonconsenting individuals or communities. But it is far from clear that a lenient legislative line on selecting 'deaf embryos' would honour the stated caveat. If disabilities are harmed conditions and if deafness is a disability, the practice would allow the creation of future individuals in harmed conditions, which has a definite ring of allowing the production of future harm. This impression is fortified by Savulescu's contention that the 'wrong' choices can and should be allowed only because so few

---

[42] See, e.g. Sonia M. Suter, 1998, 'Value neutrality and nondirectiveness: Comments on "Future directions in genetic counseling"', *Kennedy Institute of Ethics Journal* 8: 161–3; Glyn Elwyn, Jonathon Gray, and Angus Clarke, 2000, 'Shared decision making and non-directiveness in genetic counselling', *Journal of Medical Genetics* 37: 135–8; and Fuat S. Oduncu, 2002, 'The role of non-directiveness in genetic counseling', *Medicine, Health Care and Philosophy* 5: 53–63.

[43] E.g. Elwyn, Gray, and Clarke, 2000, p. 135.

[44] Cf. Heta Häyry, 1991, *The Limits of Medical Paternalism* (London: Routledge), pp. 106–7.

parents would probably make them.[45] What if many parents decided to aim at conditions that consequentialists define as disabilities? By the logic of Savulescu's argument, this would call for legal prohibitions.

In a similar manner, the social view is inclined to move towards the other legislative extreme. This inclination manifests itself, in our current context, indirectly. Champions of the model often regard the general principle of parental freedom as an individualistic ploy that conceals the rise of what they see as a new and frightening form of eugenics.[46] Governments do not prevent the reproduction of 'unfit' citizens any more,[47] but under the cloak of individual autonomy and the freedom of the health market people are led to believe that all available genetic tests should be used to exclude unwanted hereditary conditions. Since the situation is, so the argument goes, inherently coercive and detrimental to the interests of people with disabilities, parents should not be encouraged to make use of genetic testing. Yet this is exactly what legal leniency invites them to do, and this is why it should not be condoned. Parents should not be allowed to choose children without specific conditions like the ones probably leading to lack of hearing. Indirectly this means that in some situations people are legally required to choose the 'deaf embryos'. When the probability of deafness is very high to begin with, and PGD and ES are banned, the likeliest outcome is that the potential parents are forced by law to have deaf children if they want to have children at all. This is how the logic of the social view leads to legal requirements.

4.11 The nondirective compromise

The starting point of the nondirective compromise is that the moral reasons for and against selecting 'deaf embryos', different as they are, have roughly equal weight, which means that the practice is genuinely morally contested. Since honest genetic counselling should reflect this situation, it cannot favour either the medical view or the social view. Rather than avoiding the ethical issues, however, comprehensive and honest counselling should convey the main thrust of both models to the potential parents. Instead of striving for artificial neutrality, the advice given can be 'multi-directive': in the interest of the 'wisdom of the process' two practitioners could try to make equally strong cases for the opposing views. The

---

[45] Savulescu, 2002b, p. 773.   [46] Reindal, 2000; Koch, 2005.
[47] On the 'old eugenics', see, e.g. Allen Buchanan, Dan W. Brock, Norman Daniels, and Daniel Wikler, 2000, *From Chance to Choice: Genetics and Justice* (Cambridge: Cambridge University Press).

process itself could then ideally become nondirective in the sense that I defended in Section 4.10.

The nondirective compromise is compatible with legal permissiveness regardless of the approach taken to the relationship between law and morality (the alternatives are described in Section 4.3). Natural law theorists would expect legislators to prohibit serious and unmistakable moral wrongs, but selecting 'deaf embryos' cannot be counted among these. Legal positivists need to see that the law has, by following its own historical logic, come to the permissive conclusion, which in many countries it has. And liberals require, and seem to be satisfied, that no serious harm is inflicted on innocent third parties.

The acceptance of the moral contestedness of selecting 'deaf embryos' suggests strongly the nondirective compromise, and the legal permissiveness that goes with it appears to be supportable from most angles. This is why the opposing parties would be wise to assume the compromise.[48]

4.12   Contested rationalities

Let me now return to the threads that I left untied while developing the argument for my suggestion. Although there is a sense in which the quoted supporters of the medical and social views would be wise to opt for moral contestedness, they are probably not inclined to do so. A reconstruction of their views shows the elements that are needed in their notions of rationality and morality in order to keep their positions intact. A reconsideration of my argument, in its turn, reveals how, instead of rising above the debate, it merely introduces the missing middle stance into it.

In his defence of the medical view, Harris uses the analogy of deafening a hearing child and selecting a 'deaf embryo'. This argument can only succeed if three premises are assumed. First, acts and omissions must have the same moral value if they have the same consequences.[49] Secondly, intentions cannot matter, if the outcome would be the same. And thirdly, existence at the time of the choice does not matter – only existence that ensues from our decisions does. With these additions, his case becomes consequentialist. Although no one would be harmed or wronged by any selective choice, the world becomes a better place if 'hearing embryos'

---

[48] An earlier version of the argument of this chapter so far has been presented in Matti Häyry, 2009a, 'The moral contestedness of selecting "deaf embryos"', Kristjana Kristiansen, Simo Vehmas, and Tom Shakespeare (eds), *Arguing About Disability: Philosophical Perspectives* (London: Routledge): 154–68.

[49] This is required by the two other steps in Harris's analogy, see Section 4.4.

are chosen. This is where the callous judgement comes into play. If Harris says, 'The world would be better if hearing people are produced' can he avoid saying, 'The world would be better if deaf people did not exist'? Since he thinks that he can, the task is to understand how, and an example could be helpful in this.

Imagine that you are stranded on a desert island with all the supplies that you need for living – and with one person. In scenario one this is an ordinary dull person with whom you can have the occasional conversation but with whom you will be bored most of the time. In scenario two the other person is an excellent storyteller who will keep you entertained during your long days and nights by relating tale after fascinating tale. If you end up in scenario one, it would seem possible to regret this without saying anything particularly insulting about your unexciting companion. 'It would be better to have the storyteller than you' does not necessarily imply 'It would be better that you did not exist'. The former is a slightly rude and probably unwise comment under the circumstances, but it does not come even near to the potentially threatening tone of the latter.

If Harris has something like this in mind, then the additional premise he requires is that deaf people should not take comments about their qualities personally. They should see hearing as an ability that they lack – like the boring companion lacks the ability to tell engaging tales – and simply recognise their shortcoming without making a big deal of it. In the Harris world, the fact that some people disagree with this description of the matter is irrelevant, because by doing so they just show their irrationality.

Now that the analogy has been made to work, Harris has another challenge. According to him, parents are legally permitted to make the immoral choice of bringing a deaf child into existence. Does this mean that parents should also be legally permitted to deafen their hearing children, say, when they are reaching adolescence? The answer seems to be 'no' on the grounds that morality and the law follow their own logics, and this makes the difference between the cases at the level of law but not at the level of morality. Behaviour that wrongs and harms others is legally as well as morally forbidden, and deafening a hearing child falls under this category. But the 'deaf embryo' is not wronged or harmed by bringing it to existence (it will have a life worth living that it would otherwise not have had), although its 'harmed condition' makes its creation suboptimal (in the consequentialist sense) and hence immoral. This is why parents, according to Harris, are legally allowed to make the immoral prenatal choice but not to harm their existing child.

Moving on to the opposite camp, the defence of the social view, in the context of choosing deafness, calls for two stipulations on ethical decision making and a prescriptive postulation on resource allocation.

The first stipulation is that whenever parents estimate that a sufficient deaf culture exists, it does. This is needed to counter the criticism that, apart from a few well-established communities such as Gallaudet, deafness as a way of life is too precariously founded to guarantee the good life of deaf children.[50] In response, the stipulation makes it the parents' business to assess the situation. What is 'sufficient' cannot be evaluated with total neutrality anyway, so it is best to put in charge individuals who are most closely affected by the choice. Letting other people or society as a whole interfere would, according to this line of thought, be irrational.

The second stipulation is that if possible undesired outcomes are exceedingly improbable, they need not be taken into account in reproductive decision making. This is directed against the comment that deafness combined with the loss of sight and touch would make a person totally unable to communicate with others. While the comment can be valid, the condition is so rare that taking it into consideration would, so the stipulation dictates, be irrational. Human choices would become impossibly difficult if very small risks like this should always be averted in the name of morality.

The prescriptive postulation on resource allocation is that all needs should be catered for equally and without discrimination. This is against the argument that the 'special' needs of deaf children would drain resources required to meet the normal needs of others. The question is, why would only some needs be defined as 'normal'? Different people have different needs, and if society assumes a responsibility for their satisfaction, there is no legitimate reason to exclude one group of people, present or future, by claiming that their requirements are 'special'. Such distinctions are, as far as the postulation goes, irrational or immoral.

The final observation of this chapter concerns the rationality exemplified by my own argument for the nondirective compromise. In presenting this, I have used the logic of the middle position between more extreme (in this case 'social' and 'medical') views. The solution seemed natural, because the viewpoint is all but missing in current debates. Following this logic, it would be reasonable to accept morally the notion that has already

---

[50] This stipulation is needed (only) when the specific argument of deafness as a culture is used. Other supporters of the social view could bypass this step and say that just societies should provide sufficient services for citizens both with and without disabilities so that they can live flourishing lives.

been recognised legally, namely that neither of the opposing views can decide the matter to everybody's satisfaction. Legal permissiveness could then be complemented with the admission that the practice is morally contested. In defending the stance I have appealed to reasons that are likely to come up in public discussions, in the way that representatives of the middle position often do. The rationality involved is, to a great extent, the rationality of communication and negotiation, although the results are bound to vary according to the mix of people around the table and the arguments taken into account.

Saviour siblings and treating people as a means

In this chapter, I analyse the morality of creating children who could become tissue donors for their older siblings. After an examination of harms, benefits, consent, and privacy, I study in detail the argument that the production of saviour siblings involves, wrongfully, the treatment of people as mere means.

5.1 Facts and regulations

When parents need a matching donor for a seriously ill child, they can try to produce one by using reproductive technologies. Preimplantation genetic diagnosis (PGD) following in vitro fertilisation (IVF) reveals an embryo's immune – human leucocyte antigen (HLA) – profile and whether or not it could become a suitable donor for its existing sibling. In a favourable case, a healthy and matching embryo can be implanted in the potential mother's uterus and if all goes well, a suitable donor is born. Stem cells are retrieved by collecting placental or umbilical cord blood and these are injected into the ailing child in the hope of providing a cure. Donation of blood, bone marrow, and organs is also a viable option for other treatments that may be required later.

The conditions for which healthy matching donors have been sought so far include Fanconi's anaemia,[1] thalassaemia,[2] and Diamond–Blackfan anaemia (DBA),[3] all diseases with bleak prognoses if stem cell therapies enabled by saviour siblings cannot be used. Fanconi's anaemia causes

---

[1] Y. Verlinsky, S. Rechitsky, W. Schoolcraft, C. Strom, and A. Kuliev, 2001, 'Preimplantation diagnosis for Fanconi anemia combined with HLA matching', *Journal of the American Medical Association* 285: 3130–3.

[2] Naveen Qureshi, Drucilla Foote, Mark C. Walters, Sylvia T. Singer, Keith Quirolo, and Elliott P. Vichinsky, 2005, 'Outcomes of preimplantation genetic diagnosis therapy in treatment of β-thalassemia: a retrospective analysis', *Annals of the New York Academy of Sciences* 1054: 500–3.

[3] Y. Verlinsky, S. Rechitsky, J. Cieslak, I. Tur-Kaspa, R. Morris, and A. Kuliev, 2005, 'Accuracy and outcomes of 3631 preimplantation genetic diagnosis (PGD) cycles performed in

shortness, skeletal anomalies, tumours, leukaemias, and bone marrow failure; some forms of thalassaemia require constant heavy medication and regular blood transfusions; and DBA is associated with congenital malformations, thumb and upper limb abnormalities, cardiac defects, urogenital deformities, and cleft palate. Successful treatments have been reported at least in the United States, in the United Kingdom, and Belgium. Widely reported cases in the saviour sibling discussion are those of the Nash family in Colorado, United States (the first saviour sibling, provided a successful cure for Fanconi's anaemia in 2000);[4] in Great Britain, the Hashmi family (legal battle to produce a saviour sibling for thalassaemia (2000–2005), family stopped trying in 2004);[5] the Whitaker family (travelled to Chicago in 2002 to produce a matching donor for DBA);[6] and the Fletcher family (the first British saviour sibling, donor for DBA, born in 2005).[7]

The regulation concerning the creation of saviour siblings is currently in a state of flux in most countries, and there are marked differences. In the United States, genetic testing is gradually becoming an industry,[8] and there are few restrictions, despite arguments for their desirability.[9] In Australia, PGD and HLA testing have been used with official approval.[10] In Europe, nation states have assumed a variety of approaches from total bans to relatively permissive policies.[11] In the United Kingdom, a

one center', *Fertility and Sterility* 84: S98; A. Kuliev, S. Rechitsky, I. Tur-Kaspa, and Y. Verlinsky, 2005, 'Preimplantation genetics: improving access to stem-cell therapy', *Annals of the New York Academy of Sciences* 1054: 223–7.
[4] Deborah Josefson, 2000, 'Couple select healthy embryo to provide stem cells for sister', *British Medical Journal* 321: 917.
[5] Sally Sheldon, 2005, 'Saviour siblings and the discretionary power of the HFEA', *Medical Law Review* 13: 403–11.
[6] Margaret R. Brazier, 2006, 'Human(s) (as) medicine(s)', Sheila MacLean (ed.), *First Do No Harm: Law, Ethics and Healthcare* (Aldershot: Ashgate): 187–202, p. 198.
[7] Kirsty Horsey, 2005, '"Saviour sibling" born to Fletcher family', *IVF News*, 23 July 2005 – www.ivf.net/ivf/saviour_sibling_born_to_fletcher_family-o1555-en.html. See also Gail Edgar, 2008, 'The saviour sibling', *Belfast Telegraph*, 18 May – www.sundaylife.co.uk/news/article3714984.ece.
[8] Susannah Baruch, David Kaufman, and Kathy L. Hudson, 2008, 'Genetic testing of embryos: practices and perspectives of US in vitro fertilization clinics', *Fertility and Sterility* 89: 1053–8.
[9] E.g. Bratislav Stanković, 2005, '"It's a designer baby": Opinions on regulation of preimplantation genetic diagnosis', *UCLA Journal of Law and Technology* 3 – www.lawtechjournal.com/articles/2005/03_050713_stankovic.php.
[10] Merle Spriggs and Julian Savulescu, 2002, 'Saviour siblings', *Journal of Medical Ethics* 28: 289; Australian Stem Cell Centre, 2009, 'What are stem cells?' – www.nscc.edu.au/public-education_what-cells_cord.aspx.
[11] Anniek Corveleyn, Eleni Zika, Michael Morris, Elisabeth Dequeker, James Lawford Davies, Karen Sermon, Guillermo Antiñolo, Andreas Schmutzler, Jiri Vanecek, Fransesc Palau, and

specific governmental agency, the Human Fertilisation and Embryology Authority (HFEA), has been in charge of granting licences for the use of reproductive technologies.[12] The production of saviour siblings was accepted by Parliament in May 2008.[13]

5.2   The logic of the case

The moral logic of the saviour sibling case can be presented as a series of yes-or-no questions, together with answers to them. The starting point is that a problem is detected in an existing child; and the first question is whether or not there is a cure that does *not* involve the use of donors. If a therapy or drug can be found, the problem is solved. On the other hand, if it cannot, and if donor-related treatment is not an option either, the situation remains unresolved.

In a case in which a donor could help, the next question is, can an already living one be found (and the creation of a new individual thereby avoided)? This is where medical teams, at the request of the parents, canvass all available records to find a tissue-type match. A positive result, while encouraging to the ailing child, will lead to a cluster of side issues - which are not exactly similar to, but which resemble closely, some aspects of the saviour sibling debate. Matching individuals can be competent adults who consent to the procedure, and if this is the case, a potential solution has been identified. But if they are competent adults who do *not* consent, what should be done? Should coercion or persuasion be used? What if their tissue could be used without their knowledge and with no tangible detriment to them? Alternatively, what if the possible donor is a child or an incompetent adult? Legal solutions have been devised for such cases, but what kinds of reactions would be rational and moral? Is there a moral distinction between family members and total strangers as donors? These are all questions that need to be kept in mind, also in the ethical assessment of the combination of IVF, PGD, and HLA typing.

If suitable donors, living or dead, cannot be identified, it is time to ask whether a saviour sibling could be produced. In a negative case, the child's ailment remains, regrettably, uncured. An affirmative reply, in its turn, raises one final yes-or-no question, which is shared with the already-existing-donor

---

Dolores Ibarreta, 2007, *Preimplantation Genetic Diagnosis in Europe* (Executive Summary), EUR 22764 EN – www.eurogentest.org/web/files/public/unit1/pgd/22764-ExeSumm.pdf.

[12] Human Fertilisation and Embryology Authority – www.hfea.gov.uk/.

[13] BBC News, 2008, 'MPs reject "saviour sibling" ban', 19 May – www. news.bbc.co.uk/2/hi/uk_news/politics/7409264.stm.

situations. Is the procedure that is required for the eventual treatment invasive? Queries and responses continue in either case, but they are different, and often asked and answered by ethicists of different schools.[14]

The procedures are, to varying degrees, invasive at least when bone marrow, blood, and organs have to be retrieved to produce a cure. In these cases, the next question is, what could justify the related violations of bodily integrity, infringements of privacy (in other senses), and lack of consent? The donor's own best interest and the existing child's needs have been cited as sufficient reasons, but these lead to further challenges concerning the rightful limits of medical paternalism and the legitimacy of sacrificing one human being to benefit other individuals. Section 5.3 investigates such questions.

The procedure is arguably noninvasive when placental or umbilical cord blood can be used.[15] In addition, the utilisation of loose hair, skin, saliva, and other detached parts or extracts of the body would belong to this category. Since no physical contact with the donor is needed, the natural question here is almost diametrically opposite to the earlier enquiry, and this is, what could be wrong with this? If a child's life and health are in danger, why not go ahead and exploit whatever bits and pieces are found lying around unused?

One set of answers states that the moral mistake has already been made in the creation of the saviour sibling. By handpicking the new individual, parents have resorted to designing life and this is wrong for psychological as well as metaphysical reasons. This is a response that I will discuss first briefly in Section 5.4 and then in more detail in Chapter 6. Another objection is that by discarding unsuitable embryos in the process of producing the desired child, parents and medical professionals violate their sanctity of life. I will return to the question of life's inviolability in Chapter 7. And lack of consent can be used as a reason against both testing and selection. This point is connected to the design and privacy arguments and will be examined together with them in Chapter 6 and in Section 5.5.

Another set of answers concerns the treatment of individuals when they are already in existence. The issues of lack of consent and violations of

[14] Consequentialists are primarily interested in the harm possibly inflicted by invasive methods; nonconsequentialists also raise more abstract ethical concerns.
[15] Arguably *all* testing that involves PGD is invasive, as one cell of the tested embryo is removed to prepare the diagnosis. See Section 5.3 and, e.g. Bruce Goldman, 2007, 'Reproductive medicine: The first cut', *Nature* 445: 479–80; Maria-Elena Torres-Padilla, David-Emlyn Parfitt, Tony Kouzarides, and Magdalena Zernicka-Goetz, 2007, 'Histone arginine methylation regulates pluripotency in the early mouse embryo', *Nature* 445: 214–18.

genetic privacy are not only relevant in the use of placental and umbilical cord blood, but also in reproductive selection and invasive tissue retrieval. These will be dealt with in Section 5.5. But the main topic of this chapter, and the one specified and delimited by all the preceding considerations, is the problem of *instrumental use*. When saviour sibling tissue or other materials are employed in restoring the health of an existing child, is the newborn (or its mother) used merely as a means to serve the ends of others? And if so, is this wrong; and if it is, in what way? My examination of these questions will occupy Sections 5.6, 5.7, 5.8, and 5.9, and I will sum up the findings of this chapter in Section 5.10.

5.3   What could justify invasive procedures?

Both the creation and the use of saviour siblings can be invasive. PGD involves the removal of one of the six to eight cells of the tested embryo, and there is no precise knowledge of the long-term effects of this operation on the resulting individual. Experts used to assume that the remaining cells are totipotent and will secure the normal development of the human body, but this assumption has recently been challenged.[16] And when the new individual is born, the procedure by which the older sibling is helped can require physical intrusion. This is the case if bone marrow or other tissues or organs are needed.

How can these invasions be justified? Medical ethics does not usually allow breaches of physical integrity without good grounds – which include consent, the recipient's own best interest, and other people's legitimate interests. Can these be appealed to in this case?

Saviour siblings cannot, as embryos or neonates, give their *actual* consent to cell or tissue retrieval. Although this is hardly encouraging, it is not the end of the story, either. Apart from this type of approval, in which the recipients genuinely give their permission to invasive procedures, many other types of 'consent' are in regular use in medical situations.[17] *Assumed* consent has been secured when we believe, for reasons which make sense to us, that the recipients would have permitted the activity had they been able to form and express their opinion at the time. *Rational* consent is in

---

[16] Goldman, 2007; Torres-Padilla, Parfitt, Kouzarides, and Zernicka-Goetz, 2007.

[17] The classification of forms of consent can be made in a variety of ways. My list includes the types that I think are relevant in the current context, but it would in other surroundings be incomplete. The names used for different kinds of consent can also vary, so someone else can refer to one of my categories by a different name; and the names I have used can mean something else in other people's listings.

place when we think that the recipient ought to permit the activity in the name of logic and morality. And *proxy* consent is used when the recipient is bypassed in the decision making altogether and the permission is given by someone else – a parent, relative, friend, expert, or authority. The common denominator of all the non-actual forms of consent is that they need to be justified further by those assuming, reckoning, or sidestepping the will of the object of the intervention. Considerations of interests find a natural function here.

For the evaluation of the saviour sibling's own best interest, two stages of the process should be distinguished: the use of PGD and the retrieval of tissue for the ailing child. To start with, the created individual will *not* be made healthier or more useful to others by PGD. There is no *subjective* comparison between a life with thalassaemia and without it; or between a life as a matching donor or not. Saviour siblings are born *because* they have the required qualities; and the natural (but objective) point of comparison is with other possible individuals who were *not* brought into existence because they had the genetic mutation or did not match the tissue type of the sick child. So the object of the intervention cannot think afterwards, 'Lucky for me that they decided to use PGD, because otherwise I would have had thalassaemia.' This would be conceptual nonsense.

There is one subjective criterion of assessment, though, and this is between life as saviour sibling and no life to begin with. From the viewpoint of the new individual, it is possible that the parents would have had a different child, or no child at all, without the new prospects provided by PGD. As the PGD-favoured choice, the saviour sibling has been given a life that might not or would not otherwise have been on offer. If life is better than nonexistence, PGD is in this sense in the new individual's own best interest.[18]

Similarly, the invasive transplantation procedure does not directly make the saviour sibling healthier or longer lived. On the contrary, the retrieval of cells or tissue can be, to varying degrees, harmful. Blood can be obtained without much risk; organ donation can be positively

[18] For alternatives to this view, see David Benatar, 2006, *Better Never to Have Been: The Harm of Coming into Existence* (Oxford: Clarendon Press); Matti Häyry, 2004c, 'A rational cure for pre-reproductive stress syndrome', *Journal of Medical Ethics* 30: 377–8; Matti Häyry, 2005c, 'The rational cure for prereproductive stress syndrome revisited', *Journal of Medical Ethics* 31: 606–7; Matti Häyry, 2009b, 'An analysis of some arguments for and against human reproduction', Matti Häyry, Tuija Takala, Peter Herissone-Kelly, and Gardar Árnason (eds), *Arguments and Analysis in Bioethics* (Amsterdam: Rodopi): 147–54.

detrimental; and bone marrow is, in terms of risk and invasiveness, a case in between. It is possible that the saviour can indirectly earn *social* benefits by offering medical assistance to the existing child. These benefits, if they are forthcoming, will be intertwined with the promotion of other people's interests – families and societies may or may not favour individuals who have been useful to their siblings in this way.

Would it be in the saviour sibling's own best interest to 'try' to make the ailing child healthy and the parents happy by 'donating' matching tissue?[19] It can be, if the operation is successful in two ways: the process does not inflict harm on the donor *and* the therapy works. If either of these elements is missing, however, the situation can be different. Parental attitudes can change if the new individual fails to bring about the desired cure. And harm or inconvenience to the donor calls for at least a balancing exercise between the good and bad outcomes of the procedure to all the parties involved.

The idea of risking harm on newly born children or interfering with their physical integrity expressly to make their parents happy may sound far-fetched, but it is sometimes seen as justified in medical contexts. Male circumcision is accepted in many jurisdictions at parental request on religious or cultural grounds. As for exposing children to harm to benefit their relatives, the use of minors as donors for organ transplantation is not always seen as an impossible alternative.[20] And individual children's inclusion in medical research has in certain jurisdictions been made obligatory because of its benefits to children in general.[21]

It seems, then, that the case for invasive procedures is based on two premises. First, either life as such or life as encountered by the saviour sibling in question must be preferable to not being born at all. Most philosophers seem to go along with this assumption. Secondly, however, consistency requires that if it is all right to use infants in medical treatments without their consent then it should also be morally acceptable to use adults in the same way in similar situations. Although this is a trickier position to defend, John Harris, for instance, has done exactly so in

---

[19] The words 'try' and 'donate' are placed in quotes in this sentence to highlight the fact that no intentional choice on the part of the saviour sibling is involved.

[20] Francis L. Delmonico and William E. Harmon, 2002, 'The use of a minor as a live kidney donor', *American Journal of Transplantation* 2: 333–6; Cordelia Thomas, 2004, 'Preimplantation testing and the protection of the "saviour sibling"', *Deakin Law Review* 9 – ww.austlii.edu.au/au/journals/DeakinLRev/2004/5.html.

[21] See, e.g. National Institute of Health, 1998, *NIH Policy and Guidelines on the Inclusion of Children as Participants in Research involving Human Subjects* – http://grants.nih.gov/grants/guide/notice-files/not98-024.html.

relation to organ donation and medical research, thereby proving that the position can be backed up with at least one kind of rationality.[22]

5.4   Why would noninvasive procedures be a problem?

The production and use of saviour siblings can be seen as noninvasive, if PGD does not present a threat to the developing embryo and if placental or umbilical cord blood is sufficient for the required treatment. The question in this case is, why would this be problematic? What could legitimise a failure to cure a seriously sick child with discarded biological materials?

Some ethicists believe that the creation of saviour siblings is wrong because it is another step towards the direction of having babies by design.[23] Reproductive selection aimed at eliminating genetic diseases started this process by citing the best interest of the eventual child as a palatable justification. Selection intended to find a cure for an existing individual would take the idea a notch further by making a possibly agreeable appeal to the interests of others. But the wider the range of accepted reasons becomes, the harder it will be to resist other, hitherto foreclosed, uses of the technique, especially when these can be seen as arising from benign motives. If intelligence is a good overall quality, would it not be in anybody's interest to have more of it? If brown-eyed individuals are more popular in a community, would it not be a service to prospective children to make sure that they meet this criterion? If girls are undervalued in a society, would it not be kinder to have boys? But the forms of selection aimed at determining intelligence, eye colour, and sex are infested with ethical questions.[24]

One consideration is psychological harm. Parental expectations can lead to pressures in successful cases and disappointments in others and these will arguably lower the experienced life quality of the child produced. In mild occasions this can lead to tensions in one's self-image (should I be what I am or what mum and dad ordered?) and in worse scenarios to anxiety and depression. Defenders of selection are quick to point out that expectations are present in every parental–filial relationship; that it is not considered too harmful in 'normal' cases; and that it should not, in the name of consistency, be so considered in the saviour

---

[22] John Harris, 1975, 'The survival lottery', *Philosophy*, 50: 81–7; John Harris, 2005, 'Scientific research is a moral duty', *Journal of Medical Ethics* 31: 242–8.

[23] E.g. Samuel Hensley, 2004, 'Designer babies: One step closer', *The Center for Bioethics and Humanity*, 1 July – www.cbhd.org/resources/genetics/hensley_2004–07–01.htm.

[24] E.g. Caroline Berry and Jacky Engel, 2005, 'Saviour siblings', *Christian Medical Fellowship Files* Nr 28 – www.cmf.org.uk/literature/content.asp?context=article&id=1317.

sibling or designer baby cases.[25] It is by no means clear, they continue, that the new practices would raise the level of harm sufficiently to distinguish the instances. But their opponents can counter these comments with a series of observations. Perhaps the involvement of parents in their children's lives is already too extensive and should be limited; and if this is the case, the analogy argument fails to work. Or perhaps the situation is acceptable now but does not bear even minor changes: the fact that a bad thing can be tolerated to some degree does not mean that it should be knowingly boosted.[26] As to increases in the level of pressures and anxieties, it is true that there is no evidence for it – but there is no evidence against it either, and it could be safer to place the burden of proof on those who want to change the prevailing practices which have served humankind reasonably well so far.[27]

Another ethical question is unfairness to the children whose qualities are *not* handpicked. If only some are benefited by design, the rest will have to live with a disadvantage that they have in no way deserved. Here the champions of saviour siblings and designer babies are keen to remark on an apparent contradiction in arguing from harm and fairness at the same time. If selected children are harmed by the choice, then what possible loss could there be in not being selected? The contradiction is, however, only apparent. Some children can be better off as a result of design, while others can be harmed or untouched by it. The unfairness is then manifested in comparisons between the two main groups. Individuals who fare worse than the luckiest ones are left with a relative congenital disadvantage, which would not have existed without selection.[28]

Yet another concern is discrimination against those who do not fulfil the criteria of prenatal choice. Will the less intelligent (whatever the manner of measurement), the blue-eyed (or, to be more precise, the non-brown-eyed), or women (young or old) suffer due to the technique that enables their exclusion and due to the political climate that allows this? Proponents of designer babies say 'no' because embryos and fetuses do

[25] Sally Sheldon and Stephen Wilkinson, 2004, 'Should selecting saviour siblings be banned?', *Journal of Medical Ethics* 30: 533–7; Sally Sheldon and Stephen Wilkinson, 2005, '"Saviour siblings": Hashmi and Whitaker – An unjustifiable and misguided distinction', *Pro-Choice Forum* – www.prochoiceforum.org.uk/irl_rep_tech_2.asp.

[26] This leaves untouched the view that there is never too much parental control or that at least the critical level is not reached by genetic selection. Those who have doubts concerning the creation of saviour siblings are not likely to share this position, though, so it remains an external form of criticism.

[27] I will return to the relative merits of hope, fear, and caution in Chapter 8.

[28] I will return to design arguments in Chapter 6.

not count and people with the avoided features should not see a symbolic threat where none is intended. Opponents respond that it is difficult not to take seriously the loss of human life and not to take personally clear messages stating that one's replacement with another kind of human being would make the world a better place.[29]

5.5   Rational consent and genetic privacy

All these reflections proceed from the idea that the creation of saviour siblings in medically indicated situations is inevitably linked with the production of other kinds of designer babies on a grand scale. But what if this is not true? Let us assume, for argument's sake, that PGD can be readily limited to acceptable selection; that this includes design for sibling therapy; and that the good and bad types of planning can be kept clearly apart. It becomes immediately visible that whereas designer babies in general bring up issues of harm, unfairness, and discrimination, as shown in the last section, saviour siblings in particular all but elude them. If the removal of the one cell from the embryo does not have grave effects (which is possible) and if the parents resolve not to blame the new child for failures in the therapy (which is also possible), concrete objections to helping an existing child seem to be much weaker than those directed against a wider permission to choose offspring. Questions of fairness and justice hardly arise and concerns of harm can be addressed by meticulous research and firm family policy.

The situation can be tentatively assessed in the light of an imaginary example. Unbeknown to me, my umbilical cord has been preserved and now a medical team asks for my permission to use it in the life-saving treatment of an ailing child. What should I do? What *can* I do? A refusal would indirectly result in the patient's death. And as Jonathan Glover has noted, the 'ethical objections that would justifiably block the only means of saving a child's life have to be very impressive indeed'.[30] It seems that I have strong moral reasons to give my permission to the procedure, whatever my ethical background theory. It would undoubtedly be considered virtuous to grant the request and vicious to turn it down. My duties towards others probably include an obligation to save a life when I can do it with minimal personal effort. Outcomes favour the donation, as well. If I do not consent, I will be considered a villain; if the medical team

[29] See John Harris on symbolic threats in Chapter 4, Section 4.12.
[30] Jonathan Glover, 2006, *Choosing Children: Genes, Disability, and Design* (Oxford: Clarendon Press), p. 67.

cannot find me or if I am incompetent, they have every reason to assume my authorisation; and if I refuse, society has a plausible case to bypass my actual will in the name of rational consent.

Despite these initial reactions, the matter is not clear-cut. People tend to have deep-rooted intuitions about what is theirs, or what belongs to their own sphere, and interventions by others are often seen as violations of privacy.[31] I would personally not have any immediate use for my umbilical cord and I would not necessarily see it as a part of me in any meaningful sense, but needs and opinions differ in matters like these. Others could require or want the material for their own treatment, for the development of a new drug, or for cultural purposes. Respect for privacy offers protection for such requirements and wishes against the interests that outsiders may have.

Privacy as an ethical and legal principle gives me a say in who may invade my body; who may use parts of me that I do not use any more; and who may access information concerning me.[32] Violations of bodily integrity do not, by definition, occur in the noninvasive saviour sibling case and property claims in body parts have been seen as problematic.[33] It does not seem inevitably right, however, that others decide for me, without my consent, how my discarded tissue is to be used. Even the retrieval of cadaveric organs for transplantation remains controversial although strictly speaking the dead should have no interests in them.[34] In addition, there are issues of informational privacy. If I am identified as a potential donor for someone, everyone involved will have at least two pieces of knowledge about me; that I am a tissue match for the recipient, and that I do not have the disease that the recipient has. These may seem like inconsequential details, but part of the function of privacy is precisely to protect me from 'being known' like this.[35]

5.6   Means, mere means, and outcomes

Considerations of privacy provide a natural bridge to the vocabulary focal to this chapter, namely that of *treating people as a means* to the ends

---

[31] On the definition of privacy see, e.g. Graeme T. Laurie, 2002, *Genetic Privacy: A Challenge to Medico-Legal Norms* (Cambridge: Cambridge University Press), p. 6.
[32] E.g. Tony McGleenan, 1998, 'The jurisprudence of genetic privacy', *Medicine, Health Care and Philosophy* 1: 225–33; Laurie, 2002.
[33] See, e.g. Rohan Hardcastle, 2007, *Law and the Human Body: Property Rights, Ownership and Control* (Oxford: Hart Publishing).
[34] See, e.g. Charles C. Hinkley II, 2005, *Moral Conflicts of Organ Retrieval: A Case for Constructive Pluralism* (Amsterdam: Rodopi).
[35] This point will be explored further in Chapter 6.

of others. Violations of our privacy, when they are deliberate, are always motivated by the interests of others. These include a prudential interest to further the intruder's aims, a paternalistic interest to promote the recipient's wellbeing, and a malevolent interest to invade the victim's sphere. In all these cases, however, other people use something that 'belongs' to us (or make intrusions into something that 'belongs' to us) as an instrument to achieve ends that *they* have defined.[36]

It is frequently said that the creation and use of saviour siblings is wrong because they (and possibly their mothers) will be treated as a means in the process. But what does treatment 'as a means' or 'as a mere means' involve and on what grounds, if any, can it be deemed wrong? In philosophical terms, the notion is derived from Immanuel Kant's ethics,[37] and I will return to its possible meanings in that context in Sections 5.8 and 5.9. Let me first examine, however, the ways in which the idea has been formulated, criticised, and defended independently of Kant's theory.[38]

To start from the critical end of the continuum, John Harris does not see much merit in the Kantian objection as it has been used in bioethical debates.[39] When we treat others as a means we make (or knowingly let) others do something that promotes our ends; perhaps

---

[36] The word 'belongs' is in quotes to indicate that I do not primarily mean belonging in the sense of ownership – rather, my meaning is 'being a part of me or my domain'.

[37] Immanuel Kant, 1994, *Grounding for the Metaphysics of Morals* [*Grundlegung zur Metaphysik der Sitten* 1785a], in Immanuel Kant, *Ethical Philosophy*, translated by James W. Ellington, second edition (Indianapolis, IN: Hackett Publishing Company), p. 36 (§ 429). For an accessible explanation of Kant's view, see Roger J. Sullivan, 1994, *An Introduction to Kant's Ethics* (Cambridge: Cambridge University Press), pp. 65–83.

[38] One discussion on means and ends that precedes Kant is the doctrine of double effect, sometimes employed in cases where bad outcomes must be allowed in order to achieve good ones. Examples include the administration of painkillers in terminal treatment even if death can be hastened by it, and the removal of a cancerous womb with a fetus inside to save a woman's life even if the death of the fetus will ensue. The aspect that makes this discussion unhelpful in the saviour sibling case is that the effect sought for must, according to the traditional reading, always flow from the action at least as immediately as the questioned one: relieving pain before death and saving the woman before the death of the fetus in the examples. The stumbling block here is that the therapy for the ailing sibling cannot be made to precede the creation and instrumental use of the new individual. On the doctrine and literature concerning it, see, e.g. Alison McIntyre, 2004 [substantive revision 2009], 'Doctrine of double effect', *Stanford Encyclopedia of Philosophy* – plato.stanford.edu/entries/double-effect/.

[39] John Harris, 1985, *The Value of Life: An Introduction to Medical Ethics* (London: Routledge and Kegan Paul), pp. 142–5; John Harris, 1998, *Clones, Genes, and Immortality: Ethics and the Genetic Revolution* (Oxford: Oxford University Press), pp. 148–53; John Harris, 2007, *Enhancing Evolution: The Ethical Case for Making Better People* (Princeton, NJ: Princeton University Press), p. 156.

in circumstances in which we could have done something to promote those ends ourselves; when there is an inducement for others to do so.[40] As Harris notes, this kind of behaviour is commonplace and does not usually attract moral censure.[41] We do things for each other, sometimes spontaneously, sometimes on request, and sometimes for a fee; but this instrumental use is not, as a rule, seen as a problem. And although the proper Kantian formulation of treating people as *mere* means could carry more moral weight,[42] it does not help in the saviour sibling case, either, because most instances of reproduction are at least partly motivated by the good of the created child, whatever the other considerations.[43]

Harris concedes that instrumental use can be condemned if it is exploitative, or denies other people's personhood.[44] This is not, according to him, the case when services, tissue, or body parts are donated altruistically or provided in exchange for adequate payment.[45] But wrongful instrumentalisation may occur, especially in the absence of consent, if the donor is coerced or exposed to grave danger.[46] Exploitation, Harris writes, 'usually implies that the exploiter is able to apply some coercive pressure that those whom she exploits are unable, or ill equipped, to resist.'[47] The role of consent is crucial, as our own genuine permission can, Harris believes, annul allegations of coercion. In his words, 'one way of trying to ensure that we do not exploit others is to ask for their consent to what we propose and to make sure that they have a real option to refuse.'[48]

At first glance the views expressed by Harris would seem to support restrictions on the creation of saviour siblings: the ones used in promoting the ends of others have not consented; they are in no position to resist the procedures they are subjected to; and they can be harmed or inconvenienced by the process. But not so according to Harris, who has been quoted as saying, in the wake of the Fletcher case in the United Kingdom: 'There could be no better reason for having a child than to save

---

[40] Harris does not give this characterisation in so many words, but these three elements are present in Harris, 1985, pp. 142–3, which is where he gives his most detailed exposition of the expression.

[41] Harris, 1985, pp. 143–4; see also Nicholas Agar, 2004, *Liberal Eugenics: In Defence of Human Enhancement* (Oxford: Blackwell), pp. 42–3.

[42] Harris, 1998, p. 148.   [43] Harris, 2007, p. 156.   [44] Harris, 1998, p. 148.

[45] Harris, 1985, p. 143–4; Harris, 1998, p. 149.

[46] Harris, 1985, p. 143; Harris, 1998, pp. 150–3.   [47] Harris, 1985, p. 143.

[48] Harris, 1998, p. 148 (comma removed after 'others').

the life of another child … so this is genuinely a "pro-life" decision by the parents and the HFEA and they are to be congratulated.[49]

The logic Harris employs here is probably the following.[50] In his view, it would make no sense to talk about consent in the production and use of saviour siblings, because embryos and neonates are simply not capable of giving or refusing permissions. Likewise, it would make no sense to talk about coercing unborn or newly born human beings, as coercion typically involves irresistible threats or promises, and such entities, too, are beyond their comprehension. The remaining factor, then, is the net well-being generated by the decision, and since the medical needs of the ailing child clearly outweigh the risks imposed on the saviour sibling (who will be endowed with a life, anyway), the practice is not exploitative and ought to be condoned.

Glover agrees with the ethical views presented and implied by Harris, but he takes the analysis further and allows some variety in the eventual moral judgements. Treating a person merely as a means, he states, requires that there is 'a violation of his or her autonomy or else a denial of some kind of respect he or she is owed'.[51] But although the selection for implantation and the retrieval of tissue happen 'without the new child's consent', the condition is not, according to him, met: 'Because there is no capacity for choice, the issue of respecting the child's autonomy does not arise at either stage.'[52] Instead, the question boils down to the details of each individual case. If parents want to have a saviour sibling, use its cells, and then put the child up for adoption, they can be accused of wrongful instrumentalisation.[53] As Glover expresses the matter: 'Whether the child is treated merely as a means depends on how much the parents love and care for the child.'[54] Parents who are prepared to use children for spare parts and immediately abandon them, fall, apparently, outside the scope of proper parental affection. Another restriction accepted by Glover is connected with the procedures required. While he sees the acquisition of placental and umbilical stem cells as unproblematic, he would not allow parents to produce a saviour sibling 'in order to have an organ donor for the older child'.[55] Here the balance of risks and benefits would make it too

---

[49] Andy Coghlan, 2004, '"Saviour sibling" babies get green light', New Scientist, 22 July – www.newscientist.com/article/dn6195-saviour-sibling-babies-get-green-light.html.

[50] This is my interpretation. I have not found direct views on saviour siblings, apart from the quote above, in what Harris has written or said publicly.

[51] Glover, 2006, p. 67.   [52] Glover, 2006, pp. 67–8.   [53] Glover, 2006, p. 68.

[54] Glover, 2006, p. 65.   [55] Glover, 2006, p. 68.

difficult to assess how genuinely people would or should consent to the donation.[56]

5.7   Means, individuals, and values

Balancing acts between the wellbeing of the donors and recipients of advantages have also been touched on, in the more general context of social justice, in the 'deontological' (as opposed to 'consequentialist') liberal discussion. And such weighing exercises have been unequivocally rejected by some proponents of the 'deontological' and 'teleological' approaches to the genetic challenge.

In a Kantian criticism of utilitarianism, John Rawls argues that aiming at the greatest average happiness in society will create a 'tendency to regard men as means to one another's welfare'.[57] This is prone to lead to lack of self-respect and self-esteem; and this is not what rational agents would condone in choosing their rules of cooperation.[58] According to Rawls, the right reaction here is that in 'the design of the social system we must treat persons *solely as ends and not in any way as means*' – an intensified Kantian task that Rawls believes his principles of justice can accomplish.[59] Within his view, 'to regard persons as a means is to be prepared to impose upon them lower prospects of life for the sake of higher expectations of others',[60] and this is something that his 'difference principle' can prevent from happening by requiring that social and economic inequalities 'are to be arranged so that they are ... reasonably expected to be to *everyone's* advantage'.[61]

Robert Nozick agrees with Rawls that the use of persons to benefit others must be rejected.[62] He contrasts minimising the use of people as means (favoured by consequentialist thinkers) and prohibiting it altogether (as an absolute side constraint) and argues that the latter solution is the right one in political arrangements. Utilitarians note that we are willing to make all sorts of temporary sacrifices to promote our own long-term good and claim that the same idea can be extended to

---

[56] Glover uses the form 'would', which seems to imply that he is talking about the *actual* consent of the infant. Since this has been ruled out, however, by his comments on the lacking 'capacity for choice' in small children, I believe that 'should', implying *rational* consent, is the correct choice.

[57] John Rawls, 1972, *A Theory of Justice* (Oxford: Oxford University Press), p. 183.

[58] Rawls, 1972, p. 181.   [59] Rawls, 1972, p. 183 (my emphasis).

[60] Rawls, 1972, p. 180.   [61] Rawls, 1972, pp. 60, 180 (my emphasis).

[62] Robert Nozick, 1974, *Anarchy, State, and Utopia* (Oxford: Blackwell), pp. 31–3.

sacrifices that members of society make for society as a whole.[63] Nozick argues, however, that the analogy breaks because 'there is no *social entity* with a good that undergoes some sacrifice for its own good.'[64] Instead, there 'are only individual people, different individual people, with their own individual lives', and using 'one of these people for the benefit of others, uses him and benefits the others', nothing more.[65] And although Nozick, unlike Rawls, believes that treatment as an end and treatment as a means can be legitimately combined in economic transactions,[66] his overall conclusion is that even rules such as Rawls's 'difference principle' eventually fail to justify the involuntary transfer of benefits from one distinct person to another.

What would the political theories of Rawls and Nozick say about the moral choice of producing saviour siblings? The application is not straightforward, but some points can be derived with relative confidence. Rawls could be anticipated to support the prescriptions laid out by Glover (although not, of course, on the same grounds). Arguably, the use of PGD and placental or umbilical cord blood can be 'reasonably expected to be to everyone's advantage', whereas having a matching child and putting it up for adoption or using it as an organ donor would not. The only difference here could be terminological: Rawls would insist that in acceptable cases saviour siblings are treated solely as ends in themselves, while it would be more natural to Glover to say that they are treated as a means but justifiably so.[67] Nozick, in his turn, could go further and reject the practice in its entirety as wrongfully instrumental. Going inside the embryonic or newly born body of an individual (who cannot consent or dissent) in order to benefit another individual clearly violates the distinctness of persons, and if this distinctness is seen as an absolute moral constraint to our actions, as Nozick does see it, saviour siblings should not be created with the help of PGD or used invasively to help others.[68]

Jürgen Habermas and Michael Sandel come, via different routes, to the same normative conclusion that Nozick might reach. Habermas starts from liberal premises but goes on to remark that genetic 'programming of desirable traits and dispositions ... gives rise to moral misgivings as soon as it commits the person concerned to a specific life-project or ... puts

---

[63] Nozick, 1974, p. 32.   [64] Nozick, 1974, pp. 32–3.
[65] Nozick, 1974, p. 33.   [66] Nozick, 1974, p. 31.
[67] See also the brief case for liberal eugenics in Rawls, 1972, pp. 107–8.
[68] Cf., however, the thought experiment of a 'genetic supermarket' in Nozick, 1974, p. 315 n.

specific restrictions on his freedom to choose a life of his own'.[69] Since it stands to reason that being a saviour sibling is a commitment that curtails an individual's self-definition,[70] this use of PGD should be morally condemned. Sandel's thinking on the matter is slightly more difficult to read, since his fundamental premises seem to support both permissions and bans.[71] One of the 'human goods embodied in important social practices' that he wants to safeguard in his theory is 'a willingness to share the fruits of good fortune through institutions of social solidarity',[72] and this would seem to push us into the direction of altruistic donations when others are in need of our tissue or organs. On the other hand, however, he also advocates 'norms of unconditional love and an openness to the unbidden' in parenting,[73] and rejects as 'morally abhorrent ... harvesting organs from a baby to save other people's lives'.[74] Given his general reluctance to accept genetic engineering, it seems safe to infer that Sandel would oppose the creation of saviour siblings.

Habermas and Sandel's views on the role of consent are different from the ideas of more outcome-oriented ethicists. Harris, Glover, and Rawls do not seem to mind that people subjected to laws and medical procedures have not actually agreed to be regulated or treated in the ways decreed by the authorities. Rational consent is sufficient for them, and this can be assumed as long as the choices made and enforced are compatible with their moral theories. Habermas is more sensitive to the fact that genetically selected future individuals cannot participate in the decision-making process leading to their existence. Instead of ignoring 'embryonic' consent, he makes the lack of it one of the cornerstones of his criticism of reproductive technologies.[75] Sandel agrees with Harris, Glover, and Rawls that the requirements of morality trump personal assent, but he founds morality in tradition rather than theory.[76] As a result, he does not place much value on either actual or rational (individual-liberty-driven) consent: in his view, proper behaviour accords with and supports good social and communal practices.

---

[69] Jürgen Habermas, 2003, *The Future of Human Nature*, translated by William Rehg, Max Pensky, and Hella Beister (Cambridge: Polity Press), p. 61.

[70] Whatever good and altruistic aspects it might otherwise have.

[71] Michael J. Sandel, 2007, *The Case Against Perfection: Ethics in the Age of Genetic Engineering* (Cambridge, MA: The Belknap Press of Harvard University Press).

[72] Sandel, 2007, p. 96.   [73] Sandel, 2007, p. 96.

[74] Sandel, 2007, p. 113. It is not clear what 'harvesting' here means, though, so it is remotely possible that I am quoting this line out of context. But this should not alter Sandel's normative conclusions.

[75] Habermas, 2003, pp. 60–6.   [76] Sandel, 2007, pp. 96–7.

5.8   Green's three readings of Kant

The wrongness of using people as a mere means is an essentially Kantian notion, which is presumably why Rawls, Nozick, and Habermas, who all draw on Kant's thinking have found it useful in their political theories. A more direct link to moral (insofar as this can be distinguished from political) philosophy and bioethics is provided by Ronald Green, who argues that Kant's doctrine on treating persons properly can be interpreted in competing ways, only one of which offers reasonable grounds for normative judgements.[77]

Green starts with Kant's relevant (second) formulation of the categorical imperative, which advises moral agents to 'Act so as to treat humanity, whether in your own person or in that of another, always as an end and never as a means only.'[78] After pointing out the difficulties of applying this concise rule to complicated bioethical issues, he sets out to give it the three readings that he believes are used and confused in current debates.

The first reading condemns offences against reasoned willing.[79] As thinking and willing beings we would contradict ourselves by turning against our own processes of thought and judgement. This can be done at least in two ways; by taking our own lives we totally annihilate the mental and moral basis of our being; and by using the wrong kinds of intoxicating substances we obliterate or distort our consciousness. In both instances we use ourselves as mere means, the end in the case of suicide being the avoidance of pain and suffering and in the case of intoxication anything from the simple pursuit of pleasure to the metaphysical evasion of life's intolerability.

Green sees this interpretation as problematic and surmises that its motivation is in Kant's Christian heritage.[80] Christianity forbids suicide and Kant had to twist his ethical theory to accommodate this, even at the expense of contradictions. He accepted the self-inflicted death of persons who sacrifice themselves for the sake of others, although they eliminate their reasoned willing as surely as those who want to avoid pain.

---

[77] Ronald M. Green, 2001a, 'What does it mean to use someone as "a means only": Rereading Kant', *Kennedy Institute of Ethics Journal* 11: 247–61. See also Ronald M. Green, 1991, 'The first formulation of the categorical imperative as literally a "legislative" metaphor', *History of Philosophy Quarterly* 8: 163–79.

[78] Immanuel Kant, 1959, *Foundations of the Metaphysics of Morals* [1785b], translated by Lewis White Beck (Indianapolis, IN: Bobbs-Merril), p. 47 (§ 429) – quoted in Green, 2001a, p. 248.

[79] Green, 2001a, pp. 251–2.   [80] Green, 2001a, p. 252.

Cultural views are also visible in Kant's views on recreational drugs. He commended the use of alcohol, as wine consumed in moderation stimulates social skills and clever conversation. Opium, on the contrary, was on Kant's black list as a cause of stupefaction. He found in this a reason to criticise cultures that ban wine and permit opium in its place.

Whatever the facts and values of this reading, it is not obviously applicable to the creation and use of saviour siblings. The lives of the children who are eventually born are not deliberately put in jeopardy, and neither are the lives of their mothers. And even if the minds of the new individuals can be confused by the circumstances of their coming into being, this does not necessarily constitute a concrete threat to their reasoned willing later in life.

Green's second reading proceeds from the notion that, according to Kant, human dignity and integrity forbid us to use our body parts as instruments of commerce or gratification.[81] We are both spiritual and physical beings, and the practices of self-mutilation, sale of teeth, prostitution, extramarital sex, and masturbation dent our worth by treating parts of our humanity as mere means in the pursuit of lower ends like pleasure.

Again, Green sees flaws in this line of thinking.[82] It is permissible, says Kant, to amputate a limb to save one's life and to sell one's hair to make ends meet. Green asks how these can differ from 'selling a tooth to help oneself out of serious financial difficulties' so radically that they are allowed but tooth selling condemned.[83] Similar tensions can be pointed out between extramarital sex (forbidden because one person uses the other as a means) and marital sex (permitted because both use the other equally as a means); and between prostitution (wrong) and dangerous manual labour (right). Green reckons that this interpretation, like the first, is overshadowed by Kant's conservative views, which is why these two formulations are 'not the best embodiments of Kant's moral philosophy'.[84]

Green's third, and in his own view most promising, reading links wrongful instrumental use to the idea of 'impartial co-legislation'.[85] According to this, 'persons are used as "means only and not as ends", when they are treated in ways they could not accept under conditions of informed, impartial, and rational choice as a rule of conduct to everybody'.[86] Green takes his lead from Kant's analysis of making false promises. These are deemed wrong because the deceived person 'cannot possibly assent to my

---

[81] Green, 2001a, p. 252.   [82] Green, 2001a, p. 253.   [83] Green, 2001a, p. 253.
[84] Green, 2001a, p. 253.   [85] Green, 2001a, p. 253.   [86] Green, 2001a, p. 254.

mode of acting against him and cannot contain the end of this action in himself'.[87] More generally, when we violate other people's rights, we use them 'merely as a means, without considering that, as rational beings, they must always be esteemed at the same time as ends, i.e., only as beings who must be able to contain in themselves the end of the very same action'.[88]

The more general formulation, according to Green, is introduced by Kant to bypass the *actual* assent of the objects of our conduct, as otherwise we would have to heed, for instance, to the will of criminals who disagree with judges about their sentences.[89] We can frustrate the expressed will of others without treating them as mere means as long as we can confidently assume that, *as rational beings*, they would (or should) share the ends of our action. In the case of criminals, this means understanding that society needs rules which must be enforced even against the preferences of those who break them. And in healthcare contexts, the move provides a justification for many kinds of medical paternalism.

Green favours the third formulation, because he thinks that the other two 'are largely expressions of Kant's received moral opinions and prejudices', and because in his opinion arguments 'for not eclipsing our rational willing or for not debasing ourselves by commodifying our bodies … must finally be passed before the bar of informed, rational, and impartial co-legislation'. It is possible, Green concedes, that the use of certain drugs or the sale of sexual favours should in the final analysis be forbidden, but this, he argues, should be demonstrated by careful considerations of harm, self-harm, and exploitation, rather than deduced from untutored reactions to trespasses on human dignity and integrity.

A commitment to the third reading implies, among other things, that the creation and use of saviour siblings cannot be straightforwardly rejected as a form of treating individuals merely as a means. The new children can and probably will be loved by their parents in their own right, and instrumental use as such is not morally condemnable.[90] According to Green, I use people merely as a means 'not when I employ their bodies or their talents primarily as an instrument of my purpose, but only when I do so in ways that they could not also impartially accept'.[91] And although saviour siblings could as adults complain about their origins and role, it is more likely that, as rational beings, they would recognise the propriety of PGD and the life-saving use of their cord blood.

[87]   Kant, 1959, p. 48 (§ 430) – quoted in Green, 2001a, p. 254.
[88]   Kant, 1959, p. 48 (§ 430) – quoted in Green, 2001a, p. 254.
[89]   Kant, 1959, p. 48 note 14 (§ 430) – quoted in Green, 2001a, p. 254
[90]   Green, 2001a, pp. 255–6.   [91]   Green, 2001a, p. 256.

5.9   Ends *and* means: two different principles?

What Green and others have to say about instrumental use is interesting – but somehow not entirely satisfactory. The three readings of Kant of the preceding section can be accurate and Green may have formulated the most sensible Kantian answer to the question at hand. Perhaps impartial co-legislation is the answer to the rightness and wrongness of saviour sibling decisions, and perhaps all the outcome-, rule-, and tradition-based observations presented by others and paraded in this chapter can be usefully employed by the co-legislators in their imaginary meetings. But does this shed any light on the evils of *instrumental* treatment as opposed to *any other* kind of immoral behaviour towards oneself or others? I am not convinced that it does.

If I kill someone for no particular reason, I act immorally. If I seize an unclaimed human corpse and sell it, I use it as a means to promote my financial ends. If I kill someone and sell the body to the highest bidder, I act immorally *and* use the victim's body as a means to my ends. If I confuse people's minds for no particular reason, I act immorally. If I find a group of confused people and incite them to champion my ideals, I use them as a means to promote my political ends. If I intentionally confuse people's minds so that they feel compelled to further my cause, I act immorally *and* use the victims' minds as a means to my ends. All the theoretical views surveyed so far recognise most of the ethically problematic dimensions of these courses of action. But none of them gives a proper account of the difference between the acts that are 'just' immoral, 'just' instrumental, or both. I believe that one more attempt is needed to tease out these distinctions and to assess their implications and requirements on the rationalities involved.

Starting again from Kant's reflections, he gave (at least) three formulations to the moral law, or his categorical imperative.[92] The first says that the principles on which we act must be universalisable; that they must be applicable to all rational agents alike.[93] The second is the one concerning ends and means.[94] And the third requires that our principles must be acceptable to all rational agents in an ideal world in which we give moral

---

[92] There might be four, but the three that are explicitly expressed by Kant himself and traditionally recognised give enough variety for my purposes here. For a general exposition of the formulations, see, e.g. Robert Johnson, 2004 [substantive revision 2008], 'Kant's moral philosophy', *Stanford Encyclopedia of Philosophy* – http://plato.stanford.edu/entries/kant-moral/.

[93] Kant, 1994, p. 30 (§ 421).   [94] Kant, 1959, p. 36; Kant, 1785b, p. 47 (§ 429).

laws in unison.[95] The remarkable detail here is that while the first and third formulations demand equal applicability to and equal acceptance by all reasonable people, the second wording manifestly does *not* advocate equal treatment to all. It does not advise us to act so as to treat every agent as a capable follower and giver of the moral law. Instead, it makes something *in* us – humanity – central to our proper treatment. This awe-inspiring element within us but not quite within our reach is the entity that should always be treated as an end in itself, never as a mere means.[96] But how exactly can we fail to treat humanity as an end? And how can we treat it as a means? It is illuminating to examine these two questions separately.

We can fail to treat humanity in rational (willing) agents as an end by annihilating their will (killing is the paradigmatic example); by confusing their will (deception and mind altering could be used); and by restricting their will (by not letting them pursue their own goals as they see fit). These are the mental aspects of our humanity and for them to be treated appropriately as an end, the wills of persons need to continue to exist and they need to do so in an unperplexed and unencumbered state. To ensure that they do, certain acts against our physical person must be prohibited. Murder and suicide destroy the body and simultaneously obliterate the mind. Intoxicating substances influence the brain and baffle the psyche. And involuntary restrictions and interventions affect the will through the body. Consequently, we should not take our own life or the life of another, intoxicate ourselves or others, or curtail people's freedom of choice and action.

This, however, is where the plot thickens. What about *voluntary* masturbation, extramarital sex, prostitution, or tooth selling? How can restrictions of liberty be justified in these instances? Given Kant's views on hair sale and life-saving amputations, an argument could be made that he wanted to protect individuals from harm. Masturbation was believed to cause mental illness; casual sex is a potential health hazard; prostitution can be harmful to the service providers and to society as a whole; and giving up a nonrenewable organ deteriorates a person's physique. But this could all be stated in terms of treating or failing to treat people as ends. If the will's existence or clarity is in danger, its freedom from constraint could be subordinated to these higher ends by simply stipulating that they

---

[95] Kant, 1994, p. 38 (§ 432).
[96] I have studied this element in Matti Häyry, 2005a, 'The tension between self-governance and absolute inner worth in Kant's moral philosophy', *Journal of Medical Ethics* 31: 645–7.

must be considered first. Kant's solution, in contrast, was to introduce the concept of treating humanity merely as a means.

Many people today are unmoved by Kant's original examples of using people as a mere means. The idea of using one's genitals for sexual gratification or financial gain is not as shocking to all participants of current bioethical debates as it was to the eighteenth-century small-town professor. The ethical issues, however, remain, although sometimes in different forms. The sale of organs has been intensely discussed during the past decades;[97] and if I make a will donating my earthly remains to be used as dog food, all kinds of objections are likely to crop up. Some arguments in these contexts are linked with global injustice, coercion, exploitation, and the validity and freedom of the agent's consent. These, however, are not of interest in the present context, because they can be expressed in terms of humanity as an end. Unfairness, compulsion, and pressures on decision making are all arguably failures to treat the recipient's humanity as an end. In the assessment of these objections, no mention of treatment as a means is needed. Why, then, would the sale of organs and the use of humans as dog food be wrongfully instrumentalising? Two answers naturally offer themselves.

First, the sale of organs *commodifies* human beings – assigns a price to the human body and its parts. The human body, however, is inexorably linked with the human mind, the locus of our rational agency, humanity, and dignity. These can only be evaluated in terms of their absolute inner worth, which makes them priceless and out of the bounds of commercial activity. Our strength, skills, and work are ours to use and they are a part of and the basis for our legitimate property, but *we* do not belong to ourselves in this sense. We can sell our efforts and our belongings but not our persons, including our body parts.[98]

Secondly, feeding our remains to dogs arguably constitutes an *improper use* of the human body. This charge is difficult to analyse any further, although its existence is probably universal. It can be linked with cultural taboos, feelings of moral disgust, and physical and emotional 'yuk' reactions; but it should not be dismissed too swiftly because of these connections. We can extinguish our sensitivities in most issues (and philosophers often do), but whether or not this is a good thing is another matter. Intuitive responses can lead to ethical and legal overreactions,

---

[97] See, e.g. Hinkley, 2005; Stephen Wilkinson, 2003, *Bodies for Sale: Ethics and Exploitation in the Human Body Trade* (London: Routledge).

[98] See, e.g. Sandel, 2007, p. 94.

but they can also show the limits within which people feel safe and can comfortably live as societies and communities.[99]

The ideas of commodification and improper use show that the formulation of treating people 'as a mere means' can eventually turn out to be a red herring in Kantian ethics. It does not really matter in these cases if people are treated as ends or not; the decisive factor is whether they are treated 'wrongfully as a means'. And if this immorality is limited, as the literature suggests, to commercial and disgusting use of body parts, the objections from commodification and improper use do not necessarily affect the creation and recruitment of saviour siblings for immediate medical purposes. The new individuals are not sold or bought, and nor is a price attached to them, although die-hard opponents of the practice can still complain about 'reification' and claim that saviour siblings are regarded indecently as 'things'. Charges of improper use, as things or otherwise offensively, may have some force, but this force varies according to the invasiveness of the procedure and the rationality and morality evoked. If the child is produced also for its own sake and placental or umbilical cord blood is used, the case remains, from most ethical angles, abstract.

5.10   Saving rationalities

The considerations of this chapter have shown that there are at least five main objections to the creation and use of saviour siblings. Possible lives are lost and wills annulled when unsuitable embryos are discarded based on PGD. Future and nascent wills are denied and restricted when cells are removed and parts of the new individual used in treatments. Human beings are involuntarily exposed to physical and mental risks when they are probed and put to the service of their older siblings. Individuals are reified and made exchangeable when their loss of body parts is judged less important than other people's health needs. And humanity in general is insulted and undermined when embryos and newborns are treated in improper ways. Different rationalities weigh, of course, the strength of these objections differently.

Harris and Glover flatly deny them all. For them, it is not rational to discuss the lives and wills of the unborn or the newly born, because they

---

[99] Cf. Matti Häyry, 2003b, 'Deeply felt disgust – a Devlinian objection to cloning humans', in Brenda Almond and Michael Parker (eds), *Ethical Issues in the New Genetics: Are Genes Us?* (Aldershot: Ashgate): 55–67.

are either not yet worthy of moral consideration or not constitutionally capable of formulating or expressing their preferences. Physical and mental risks could be a consideration in organ transplants but not in less invasive operations. Judging people's needs equally and then prioritising the most pressing demands is seen by Harris and Glover as a basic moral axiom. Insults and indecencies, especially if they are based on emotions or traditions, are deemed by them irrational.

Green could, judging by his methodology of informed and impartial co-legislation, be interested in all possible arguments for and against suggested lines of action. In practice, he seems to settle for the less ambitious task of proving that some readings of Kant are not helpful in some saviour sibling situations. The torch of Kantian ethics is carried forward by Habermas who embraces all five objections. For him, the decisive factor is that the wills of future people are denied, but he is also concerned about loss of life, reification, and improper use. All these have, according to him, a tendency of distorting our self-image as a species; and changes in this self-image would probably lead to the end of morality as we know it.

Sandel is less interested in the threats posed on individual minds and bodies and more keen to safeguard traditional ways of thinking about reproduction, social arrangements, and morality. For him, reification and improper use provide good arguments against the production of saviour siblings. This type of thinking is also in line with the ideas that Leon Kass has concerning the right and wrong uses of sexual organs. Although definitely not a Kantian, Kass comes closer to Kant's original views on sexual and reproductive behaviour than any of the other moralists discussed in this chapter.

6

Reproductive cloning and designing human beings

In this chapter, I study ethical views on human reproductive cloning by the nuclear transfer method. A brief account of permissive ideas based on liberty and the avoidance of harm is followed by an exploration of arguments that oppose cloning as a detrimental practice of designing people.

6.1 An almost universal condemnation

Human reproductive cloning became an ethical and legal issue in February 1997, when Ian Wilmut and other researchers at the Roslin Institute in Scotland reported that they had successfully produced the first mammalian clone by using the method of somatic cell nuclear transfer.[1] They had 'emptied' 277 sheep ova by removing their nuclei and then fused them, by using electricity, with mammary gland cells taken from other sheep. This produced 29 growing embryos, and their implantation in surrogate mother sheep resulted in 13 pregnancies. In the end, one healthy lamb, Dolly, was born on 5 July 1996.

Following the announcement of Dolly's birth, the media was quick to note the connection with human cloning – if the process worked for sheep, what would stop scientists from mass producing copies of human beings? Wilmut himself went on record early on stating that his work did not 'have anything to do with creating copies of human beings' and that he found the idea of cloning humans 'repugnant'.[2] But the door had been opened to the possibility, and lawgivers and policy makers all over the world sprang into regulative action.

Already in 1997, human reproductive cloning was condemned by the United Nations Educational, Scientific and Cultural Organization

[1] I. Wilmut, A. E. Schnieke, J. McWhir, A. J. Kind, and K. H. S. Campbell, 1997, 'Viable offspring derived from fetal and adult mammalian cells', *Nature* 385: 810–13.
[2] Michael Specter with Gina Kolata, 1997, 'After decades of missteps, how cloning succeeded', *The New York Times*, 3 March – http://query.nytimes.com/gst/fullpage.html?res= 9A04E0D71F31F930A35750C0A961958260.

(UNESCO)[3] and in the same year or before, it was prohibited by the national legislations of Argentina, Austria, Brazil, Denmark, Georgia, Germany, Iceland, Mexico, Norway, Peru, Slovakia, Spain, South Africa, and the United Kingdom. Some of these legal bans were directly prompted by the cloning of Dolly, while others were applications of existing laws to the new situation. By 2004, human reproductive cloning had been explicitly or implicitly banned in at least 30 countries and legislative preparations for further prohibitions are underway.[4] In March 2005, the United Nations General Assembly adopted a declaration against human cloning, but instead of unanimity, this was accepted by a vote of 84 in favour, 34 against, and 37 abstentions. The document is not binding on the member states.[5]

6.2   Distinctions and politics

The failure of the United Nations General Assembly to adopt the *United Nations Declaration on Human Cloning* unanimously does not mean that the cloning of human embryos *to produce new adult human beings* was accepted in the dissenting and abstaining countries. The message is, rather, that some countries wanted to ban the production of human embryos by nuclear transfer in all circumstances and for any purposes, whereas others wanted to retain the possibility of 'therapeutic cloning' for human embryonic stem cell research and treatments.

The method of cloning human beings by nuclear transfer to create clones who will grow up to be adults, if it is used, is exactly the same as for the creation of embryos for research or therapy. Since in both cases an early human being is produced, the semantic argument can be made that both modes of cloning are in fact 'reproductive'. In this spirit, the United States President's Council on Bioethics proposed in 2002 the terms 'cloning-to-produce-children' and 'cloning-for-biomedical-research'.[6] Although these names are accurate, they have not caught on, and I will stay with

---

[3] *Universal Declaration on the Human Genome and Human Rights*, 1997, adopted by the General Conference of UNESCO at its 29th session on 11 November.

[4] United Nations Educational, Scientific and Cultural Organization, 2004, *National Legislation Concerning Human Reproductive and Therapeutic Cloning* (Paris: Division of Ethics of Science and Technology).

[5] United Nations Press Release GA/10333, 2005 – www.un.org/News/Press/docs/2005/ga10333.doc.htm.

[6] President's Council on Bioethics, 2002, *Human Cloning and Human Dignity: An Ethical Inquiry*, (Washington, DC, July) – bioethicsprint.bioethics.gov/reports/cloningreport/fullreport.html.

the expressions 'cloning' and 'reproductive cloning' for endeavours to produce children in this way and 'stem cell creation' or 'therapeutic cloning' for practices related to stem cell research and therapies. Despite a few attention-seeking claims to the contrary, so far there have not been any verified reports on successful (reproductive human) cloning (by nuclear transfer).[7]

Living beings can be cloned not only by somatic cell nuclear transfer, but also – and this has been more common in agricultural biotechnology – by duplication, or embryo splitting.[8] In this method, an existing embryo is mechanically divided into two or more embryos and the resulting entities are allowed to continue their development normally. Identical twins have, even before advances in reproductive medicine, been the result of spontaneous duplication. The ethical problems of producing new human beings in this way are arguably fewer, and the practice has been accepted in fertility treatments by the American Medical Association.[9] Others have disagreed, however, and in the United Kingdom, for instance, such treatments are illegal.[10] In this chapter, I will focus on reproductive cloning by nuclear transfer, because when this method is used the chances of designing the clone's qualities are far more extensive as well as far more hotly debated. The issue of producing duplicates and destroying them for research purposes will be discussed in Chapter 7, which concentrates on therapeutic cloning.

The reason for the disagreement on the United Nations declaration was that different countries wanted different results out of the process.[11] Nations with a more permissive stand on stem cell research aimed at a focused ban on reproductive cloning to clarify the situation and to create protected working conditions for their life scientists. This stance was represented by the United Kingdom, a country which 'strongly supports stem

[7] Human embryos *have* been produced by nuclear transfer, but these experiments have been more closely related to advances in stem cell research and therapies than to attempts to create children.

[8] See, e.g. James A. Byrne and John B. Gurdon, 2002, 'Commentary on human cloning', *Differentiation* 69: 154–7.

[9] Council of Ethical and Judicial Affairs, 1994, *Pre-Embryo Splitting*, American Medical Association.

[10] Human Fertilisation and Embryology Authority, 2004, *Embryo Splitting & Cloning Statement*, 15 January – www.hfea.gov.uk/hfea/rss/791.html.

[11] See, e.g. Rosario M. Isasi and George J. Annas, 2003, 'Arbitrage, bioethics, and cloning: The ABCs of gestating a United Nations cloning convention', *Cape Western Reserve Journal of International Law* 35: 397–414.

cell research'[12] but which had already in 2001 enacted a law 'to prohibit the placing in a woman of a human embryo which has been created otherwise than by fertilisation.'[13] Nations with more restrictive views, on the other hand, pursued a universal ban on stem cell research as well as reproductive cloning and hoped to use the strong international attitude against the latter as an instrument to prohibit the former.

A similar split can be seen in regional and national attempts to regulate cloning. An early ban on cloning was accepted by 19 countries of the Council of Europe in 1998, but the signatories did not include Germany ('too permissive') or the United Kingdom ('too restrictive').[14] Three years later, the European Parliament rejected a move to ban all cloning in the European Union.[15] The United States government, too, has been unable to pass any federal laws on the prohibition of cloning. In 2001–2009 federal funding of stem cell research was banned, but otherwise the regulation was up to the individual states; and some states have rejected either reproductive or therapeutic cloning whereas some have rejected both.[16] Globally, national legislations are diverse and keep changing with advances in the relevant technologies.[17]

6.3   The case for cautious progress

Legislators have, by and large, assumed a restrictive attitude towards human reproductive cloning, but this has not stopped philosophers from studying critically the potential reasons for as well as against the practice. The most permissive view that has emerged from this exercise so far

[12] Department of Health, 2005, 'UK to vote against UN human cloning decision', *News Releases*, 7 February – www.dh.gov.uk/en/Publicationsandstatistics/Pressreleases/DH_4105348.

[13] *Human Reproductive Cloning Act*, 2001 – www.opsi.gov.uk/ACTS/acts2001/ukpga_20010023_en_1.

[14] *CNN World News*, 1998, '19 European nations sign ban on human cloning', 12 January – edition.cnn.com/WORLD/9801/12/cloning.ban/video.html.

[15] *BBC News*, 2001, 'Europe rejects human cloning ban', 29 November – news.bbc.co.uk/1/hi/sci/tech/1682591.stm.

[16] *National Conference of State Legislatures*, 2008, 'State human cloning laws', January – www.ncsl.org/programs/health/Genetics/rt-shcl.htm.

[17] See, e.g. Kirstin Matthews, 2007a, 'Overview of world human cloning policies', *The Connexions Project*, 3 August – cnx.org/content/m14834/latest/; Kirstin Matthews, 2007b, 'World cloning policies', *The Connexions Project*, 3 August – cnx.org/content/m14836/latest/. See also Global Lawyers and Physicians, 2005, 'Database of global policies on human cloning and germ-line engineering' – www.glphr.org/genetic/genetic.htm.

states that although cloning would be too dangerous now it should not be completely rejected lest some of its possible benefits be unnecessarily lost in the process. In some more detail, the case for cautious progress can proceed by first listing the positive aspects of the practice and then assessing the weight of its negative sides.[18]

Cloning as a form of assisted reproduction could, so the argument goes, help otherwise childless couples and individuals to have children. Spouses may wish to clone an infant that they have just lost. A sterile husband or partner may desire offspring who would be biologically his own. A lesbian couple may want to have genetic offspring together. And a single woman could yearn to have a child by herself. In addition, research into cloning would probably accelerate development in other areas of biology and reproductive medicine. More might be learned about life's beginnings, fertility problems, and the human ageing process. Cloning and research into it could, directly and indirectly, meet reproductive needs, fulfil parental desires, satisfy preferences, reduce suffering, and promote people's health.

A permission to clone human beings, perhaps regulated in appropriate ways, would, the argument continues, respect individual and reproductive freedom. This is a good thing, because freedom of choice in general should be allowed when no one else is harmed; rational decisions should be protected from restrictions; and procreative autonomy in particular can be regarded as a human right. A permission to conduct research in this field would also respect the liberty of life scientists and their voluntary collaborators. Restrictions on science are restrictions on freedom of thought, belief, speech, and action, and as such suspect. And if people want to donate materials, including embryos, to research, they should be allowed to do so. Moderate regulation on cloning, as opposed to wholesale bans, could reduce suffering, increase wellbeing, promote autonomy, and further justice.

[18] Since my focus in this chapter is on cloning and design, I will not present an extended analysis of the cautiously permissive view (what follows is only an impressionistic sketch). For one version of it, see, e.g. John Harris, 2004, *On Cloning* (London: Routledge). My earlier work on the topic, indirectly defending the view, is reported in Matti Häyry, 2001c, 'But what if we *feel* that cloning is wrong?', *Cambridge Quarterly of Healthcare Ethics* 10: 205–8; Matti Häyry and Tuija Takala, 2001, 'Cloning, naturalness and personhood', David C. Thomasma, David N. Weisstub, and Christian Hervé (eds), *Personhood and Health Care* (Dordrecht: Kluwer Academic Publishers): 281–98; Matti Häyry, 2003c, 'Philosophical arguments for and against human reproductive cloning', *Bioethics* 17: 447–59; Matti Häyry, 2003b, 'Deeply felt disgust – a Devlinian objection to cloning humans', Brenda Almond and Michael Parker (eds), *Ethical Issues in the New Genetics: Are Genes Us?* (Aldershot: Ashgate): 55–67.

Cloning and research into it, proponents of the practices can also claim, are consistent with some deeply human character traits and encourage people to develop these as virtues. A drive to reproduce is a very natural drive and a family with children is an ideal context for the development of one's personality and social skills. By helping people to have children and found a family, cloning would assist them to become better human beings and more productive members of communities. A need to understand the mechanics of the world is also a natural part of the human condition, and science is the best-known method to acquire reliable knowledge and thereby to satisfy this need. Research should have its limits, but these can be set by regulation without resorting to bans and prohibitions.

These considerations show that at least an initial case exists for allowing cloning and research into it. Other factors can reverse or modify this judgement, but to achieve this they must be clearly presented and have sufficient weight in the balancing of the advantages and disadvantages of the practice. These other factors can be divided into two groups: the tangible and the intangible.

Tangible arguments against cloning have to do with risks and dangers. Since Dolly was the only healthy lamb produced after 277 attempts, and since the other 276 candidates all had lethal problems of some sort, the method was at that stage clearly not safe enough for use in human reproductive medicine. Another question mark is that Dolly died young for its species, and some experts have thought that this had something to do with the age of the somatic-cell donor.[19] This topic will be addressed again in Chapter 9, when considerable life extension is discussed, but the gist of the matter is that the cells of an organism can have a natural life span, part of which may already have been spent by the adult donor. The physical risks of nuclear transfer are, moreover, complemented by psychological and political dangers. It could be mentally challenging for a child to be a clone, let alone the first human clone. And nonprohibitive solutions can leave room for local policy exceptions and eventually lead to dangerous experimentation at the expense of individual lives and collective values.

Intangible arguments against cloning come in many shapes and sizes. Some say that cloning is unnatural; others that scientists involved in it are playing God. According to some critics, clones would lack freedom

---

[19] Jim Giles and Jonathan Knight, 2003, 'Dolly's death leaves researchers woolly on clone ageing issue', *Nature* 421: 776.

as individuals and persons; and according to others, the mere idea of producing duplicate humans is repulsive.[20]

Champions of cautious progress admit the partial relevance of tangible factors and possibly the indirect significance of intangible ones.[21] As long as the method is unsafe, they say, it should not be used on humans, and hence a moratorium on cloning itself might be accepted. Regulated research should, however, continue, and the moratorium be made conditional on the state of scientific advances in the area. When the method is safe, experiments must no longer be stalled on account of psychological, political, or intangible reservations. Being born as the first 'test-tube baby' did not hurt Louise Brown, so why should it hurt someone to be the first human clone? Regulations suffice to set proper limits for research. Since, the case continues, all the intangible arguments are too sentimental, religious, traditional, or vague to be taken seriously, the conclusion must be that moratoria and regulations, not bans and prohibitions, are the correct response to cloning and research into it.

6.4   Arguments for an absolute prohibition

Advocates of prohibition can seek support from an array of arguments presented in ethical discussions and popular media. Cloning would be playing God, unnatural, or disgusting. It would be inherently dangerous to the products of the procedure and to others involved; it would have a detrimental effect on human evolution; and it would make men redundant. As an inappropriate extension of technology, it would violate human dignity, corrupt humanity, and jeopardise individual freedom. As a new form of having offspring, it would confuse people's identities, complicate family relations, and change attitudes towards children. It would also take sex out of reproduction; endorse illusions of human control; drain scarce resources; and open the door for new forms of eugenics.[22]

Some of the fundamental concerns behind these arguments have to do with the destruction of early human life; the speed at which science and technology change the world; and the anticipated loss of life's meaning

---

[20] For a more extensive list, see Section 6.4.

[21] An early expression of this view can be found in Ruth Chadwick, 1982, 'Cloning', *Philosophy* 57: 201–9.

[22] See, e.g. Leon Kass and James Wilson, 1998, *The Ethics of Human Cloning* (Washington, DC: The AEI Press); Gregory E. Pence (ed.), 1998, *Flesh of My Flesh: The Ethics of Cloning Humans. A Reader* (Lanham, MD: Rowman & Littlefield); William Dudley (ed.), 2001, *The Ethics of Human Cloning* (San Diego, CA: Greenhaven Press).

as we know it. These concerns will be addressed in detail in Chapters 7, 8, and 9. In what follows, I will concentrate on the claim that cloning is wrong because it involves *designing* human beings. According to this notion, human design would, in one way or another, produce defective individuals (Section 6.5), distorted families (Section 6.6), misshapen communities (Section 6.7), perverted societies (Section 6.8), and a disturbed human race (Section 6.9). After examining these charges, I will contrast them with the idea that progress can be desirable even if it takes us beyond the current boundaries of humanity (Section 6.10), and conclude the chapter by summarising the rationalities involved in the conflicting views (Section 6.11).

Most arguments from design fall within the category of 'intangible' objections, dismissed by proponents of cautious advances as 'sentimental', 'religious', 'traditional', or 'vague'. The challenge, then, is to see how they can be formulated in a relatively precise, reasonable, and generally understandable way, avoiding excessively controversial customary or ideological assumptions where this is possible.

6.5   Lack of limits and defective individuals

Everybody seems to agree that cloning should not be attempted now, because it would be too dangerous for the resulting individuals, physically or mentally. The argument against human design goes further and states that even if immediate health risks could be controlled, clones would still suffer from flaws in their constitution. Our skills do not match those of God or nature, and there are limits beyond which it would be unsafe for us to go.

It should be noted that 'God' and 'nature' need not be seen as intentional agents here. The point of departure is merely that there are things in this universe that we have not made. Mountains and human beings belong to this category. With the help of technology, we can, if we so choose, make or simulate some of these things; and it is in some cases wise and in other cases unwise to do so. The argument says that it would be unwise to manufacture human beings.

The dividing line between nature-born (natural, given, good) and human-made (artificial, manufactured, bad) in reproduction is already, to an extent, a matter of negotiation and agreement. Human life can be started by heterosexual intercourse leading to the union of an egg and a sperm inside a woman. It can also be begun by combining the egg and the sperm in a Petri dish. Using the Dolly method, a human life could commence when a somatic cell and an emptied ovum are exposed to electricity in a laboratory. And in theory at least gametes or embryos could be constructed mechanically to create new life.[23] Many people felt that the relevant boundary was already crossed by the production of the first test-tube babies; but others argued that conception in one place (Petri dish) is as natural as conception in another (woman). At the other end of the continuum, most of us would probably list the use of mechanical gametes as artificial, although some might actually welcome the technology. The argument scrutinised here draws a line between the union of two genomes in conception and the replication of one existing genome by cloning: the spontaneous fusion of egg and sperm is seen as natural and acceptable; but the electricity-induced collision of the somatic cell and the drained egg is seen as artificial and suspect.[24]

The danger that we invoke by overstepping the bound can be described in general or particular terms. The charges of 'acting unnaturally' or 'playing God' evoke lofty images of environmental disaster and divine punishment. If we change the course of rivers or move mountains, the long-term cumulative consequences can be catastrophic in ways that we cannot precisely define in the light of our current knowledge. And if we choose to produce 'abominations' like animal–human hybrids, clones, or parentless children, not only are the material outcomes unpredictable, but we may also have to confront the wrath of gods.[25] I will study the idea of precaution in the face of the unknown in more detail in Chapter 8.

A more specific moral and political argument states that we should not unnecessarily blur boundaries that we find otherwise indispensable in our mutual dealings. The borderline between human beings and everything else is a prominent example of this. Some prefer to define this divide in terms of a distinct soul, possessed by us but not by other entities: they can claim that clones would lack this essential feature of humanity. But the relevance of the separation extends beyond theological and metaphysical considerations. Eventually, it determines the types of right we can grant to various beings and things.

---

[23] See, e.g. Ainsley J. Newson and Anna C. Smajdor, 2005, 'Artificial gametes: new paths to parenthood?', *Journal of Medical Ethics* 31: 184–6.

[24] Note the Frankensteinian image of human parts brought together and electrically shocked into action.

[25] I have studied these two arguments in Matti Häyry, 1994a, 'Categorical objections to genetic engineering – A critique', Anthony Dyson and John Harris (eds), *Ethics and Biotechnology* (London: Routledge): 202–15.

Advances in science will in the future produce entities that cannot readily be told apart from human beings. This is not to say that there is no difference; only that the difference cannot necessarily be detected. A computer or a robot with a human form and sufficient conversational skills would be a case in point. As already observed by Alan Turing in 1950, it would, even by using relatively simple technology, be very difficult without visual contact to judge whether one is exchanging written messages with a human being or with a digital computer programmed to imitate one.[26] While this does not prove that machines are people (or that they are intelligent, which was closer to the original point of the 'Turing test'), it does suggest that making the distinction can be problematic. And this, in its turn, has some intriguing conceptual and ethical implications.

As things stand, I have no qualms about selling my computer or switching it off or sending it to recycling. It is an artificial nonhuman entity and not a proper object of my moral respect. In contrast, I do have qualms about killing or enslaving other people. They are natural human entities and they do belong to the class of revered objects, as 'natural' and 'human' seem to command respect in a way that artificial and nonhuman do not. The situation could be different if someone had programmed my computer to pass the Turing test. If it could convince me in conversation that it is in fact a living being with thoughts and ideals, I might well give its 'humanity' the benefit of the doubt and refrain from turning it off. Other people could, of course, reasonably disagree with me on this.

When it comes to clones and their reification, I would have the same qualms as I would have with any human being. Clones, I assume, could easily pass the Turing test and convince me of their 'humanity' in the same sense that my upgraded computer could. They would also have a human genome, which many people see as the decisive factor. But they would be manufactured in a sense that naturally conceived individuals are not, and some say that this would make them less than fully human. One repercussion of this is that their rights to life, freedom, and other good things could feasibly be contested.

The ethical issue created by pushing the boundaries of humanity is inescapable and cannot be limited to the debate on cloning. We can include people produced by somatic cell nuclear transfer in the human family, but a line must still be drawn somewhere if we do not want to end up granting rights to digital computers or personable household appliances. At some point, we must say that an entity of our own making

---

[26] Alan Turing, 1950, 'Computing machinery and intelligence', *Mind* 59: 433–60.

is not our equal in moral and political terms, despite its appearance, conversability, or constitution. The argument from design against cloning states that the proper criterion for the distinction is biological origin in a relatively unmanipulated conception and that if we fail to observe this standard, humanity as a distinct and understandable ethical category ceases to exist.

6.6   Asexual reproduction and distorted families

Another variant of the design argument states that cloning people presents a threat to the family as the cornerstone of human reproduction and social life. The essential features of this view are presented in an early exchange between Leon Kass and James Wilson. Both stress the import- ance of the family, but in slightly different ways and with radically diver- gent conclusions.[27]

Denying the validity of utilitarian arguments for or against cloning, Kass maintains that, 'even if no one complains' (even if no immediate concrete harm can be detected), cloning is still 'a form of child abuse ... and a deep violation of our given nature as gendered and engendering beings'.[28] This is something revealed to us by our 'repugnance',[29] or 'a prearticulate human moral sense'[30] echoed in the teachings of Anglican, Methodist, and Catholic Christianity, but forgotten or ignored by society as a whole.[31] Moral sense tells us that reproductive technologies 'lead ... to the continuing erosion of respect for the mystery of sexuality and human renewal'[32] and 'obscure the deeper meaning of naturally significant rela- tions among embodiment, sexual differentiation, and procreation'.[33] The fact that technological reproduction has become socially acceptable pro- vides, according to Kass, no more moral evidence in its favour than 'the growing social acceptability of sodomy and adultery [constitutes] a refu- tation of Leviticus 18:22 or the Seventh Commandment'.[34] Although nat- ural teleology has been largely dismissed by modern science and 'nature in its possibly normative pointings has become invisible' to many people, Kass can see that cloning is nonetheless 'contrary to nature'.[35]

Starting from what he calls the 'ontology of sex', Kass argues that sex- ual reproduction gives our existence its meaning. Human life would not

---

[27] Kass and Wilson, 1998.   [28] Kass and Wilson, 1998, p. 78.
[29] Kass and Wilson, 1998, p. 78.   [30] Kass and Wilson, 1998, p. 79.
[31] Kass and Wilson, 1998, p. 80.   [32] Kass and Wilson, 1998, p. 80.
[33] Kass and Wilson, 1998, pp. 80–1.   [34] Kass and Wilson, 1998, p. 80.
[35] Kass and Wilson, 1998, p. 81.

have been possible without sexuality, Kass submits, because only 'sexual animals can seek and find complementary others with whom to pursue a goal that transcends their own existence'.[36] Other kinds of beings see the world only as food and enemies. The human animal is also, he contends, the sexiest and most intelligent of creatures. Since the female of the species does not go into heat but is 'receptive throughout the estrous cycle', the male of the species 'must therefore have greater sexual appetite and energy to reproduce successfully', and this accounts for the unrivalled human features of ambition, sociability, openness, and intelligence.[37]

According to Kass, when women and men have sex, they simultaneously accept and try to overcome their own mortality. Organisms that reproduce asexually can be seen to act in self-preservation, as the same genome continues its life in new individuals. Sexual reproduction, in contrast, creates a new variation of life that is known, in the normal course of events, to outlive its parents.[38] It also produces an object of generosity, care, and love for the woman and the man, and unites them in parenthood with a bond that mere sexual intercourse cannot achieve. While sex allows the conception of a human being who signals the mortality of its procreators, it also initiates a project that carries their inheritance, beliefs, and ideals beyond the grave.[39] Kass believes that there 'is wisdom in the mystery of nature that has joined the pleasure of sex, the inarticulate longing for union, the communication of the loving embrace, and the deep-seated and only partly articulated desire for children in the very activity by which we continue the chain of human existence and participate in the renewal of human possibility'.[40]

On the basis of these considerations, Kass argues that cloning is wrong. The natural wellbeing of children and their parents can only be guaranteed by sexual reproduction and traditional child rearing in stable, heterosexual, two-parent families.[41] Cloning is a form of asexual reproduction, and as such it 'is a radical departure from the natural human way, confounding all normal understanding of father, mother, sibling, and grandparent and all moral relations tied thereto'.[42]

In his critical comment, Wilson disagrees with the conclusions reached by Kass. He argues that in most cases of artificial procreation, including cloning, the mother–child relationship and other family relations can be settled in a satisfactory manner, and contends that these factors are more

---

[36] Kass and Wilson, 1998, p. 28.   [37] Kass and Wilson, 1998, pp. 28–9.
[38] Kass and Wilson, 1998, p. 29.   [39] Kass and Wilson, 1998, p. 30.
[40] Kass and Wilson, 1998, p. 31.   [41] Kass and Wilson, 1998, pp. 24–6, 81–2.
[42] Kass and Wilson, 1998, p. 26.

significant than the way in which conception is arranged. He presents studies and statistics to support the view that children adopted within a short period of time after their birth and children produced by artificial insemination or in vitro fertilisation seem to fare approximately as well as children conceived naturally and reared by their biological parents.[43] Surrogate motherhood presents a problem when the bearer wants to keep the child, and it should not, in Wilson's view, be legally endorsed.[44] But when the special relationship between mother and child can be established and the child can grow up in an intact, two-parent family, all is well and even cloning can be condoned.[45]

Kass objects to Wilson's model because it is based on a utilitarian assessment of the wellbeing of individuals.[46] He would rather like to defend 'the institution of marriage and the two-parent family' (against the perils of ignoring 'the *natural* (hetero)*sexual* ground of parenthood'),[47] safeguard newborn girls from being their mother's twin sisters ('not ... exactly a normal mother–daughter relationship'),[48] and live in a society that has not 'forgotten how to shudder' and does not 'always [rationalize] away the abominable'.[49] None of these concerns can, respecting the views presented by Kass, be estimated by alternative outcomes. The gist of his view must, then, be that moral sense indicates and natural facts of reproduction confirm that children should not be produced by cloning. The idea of doing so is repugnant and closer examination shows that cloning is a threat not only to family life but also to what it means to be human.

6.7   Project of mastery and misshapen communities

Michael Sandel believes, like Kass, that cloning is wrong; but he also believes that its wrongness cannot be adequately explained either by appeals to rights and risks or by considerations of sexual morality. Instead, he thinks that cloning is wrong because 'its primary purpose is to create children of a certain kind'.[50]

Sandel starts out by postulating a situation in which the production of human clones has been made as safe as any other form of reproduction. Individualistic notions of liberty, rights, and autonomy cannot, he notes,

---

[43] Kass and Wilson, 1998, pp. 92–5.   [44] Kass and Wilson, 1998, pp. 95–7.
[45] Kass and Wilson, 1998, pp. 91–2, 99–100.   [46] Kass and Wilson, 1998, p. 78.
[47] Kass and Wilson, 1998, p. 82 (emphasis by Kass).   [48] Kass and Wilson, 1998, p. 83.
[49] Kass and Wilson, 1998, p. 87.
[50] Michael J. Sandel, 2005b, 'The ethical implications of human cloning', *Perspectives in Biology and Medicine* 48: 241–7, p. 242.

under such circumstances be used to condemn cloning. The reproductive freedom of potential parents entitles them to decide when and how they want to have children. The children themselves are not asked what qualities they would like to have, and this is why some ethicists claim that their autonomy is thwarted in the process. But Sandel counters this accusation by pointing out that people do not get to choose their genetic features in other modes of procreation, either. If our parents do not make the decisions, the selection of our inborn qualities is left to blind chance – the 'genetic lottery'.[51]

The argument that cloning is wrong as an asexual form of reproduction does not impress Sandel much, either. According to him, deviation from the historical way of making babies does not threaten the attraction between women and men. As he writes: 'Sex will survive perfectly well on its own – without the help of federal legislation.'[52] Similar observations can presumably be extended to family role names like mother, father, aunt, sister, and grandparent, which will probably not be greatly confused by the occasional production of clones.

In his own dismissal of cloning, Sandel returns to the basic views that he has levelled against genetic selection and engineering in general.[53] All these practices involve the creation of children with features and qualities that parents or society would like them to have. And this attempt to design lives, Sandel states, is an 'assault on the understanding of children as gifts rather than possessions, or projects of our will, or vehicles of our happiness'.[54] As a result, people's attitudes towards their children become disfigured, and this contributes to the corruption of all relations within communities. The eventual outcome, in Sandel's view,[55] is that people lose their humility and sense of responsibility, and this loss will serve a fatal blow to our already endangered institutions of solidarity.[56]

This line of thinking has been criticised for its apparent lack of realism in the world in which we live. Parents already control the lives of their children by making early educational choices for them and by organising their leisure-time activities. Schools and hobbies are selected for and imposed on youths regardless of their own views and wishes; and parental ambition rather than self-direction accounts for many decisions that mould the lives of young people.

---

[51] Sandel, 2005b, pp. 242–3.   [52] Sandel, 2005b, p. 243.
[53] Michael J. Sandel, 2007, *The Case Against Perfection: Ethics in the Age of Genetic Engineering* (Cambridge, MA: The Belknap Press of Harvard University Press). See Sections 2.3, 3.3, 3.8, and 5.7.
[54] Sandel, 2005b, p. 242.   [55] As described in Section 2.3.
[56] Sandel, 2005b, p. 243; Sandel, 2007, pp. 89–92.

Sandel sees this phenomenon as reinforcing, not weakening, his view. The counterargument presupposes that although parental control has steadily increased, nothing detrimental has come out of the development, and suggests that the addition of cloning into the equation does not produce a qualitative leap in the trend. Sandel agrees that genetics does not introduce an abrupt break into what is going on, but argues that what is going on is in itself alarming. He believes that what 'is most troubling about human cloning and bioengineering is not that they represent a radical departure, but that they carry to full expression troubling tendencies already present in our culture, especially in the way we regard and treat children'.[57] We should not allow cloning, and if this means that some current parental activities must in the name of coherence and consistency be reviewed and possibly curtailed, it should also be done to rescue feelings and practices of solidarity in our modern communities.

6.8   Loss of mystery and perverted societies

The next design argument against cloning shifts the focus from defective individuals, distorted families, and misshapen communities to the wider realm of flawed societies, perverted states, and corrupt political systems. David Gurnham has given an informative account of this type of reasoning, which in his treatment involves the concepts of 'dignity' and 'mystery' and explains them in terms of social and political arrangements and their proper limits.[58]

Gurnham 'examines the ethical objections to cloning through the relationship between the reproductive possibilities that cloning brings and its perceived implications for human dignity' and maintains that 'arguments raised against cloning imply that there are certain things about human life that should always remain mysterious and other things that should never be so'.[59] Such arguments claim, according to him, that in a dignified human life the origins of individuals should always remain a mystery while family relations must always be transparent and easy to describe. Cloning is wrong because it violates the rules on both dimensions.[60]

How, then, does cloning violate the first rule and why does it matter? Gurnham cites Jacques Derrida and Hilary Putnam, who both emphasise

---

[57]   Sandel, 2005b, p. 243.
[58]   David Gurnham, 2005, 'The mysteries of human dignity and the brave new world of human cloning', *Social and Legal Studies* 14: 197–214. Gurnham's contribution explicates rather than defends the view he formulates, although in the end he seems to assume a cautiously positive attitude towards it.
[59]   Gurnham, 2005, p. 198.   [60]   Gurnham, 2005, pp. 197–8.

the role of secrecy and mystery in ethics; Derrida as a general principle and Putnam specifically in human reproduction.[61] In Putnam's words, quoted by Gurnham, 'the unpredictability and diversity of our progeny is an intrinsic value and that a moral image of the family reflects it coheres with the moral images of society that underlie our democratic aspirations'.[62] The way in which the mystery of our origins is linked with democracy seems to be crucial to the argument, although it is not easy to understand or to explain. Human rights as a part of a political system of equality do not seem to enlighten the matter, as rights cannot be assigned to individuals who do not exist yet.[63] The idea of an unscrupulous elite cloning people to make society more efficient could carry some precautionary weight, but it cannot be extended to proposals to increase the reproductive autonomy of individual parents (all of them, not just elites) by new technologies.[64] It seems, Gurnham contends, that the answer must be found in an *intrinsic* connection between the mystery of our origins and our commitment to democracy; and it also seems that this connection does not lend itself to further analysis. The unveiling of the secret of humanity does not start an independent series of events that will, in the absence of proper regulation, eventually damage democracy. The mystery and democracy are conceptually intertwined and in our liberal way of thinking they simply stand and fall together.[65] (Some more light will be shed on this in Section 6.9.)

Violations of the other rule are easier to illustrate.[66] For our family relationships to work, we need a clear vocabulary of the roles that people have. Mothers and fathers have children, children have sisters and brothers, and when children become mothers and fathers, their children will have grandmothers, grandfathers, aunts, and uncles. Everyone knows her or his title and role in the system and the stability of the network of relationships provides a solid basis for democratic institutions. Cloning distorts this arrangement and adds mystery to links that should be comprehensible without any prior reflection. If a woman gives birth to her own clone, in genetic terms her own twin sister, she becomes the mother and the sister of the same person. Before the age of technology, she could have

---

[61] Gurnham, 2005, pp. 202–3; Jacques Derrida, 1995, *The Gift of Death*, translated by David Wills (Chicago, IL: Chicago University Press), p. 54; Hilary Putnam, 1999, 'Cloning people', Justine Burley (ed.), *The Genetic Revolution and Human Rights: The Oxford Amnesty Lectures 1998* (Oxford: Oxford University Press): 1–13, pp. 10–13.

[62] Putnam, 1999, pp. 12–13; Gurnham, 2005, p. 202.   [63] Gurnham, 2005, p. 203.

[64] Gurnham, 2005, pp. 204–6.   [65] Gurnham, 2005, pp. 206–7.

[66] Gurnham, 2005, pp. 208–11.

accomplished this only by having a child with her father. This allusion of incest, together with other instances of confused and perverted family relationships, leads Gurnham to believe that the wrongness of cloning can be to a large extent associated with the secrecy and uncertainty that it is prone to introduce into the basic units of society and political order.[67]

6.9   Forsaken self-understanding and a confused species

The widest-ranging argument against the design and manufacture of people by cloning has been presented by Jürgen Habermas. In *The Future of Human Nature*, he maintains that making replicas of extant individuals would spell the end of civilised society and humanity as we now know them.[68]

According to Habermas, the modern ethos of universality and liberal democracy requires that all people are treated as moral equals. For all people to be treated as moral equals, again, their bodily and personal integrity must always be respected. But how, exactly, can we do this? How can we properly respect the bodily and personal integrity of human beings? Habermas argues that the crux of the matter is to understand the dual nature of human persons as partly 'grown' and partly 'made'.[69]

Many aspects of our being have, at some point in our lives, been selected, changed, or negotiated by ourselves (or by others). These aspects constitute us as made, and they can include education, work, lifestyle, and values. There are, however, also characteristics in our lives that we (or others) have *not* chosen. They form us as grown, and they have traditionally comprised our bodies as they are when we are born. Habermas uses the distinction of *having* a body and *being* a body, where the former, the conscious possession of a corporeal identity, is acquired at some time during our youth when we realise that we are, and have for a while been, corporeal entities.[70] What is grown in us, or at least in our physical selves, is the original body we were before our parents and healthcare

---

[67] Gurnham, 2005, p. 211.
[68] Jürgen Habermas, 2003, *The Future of Human Nature*, translated by William Rehg, Max Pensky, and Hella Beister (Cambridge: Polity Press). For a balanced description and criticism of Habermas on cloning, see Eduardo Mendieta, 2004, 'Habermas on human cloning: The debate on the future of the species', *Philosophy & Social Criticism* 30: 721–43.
[69] Habermas, 2003, pp. 44–53.
[70] Habermas, 2003, p. 50. Habermas borrows the vocabulary of 'having' and 'being' a body from Helmut Plessner, 1981, *Die Stufen des Organischen* [1927], *Gesammelte Schriften* Volume IV (Frankfurt am Main: Suhrkamp).

providers started nurturing and shaping it – and before we even knew that it existed.

The point of the distinction, in the model suggested by Habermas, is to stress that our being has two sides, both of which need to be equally respected in order to sustain a universal morality based on democratic dialogue.[71] The essence of modern liberal ethics and legislation is that persons who all live their own lives come together, assume a 'we' attitude, and go on to negotiate the norms and values that they can all reasonably accept. Respect for persons has, in this model, two facets. The people around the table must be listened to and their consent must be attained before any rules of conduct are finalised. This guarantees that their freedom as autonomous, (psychologically) self-choosing decision makers is taken adequately into account. But equally importantly, they must also be encountered as individuals with their own autonomous, (biologically) self-directing lives, which are anchored in their own inner nature, or humanity. Otherwise, they are not treated as ends in themselves in the Kantian sense.[72] Habermas finds our inner nature and humanity in the part of us that is grown and not made: traditionally, in the body in which (or as which) we were born.[73]

The possibility of cloning challenges our self-direction by threatening to eliminate what is grown in us. If our parents get to choose our genomes, our initial biological selves become human-made in a way that they have never been human-made before. Some of our features have, of course, been determined by our parents' choice of reproductive partners; and parts of our biology have been influenced by environmental factors before and after our birth. It is also possible that some of our early social influences stay with us all through our lives so that they cannot in the end be told apart from our physical drives. But cloning still represents a considerable departure from what has been before.

Despite human efforts to breed people, everyone so far has been born as a unique individual. Whatever the amount of eugenic matchmaking and selection by prenatal tests, people have been born as unpredictable surprises for their procreators. Some desired features may have turned out as expected and some feared medical conditions may have been avoided, but the new beings have still had their irreplaceable individuality, given to them by nature or God or fate or chance *but not* by other people. Even

---

[71] Habermas, 2003, pp. 53–60. [72] Habermas, 2003, pp. 55–6.

[73] As he writes, 'The capacity of being oneself requires that the person be at home, so to speak, in her own body.' Habermas, 2003, pp. 57–8.

identical twins, who share the same genome, have historically been produced by uncontrolled natural processes. In cloning, by nuclear transfer and embryo splitting alike, this ceases to be the case. Parents and scientists would select the genomes that clones would have, thereby removing the foundation of their grown corporeal selves. These people would be chosen and made by others.

The connection Habermas builds between cloning and the demise of civilised humanity utilises his own concept of the ethical self-understanding of the human species and it is best seen as conceptual, not causal.[74] Universal, democratic moral discourse between equals would necessarily come to an end with the first human clone entering the negotiations on norms and values. The morality of modern times must be accepted by every human being in circumstances in which everybody's personal (made) *and* bodily (grown) integrity is respected. Clones would not have a grown integrity to begin with, so it would not be possible to treat them equally. As a result, it would be impossible to have a morality in the sense human beings living in modern liberal societies conceive of it. Cloning would rob us of our ethical humanity.

6.10   Design for a transhuman world

All 'design' arguments against reproductive cloning share a concern that the acceptance of the technique would change our notion of ourselves. The manufacture of people is seen to blur the distinction between human and nonhuman beings; to threaten our sexual practices and family lives; to gnaw on the ties of solidarity in our communities; to unveil useful mysteries and create harmful ones; and to destroy the possibility of democratic decision making between equals.

A possible response to this is simply to question the value of humanity *as we now know it*. Our species has gone through a long history of changes and transformations, most of which do not bother us at all when we consider them retrospectively. A couple of thousand years ago people did not use soap, but those of us who now do are not particularly worried about this lost feature of our earlier humanity – on the contrary, there is a distinct feeling of superiority and relief when we look back at our unwashed relatives of the past. Why should this not be the case with

---

[74] All this, as well as the content of the preceding two paragraphs, has been distilled from the already cited pages in Habermas, 2003, but I have tried to present his argument in a form that I can understand. I hope that I am not distorting his intended line of thinking too noticeably.

further developments? We now accept the artificial alteration of our surface bacteria and body odour; so it stands to reason that future people could accept the artificial alteration of our modes of procreation. They could look back at us, relieved that they have escaped the labyrinth of the 'natural' relations that we currently have. And if democracy is based on the naturalness of our origins, perhaps future societies will work on better principles, just as we believe that democracy is a better political arrangement than the ones that have prevailed historically. We may not be human any more, but being transhuman or posthuman can, for the 'people' of the future, be a better option.[75]

Nick Bostrom and Toby Ord's ideas concerning resistance to change could possibly be applied to the situation. They claim that many attempts to improve the human lot are unnecessarily hindered by *status quo bias* – 'an inappropriate (irrational) preference for an option because it preserves the status quo'.[76] To detect when this bias is present, they suggest the following *reversal test*: 'When a proposal to change a certain parameter is thought to have bad overall consequences, consider a change to the same parameter in the opposite direction. If it is also thought to have bad overall consequences, then the onus is on those who reach these conclusions to explain why our position cannot be improved through changes to this parameter. If they are unable to do so, then we have reason to suspect that they suffer from status quo bias.'[77] Applied to the cloning issue, this argument could state that if *increasing* our procreative powers by nuclear transfer techniques is seen to be bad, we should ask whether *decreasing* our procreative powers to an equivalent degree would be any better. If, then, the idea of forgoing all the advantages of modern reproductive medicine is seen as an equally bad option, the opponents of cloning have arguably succumbed to the conservative bias.

It seems, however, that the success of this argument depends on our definition of the relevant parameters and the nature of the status quo we have in mind. The objections from design postulate that, at the current speed of technological advances, morality is changing so rapidly that our self-image and societal arrangements cannot keep up with the developments. Put in these terms, the transhumanist view states that *slowing the pace down* by bans and regulations will have bad overall consequences flowing from lost opportunities to make the most of scientific innovations. The

---

[75] See, e.g. Nick Bostrom, 2005, 'In defence of posthuman dignity', *Bioethics* 19: 202–14.
[76] Nick Bostrom and Toby Ord, 2006, 'The reversal test: Eliminating status quo bias in applied ethics', *Ethics* 116: 656–79, p. 658.
[77] Bostrom and Ord, 2006, pp. 664–5.

reversal test here would be to ask whether considerably *accelerating the change* of morality would have better consequences; and defenders of our current ethos could suggest that not even the most reckless advocate of progress could reasonably choose to believe this. People need at least some familiar elements of ethical and political thinking to flourish, and change should be controlled accordingly. Given these considerations, those who support cloning should, in view of Bostrom and Ord's test, explain why only the current 'dynamic status quo' – the tempo of development that we now experience – is acceptable.

Eventually, the question of humanism and transhumanism boils down to different attitudes towards change. Some believe that haste is dangerous for our self-understanding and others think that timidity prevents us from improving our condition. I will return to these issues in Chapter 8.

6.11   Cloning rationalities

In this chapter, I have examined the three main approaches to the ethical debate about human reproductive cloning by nuclear transfer, each with its own distinct rationality, or background presuppositions.

The first approach emphasises individual decision making and sees safety as the only obstacle in the way of cloning human beings once the technique has been made to work. The physical and mental wellbeing of children born by cloning should be guaranteed; and any reasonably expected harm to family and social structures must also be carefully considered. But more abstract injuries like offended feelings and corruption of morality ought to be dismissed as the alarmist nonsense that they are. Concerns which are not supported by science or people's immediate welfare are, according to this view, irrational. Besides, supporters of the model say, people will in time get used to new things and the moment of initial opposition will pass.

The second approach stresses the value of humanity and morality as they now are and sees cloning, genetic selection, and germ-line gene therapies as a threat to them. People will, as predicted by the proponents of cloning, change their minds and come to condone new technologies, but this, far from being a neutral evolution of attitudes, is a temptation to be resisted, because it will inevitably lead to the demise of family relations, solidarity, and democracy. The wellbeing of individuals is important, but it would be unwise – irrational – to pursue it at the expense of our most cherished moral, social, and political institutions. Radical change should be opposed in the name of preserving our humanity.

The third approach welcomes radical change and in a sense also the possibly ensuing end of humanity, and hails new technologies like cloning as heralds of progress. If advances in science and its applications can take us beyond our current limitations, we should greet the new transhuman world with open arms, even if this would mean giving up some of our current physical and moral features. As the physical traits that we should have to abandon are mainly bodily imperfections and weaknesses, it stands to reason to think that the moral norms that we would be giving up can equally be counted as unnecessary ethical hindrances. It would be irrational, within this view, to hold on to these in the face of long-awaited changes for the better.

Cloning can be approached from other angles, as well, but in this chapter I have concentrated on the case for cautious progress; on its various critics who argue that designing human beings is wrong because it changes humanity; and on those who do not regard change as problematic. The main features of the other views will be covered, or have been covered, in the other chapters.

7

Embryonic stem cells, vulnerability, and sanctity

In this chapter, I examine two aspects of the morality of human embryonic stem cell research. The first is the role of women in the acquisition of eggs for embryo creation. The second is the moral status of embryos that perish in destructive modes of stem cell research.

7.1   What, why, and how regulated?

The possibility of research on human embryos and embryonic stem cells shifts the focus of discussion drastically from making better *people* (creating new individuals) towards making people *better* (improving the health of existing individuals). Embryos and their early parts are, if implanted and nurtured properly, capable of developing into adult human beings, but this development is disallowed in most forms of embryo experimentation. The aim of the practice is not reproduction but rather the accumulation of biological and medical knowledge for the benefit of the population.

Embryonic stem cells can be acquired from embryos produced by in vitro fertilisation (IVF), somatic cell nuclear transfer (the Dolly method), or duplication. Although embryos created by IVF for fertility treatments but left unused can provide good materials for research, future stem cell treatments would ideally also seem to require cloning by nuclear transfer. Donor stem cells can be rejected by the recipient's immune system, but this could be prevented by creating an embryonic clone of the patient and harvesting this for therapeutic and immunologically compatible stem cells. The difference between 'therapeutic' and 'reproductive' cloning would then be that in one the embryo is destroyed to provide a cure and in the other it is implanted to make a baby.

Fertilised eggs, products of successful nuclear transfer, and cells of the clusters produced by their first divisions (morulas) are *totipotent*, which means that they can develop into new human beings in an adequate

146

environment provided by a natural or an artificial womb.[1] The inner cells of four- to five-day-old embryos (blastocysts) are *pluripotent*, and they can become any tissue of the body but not the placenta. Embryonic stem cell research has to date been concentrated on human and mouse embryonic *stem cell lines* – cultures of cells which have been derived from early pluripotent embryos. Such human cell lines have been successfully produced since 1998.[2]

Embryonic stem cell research is motivated by scientific curiosity and an urge to overcome hitherto incurable diseases. So far the practical results have been fairly tentative – no treatments have been completed and no clinical trials have been accepted. The challenges of ongoing work in this field include avoiding transplant rejection and controlling cell differentiation. For instance, pluripotent stem cells injected directly into recipients tend to fulfil their function by developing into many kinds of tissue, causing teratomas ('monstrous' tumours containing hair, teeth, bone, and other body parts). Scientists hope, however, that once these problems have been solved, embryonic stem cells can be used to offer unique relief for conditions that require tissue regeneration and replacement.[3]

Human embryonic stem cell lines have during the first decade of their existence been mainly created by destroying human embryos; their survival over time in an undifferentiated state has depended on cloning by duplication, and their therapeutic utilisation may require cloning by somatic cell nuclear transfer. These links with reproduction and beginning lives, and the conflicting normative views on the two issues, have led to considerable variation in the regulation of stem cell research worldwide. Some legislators would like to prevent all mechanical production of people; others only want to avoid the unnecessary annihilation and disrespectful use of early humans and their parts; and still others argue that since embryos are not full-blown persons, all useful experimentation should be allowed.

The United Kingdom has taken one of the most permissive views on research into embryos and their parts. Up until the fourteenth day of

---

[1] On the current state of artificial-womb technologies, their future prospects, and their ethical issues, see, e.g. Scott Gelfand and John R. Shook (eds), 2006, *Ectogenesis: Artificial Womb Technology and the Future of Human Reproduction* (Amsterdam: Rodopi).

[2] James A. Thomson, Joseph Itskovitz-Eldor, Sander S. Shapiro, Michelle A. Waknitz, Jennifer J. Swiergiel, Vivienne S. Marshall, and Jeffrey M. Jones, 1998, 'Embryonic stem cell lines derived from human blastocysts', *Science* 282: 1145–7.

[3] D. C. Wu, A. S. Boyd, and K. J. Wood, 2007, 'Embryonic stem cell transplantation: potential applicability in cell replacement therapy and regenerative medicine', *Frontiers in Bioscience* 12: 4525–35.

embryonic development, almost any kind of work is allowed, provided that it is licensed by the Human Fertilisation and Embryology Authority. Some of the more controversial licences have been granted for the study and duplication of embryos produced by IVF; for the creation of human–animal hybrids; and for the cloning of embryos for research purposes by somatic cell nuclear transfer.[4]

Other countries have chosen to draw the lines differently. Some ban therapeutic cloning or human–animal hybrids, or both, or permit only the use of supernumerary embryos originally produced for fertility treatments. Others allow the use of older human embryonic stem cell lines but outlaw the creation of new ones, or forbid the use of public funds for this type of research, or accept experimentation for a time period of less than fourteen days. In the United States, individual states are free to regulate stem cell research as they wish, but during 2001–2009, federal resources could not be used except for work on some early lines which were in existence when the ban was enacted. In Europe, the strictest rules prevail in France and Germany. Many nations all over the world have to date left stem cell research unregulated, partly because the science is developing so rapidly and partly because the connection between therapeutic and reproductive cloning remains disputed.[5]

7.2   Alternatives and conjectures

The acquisition of optimal stem cells for research and therapy has involved the destruction of human embryos, and their antecedent creation for the purpose. Those who place value on early human lives argue that both practices are wrong and should be stopped. Since, however, stem cells are a promising subject of scientific enquiry, some of them are prepared to make concessions in special cases. Roughly speaking, embryos produced in nonresearch contexts may, even according to some cautious views, be studied if they are already dead, or nonviable, or unlikely to see the light of day anyway.

Legislators in the United States and in Germany have taken the view that research on human embryonic stem cell lines that pre-date the relevant national regulation can be considered acceptable even if the establishment of new lines is banned. The logic here is that potentially valuable

---

[4] Human Fertilisation and Embryology Authority – www.hfea.gov.uk/index.html.
[5] See, e.g. Kirstin Matthews, 2007c, 'Stem cells: A science and policy overview'– cnx.org/content/col10445/1.1.

scientific activity is allowed, but it is limited, in the words of George W. Bush, to situations 'where the life and death decision has already been made'.[6] Since nothing can bring back the destroyed embryos, we might as well make their sacrifice meaningful by letting researchers study them, increase our knowledge about life's beginnings, and try to develop treatments for diseases infesting humanity.

Nonviable IVF embryos detected by preimplantation genetic diagnosis (PGD) are another source of material that can be considered legitimate. Even if implanted, these entities would not, by definition, be capable of developing into fetuses, infants, and adult human beings, so arguably nothing would be lost by allowing their use in research. Depending on the specific conditions that individual embryos of this kind have, their utility may be restricted. Still, many of them can yield solid information, acquired without raising too many ethical questions, provided only that the 'parents' consent to the use of their offspring.[7]

Many legislatures permit research on 'supernumerary' IVF embryos but not their creation deliberately for scientific purposes. IVF treatments usually generate more embryos than are implanted to produce children, and the excess ones are often frozen for future operations. Sooner or later, though, they are not needed any more, and they are either destroyed or stored indefinitely. The use of these 'surplus' or 'spare' embryos is often seen as ethically more tenable than the production of new human beings for the purposes of research. Again, the argument is that something is gained and nothing is lost when scientists dissect an entity that would otherwise have gone to waste, immediately or eventually.

All these distinctions can be challenged on conceptual and factual grounds. The 'already dead' position gives rise to a range of issues regarding consistency and complicity – can it really be right to destroy embryos on 28 February but not 1 March and will researchers get their 'hands dirty' by benefiting from past wrongdoing?[8] The 'sacrifice the non-viable' view sounds feasible as long as it is thought of in terms of a triage: if resources are scarce and not all can be saved, then let us

[6] 'President discusses stem cell research' – usgovinfo.about.com/blwhrelease16.htm.
[7] For a Harvard Stem Cell Institute advert asking couples to donate their affected embryos for research, see, e.g.: Participating in stem cell research – www.hsci.harvard.edu/participating-stem-cell-research.
[8] For a critical analysis of these issues, see, e.g. Tuija Takala and Matti Häyry, 2007, 'Benefiting from past wrongdoing, human embryonic stem cell lines, and the fragility of the German legal position', *Bioethics* 21: 150–9.

abandon those who would not make it anyway. But since resources are not that scarce, no one needs to be deserted. Embryos with lethal and currently incurable conditions could be frozen to wait for future medical advances which may one day provide a treatment for them. The 'spare embryo' approach, in its turn, is more rhetorical than based on objective facts. Fertility treatments do not produce excess material unless physician-scientists decide that they do and act accordingly. It would be equally possible to retrieve only the ova and fertilise only the eggs that are implanted, leaving no surplus after the procedure.[9] Fertility clinics have, in fact, for 30 years produced embryos for research purposes by creating more of them than is strictly needed.[10] If the protection of early human life is taken seriously, supernumerary embryos that already exist should perhaps be rendered unavailable to science by freezing them to wait for ectogenesis to come online; or they could be given a chance of a life now by embryo adoption.[11]

Complicated rescue operations for embryos make little sense unless their existence has moral value in the same way that the lives of born human beings do. This idea has been both defended and criticised in bioethical literature concerning abortion, fertility treatments, and embryo experimentation. Some claim that all human lives are sacred from conception and that the destruction of embryos is tantamount to murder. Others counter that fertilised eggs, morulas, and blastocysts are no more persons with rights than acorns are oak trees with roots. Still others say that early human beings have some worth and ought to enjoy a certain degree of protection, although they recognise that if fire breaks out in a fertility clinic most of us would probably save an unconscious child rather than a Petri dish containing an embryo.[12] These views will be discussed in Sections 7.7, 7.8, and 7.9.

---

[9] The standard objection to this is that women have to go through additional cycles of egg retrieval, if the first attempts prove unsuccessful. But this, of course, is hardly a sufficient reason for sacrificing humans with a right to life.

[10] For an early contribution dissecting this rhetoric, see Søren Holm, 1993, 'The spare embryo – A red herring in the embryo experimentation debate', *Health Care Analysis* 1: 63–6.

[11] For a defence, see, e.g. Reginald Finger, 'Embryo adoption: A life-affirming parenthood choice' – www.cmdahome.org/AM/Template.cfm?Section=Home&TEMPLATE=/CM/ContentDisplay.cfm&CONTENTID=11075. For some of the questions, see, e.g. Susan L. Crockin, 2001, 'Embryo "adoption": A limited option', *Reproductive BioMedicine Online* 3: 162–3.

[12] Example by George J. Annas, 1989, 'A French homunculus in a Tennessee court', *Hastings Center Report* 19: 20–2; Michael J. Sandel, 2005b, 'The ethical implications of human cloning', *Perspectives in Biology and Medicine* 48: 241–7.

There are three main ways to avoid the destruction of embryos and still retain some or most of the benefits promised by stem cell research. These ways involve work on adult cells as they are, reprogrammed adult cells, or embryonic cells removed without ending the life of the original organism. First, the use of adult stem cells is relatively uncontested in the ethical sense, and its results have been moderately encouraging.[13] Treatments with the patient's own stem cells are currently being offered at least for autoimmune diseases, cerebral palsy, diabetes type 2, heart failure, multiple sclerosis, osteoarthritis and other degenerative joint diseases, Parkinson's disease, rheumatoid arthritis, and stroke. One option would be to concentrate all resources on this area.

Secondly, it is now possible to 'reprogramme' adult human stem cells to act like their embryonic counterparts.[14] Already differentiated cells are manipulated so that they 'de-differentiate' into *induced pluripotent cells* (iPCs). This stimulated return to the blastocyst stage can produce entities with characteristics desired in embryonic stem cells without giving rise to the controversies related to the actual use of unborn human beings. Directing research into the creation and use of iPCs should arguably be preferred by all those who believe that embryos have more moral value than somatic human cells.[15]

Thirdly, a group of scientists has reported that they have been able to derive human embryonic stem cell lines without the destruction of embryos.[16] These scientists used a PGD technique to remove a single cell (blastomere) from an embryo at the eight-cell stage and then used the blastomere for the derivation of a stem cell line. They left the original

[13] Richard K. Burt, Yvonne Loh, William Pearce, Nirat Beohar, Walter G. Barr, Robert Craig, Yanting Wen, Jonathan A. Rapp, and John Kessler, 2008, 'Clinical applications of blood-derived and marrow-derived stem cells for nonmalignant diseases', *Journal of the American Medical Association* 299: 925–36.

[14] K. Takahashi, K. Tanabe, M. Ohnuki, M. Narita, T. Ichisaka, K. Tomoda, and S. Yamanaka, 2007, 'Induction of pluripotent stem cells from adult human fibroblasts by defined factors', *Cell* 131: 861–72; Junying Yu, Maxim A. Vodyanik, Kim Smuga-Otto, Jessica Antosiewicz-Bourget, Jennifer L. Frane, Shulan Tian, Jeff Nie, Gudrun A. Jonsdottir, Victor Ruotti, Ron Stewart, Igor I. Slukvin, and James A. Thomson, 2007, 'Induced pluripotent stem cell lines derived from human somatic cells', *Science* 318: 1917–20; Sabine Conrad, Markus Renninger, Jörg Hennenlotter, Tina Wiesner, Lothar Just, Michael Bonin, Wilhelm Aicher, Hans-Jörg Bühring, Ulrich Mattheus, Andreas Mack, Hans-Joachim Wagner, Stephen Minger, Matthias Matzkies, Michael Reppel, Jürgen Hescheler, Karl-Dietrich Sievert, Arnulf Stenzl, and Thomas Skutella, 2008, 'Generation of pluripotent stem cells from adult human testis', *Nature* 456: 344–9.

[15] See, e.g. Søren Holm, 2008, 'Time to reconsider stem cell ethics – the importance of induced pluripotent cells', *Journal of Medical Ethics* 34: 63–4.

[16] Young Chung, Irina Klimanskaya, Sandy Becker, Tong Li, Marc Maserati, Shi-Jiang Lu, Tamara Zdravkovic, Dusko Ilic, Olga Genbacev, Susan Fisher, Ana Krtolica, and Robert

embryo otherwise intact so that it could have been, in principle, implanted to produce a new individual. The utilisation of research embryos for reproduction is not currently accepted, but the organisms involved in these experiments are similar to the diagnosed embryos that are implanted routinely.

The remaining question in all these cases concerns the actual or potential power of stem cells to produce new human individuals. If the blastomeres removed by the PGD method in the third alternative are totipotent, then they could, and perhaps should, be seen as human beings who according to some views are worthy of protection or bearers of rights. And if, eventually, all the multipotent and pluripotent stem cells of the first and second alternatives can be reprogrammed back to totipotency, how should we assess the moral status of these 'induced embryos'?

7.3   Connections with ethical challenges

If usable stem cells can be produced without destroying embryos, why would anyone want to dissect embryos for research purposes? Why risk causing moral offence by doing something that does not seem to be, strictly speaking, necessary? The consequentialist answer to this question is that 'necessity' comes in varying degrees. Some good work can, no doubt, be done with iPCs and the like, but more and better work could probably be done by using genuine embryonic stem cells. Speed and efficiency are important because people suffer and die every day from diseases that could be stopped by stem cell treatments. If nothing of true value is lost by destroying embryos, then moral offence makes a poor case against a practice that can save lives and improve life quality.[17] If we do not allow scientists to conduct embryonic stem cell research now, the claim goes, we may become 'responsible for the deaths of many people who perished while we delayed the development of treatments'.[18]

Lanza, 2008, 'Human embryonic stem cell lines generated without embryo destruction', *Cell Stem Cell* 2: 113–17.

[17] John Harris, 2003b, 'Stem cells, sex, and procreation', *Cambridge Quarterly of Healthcare Ethics* 12: 353–71, p. 361; Guido Pennings and André Van Steirteghem, 2004, 'The subsidiarity principle in the context of human embryonic stem cell research', *Human Reproduction* 19: 1060–4; Katrien Devolder and Julian Savulescu, 2006, 'The moral imperative to conduct embryonic stem cell research', *Cambridge Quarterly of Healthcare Ethics* 15: 7–21. Interestingly, Devolder and Savulescu's argument for haste in stem cell research is, as far as facts are concerned, partly based on the results of Woo Suk Hwang, the South Korean biomedical scientist whose work was later exposed as rushed, unsubstantiated, and fabricated.

[18] Devolder and Savulescu, 2006, p. 12.

I will examine the arguments from potential benefit and potential harm in Chapter 8. It is clear, however, that the strength of the consequentialist necessity defence will depend on the view taken on the moral status of the embryo. It is one thing to make use of a collection of cells with no particular significance and quite another to sacrifice unborn human beings in order to advance medicine. There are points of view from which both can be endorsed, but these are not readily acceptable to all.

The distinctive role of sanctity-of-life considerations in stem cell research can be highlighted by looking at the practices presented in the foregoing chapters and the sources of moral contention in them. Genetic selection, the creation of saviour siblings, and reproductive cloning can, of course, be tangentially linked with the worth of beginning lives in that they all involve the demise of unfit or unsuccessful human entities. But these activities also have dimensions that make them subject to other, in their own context possibly more important objections. Attempts to make the best babies can be criticised as a failure to grasp the true nature of parental responsibility: children should be loved for what they naturally are and not for what parents want them to be. The selection of only hearing children can be questioned as an attempt to annihilate deafness as a culture. Cloning can be seen as the ultimate instance of designing human beings. And the production of saviour siblings can be challenged for its instrumental motives.

The first three of these complaints cannot be applied to stem cell research at all. Since babies are not born, questions of parental responsibility, cultural diversity, and the manufacture of adult human beings do not arise. Embryos, like children, can be used as means, though, and so can women who produce eggs for IVF, therapeutic cloning, or experiments in parthenogenesis.[19] Instrumentalisation, then, can be an issue in human embryonic stem cell research. I will start my analysis with the treatment of women, because without them embryos (whatever their moral status) would not exist.

7.4   Would women be unnecessarily used?

Embryo creation requires eggs and eggs come from female bodies. They do not, however, come from female bodies as easily as sperm comes from

---

[19] It should also be possible to instrumentalise men in the procurement of fertilised eggs (which need sperm to come about) but the literature seems to be silent on this point, perhaps because the method of acquiring eggs is rather less convenient and more dangerous for women than acquiring sperm is for most men.

male bodies and somatic cells could come from nuclear transfer donors. They have to be extracted by a surgical procedure under anaesthesia, and the operation is preceded by multiple hormone injections with a plethora of side effects and a number of less than fully studied but possibly harmful long-term health effects.[20] The side effects of hormonal stimulation range from moodiness and minor infections to a condition called ovarian hyperstimulation syndrome – which can necessitate hospitalisation. The long-term risks are not well understood, and there is concern that some drugs commonly used in the procedure have either not been approved for the purpose at all or have been approved but without precise knowledge of the future consequences on the treated women and their offspring.[21]

If egg retrieval can be dangerous for the providers and their children, why is it done and how can it be legitimised? In the context of fertility treatments, the answer to both questions is the same. The desire and intention to make babies provides both an explanation and a justification for procuring eggs despite the risks. But what about research? Can advances in science account, and give moral reasons, for ova harvesting?

Estimates on the potential benefits of human embryonic stem cell research and therapies vary considerably. The most positive views can be found in philosophical contributions.[22] Guido Pennings and André Van Steirteghem, for instance, assert that stem cells 'are considered to have great therapeutic potential' and that researchers 'all over the world emphasize the enormous possible benefits stem cells may have for the treatment of diseases'.[23] John Harris, writing in defence of embryo research as opposed to its alternatives, contends that 'we do not yet know whether adult cells will prove as good as embryonic cells for therapeutic purposes' and that '[at] the moment there is simply much more accumulated data and much more therapeutic promise from human embryonic

[20] For an accessible description of the method, see, e.g. Robert Steinbrook, 2006, 'Egg donation and human embryonic stem-cell research', *The New England Journal of Medicine* 354: 324–6. See also Donna Dickenson and Itziar Alkorta Idiakez, 2008, 'Ova donation for stem cell research: An international perspective', *International Journal of Feminist Approaches to Bioethics* 1: 125–44.
[21] E.g. Helen Pearson, 2006, 'Health effects of egg donation may take decades to emerge', *Nature* 442: 607–8; Diane Beeson and Abby Lippman, 2006, 'Egg harvesting for stem cell research: medical risks and ethical problems', *Reproductive Biomedicine Online* 13: 573–9.
[22] This is especially true of philosophical contributions that do not cite reliable scientific literature in support of their claims – see following text and notes.
[23] Pennings and Steirteghem, 2004, p. 1060. The authors give no scientific references for these views.

stem cells'.[24] Recently, Katrien Devolder and Julian Savulescu cited the publicised research of Woo Suk Hwang and others, noting that this 'is indisputable evidence of cloning of human embryos' and observing that the 'recent research involving cloning of human embryos is of enormous significance to humanity'.[25] However, Hwang's results were shortly afterwards shown to be fabricated.[26]

The approach chosen by the champions of human embryonic stem cell research is perhaps best summarised by Dan Brock, who writes: '*I will take for granted* the dominant view in the scientific community that this research has great scientific and medical promise for the understanding and treatment of a wide range of human diseases such as Type 1 diabetes and Parkinson's disease.'[27] What Brock and other proponents of embryonic research 'take for granted' about future prospects could be true and to insist on further evidence on the popularity and justification of this belief in scientific circles can be futile. But the point is that on this level of generality the 'promise' referred to is not only difficult to evaluate but also practically impossible to apply to individual cases of egg retrieval.

Opponents of ova harvesting for research purposes have suggested a simpler test for the assessment of risks and benefits. Judy Norsigian observes that whereas in the case of fertility treatments 'women undergoing multiple egg extraction ... do know that there is a clear potential benefit, and one that is of inestimable value: a baby', for women who are asked to undergo the same procedure to create embryos for research the 'risk/benefit ratio is vastly different [as] the possible benefits ... are quite hypothetical at this stage'.[28] Also comparing women in the same two groups, Diane Beeson and Abby Lippman echo the point by noting that '[one] has a 10–40% chance of producing a baby either for herself or another [woman], while the other is but a subject in a research project

[24] Harris 2003b, p. 361. Harris refers to some studies showing promise in embryonic stem cell research but includes no comparisons with adult stem cell research and its prospects. Others, e.g. Burt et al. 2008, seem to have some confidence in the latter.

[25] Devolder and Savulescu, 2006, pp. 8, 10.

[26] In a subsequent contribution, Savulescu has analysed what went wrong in the Hwang case. He does not comment on the possible misconceptions created by ethicists who rest their cases on unverified scientific data. See Rhodri Saunders and Julian Savulescu, 2008, 'Research ethics and lessons from Hwanggate: what can we learn from the Korean cloning fraud?', *Journal of Medical Ethics* 34: 214–21.

[27] Dan W. Brock, 2006, 'Is a consensus possible on stem cell research? Moral and political obstacles', *Journal of Medical Ethics* 32: 36–42, p. 36 (italics added). This passage in an academically esteemed bioethics journal contains no references to academic literature.

[28] Judy Norsigian, 2005, 'Egg donation for IVF and stem cell research: Time to weigh the risks to women's health', *Different Takes* 33 – popdev.hampshire.edu/projects/dt/33.

with still uncertain benefits'.[29] Norsigian, Beeson, and Lippman focus particularly on the limited utility of therapeutic cloning, and find support for their views from Evan Snyder and Jeanne Loring, authorities in stem cell research, who in the aftermath of the Hwang incident conceded that somatic cell nuclear transfer 'plays only a minor role in the wider discipline of stem-cell biology – a branch of developmental biology that has no lack of other challenges to occupy its practitioners' time'.[30]

Norsigian goes on to suggest that research could usefully go on by 'studying embryo stem cells derived from "conventional" embryos that would otherwise be discarded by couples who are no longer pursuing IVF at an infertility clinic.'[31] But the eggs for these 'leftovers' have also come from female bodies, arguably not by accident, and this proposal is therefore not inevitably neutral when it comes to women's health.[32]

The relevant finding here, however, is that the 'necessity' argument for human embryonic stem cell research on donated eggs and their post-IVF, post-parthenogenesis, and post-cloning descendants needs to be fine-tuned. Advocates of the practice can either claim that when benefits are potentially enormous research should go on despite predicted risks (this solution will be discussed in Chapter 8); or they should admit that when both promises and dangers are uncertain, the justification must be reformulated. The latter option will be studied in the following two sections, first from the viewpoint of harm prevention and justice, then from the perspective of liberty.

7.5   Would women be unfairly used?

It would be unfair to systematically expose one group of people to risks that other people do not have to take, especially if the benefits flowing from the practice can be enjoyed by all alike. In egg harvesting, women are asked to face health dangers that men are not asked to face, although the anticipated results of the research on ova and embryos can benefit both. The case can be made that egg retrieval is discriminatory and unfair.

In a more general context, Harris has outlined, albeit unwittingly, an answer to this criticism. His argument is that everyone, regardless of

---

[29] Beeson and Lippman, 2006.

[30] Evan Y. Snyder and Jeanne F. Loring, 2006, 'Beyond fraud – stem cell research continues', *The New England Journal of Medicine* 354: 321–4, p. 323.

[31] Norsigian, 2005. See also Judy Norsigian, 2004, 'Stem cell research and embryo cloning: Involving laypersons in the public debates', *New England Law Review* 39: 527–34.

[32] On the idea of messages sent by policies like this, see, e.g. Takala and Häyry, 2007.

gender or group membership, has a moral duty to participate in 'serious scientific research'.[33] This duty, according to him, is based on *beneficence* and *fairness*. When it is probable that our actions can prevent grave harm to others and when the balance of risk to ourselves and benefit to others is reasonable, we should act, 'because to fail to do so is to accept responsibility for the harm that then occurs'.[34] And when we have benefited from the existence of a social practice, and continue to 'accept these benefits, we have an obligation of justice to contribute to the social practice which produces them'.[35] Since medical research has the potential of preventing and alleviating harm, and since we have all profited and carry on profiting from it, we all have a duty to participate in it, as study subjects if needed. Other things being equal, then, women should donate eggs, and men should do something equally onerous for scientific research to ward off the threat of gender imbalance.

The idea Harris suggests, and especially its application to ova harvesting,[36] can be challenged from at least three angles. The existence of the duty he evokes can be questioned; the role of risk in the model can be queried; and the feasibility of the required gender neutrality can be doubted. Let me flesh out these concerns, and possible responses to them, one by one.

In an analysis of Harris's view, Sandra Shapshay and Kenneth Pimple argue that although the duty he introduces does exist, it only exists in such a weak form that it cannot justify a universal obligation to participate in medical research.[37] They begin by introducing levels of moral stringency for beneficence, or 'the rule of rescue', and distinguish between views that require us to prevent *all serious harm* that we reasonably can; *the most serious harm* we can; or just *some serious harm* of our own choosing.[38] If we select the last reading, participation in scientific research is one, but only one, of the countless ways in which we can help others and thereby do what we ought to do.[39] If we go for the middle reading, we cannot fulfil our obligation of beneficence without doing *some* sacrifices for others, but health problems which can be solved by biomedical research still have to compete for our moral attention with other major social and global

[33] John Harris, 2005, 'Scientific research is a moral duty', *Journal of Medical Ethics* 31: 242–8.

[34] Harris, 2005, p. 242.   [35] Harris, 2005, p. 243.

[36] Harris does not discuss this in his paper, so some of the criticisms are to Harris-like rather than actually Harris-related views.

[37] Sandra Shapshay and Kenneth D. Pimple, 2007, 'Participation in biomedical research is an imperfect moral duty: A response to John Harris', *Journal of Medical Ethics* 33: 414–17.

[38] Shapshay and Pimple, 2007, p. 415.   [39] Shapshay and Pimple, 2007, pp. 415–16.

issues – poverty, hunger, illiteracy, and injustice, to name but a few.[40] The strict duty Harris seems to postulate must, then, be grounded on the first interpretation, but an obligation to spend our entire lives minimising harm on others is arguably too demanding to allow us to live meaningful lives ourselves.[41] In a similar vein, Shapshay and Pimple argue that although fairness in the sense of not 'free riding' in society is important, as Harris says, we can reciprocate other people's contributions in many alternative ways without becoming subjects for biomedical research.[42]

A possible response to this criticism is that the weaker duty would nonetheless provide responsible citizens with good moral reasons to promote science. Even if our obligation is 'only' to prevent the most serious kinds of harm to our fellow beings when we reasonably can, this still implies that we have a strict duty to fight *either* disease *or* poverty *or* hunger *or* illiteracy *or* injustice. We can choose the way in which we practise our beneficence and fairness towards other people, but doing none of the above is not an option.[43] Those of us who are not active in politics or charities aiming to reduce need and suffering could, in the last analysis, serve others best by becoming subjects of human experimentation.

Another concern raised by the use of the Harris model in embryonic stem cell research is that the risks of egg retrieval as such remain the same whether or not we accept the universal duty to help others: 'fairness' is pursued by exposing new groups of people to the levels of danger that now face ova donors. These levels of danger could, of course, become lower if everyone participated in biomedical research. The IVF procedure is safer and more efficient now than it was 30 years ago; and the medical profession's ability to deal with emerging health issues is constantly improving through scientific work. But can hazardous activities be justified by saying that they are designed to relieve their own harmful effects? An example clarifies the point. The synthetic oestrogen diethylstilbestrol (DES) was used from the early 1940s until the early 1970s to reduce miscarriages (ineffectively, as it transpired), but one of the long-term effects is that the daughters of women treated by DES experience infertility problems.[44] The situation – as early as in 1987 – prompted Robyn Rowland to opine that it 'is the "natural progression of science" that *in vitro* fertilisation is

---

[40] Shapshay and Pimple, 2007, p. 416.   [41] Shapshay and Pimple, 2007, p. 415.
[42] Shapshay and Pimple, 2007, pp. 416–17.
[43] The list can, of course, go on, but it is, within the argument from rule of rescue, limited to causes of serious harm.
[44] Roberta J. Apfel and Susan M. Fisher, 1984, *To Do No Harm: DES and the Dilemmas of Modern Medicine* (New Haven, CT: Yale University Press).

now hailed as a solution to the problems of DES'; and that 'DES daughters are being offered IVF pregnancies to overcome their infertility caused by medical mismanagement and experimentation on their mothers.'[45] When this history is combined with the currently unknown risks of hormonal stimulation preceding IVF, a pattern starts to emerge. Is it sensible that the medical mistakes of yesteryear are corrected by new mistakes which need to be corrected tomorrow? The model certainly does not seem to reduce the long-term risks in any obvious way.

The most natural response to these observations is that despite minor hiccups biomedicine has made, and continues to make, many people's lives are better than they would have been without advances in science. Iatrogenic morbidity and mortality are not uncommon, but they are the result of bad science and sloppy healthcare practices, not of serious research. The unhindered progress of new medical procedures and technologies is the best way to promote human health and wellbeing. (Again, I will examine the presumptions of this line of argument further in Chapter 8.)

An alternative answer to the question of risk is to argue, as Harris in fact does, that danger does not remove our duty to help others. As he writes, when 'the risks to research subjects are significant and the burdens onerous but ... the benefits to other people are equally significant and large', it would probably be wrong to *force* people to participate; but this is not 'to say that individuals should not be willing to bear such burdens nor is it to say that it is not their moral duty to do so'.[46] This brings to sharp focus the remaining concern about his proposal, the issue of gender neutrality. We do not live in a perfectly just world, where women and men alike would be likely to volunteer for arduous experimentation in order to improve other people's chances to have babies or conquer diseases. The request for ova to study embryos and embryonic stem cells is directed at women – and in many instances at women undergoing infertility treatments, who are under emotional and social pressure to contribute to the practice they are seeking help from.

The likeliest comeback from the science-friendly camp is that while gender inequality is wrong and coercion in the IVF situations should be

---

[45] Robyn Rowland, 1987, 'Making women visible in the embryo experimentation debate', *Bioethics* 1: 179–88, pp. 185–6. On the use of IVF to overcome DES problems, Rowland refers to Suheil Muasher, Jairo Garcia, and Howard Jones, 1984, 'Experience with diethylstilbestrol-exposed infertile women in a program of in vitro fertilisation', *Fertility and Sterility* 42: 20–4, p. 22.
[46] Harris, 2005, p. 246.

avoided, it would still be desirable to have egg donations for embryonic stem cell research. Wider questions of justice must, of course, be addressed, but since they are the cause, not the result, of practical inequalities in research subject recruitment they should not be employed against useful biomedical work. Women can be informed of all the factors relevant to ova retrieval, but in the end they should be allowed to decide for themselves whether to discharge their broad duty of beneficence in this or some other way.

7.6   Would women be wrongfully used?

The proposal on the table, then, is the following. People have a moral duty to do something to benefit their fellow beings, and participation in bioscientific research is one good way of discharging this duty. There can be risks, but when the benefits are proportional to these, the moral obligation remains (even if its legal enforcement would be questionable). It is possible that women will be burdened more than men in the process, but that should be counteracted by promoting gender equality generally, not by hindering experimentation. If women want to participate in embryonic stem cell research as egg providers, voluntarily and in possession of adequate information on its nature and effects, they should be free to do so.

Few participants in the ethical discussion on egg retrieval would oppose this proposal as such, as opposition would mean undermining women's standing as competent decision makers. But many argue that the conditions stated in the suggestion are not met in real life. Most ova providers want money for their services; a transaction that, for instance, law in the United States does not allow for research purposes (although it does allow it for fertility treatments). In the United Kingdom, direct payment is also ruled out (albeit that the price of IVF treatments can be reduced for women who assign some of their harvested eggs for research). Without financial incentives, however, women seem to be unwilling to donate ova to science except when they have been poorly informed or are under undue pressure. Infertility treatments can create an emotional impulse to help the physician-researchers in their ongoing work; and family members or friends suffering from conditions that human embryonic stem cell research could address can build social expectations. If none of these coercive elements is present, women want to be paid for their eggs. But economic encouragement over and above the reimbursement of expenses and a token compensation for the inconvenience endured is widely banned.[47]

Payment for egg retrieval is thought to be wrong, because it would make possible the exploitation of defenceless groups. Like emotional and social pressure, economic inducement can play on the vulnerabilities of young women, low-income women, women from ethnic minority communities, and women in the developing world.[48] Thomas Papadimos and Alexa Papadimos have presented a case against using young American college students as ova providers; and their reasoning can easily be extended to more, and differently, disenfranchised women, as well.[49] They maintain that young female students cannot properly consent to selling their eggs either to help others to have children or to assist scientists in their work. To support this claim, they present four elements needed for informed consent to be valid – voluntariness, capacity, understanding, and disclosure – and argue that none of these is robustly present when budding young adults make far-reaching decisions under the pressure of rising tuition costs.

Voluntariness, according to Papadimos and Papadimos, is possible only if the decision maker is not under the undue control of others. The forms of control they recognise are coercion by direct threats (which is not normally present in egg trade); persuasion, or engagement with the other's reason or emotion (appeals to reason are acceptable, appeals to emotion are not); and manipulation, which stands for lying, withholding information, emotional blackmail, and the like (all unacceptable). The authors say that 'trying to persuade someone to trade their genes for tuition cannot be based on reason', that such 'persuasion invariably invokes an emotional response', and that when 'one is "in need" reason may not prevail'.[50] The implication seems to be that even without coercion or manipulation, an offer of money in exchange for ova will automatically foreclose the possibility of voluntariness.

---

[47] Françoise Baylis and Caroline McLeod, 2007, 'The stem cell debate continues: the buying and selling of eggs for research', *Journal of Medical Ethics* 33: 726–31; also Harris, 2005, p. 247; Beeson and Lippman, 2006; Brock, 2006, p. 41; Steinbrook, 2006, pp. 325–6; Debora Spar, 2007, 'The egg trade – Making sense of the market for human oocytes', *The New England Journal of Medicine* 356: 1289–91.

[48] Beeson and Lippman, 2006; Spar, 2007, p. 1299.

[49] Thomas J. Papadimos and Alexa T. Papadimos, 2004, 'The student and the ovum: The lack of autonomy and informed consent in trading genes for tuition', *Reproductive Biology and Endocrinology* 2: 56 – pubmedcentral.nih.gov/articlerender.fcgi?artid=479702.

[50] Papadimos and Papadimos, 2004.

Capacity, as defined by Papadimos and Papadimos, 'involves the psychological, social, and physical wherewithal to make a [legally] competent decision', and its 'determination [is] usually made by a health care provider'.[51] They argue that although a female university student is normally competent to decide for herself, in the ova retrieval case 'she may lack the capacity to make this choice because she is in need of financial resources and she has been presented with a "fix" for her dilemma', which can render her 'psychologically unable to refuse'.[52] The capacity for autonomous decision making, then, can be absent in this setting.

Understanding is another requirement that financial arrangements for ova retrieval can leave unmet. Papadimos and Papadimos refer to studies showing that patients, at times, 'do not acquire, process, or retain the information related to risks presented to them preoperatively' and note that this can reduce 'the morality of informed consent before surgery ... especially ... when dealing with a decision concerning the reproductive health of females who only recently reached adulthood and now face a financial dilemma with a seemingly easy solution for its resolution'.[53] A college student can, on an abstract level, understand what risks are involved in egg harvesting, but 'can she actually accept the fact that she has a remote, yet possible chance of getting cancer or dying?'[54]

Disclosure also causes ethical qualms for Papadimos and Papadimos. The standards used in deciding what to tell patients or study subjects about invasive procedures and their effects range from what professionals would usually say to what each individual would subjectively need to know. The authors deem the professional approach too technical or medical to be used in a personal matter like ova collection; and the subjective preferences too difficult to define to be of practical use. The remaining test is what a 'reasonable person' would like to know, but this is found unhelpful 'because a standard for a "reasonable" university student cannot be gleaned from the collective masses'.[55]

The argument presented is that while autonomous choices to donate eggs could be accepted, female university students who are offered money for their ova are incapable of making such choices and thereby unable to give their informed consent to the transaction. If economic inducements are allowed, Papadimos and Papadimos write, 'young women, essentially our daughters, and in some cases our wives, who trade their genes for tuition, effectively, are being exploited'.[56] And their concern is extended

---

[51] Papadimos and Papadimos, 2004.   [52] Papadimos and Papadimos, 2004.
[53] Papadimos and Papadimos, 2004.   [54] Papadimos and Papadimos, 2004.
[55] Papadimos and Papadimos, 2004.   [56] Papadimos and Papadimos, 2004.

to current and future recruitment of other groups, as well. Women of lesser means, in affluent and especially in developing countries, face the same situation regardless of their academic status. Vigilance is needed, they argue, lest the global ova industry transform women into mere providers of biomaterial.

Those who advocate fees for research participation can observe that the view on autonomy offered by Papadimos and Papadimos is incompatible with many practices that are presently accepted in our societies. Even young people can donate kidneys for altruistic reasons,[57] and research subjects are often compensated when invasive procedures, say, bronchoscopy or endoscopy are involved.[58] Talking about emotionally and economically laden situations, students are allowed to get married, have children, terminate their studies, and commit themselves to jobs that they do not value. And if these choices are not dangerous enough for comparison, they are also permitted to take on downhill skiing, ocean sailing, mountain climbing, and body building. All the choices in the first list are related to strong emotions and long-lasting economic implications, which should reduce voluntariness and capacity; whereas the low but existing risk of death in sports should make proper understanding and disclosure impossible. Unless Papadimos and Papadimos want to ban all these, proponents of fees can suggest that their notion of the mental abilities of female university students can be described as paternalistic and discriminatory.

It is possible that the authors have inadvertently overstated the role of autonomy in their argument and that they could have done better by concentrating on the *type of action* discussed. Donating vital organs, getting married, producing offspring, landing a job, and possibly being involved in sports are all good and respectable activities, and no one seems to care if young adults assume the dangers related to *these* with less than full capacity or understanding. Other kinds of conduct, such as drug taking, disorderly behaviour, and prostitution, on the contrary, are not seen as equally acceptable, and they attract moral censure more easily. One explanation for this is that drugs are thought to have long-term health effects, rioting can harm others, and commercial sex is considered depraved. If young persons are mixed up in these, parents tend to claim that they are not thinking straight and have to be protected from their own irrational and immoral choices. Lack of autonomy, it seems, makes a difference only when members of protected groups are prone to damage themselves or

[57] Brock, 2006, p. 41.   [58] Steinbrook, 2006, p. 325.

others, physically or spiritually; and arguably it is the expectation of *harm* that makes the harvesting of eggs suspect, too.

Seen in this way, the disagreement between opponents and proponents of commercial ova acquisition becomes focused on the immediate and forthcoming effects of the arrangement. Critics say that the wellbeing of egg providers and their offspring is jeopardised for a vague promise of future benefits; and that the integrity of vulnerable women is compromised by exploitation.[59] Defenders hold that research subjects make certain small personal sacrifices for potentially enormous advances in science; and that women participating in this activity should be commended for their decency and civic virtue.[60]

When it comes to the inconvenience and consequences of ova retrieval, some consensus could be reached by empirical studies into IVF women's experiences and views. But some of the outcomes cannot be known yet and opinions are bound to vary, so the assessment of physical and psychological harm remains contested. What is more, the description of egg suppliers as exploited victims in one camp and upright citizens in the other opens a gap along the lines discussed in Chapter 5, in the context of using people as a mere means. Putting a price on human body parts can be seen as 'commodifying' and their use in stem cell research 'improper'.[61] Commodification, however, is not an obstacle for champions of fees, who can point out that blood and sperm are already tradable in the market yet this is not a problem for most. And use for research is, presumably, improper in the way intended in the using-people-as-mere-means argument only if (research destroys embryos and) the destruction of embryos is wrong. But is it, and if it is, on what grounds?

7.7   The destruction of embryos is always wrong

According to a traditional European view, the intentional killing of innocent human beings is wrong, regardless of the age of the human being in question. If people die naturally and without our active and deliberate involvement, this can and in some cases must be accepted. And different rules can apply to individuals who present a threat to others or who are guilty of serious offences. But from the beginning to the end of human life, innocent people should not be killed on purpose.

---

[59] Papadimos and Papadimos, 2004; Beeson and Lippman, 2006; Baylis and McLeod, 2007.
[60] Harris, 2005; Brock, 2006; Steinbrook, 2006.   [61] These were discussed in Section 5.9.

Since the beginning of human life in its morally significant form can be defined in different ways, some views extend their protection to embryos but others do not. Three 'sanctity-of-life' arguments that accommodate embryos make appeals to their *souls*, *bodies*, and *futures*, which according to these ethical explications are similar to ours. Once this has been established, requirements of sympathy, fairness, solidarity, and universality do the rest of the normative work and lead to the conclusion that embryo destruction would be wrong.

The first view can be expressed in the Aristotelian language of goals and their actual and potential achievement. According to Aristotle, all beings move or develop towards an end state that can be different for various kinds of beings. Heavy objects fall down, light ones rise up, and living beings move into the direction of their maturity (and eventual demise). In human beings, the driving force behind this movement is the soul, which is the form or the blueprint of what our bodies can become. The actual people that we now are have been present, as potential for growth, in our souls from the time that they became the formative part of our bodies. Aristotle and some later philosophers believed that 'ensoulment' occurs several weeks into fetal development, but many Christian thinkers have identified the formation of the soul with conception. When the latter route is chosen, human life is sacrosanct from its biological beginning, because the *soul with its potential* is already present in the embryo.[62]

The second view has been recently formulated by Patrick Lee and it focuses on our corporeal rather than spiritual being.[63] Lee's argument is that we are intrinsically valuable because of what we are (essentially); that we are (essentially) physical organisms; that we have been the same physical organisms since conception; and that therefore we have been intrinsically valuable since conception. The intrinsic value that we now have makes us subjects of rights, including a right to life, and we should not, due to this right, be killed. And as we have had the intrinsic value and its adjacent rights already as embryos, it would have been wrong to kill us at any time after conception. According to Lee, this reasoning is not dependent (like the foregoing reading of Aristotle might be) on the *potential* of the soul in human beings who are currently at an embryonic

---

[62] See, e.g. Norman Ford, 2001, 'The human embryo as person in Catholic teaching', *The National Bioethics Quarterly* 1: 155–60; John R. Meyer, 2006, 'Embryonic personhood, human nature, and rational ensoulment', *The Heythrop Journal* 47: 206–25.

[63] Patrick Lee, 1996, *Abortion and Unborn Human Life* (Washington, DC: Catholic University of America Press); Dean Stretton, 2000, 'The argument from intrinsic value: A critique', *Bioethics* 14: 228–39; Patrick Lee, 2004, 'The pro-life argument from substantial identity: A defence', *Bioethics* 18: 249–63.

stage. As he writes, 'Right *now* the human embryo is a substantial entity with the basic, natural capacities to reason and make free choices, though it will take some time for her to actualise those capacities.' And, he concludes, 'Right *now* the human embryo is an entity with the same *substantial nature* as, and so an equal in dignity with, you or me'.[64]

The third view, most notably advocated by Don Marquis in the context of abortion, sets aside both souls and bodies and concentrates on future experiences and activities. Marquis starts from the premise that we should not kill each other – that it would be seriously wrong to take the lives of adults, adolescents, children, and infants unless there are strong moral reasons for doing so. He then goes on to claim that 'the best account for the wrongness of killing adults and children is that killing us deprives us of our valuable futures, of all the goods of life that we would have experienced if we had lived out our natural life spans'.[65] The immorality of causing death is not identified with the destruction of the body or the annihilation of the soul, but with the denial of a future of value to the individual whose life is ended. Marquis extends his model from regular homicide to terminations of pregnancy, arguing that 'abortion is wrong, for abortion deprives a fetus of a future like ours'.[66] And it is possible, although not inevitable,[67] to go one step further and say that embryos should also be included.

If any of these views is tenable, the question of destructive embryonic stem cell research is easily answered: embryos are human beings in the same morally significant sense as we are and should not be killed. Stem

---

[64] Lee, 2004, p. 262.

[65] Don Marquis, 2002, 'A defence of the potential future of value theory', *Journal of Medical Ethics* 28: 198–201, p. 198.

[66] Marquis, 2002, p. 198. Cf. Don Marquis, 1989, 'Why abortion is immoral', *The Journal of Philosophy* 86: 183–202; Mark T. Brown, 2000, 'The morality of abortion and the deprivation of futures', *Journal of Medical Ethics* 26: 103–7; Don Marquis, 2001, 'Deprivations, futures and the wrongness of killing', *Journal of Medical Ethics* 27: 363–9; Julian Savulescu, 2002a, 'Abortion, embryo destruction and the future of value argument', *Journal of Medical Ethics* 28: 133–5; Mark T. Brown, 2002a, 'A future like ours revisited', *Journal of Medical Ethics* 28: 192–5; Simon J. Parsons, 2002, 'Present self-represented futures of value are a reason for the wrongness of killing', *Journal of Medical Ethics* 28: 196–7; Mark T. Brown, 2002b, 'Abortion and the value of the future: A reply to a defence of the potential future of value theory', *Journal of Medical Ethics* 28: 202; Keith Allen Korcz, 2002, 'Two moral strategies regarding abortion', *Journal of Social Philosophy* 33: 581–605; Don Marquis, 2004, 'Korcz's objections to the future-of-value argument', *Journal of Social Philosophy* 35: 56–65; Don Marquis, 2005, 'Savulescu's objections to the future of value argument', *Journal of Medical Ethics* 31: 119–22.

[67] Arthur Kuflik, 2008, 'The "future like ours" argument and human embryonic stem cell research', *Journal of Medical Ethics* 34: 417–21.

cell research must, according to this position, be conducted without ending embryonic life, if at all.

7.8 The destruction of embryos is never wrong

Opponents of the sanctity-of-embryonic-life doctrine usually accept the notion that people should not be unnecessarily killed, and they agree that people like us have intrinsically valuable lives and a right to continue living them. A point of disagreement, though, is the question, who count as people like us? The standard answers link the similarity to mental or rational abilities that most human adults and children have but all embryos lack.

Philosophical proponents of embryo research usually call the holders of morally significant abilities *persons*, and some of the main suggested criteria for belonging to this privileged group include consciousness, self-awareness, continuous mental life, interests, agency, and rationality. No precise definition of 'personhood' (in the sense of choosing specific items on the list) is needed where embryos are concerned, because it is clear that they do not have any of the requisite abilities.[68] Embryos are not aware of themselves at any level; they do not have beliefs, hopes, memories, or conscious interests; and they do not act or think.[69] This is why, so the argument goes, it is safe to deny them the protection that more mature humans enjoy and regard them as useful and legitimate material for life-saving and health-promoting scientific research.

Those who disagree with this conclusion have often made appeals to the potential, capacities, and prospects of even unborn human beings. If embryos are allowed to develop normally, they will become fetuses, children, and eventually adults. They already have, in their embryonic bodies, all the dormant capacities for feeling, thinking, and action that we have in more active forms. And their futures lie ahead of them just like our futures lie ahead of us if our lives are not abruptly terminated. Let me sketch some of the ways in which responses to these claims and comments have been formulated.

---

[68] E.g. Michael Tooley, 1998, 'Personhood', Helga Kuhse and Peter Singer (eds), *Companion to Bioethics* (Oxford: Blackwell): 117–26, p. 120. For one of the original views on 'personhood', see Michael Tooley, 1972, 'Abortion and infanticide', *Philosophy and Public Affairs* 2: 37–65.

[69] For two more early formulations of 'personhood' in this sense, see Peter Singer, 1979, *Practical Ethics* (Cambridge: Cambridge University Press); John Harris, 1985, *The Value of Life: An Introduction to Medical Ethics* (London: Routledge and Kegan Paul).

Appeals to potential abilities, latent capacities, and future expectations can be countered by a *reductio ad absurdum* – an argument that applies the opponent's premises to a new situation and shows how they will yield results that cannot be valid. In our case, four examples have been used. First, an egg and a sperm have (jointly) the same prospects as the early embryo has. Secondly, ova can (probably) be stimulated to become an embryo by parthenogenesis, that is, without the involvement of other gametes or somatic cells. Thirdly, any cell of the body can (possibly) be reprogrammed to return to the totipotent stage, after which it can develop into a new individual. And fourthly, for every live birth produced by unassisted sexual reproduction, at least three embryos are lost or miscarried. If it is wrong to thwart lives that have a chance of becoming one of us, all these entities should presumably be cherished with the same zeal as would-be research embryos. All compatible eggs and sperm ought to be brought together to actualise their potential; all suitable ova and somatic cells ought to be stimulated to transform into the human beings that they can be; and unprotected as well as protected sexual intercourse between fertile women and men should be strictly avoided. Since all these implications of the sanctity-of-life view are bizarre, its definitions of morally significant human life must, according to its critics, be rejected.[70]

A closer examination of the future-of-value notion reveals another distinction that marks a difference between the 'sanctity' and 'personhood' views. In defining the wrongness of killing, Marquis emphasises the objective value of life and describes the lack of it as a deprivation even without anyone experiencing it yet.[71] Harris, a renowned advocate of personhood as an ability to value one's existence, stresses the role of individuals and their subjective valuations of their own lives.[72] Marquis is led by his model to believe that the primary wrong in killing people is the *impersonal* cancellation of future lives; whereas the approach chosen by Harris is more open to the possibility that it is wrong to kill people because (or in case) they *personally* value their lives and want to go on living. Only the former rationale can be used in considering the fate of embryos.

In any case, if personhood in the sense that excludes embryos is the decisive criterion of intrinsic value and rights, and if potential, capacity,

---

[70] Tooley, 1998, pp. 122–3; John Harris, 2007, *Enhancing Evolution: The Ethical Case for Making Better People* (Princeton, NJ: Princeton University Press), pp. 166–77; Harris, 2003b, pp. 362–4.

[71] Marquis, 1989.

[72] John Harris, 1999b, 'The concept of the person and the value of life', *Kennedy Institute of Ethics Journal* 9: 293–308.

and prospects do not change the moral standing of embryos, then the universally accepted wrongness of deliberately killing innocent people cannot be used as a justification for banning human embryonic stem cell research.

7.9   The destruction of embryos is sometimes wrong

The 'sanctity' and 'personhood' doctrines both produce corollaries which, in the eyes of their opponents, make them less than fully credible. As noted, for instance, by Søren Holm, strict adherence to the first view forecloses abortions for any reason (including the humanitarian indications of rape and extreme youth) as well as the use of the intrauterine device for contraception (it prevents embryonic human lives from continuing in the womb); while the second view can be evoked to support embryo research for less than vital purposes like the development of cosmetics (if they have no value, they can be used for anything) and infanticide (infants do not have the abilities required for personhood, either).[73] These logical outcomes do not necessarily deter theorists who are strongly committed to their particular views, but Holm suggests that wider support might not be forthcoming for ethical notions that seem to contradict ordinary people's moral intuitions in modern societies.

Holm himself believes (as he believes most people to believe) that 'human life is intrinsically valuable at all stages of life, [but that it] becomes more valuable during the development from fertilized egg to adult human being'. The basic idea of this 'gradualist' view is that 'as the developing human being acquires new characteristics the act of killing it entails more and more wrong-making features'.[74] Embryos have some worth, developing fetuses have progressively more, and later milestones like viability or birth mark the point at which the full 'adult' value is reached. The normative implication in our present context is that destroying embryos for research is initially wrong and should not be done lightly, although good reasons can justify it. It is, in Holm's words, 'up to the scientists to present convincing arguments that destructive embryonic stem cell research is necessary to produce cures and treatments for important human

---

[73] Søren Holm, 2003a, 'The ethical case against stem cell research', *Cambridge Quarterly of Healthcare Ethics* 12: 372–83, pp. 372–3, 377.

[74] Holm 2003a, p. 376; See also Søren Holm, 1996, 'The moral status of the pre-personal human being: The argument from potential reconsidered', Donald Evans (ed.), *Conceiving the Embryo: Ethics, Law, and Practice in Human Embryology* (Dordrecht: Kluwer): 193–220.

diseases'.[75] Due to current uncertainties concerning the advantages of embryonic stem cell research, he himself remains sceptical.

Human beings go through many kinds of transformations during their lifetimes and their relationships with their surroundings change biologically, psychologically, socially, and institutionally. From one-cell zygotes we develop into fetuses, children, and adults, if many intertwining internal and external factors make this possible. At some stage we become sentient, at other points our consciousness and self-awareness come into being, and most of us eventually learn how to think rationally and act morally. Our parents' attachment to us often grows during our fetal development due to the probability of our survival, our visibility in ultrasound images, and our liveliness in the womb. Finally, other people and laws recognise us step by step as unborn offspring, family members, relatives, dependents, rational agents, competent decision makers, citizens, and members of moral communities.

The associated ideas of increasing worth and wrong-making features can be theoretically backed up by at least three lines of thinking. The first of these refers to social perceptions and other people's attitudes and commitments; the second makes an appeal to emerging potential and its connection to future possibilities; and the third distinguishes between the kinds of harm that can befall beings at their different stages of development.

Gradual additions to the perceived value of embryonic and fetal life can be explained, in the first model, by biological changes combined with the evolution of family and community responses to new individuals. Birth, for instance, may mark no significant difference in the human being itself, but it is a process by which a fetus becomes a baby and the unborn human being turns into a member of society. Intuitive notions like this support the gradualist view on the factual level: people often do, as a matter of fact, value their fellow beings more when they can feel them, name them, see them, and communicate with them. It is not clear, however, that this phenomenon can lend any support to gradualism as a moral doctrine in the present context. If we want to respect humanity in itself, as Holm and others do,[76] we cannot allow people's attitudes and commitments

---

[75] Holm 2003a, p. 381.

[76] See, e.g. Holm's views expressed during the *Examination of Witnesses (Questions 805–819) before the Joint Committee of the Human Tissue and Embryos (draft) Bill*, 2007, 26 June – www.publications.parliament.uk/pa/jt200607/jtselect/jtembryos/169/7062608. htm; and more generally, e.g. Kathryn Ehrich, Bobbie Farsides, Clare Williams, and Rosamund Scott, 2007, 'Testing the embryo, testing the fetus', *Clinical Ethics* 2: 181–6.

to influence our right to life – that right must be based on our essential inborn features rather than on contingent facts depending on our prominence and popularity.

Holm himself prefers the second model, in which potential instead of social perceptions gives the developing human being its moral status. His argument takes the following form: 'X is a biological entity with poten- tial for personhood. ... The core harm in killing (i.e. the depriving of a life-like-ours) is involved in any killing of an entity with potential for per- sonhood. ... This harm is of sufficient magnitude to ground a *prima facie* right to life. *Therefore* ... X has a *prima facie* right to life.'[77] Substituting 'embryo' for 'X' in this inference, he then goes on to state that only serious moral reasons can justify destructive research on early human beings.[78] The question mark in this model, seen from more restrictive points of view, is the reduced value that potential is allowed to assign to embryos as opposed to fetuses, children, and adults. The future 'life like ours' is the same in all cases, and unless probabilities are given a crucial role,[79] it seems inexplicable (seen from the sanctity angle) that conception does not give human beings *full* protection against its deprivation. In the other extreme, defenders of embryo research are prone to find Holm's version of the gradualist view as unconvincing as all other appeals to potential rather than actual personhood.

In a parliamentary hearing on the status of human embryos, Holm seems to have hinted at the third model, which acknowledges that differ- ent beings can be exposed to different harms according to their level of development. As he explains his gradualism, 'There are things that can harm a late foetus that cannot harm an embryo; late foetuses, in my view, have more moral status and at some point before birth they essentially get the same moral status as we have'.[80] He then comments on the abil- ity of embryos and fetuses to be harmed by pain: 'I think that sentience matters simply because there are specific kinds of harms that are linked to sentience. Unless you can feel pain I cannot cause you pain in the pro- cedures I do on you; I do not have to consider whether they cause you pain or not'. [81] Advocates of the 'personhood' view are happy to adopt this strat- egy and argue that rights can indeed be accumulated gradually: sentient beings have a right to avoid intentionally inflicted pain (because they can feel it); persons have a right not to be killed (because they are aware of their lives and want to continue them); and autonomous persons have a right

---

[77] Holm, 1996, p. 216.   [78] Holm, 2003a, p. 376.
[79] This does not seem to be Holm's preferred solution – see, e.g. Holm, 1996, pp. 200–1.
[80] *Examination of Witnesses*, 2007.   [81] *Examination of Witnesses*, 2007.

to make their own choices (because their ability to do so would otherwise be overlooked). Holm disagrees with this extension and stipulates that losing one's life can harm embryos as well as more mature human beings. This associates him with Marquis in the belief that intrinsic value is an impersonal quality, not necessarily felt by the individual having it. It also opens his thinking, again, to the 'sanctity' challenge. If loss of life harms embryos, why is this loss not sufficient to grant them *absolute* protection?

7.10   Embryonic rationalities

The question of human embryonic stem cell research has two distinct ethical dimensions: the treatment of women as egg providers and the moral status of research embryos. Both issues can be approached from different angles, relying on competing rationalities. I will first summarise the status alternatives and then outline the treatment options.

The three main views on the moral status of embryos follow, by and large, the three rationalities sketched in Chapter 2. Sanctity of life is a traditional concept, much like the notions of 'dignity' and 'giftedness' used by Leon Kass and Michael Sandel; personhood is at the core of the model advocated by Jonathan Glover and John Harris; and gradualism is compatible with the idea, championed by Ronald Green and Jürgen Habermas, that moral boundaries should be seen as matters of practical negotiation rather than theoretical definition. The connection may not be immediately visible, because the doctrines of sanctity, personhood, and gradual development seem to be focused on one commensurable entity, namely the intrinsic value of human life, whereas the three rationalities lean into three separate directions: opaque moral transcendence, transparent material outcomes, and joint decision making. On the surface the impression is true, but the justifications given to the ideas concerning life's value reveal links to the background theories on what is rational and reasonable. The sanctity view cannot shed its traditional basis in religion, because there is no other obvious way to make sense of the existence of moral 'humanhood' in the fertilised egg. The personhood view is at the core of maximising the good as experienced by individuals. And the gradualist view steers clear of the extremes as defined by the other views and stresses the importance of taking varied biological (and possibly social) factors into account in ethical decisions and political choices.

In the consideration of women as egg providers, the main questions concern the utility, fairness, and decency of ova retrieval and sales. Proponents of the practices argue mainly along the lines of the 'rational tangibility' view defended by Harris. According to him, human embryonic stem cell research must be pursued, because it is the best way to invent new therapies for otherwise incurable diseases. The risks of egg harvesting do not present insurmountable obstacles as long as everybody's duty to participate in research is recognised and the providers are adequately compensated and not coerced. Opponents of the practices, in their turn, eventually assume the 'moral transcendence' view, with appeals to justice and solidarity. It would, they argue, be unfair to expose women to risks which will not be taken by men; and vulnerable women would be exploited by making them financial offers that they cannot reasonably refuse.

A middle view can be constructed by combining all these concerns and weighing them conveniently. If some types of human embryonic stem cell research can be identified as more useful than others, if the risks to women of ova harvesting can be reduced, and if eggs are donated or sold voluntarily by fully informed and competent women in adequately just societies, then their treatment need not be an obstacle to these particular types of experimentation (although the moral status of embryos might, if their destruction is a part of the procedure).

An important remaining question concerns the estimated risks and benefits of stem cell research. Proponents claim that the risks are negligible and the benefits huge; opponents maintain that the reverse is the case; and defenders of the middle view see some truth in both accounts but insist on a case-by-case assessment. Ideological as well as factual elements feature in these judgements, and it is not clear how they could be appropriately weighed. This challenge will be studied further in Chapter 8.

8

Gene therapies, hopes, and fears

In this chapter, I examine how outcomes can be assessed in the context of genetic treatments. Factual background considerations and distinctions between somatic and germ-line interventions and therapies and enhancements are followed by an analysis of the elusiveness of objective calculations.

8.1   Trials and errors

Genes are the basic units of heredity. They guide the production of proteins, which perform most life functions in our bodies. When alterations in genes render proteins unable to perform their functions, genetic disorders can result. These disorders can be corrected by at least four methods. In the first, a normal gene is inserted into a nonspecific location within the genome to replace a nonfunctional gene. In the second, an abnormal gene is swapped for a normal one through homologous recombination, also known as DNA crossover. In the third, the irregular gene is repaired by selective reverse mutation, which restores normal functionality. In the fourth, the mechanism that turns the affected gene on and off is regulated for the desired result.

In most studies conducted so far, the first method has been used, that is, a normal gene has been inserted into a defective genome. A carrier molecule – a 'vector' – is needed in this endeavour to deliver the rectifying gene to the patient's cells. The vector has in most cases been a virus (adenoviruses and retroviruses being the commonest), although the direct insertion of DNA (or more rarely RNA) and liposomes as carriers have also been used.[1]

Between 1989 and 2009, a total of 1537 gene therapy clinical trials had been approved in 28 countries, most of them in the United States, and

---

[1] *Journal of Gene Medicine*, 2009 [updated March], 'Gene Therapy Clinical Trials Worldwide' – www.wiley.co.uk/genetherapy/clinical/.

the majority are designed to address cancer diseases, with cardiovascular, monogenic, and infectious diseases also prominently represented. Most of these trials are in their earlier stages, with 60% at phase I and 96% at phases I and II, and healthy volunteers have been tested in 2.3% of the projects.[2] In 2003, a Chinese product for neck and head cancer, Gendicine, became the first commercially licensed gene therapy product worldwide.[3] Experiments to find other uses for the product continue despite irregularities in the Chinese drug licensing agency, which have cast doubts over the firmness of research governance in that country.[4] Issues in research ethics have also been encountered in the development of gene therapies in the United States and France: for example, in the Jesse Gelsinger case in 1999 and then, since 2002, in the case of the 'bubble boy syndrome'.

Jesse Gelsinger had ornithine transcarbamylase deficiency (OTCD), a genetic liver disease that causes ammonia to accumulate in the blood. The disease is fatal in many cases; Gelsinger's condition, however, was mild enough to be controlled by a low-protein diet and medication. In 1999, when he was 18 years old, Gelsinger volunteered to take part in a phase I gene transfer experiment at the University of Pennsylvania. He knew that participation would have no therapeutic benefits for himself but he believed that the results would be helpful to future children with OTCD. Genes were infused into his body by using an adenovirus vector. Four days later Gelsinger died, probably from a reaction to the virus.[5]

The subsequent enquiry into the incident revealed several possible inadequacies: Gelsinger may not have been eligible for the trial in the first place because of his ammonia levels; and the vector that was used in the experiment had caused problems in humans and death in monkeys in preliminary studies. In the debate and lawsuit that followed, Gelsinger's father claimed that these factors had not been disclosed when the youth's consent was acquired.[6] The case was eventually settled out of court and

[2] *Journal of Gene Medicine*, 2009.
[3] E.g. Sue Pearson, Hepeng Jia, and Keiko Kandachi, 2004, 'China approves first gene therapy', *Nature Biotechnology* 22: 3–4; James M. Wilson, 2005, 'Gendicine: The first commercial gene therapy product', *Human Gene Therapy* 16: 1014; Zhaohui Peng, 2005, 'Current status of Gendicine in China: Recombinant human ad-p53 agent for treatment of cancers', *Human Gene Therapy* 16: 1016–27.
[4] Sarah E. Frew, Stephen M. Sammut, Alysha F. Shore, Joshua K. Ramjist, Sara Al-Bader, Rahim Rezaie, Abdallah S. Daar, and Peter A. Singer, 2008, 'Chinese health biotech and the billion-patient market', *Nature Biotechnology* 26: 37–53.
[5] See, e.g. Lynn Smith and Jacqueline Fowler Byers, 2002, 'Gene therapy in the post-Gelsinger era', *JONA's Healthcare Law, Ethics, & Regulation* 4: 104–10.
[6] *Gelsinger* v. *Trustees of the University of Pennsylvania*, 2000 – www.sskrplaw.com/links/healthcare2.html.

the university denied any serious wrongdoing, but clearly the informed consent procedure for the trial could have been more complete.

X-linked severe combined immunodeficiency (X-SCID) is a life-threatening condition caused by a genetic mutation and characterised by a lack of sufficient humoral and cellular immunity. Also called the 'bubble boy syndrome', it affects only males and usually leads to death within the first year of life in the absence of proper treatment. Bone marrow transplantation from a compatible donor works as a treatment, and this provides a solution in the one in three cases where a suitable donor can be found. To find a cure for the remaining sufferers, in 1998 researchers in France initiated a series of X-SCID trials, in which corrected genes originally extracted from the patients were inserted in their blood stem cells using a vector derived from a leukaemia virus.

The therapeutic results of the French trials and of those conducted in other countries were good: the gene therapy did indeed restore the immune system in boys who received the treatment. However, four of the 11 experimental patients in France and at least one of the 14 patients treated in the United Kingdom developed leukaemia as a direct result of the therapy.[7] The first three cases, which occurred in 2002, 2003, and 2005, caused concerns and led to caution and temporary bans of the therapy in France and in the United States; in the United Kingdom, researchers at the Institute of Child Health continued their work until 2007, when they reported their first case of leukaemia. The therapy is still considered promising, as X-SCID is otherwise untreatable and fatal in two patients out of three whereas leukaemia is statistically treatable in four patients out of five (three of the French boys are in remission, and one is dead). But the treatment is dangerous and gives an indication of the problems that can occur with gene therapies.

The known difficulties of these novel treatments are many and varied. Therapeutic DNA does not always 'stick', cells divide rapidly, the effects wear off, and new rounds of treatment are needed. Immune responses are tricky to control, as they need to be 'turned off' for the treatment. The use of viral vectors is associated with problems of toxicity, inflammation, and undesirable immune responses. And polygenic conditions, such as heart disease, blood pressure, and diabetes, are hard to treat because the interplay of several factors, not just one genetic mutation, has to be taken into account.

---

[7] UCL Institute of Child Health, 2007, 'Gene therapy for X-SCID; additional briefing', 18 December – www.ich.ucl.ac.uk/pressoffice/pressrelease_00592.

However, gene therapies can still have a bright future. Although they have only been studied since 1989 and only a fraction of all approved clinical trials have been in this area, some results are already promising. Most trials are in their early phases, but as they proceed further, rapid breakthroughs could be possible. These hopes, combined with the knowledge that some diseases can probably *only* be conquered in the foreseeable future by gene treatments, support the development of this branch of research, obstacles notwithstanding.

With the issues of research ethics having been properly addressed, gene therapy in its most innocuous forms seems, of late, to have become widely accepted. In the early days of the trials, people had had fears about meddling with the work of God or Nature, and many had questioned the sanity of allocating considerable resources to experiments that would not benefit the great majority for decades, if ever.[8] Now that some of the experimental treatments are actually working, therapeutic gene alterations to ailing individuals have become more popular.[9] The objections now concern genetic mutations that will be inherited by future generations; improvements that are designed to make people better than they otherwise could have been; and the way in which we should think about the consequences of new technologies. I will first consider, in Section 8.2, the nature of somatic and germ-line gene treatments; then, in Section 8.3, the distinction between therapies and enhancements; and then, in the remaining sections of this chapter, the consequence-related questions of how to construe benefits and harms (Section 8.4), how to define values (Section 8.5), how to perceive technological change (Section 8.6), how to understand human agency in technology (Section 8.7), and how to make decisions in situations of uncertainty (Section 8.8).

8.2   Somatic and germ-line interventions

So far the trials approved for humans have all been attempts to develop *somatic* gene therapies. This means that the cells targeted in the experiments have *not* been gametes or tissue involved in gamete production. In rare cases, therapeutically mutated genes have travelled to reproductive regions, but only unintentionally. In this type of medicine, the point is to

---

[8] I have examined some of these early worries in Matti Häyry, 1994a, 'Categorical objections to genetic engineering – A critique', Anthony Dyson and John Harris (eds), *Ethics and Biotechnology* (London: Routledge): 202–15.

[9] For an overview of the current legal regulations on gene therapies and their development, see Genetherapynet, 'Gene therapy clinical trials regulatory affairs and legislation' – www.genetherapynet.com/legislation.html.

provide a cure for a genetic disorder without interfering with the genetic makeup of the affected individual's offspring.

The idea of *germ-line* gene therapies, which have been tried only on animals, would be to make the genetic alteration hereditary so that it would, other things being equal, be passed on to future generations. The obvious logic of this would be to make people permanently better in the treated family line and remove the need for repeated procedures in all new individuals born into it. At the same time, of course, questions concerning the safety and efficacy of the therapies would be multiplied.

Authors like John Harris, Jonathan Glover, and Ronald Green do not have any absolute objections to either type of gene therapy. Since saving lives and restoring health are among the most important values, therapeutic somatic-cell interventions are automatically endorsed, given only that they are reasonably safe. And since therapeutic germ-line interventions are aimed at promoting the same values, similar considerations apply to them; fortified by a parental duty to provide the best possible life for one's children. This duty is arguably all the more straightforward in the present context, because selection is not involved, so giving a better life to some individuals does not entail denying life to others. Talking about future generations, Harris states that our 'obligations concerning their genetic inheritance … are part of our general obligation not to harm those who come after us'.[10] Harris sees disabling genetic disorders that we could have prevented but did not as negatively inflicted harms, and he argues that allowing such harms due to unwarranted precaution or lack of consent would be immoral.[11] Glover is slightly more cautious. He concurs with the idea that genetic disadvantages can be seen as instances of injustice, and notes that we 'owe to our children other forms of medical treatment that they need, and gene therapy … is not different in principle'.[12] He qualifies this, however, by conceding that disease and disability are not the only harms and that they should be weighed against other considerations, which include issues of the child's identity if it already has one, financial burden to the family, and risk to the mother in case of fetal surgery.[13] He also considers some general 'hubris' caveats against interfering with the genome of our

---

[10] John Harris, 2007, *Enhancing Evolution: The Ethical Case for Making Better People* (Princeton, NJ: Princeton University Press), p. 79.

[11] Harris, 2007, p. 80 – on unwarranted precaution, see pp. 34–5; on lack of consent, see pp. 81–5.

[12] Jonathan Glover, 2006, *Choosing Children: Genes, Disability, and Design* (Oxford: Clarendon Press), p. 61.

[13] Glover, 2006, pp. 61–2.

offspring, including unexpected risks of harm, past failures in projects to manage human destinies, and possible violations of our children's right to self-creation, but does not find unequivocal support for prohibitions in them.[14] Green agrees with the normative conclusion reached by Harris and Glover, although he admits that fears 'about germline gene therapy are easy to understand', since, as he writes, 'if a clinician makes a mistake in germ-line gene therapy, the clinician has created a new genetic disease that could be passed on from generation to generation, affecting uncounted numbers of people'.[15] The common tone with Harris and Glover is still found – in that all three authors conceptualise the ethical questions of germ-line gene therapies purely in terms of harms and their prevention.

Jürgen Habermas, Michael Sandel, and Leon Kass disagree with this approach and claim, on varied grounds, that while curing diseases in existing individuals by safe somatic-cell interventions can perhaps be accepted, germ-line gene therapies are another matter entirely. Permanent changes in family lines can reduce future illness, but they can also infringe rights, violate autonomy, and increase eugenic pressures. Habermas starts by recognising the initial acceptability of therapeutic gene interventions for existing individuals: 'As long as medical intervention is guided by the clinical goal of healing a disease or of making provisions for a healthy life, the person carrying out the treatment may assume that he has the consent of the patient preventively treated'.[16] But he then goes on to state that for future people the situation is different, because we cannot know what would be of value to them: 'Not even the highly general good of bodily health maintains one and the same value within the contexts of different life histories.'[17] The uncertainty, according to Habermas, compels us to forgo germ-line changes, even for therapeutic purposes. Sandel begins in a similar manner by noting that parents do have an obligation to heal their sick children and also to care for the health of their offspring more generally.[18] As he writes: 'In caring for the health of their children, parents do not cast themselves as designers or convert their children into products of their will or instruments of their ambition.'[19] The modification

---

[14] Glover, 2006, pp. 63–4, 68–72.
[15] Ronald M. Green, 2007, *Babies by Design: The Ethics of Genetic Choice* (New Haven, CT: Yale University Press), p. 57.
[16] Jürgen Habermas, 2003, *The Future of Human Nature*, translated by William Rehg, Max Pensky, and Hella Beister (Cambridge: Polity Press), pp. 51–2.
[17] Habermas, 2003, p. 86.
[18] Michael J. Sandel, 2007, *The Case Against Perfection: Ethics in the Age of Genetic Engineering* (Cambridge, MA: The Belknap Press of Harvard University Press), pp. 47–8.
[19] Sandel, 2007, p. 49.

of future individuals can, however, present problems. In Sandel's view, even beneficial 'eugenic parenting is objectionable because it expresses and entrenches … a stance of mastery and domination that fails to appreciate the gifted character of human powers and achievements'.[20] Kass, like Habermas and Sandel, sees the attractions of health promotion through genetic engineering. But he finds that the idea of changing human nature is at odds with human dignity, and argues that the distinction between somatic and germ-line therapies is untenable, concluding that all, not just some, forms of gene therapy should be regarded with suspicion.[21]

8.3   Therapies and enhancements

Distinctions like the one between somatic and germ-line interventions are used as parts of argumentation, and people holding competing views employ them in different ways. Legislators and regulators are fond of demarcation lines of this kind, because drawing them allows the inclusion of considerations from many ideological camps and creates an impression of firm yet sensitive governance of troubling issues. Scholars who defend normative 'middle' positions often also like delineations for their promise to help in the formulation of balanced and reasonable positions. Advocates of more clear-cut solutions tend to see such boundaries as blurred and use this perception as an element of their own ethical case. Harris and Kass, for instance, agree that somatic and germ-line therapies are, from the moral point of view, essentially similar. Harris continues the argument by saying that since the former is acceptable, the latter must also be accepted. Kass counters that since the latter is unacceptable, the former must also be rejected.

The distinction between therapy and enhancement is, at first glance, conceptually clear. Therapies cure diseases, alleviate ailments, and help people back to normal health and ability; enhancements are designed to improve individuals beyond their normal physical expectations. However, a closer look reveals cracks in the wall when it comes to the normative power of the divide. As noted by Green, almost 'no one is naturally immune to smallpox, polio, measles, whooping cough, or any of the other diseases that we vaccinate against', which means that vaccinations

[20] Sandel, 2007, p. 83. Sandel is slightly opaque concerning the distinction between somatic and germ-line therapies, as his own emphasis is on differentiating between therapies and enhancements.

[21] Leon R. Kass, 2002, *Life, Liberty, and the Defense of Dignity: The Challenge for Bioethics* (San Francisco, CA: Encounter Books), pp. 121–3, 130 ff.

'make us superhumans, but no one ridicules enhancements of this sort'.[22] And even if we move beyond 'forestalling disease or disability [to] pure enhancements [that] aim at gratifying the wishes of normal and healthy people for improved performance or superior capabilities',[23] it is not clear that people would like to stop or ban using what medicine has to offer. If we had the means to safely increase the height, strength, or attractiveness of our children, knowing that this would make their lot easier, why would we draw a line that would preclude us from doing so?[24]

Kass agrees with this analysis as a description of how things will develop in our current societies unless we put the brakes on by assuming a more watchful attitude towards *all* genetic advances, including thera-peutic interventions.[25] Referring to the difference between genetic and other technologies, which he sees as self-evident, he observes a 'sense that we are powerless to establish, on the basis of that difference, clear limits to [the] use' of new techniques, and envisages that the 'genetic genie, first unbottled to treat disease, will go its own way, whether we like it or not'.[26]

Harris, in his turn, welcomes the development, and so does Glover. Criticising the view that therapy brings people back to normal human performance and enhancement removes them from it, Harris points out that it is conceptually 'always true that restoring species-typical function-ing is enhancing for the individual concerned' and that therefore most 'of what passes for therapy is an enhancement for the individual relative to her [prior] state'.[27] Normalcy and distinctions based on it are not, then, for Harris the crux of the matter. Instead, he writes, 'the overwhelming moral imperative for both therapy and treatment is to prevent harm and confer benefit', and the 'remaining questions concern the detail of how to calculate where that balance lies in any particular case'.[28] Glover agrees with this conclusion, because, he argues, 'the case for reducing the inci-dence of disorders and disabilities is that they are obstacles to people hav-ing flourishing lives', which makes these good practices similar to 'other choices, including genetic ones, to remove non-medical impediments to flourishing'.[29]

Habermas and Sandel, unlike the others, believe in the distinction, especially in the context of parental choices. In a passage already quoted above (in Section 8.2), Habermas states that parents can feasibly assume their children's consent to procedures that aim at healing diseases or

---

[22] Green, 2007, p. 60.   [23] Green, 2007, p. 61.
[24] Green, 2007, pp. 62–73.   [25] Kass, 2002, p. 123.
[26] Kass, 2002, p. 124.   [27] Harris, 2007, p. 44.
[28] Harris, 2007, p. 58.   [29] Glover, 2006, p. 75.

otherwise promoting health.[30] But they most definitely cannot assume their descendants' consent to deliberate attempts to change their biological nature in ways that are not anchored in the idea of health. The value of enhancements does not necessarily outweigh the value of being 'naturally grown' and not 'made', and this is why we should resist them in the name of the autonomy of our offspring.[31] Sandel agrees that the subtle moral differences between curing diseases, using medical or educational means to enhance human features, and determining children's qualities must be recognised.[32] He disagrees with Habermas on the proper reason for this, though, since he does not believe that the autonomy of future people is the key to the issue.[33] According to Sandel, a permission to enhance children would quickly turn into a norm and an obligation to do so; this would make parents individually responsible for their own offspring; and social solidarity would gradually be corrupted.[34] For both Habermas and Sandel, the important thing is to safeguard the 'grown' or 'gifted' core of human beings (at least when it is not overtaken by serious pathological conditions).

8.4   Construing benefits and harms

The ideas of giftedness and design have been addressed in the previous chapters, and I will not return to them here. Instead, I will concentrate on what Harris dubs the '*detail* of how to calculate where the balance [of harm and benefit] lies in any particular case'.[35] I will suggest that a careful examination of this 'detail' does not necessarily lead to the effortless calculation of outcomes that Harris suggests, but rather to speculative and ideological considerations that can sway people's normative judgements more easily than any descriptive facts.[36]

What kinds of consequences could the development of gene therapies have, if left unrestricted? At least one person – Jesse Gelsinger – has died so far as a result of trials in the field. A little over ten people – the experimental 'bubble boys' – have been cured by gene therapy. After these

---

[30] Habermas, 2003, pp. 51–2; cf., however, p. 86 (esp. the passage also quoted in Section 8.2).

[31] Habermas, 2003, p. 42.   [32] Sandel, 2007, pp. 8–10, 51–2.   [33] Sandel, 2007, p. 82.

[34] Sandel, 2007, pp. 51–2, 78, 87, 91.   [35] Harris, 2007, p. 58 (italics added).

[36] I have studied this theme before in Matti Häyry and Heta Häyry, 1998, 'Genetic engineering', Ruth Chadwick (ed.), *Encyclopedia of Applied Ethics*, Volume II (San Diego, CA: Academic Press): 407–17; Matti Häyry, 2007a, 'Utilitarianism and bioethics', Richard E. Ashcroft, Angus Dawson, Heather Draper, and John R. McMillan (eds), *Principles of Health Care Ethics*, second edition (Chichester: John Wiley & Sons): 57–64.

figures, everything else is conjecture. Have genetic research centres spent an amount of money which could have fed a million people in poverty-stricken countries for the past 20 years? Not impossible. Will the research produce knowledge that will make cancer routinely treatable within the next few decades? Not impossible. Will the concentration on high-tech biomedicine effect changes in individual morality and social solidarity? Not impossible. Due to all the uncertainties, the way in which outcomes are *construed* and *weighed* becomes, at this point, all-important.

A science-enthusiastic view would stress the partial current achievements and enormous future prospects. Even experimental treatments can help volunteers whose consent justifies possible drawbacks. The question of alternative costs is a fair one, but gene therapies make, so the argument goes, the world permanently better, while feeding the hungry by conventional means is an endless task. A commitment to bioscientific research will solve food problems as well as medical problems, if only scientific advances are given the priority that they deserve. In the meantime, some people will die of poverty and hunger and this is regrettable, but when the possible advantages are close to infinite, limited disadvantages become insignificant in cost–benefit calculations. Whatever is subtracted from the immeasurable, the result remains immeasurable.

A science-friendly view could stop short of claiming that answers to all humanity's problems will be found in scientific research but still hold that the prospects are reasonably encouraging. If actual choices need to be made between gene therapies and humanitarian aid, people's acute distress should be taken fully into account, but it should not be forgotten that the agony of individuals dying of hereditary diseases is as real as anybody else's. The scarce resources at our disposal should be dispensed sensibly, with proper attention to all kinds of need around us.

A science-sceptical view would emphasise known immediate harms, unknown future disasters, questionable control arrangements, disproportionate expenses, and the profound uncertainty of any large-scale gains. People have died or contracted leukaemia as study subjects of poorly designed or recklessly executed genetic projects. If similar research endeavours are ever extended to, say, germ-line interventions, considerable damage can be done to generations to come. Ethical governance mechanisms have not, arguably, been in place so far, and consent has been obtained in the light of inadequate information or under pressure to find a cure. There are no guarantees that the situation would be different in the future. Since the financial costs are high and much of the research publicly funded, genetic research drains resources that could be used in combating more mundane problems, especially in the developing countries. And since the long-term benefits are more likely than not vastly exaggerated, all this is probably done to no avail.

A science-hostile view could go further and note that the development of gene therapies can lead to total disaster. Once somatic cures have been accepted, germ-line endeavours will follow, since there is no stopping the technological train once it has left the station. Meddling with the forces of nature can then lead either to physical catastrophes or to moral and social ruin. Minor short-term benefits cannot justify the risk, however small, of disrupting the world order so profoundly that it would spell the end of humanity as we now know it.

The question, then, is which view should guide us in the outcome assessment of genetic advances?

8.5   Defining values

Textbook accounts of consequentialism pay little or no heed to ideological differences. According to them, the action alternative that produces more net good than any other action alternative is the best and should be chosen. Definitions of the good can vary, but the assumption is that all significant outcomes of our decisions and deeds can be compared and reckoned in a neutral and objective manner. Personal opinions should not be allowed to bias the conclusions; nor should traditional moral systems be given an undue role in the calculations.[37] This purified view of outcome assessment has, however, its problems.

One of these problems is the eventual arbitrariness of the values evoked. The traditional utilitarian view, introduced by Jeremy Bentham, was that all actions and policies should be evaluated solely in terms of the pleasures and pains they cause. The only relevant factors for him were quantitative: the intensity and duration of the sensation, its certainty or uncertainty, its propinquity or remoteness, its fecundity (tendency to produce further sensations of the same kind) and purity (aptitude not to produce further sensations of the opposite kind), and the number of individuals experiencing it.[38] More contemporary one-value axiologies have, in a similar fashion, singled out

---

[37] On my views on consequentialism, see, e.g. Matti Häyry, 1994b, *Liberal Utilitarianism and Applied Ethics* (London: Routledge); Häyry, 2007a.

[38] Jeremy Bentham, 1982, *An Introduction to the Principles of Morals and Legislation* [1789], edited by J. H. Burns and H. L. A. Hart (London: Methuen), p. 38.

desires,[39] interests,[40] preferences,[41] wellbeing,[42] and needs.[43] But even within these monistic theories, there is always a temptation to say that some good things are, in and of themselves, better than the rest. John Stuart Mill famously argued against Bentham that certain 'higher' pleasures should in the utilitarian calculus count for more than others. As he wrote, 'Of two pleasures, if there be one to which all or almost all who have experience of both give a decided preference, irrespective of any feeling of moral obligation to prefer it, that is the more desirable pleasure.'[44] Similar qualifications have been added to all major utilitarian creeds, and consequently either the entities that *really* count in the listed doctrines have been reduced to *rational* desires,[45] *conscious* interests,[46] *nonfanatical* preferences,[47] and *basic* needs;[48] or legitimate trade-offs between elements of wellbeing have been left ultimately undefined.[49] The difficulty here is that much of the normative burden is in the refined theories placed on the often capricious divisions into higher and lower, rational and irrational, conscious and unconscious, nonfanatical and fanatical, or basic and nonbasic. The idea is that 'better' goods should somehow objectively be given more weight in moral assessments; yet the boundaries seem to bend to accommodate the pretheoretical moral intuitions of the philosophers advocating them. An example of this in bioethical discussion is the ranking of lives proposed by Glover and Harris into 'more', 'less', or 'not' worth living.[50]

Another problem is presented by competing ideas of value. The qualifications are introduced into the initially concrete and no-nonsense accounts of 'the good' to ward off decisions that would appear shallow, stupid, or unjust. If simple pleasure is all that counts, would we be content to live our remaining lives in an experience machine that would keep us inanely satisfied?[51] If all desires or preferences are equally

---

[39] Richard B. Brandt, 1979, *A Theory of the Good and the Right* (Oxford: Clarendon Press).

[40] Peter Singer, 1979, *Practical Ethics* (Cambridge: Cambridge University Press).

[41] Richard M. Hare, 1981, *Moral Thinking: Its Levels, Method and Point* (Oxford: Clarendon Press).

[42] James Griffin, 1986, *Well-Being: Its Meaning, Measurement, and Moral Importance* (Oxford: Clarendon Press).

[43] Häyry, 1994b.

[44] John Stuart Mill, 1987, *Utilitarianism* [1861], Jeremy Bentham and John Stuart Mill, *Utilitarianism and Other Essays*, edited by Alan Ryan (Harmondsworth: Penguin Books), p. 279.

[45] Brandt, 1979.   [46] Singer, 1979.   [47] Hare, 1981.   [48] Häyry, 1994b.

[49] James Griffin, 2008, *On Human Rights* (Oxford: Oxford University Press).

[50] See Sections 2.2 and 2.5.

[51] Robert Nozick, 1974, *Anarchy, State, and Utopia* (Oxford: Blackwell), pp. 42–5.

valuable, should we bow to a fanatic's desire or preference to make others suffer?[52] And if all interests and needs are the same, then how many people must have an urge to see a public execution to authorise the killing of an innocent person?[53] Trade-offs like these, and their intuitive clashes with common sense and decency, give rise to attempts to invent a more sensitive and sensible axiology. But once this route is taken, it is difficult to confine acceptable values solely to the realm of physical and psychological satisfaction, qualified as they may be. Already before Bentham, David Hartley suggested that our motives and reasons for action comprise pleasures and pains not only of self-interest but also of imagination, ambition, sympathy, theopathy, and the moral sense.[54] Hartley believed that these converge on sympathy, which will or should then be taken as our first guide to morality. Be that as it may, the point here is that aesthetic, entrepreneurial, theological, and ethical considerations can have a valid claim to our attention when we reckon the consequences of our actions. If some people say – like Habermas, Kass, and Sandel do – that the demise of humanity as we know it is a bad thing, their comments cannot necessarily be shrugged off just by asserting that humanity as such can have no value beyond the wellbeing of present and future individuals.

Since these difficulties are well known, some scholars have returned, more or less completely, to Bentham's original model.[55] The questions that can be put to these hedonistic utilitarians, and their answers to them, include the following. If they are asked, 'What should be done when our moral convictions conflict with the result of the pleasure–pain calculation?', they can reply that we should still act according to the calculus and admit that our convictions have in this case failed us. If they are asked, 'Is it possible to count all the pleasures and pains that our actions will, directly and indirectly, cause to all sentient beings from here to eternity?', they can admit that this cannot be done but point out that utility calculations are meant to be a criterion of morality, not a guide for action. In everyday decision making, rules of thumb can guide us, but the truth remains that *the* best choice in any situation is

[52] Häyry, 1994b, pp. 88–92.   [53] Häyry, 1994b, pp. 79–82.

[54] David Hartley, 1834, *Observations on Man, His Frame, His Duty and His Expectations* [1749], sixth edition (London: Thomas Tegg and Son), p. 261.

[55] E.g. J. J. C. Smart, 1973, 'An outline of a system of utilitarian ethics' [1961], J. J. C. Smart and Bernard Williams (eds), *Utilitarianism: For and Against* (Cambridge: Cambridge University Press); Torbjörn Tännsjö, 1998, *Hedonistic Utilitarianism* (Edinburgh: Edinburgh University Press).

the one with the best consequences overall.[56] These responses are, by and large, more acceptable to proponents of consequentialism than to its opponents.

When values are defined for outcome assessments, three main alternatives seem to emerge. Some prefer simple and concrete values and disregard the feelings of indignation or injustice that using them can cause. Others refine these simple and concrete values by qualitative distinctions to ward off intuitive criticisms, confident that these distinctions will be recognised by all who count in moral discourse. And yet others argue that more complex and immaterial spiritual or moral values should be taken into consideration. The more tangible the values advocated are, the friendlier the attitudes towards science in general and gene therapies in particular seem to be. But this is not the only dividing factor. Enthusiasm and hostility here also require specific views on the historical role of technological change (Section 8.6); the power of humankind to steer the change (Section 8.7); and the proper approach to risk-taking in this context (Section 8.8).

8.6   Technological optimism and pessimism

Technological change, including developments in medical and genetic treatments, can be seen to promote good human life – or to hinder it. Advocates of Enlightenment thinking have since the seventeenth century maintained that progress in culture, economy, science, and technology are constantly improving humanity, and that there is no end in sight for this trend. Many champions of Romanticism, on the other hand, have contradicted this and claimed that science and technology inevitably lead to misery and disaster by alienating people from their true nature, their community ties, and their traditional ways.[57] These conflicting views can be called 'technological optimism' and 'technological pessimism'.[58]

Enlightenment philosophers held that as secular reason and individual freedom triumph over religious prejudice and traditional constraint, humanity will be gradually enhanced. People will become mentally, morally, and even physically healthier; and societies will become more efficient and just. The development was seen by many as inevitable: it was thought that economic progress or ideological change force the world

[56] Cf. Häyry, 2007a, p. 58.
[57] Matti Häyry, 2008, 'The historical idea of a better race', *Studies in Ethics, Law, and Technology* 2, Article 11 – www.bepress.com/selt/vol2/iss1/art11, pp. 9–13.
[58] Häyry and Häyry, 1998, pp. 409–10.

to change almost without conscious human agency and intervention. Adam Smith is well known for his portrayal of the economic variant of this type of thinking in *The Wealth of Nations*;[59] and in France, Antoine de Condorcet presented a more ideological version in his *Sketch for a Historical Picture of the Progress of the Human Mind*.[60] Similar ideas were exercised in Germany by Georg Wilhelm Friedrich Hegel, who argued that intellectual processes are at the core of inescapable change.[61]

When people start to believe that freedom of thought and freedom of economic transactions lead to increased happiness and justice, the speculative descriptions of Enlightenment philosophers can gain considerable normative momentum. Those who promote the right kinds of transformation can be seen as good, progressive citizens, whereas those who oppose them are dubious reactionaries. In recent decades, these ideas have been employed in discussions on globalisation and freedom of research. Optimists believe that global markets and unrestricted scientific activities, including genetic advances, are the key to universal progress and wellbeing. Gene therapies are among the instruments of change towards a world with fewer diseases and better health for all. By stalling progress, their critics risk making themselves responsible for unnecessarily continued human suffering.

Philosophers of Romanticism did not believe in linear progress dictated by human reason. Instead, they emphasised the organic character of societies and communities and held that cultures have their natural life spans from birth through growth and maturity to old age and death. One of the first thinkers to introduce this idea was Johann Gottfried von Herder,[62] who compared nations to plants and maintained that, similarly to plants, the vital force of nations can be easily exhausted by a change of location. Like a tropical flower that does not flourish in the cold, a people born in one place cannot necessarily survive in another. Adjustment to new circumstances by the use of reason – the Enlightenment solution – does not, according to Herder and his fellow Romantics, work, because human beings live by emotion, feeling, will, and spirit more than by intellect

---

[59] Adam Smith, 1982, *The Wealth of Nations* [1776], edited by Andrew Skinner (Harmondsworth: Penguin Books).

[60] Marie-Jean-Antoine-Nicholas de Caritat, Marquis de Condorcet, 1955, *Sketch for a Historical Picture of the Progress of the Human Mind* [1795], translated by June Barraclough (New York, NY: Noonday Press).

[61] E.g. Georg Wilhelm Friedrich Hegel, 1857, *Philosophy of History*, translated from the third German edition by J. Sibree (London: Henry G. Bohn).

[62] Johan Gottfried von Herder, 1966, *Outlines of a Philosophy of the History of Man* [1784–1791], translated by T. Churchill (New York, NY: Bergman).

and calculation. The 'volkgeist' (national spirit) of a 'race' (a people) is a nonrational entity that steers the life of the collective largely despite the efforts of its members.

When this idea is applied to individuals, it can be easily used as a criticism of technological change. New techniques lead to new production methods and in many cases these incite people to move into industrial and urban areas. Reductions in population damage and eventually kill rural communities and spell the end of the traditions and customs by which their members lived. In cities, people wither away both morally and physically; and they become alienated and dependent on technology-driven goods and services, modern medicine among them. Since they are not, however, designed for this kind of living, gene therapies and other miracle cures do not remedy the situation, indeed, quite the contrary. Some pessimists say that genetic engineering will probably harm individuals by creating new diseases.[63] Others say that it will most certainly harm societies by encouraging injustice and by corroding solidarity in the ways depicted in such science-fiction classics as *The Time Machine* by H. G. Wells, *Brave New World* by Aldous Huxley, *The Handmaid's Tale* by Margaret Atwood, and the movie *Gattaca* directed by Andrew Niccol.[64]

8.7   Technological determinism and voluntarism

The belief that things are improving or deteriorating with time can be intensified by a conviction that this development is inevitable or inescapable. Those who hold this view can be said to subscribe to 'technological determinism' and those who deny it to 'technological voluntarism'.

Confidence in the predestination of favourable progress is obviously not a problem for those who believe in continual change towards perfection. Good things keep coming our way no matter what, so why worry? Faith in unstoppable decline is another matter: who would like to live without any hope of a better future? This is why determinism in critical comments is often linked with technological pessimism. On closer analysis, however, both ideas are equally perplexing when they are employed in attempts to guide human action. If the world develops in a pre-programmed way towards its destination regardless of what human beings do, we cannot, by definition,

[63] E.g. Walter Glannon, 2002a, 'Extending the human life span', *Journal of Medicine and Philosophy* 27: 339–54.
[64] H. G. Wells, 2005, *The Time Machine* [1895] (London: Penguin Books); Aldous Huxley, 1932, *Brave New World* (London: Chatto & Windus); Margaret Atwood, 1985, *The Handmaid's Tale* (Toronto: McClelland and Stewart); *Gattaca*, 1997 (Columbia Pictures).

do anything to alter this. This means that all ethical advice and regulation is useless – and to follow the logic to its natural conclusion, probably also dictated by the same inexorable forces of history as technological change.

To make sense of determinism, the creed must be given a more limited formulation. Moral guidance can be interpreted as saying that there is nothing human beings can do to halt the disastrous march of technology *if* a crucial boundary is crossed. The 'crucial boundary' can then be drawn between activities, for instance therapy and enhancement or somatic and germ-line treatments. This model recognises the usefulness of some advances in medical genetics but stops short of allowing everything in the name of health and wellbeing. Like the qualifications used in theories of value (Section 8.5), the doctrine sets a constraint for the assessment of consequences, arguing that all will be lost unless we refrain from certain activities, however profitable they may seem in material terms. I will continue on this theme in Section 8.8.

Voluntarists claim that people can always influence the course of history, maybe even beyond natural terminuses like the eventual demise of our solar system (humanity can move into other systems, they say). For pessimists, this is not particularly hope-inspiring, because people can make a mess of things as effectively as external circumstances could. But for optimists, the idea of progress steered by human efforts is attractive. In theory, all possible regulative options can be exercised within this umbrella notion. Good developments can be allowed and encouraged, like Glover and Harris would like to do; questionable but promising practices can be policed, like Green suggests; and sufficiently dangerous endeavours can be banned, like Habermas, Sandel, and Kass insist. In practice, however, opinions seem to be divided along the lines of friendliness and hostility to technological change. Glover, Harris, and Green clearly take the view that we can keep the train on the right track by our own efforts, whereas Habermas, Sandel, and Kass appear to lean towards the idea that only bad things can happen, and with a degree of unavoidability, if we overstep certain markers in our moral landscape.

8.8   Precaution, fear, and hope

Everyone in the ethics of technology agrees that practices which are dangerous must be at least monitored, probably also regulated, and possibly even prohibited. But how should we define 'danger' in this context? Some theorists are more apprehensive and others more relaxed in their characterisations.

Actions and choices are dangerous if we can reasonably expect and predict that they will inflict physical or mental harm on nonconsenting human beings. This view is at the core of most versions of utilitarianism and consequentialism; and it is compatible with many other ethical theories. But what if, instead of actual expectations and clear predictions, judgements are based on uneasiness and uncertainty? Champions of the so-called (and possibly misnamed) 'precautionary principle' believe that such judgements should also be recognised in ethical discussions on technological advances.[65]

The precautionary principle was originally formulated in the framework of environmental policy, but it has also been applied to medicine and genetics. When our actions could be harmful, but this harmfulness cannot be verified or falsified by scientific enquiry, the burden of proof is, according to the principle, on those who propose such actions. Until further research shows that the actions do *not* have the suspected ill effects, they should be disallowed.[66]

Opponents of the view have observed that most potentially beneficial activities could be prohibited by using this logic, given only that someone raises questions about the possible damage that they could cause. Almost all new developments in technology and policy are inherently unpredictable, because they have not been tried before. In the context of gene therapies, this is particularly true. We do not know for certain that somatic therapies will not affect the germ line, thereby making the impacts of interventions hereditary and (if the procedure is not reversed) permanent. Moreover, we do not know for certain that future generations will not be harmed by the changes in their genes. And since neither of these doubts can be scientifically disproved, no gene therapies should be permitted. But doing nothing leaves serious diseases uncured and allows removable human suffering to continue.

The idea of precaution seems to bear a likeness to the 'wager' argument for belief in the existence of God presented in the seventeenth century by Blaise Pascal.[67] Pascal argued that whether or not God actually exists, it is mathematically rational to commit oneself to the proposition that he

---

[65] The following account is mostly based on Matti Häyry, 2005b, 'Precaution and solidarity', *Cambridge Quarterly of Healthcare Ethics* 14: 199–206, pp. 199–202.

[66] The precautionary principle has many uses and interpretations in current literature on law and ethics. One of the earliest philosophical formulations can be found in Hans Jonas, 1984, *The Imperative of Responsibility: In Search of Ethics for the Technological Age* [1979], translated by Hans Jonas and David Herr (Chicago, IL: University of Chicago Press).

[67] Blaise Pascal, 1995, *Pensées and Other Writings*, translated by Honor Levi (Oxford: Oxford University Press), pp. 153–6. For a critique of the use of the 'wager' argument in gene

does. If God exists and we choose to believe it, our reward will be eternal bliss. If God exists and we deny it, our punishment will be eternal suffering. If God does not exist, belief makes us lose a few earthly pleasures that disbelief would allow us to have. As good gamblers we should see that however small the probabilities of the infinite gains and losses are, we should not let any finite considerations interfere with our choice. In a situation of uncertainty we must, according to Pascal, choose the commitment that has insignificant (finite) costs and potentially enormous (infinite) benefits. Put in negative terms, we must *not* choose the commitment that has insignificant benefits (a licence to sin) but potentially enormous costs (an eternity of torment).

Proponents of the precautionary principle seem to think along the lines of the negative formulation of Pascal's conclusion. In the absence of reliable knowledge, we should not develop gene therapies or other new techniques, lest we unleash dark forces that will bring us incalculable misery. It is worth noting that this notion contains three elements. The first is uncertainty concerning the consequences of our actions. The second is a strong intuitive feeling, or fear, of disaster. And the third is an almost lacking sense of loss for what will be missed. The third element is seldom noted in the discussion, but it can be crucial. Pascal's conviction was partly based on his nonchalance concerning the joys of secular life; and those who oppose gene therapies do not always have a particularly high regard for the cures that these might provide for a limited number of people.

Pascal's argument has often been linked with critical views on technological change.[68] With convenient assumptions, however, it could equally well be employed to defend gene therapies and other advances in genetics. Proponents of what Søren Holm and Tuija Takala have called the 'hopeful principle' claim that technological progress is a necessary condition for making people's lives better; and that prohibitions and regulations based on timidity cause more suffering than even the most hazardous innovations ever could.[69] Assuming that the better life on offer can be compared to Pascal's eternal bliss – and the champions of the principle seem to make

ethics, see Stephen P. Stich, 1978, 'The recombinant DNA debate: A difficulty for Pascalian-style wagering', *Philosophy & Public Affairs* 7: 187–205.

[68] Stich, 1978; Matti Häyry and Tuija Takala, 1998, 'Genetic engineering and the risk of harm', *Medicine, Health Care and Philosophy* 1: 61–4, p. 61; Søren Holm and Tuija Takala, 2007, 'High hopes and automatic escalators: A critique of some new arguments in bioethics', *Journal of Medical Ethics* 33: 1–4, p. 2.

[69] Holm and Takala, 2007, pp. 2–3.

this assumption – a rational gambler might want to ignore the lesser evils of technological risks and aim at the more luminous promise of a perfect future. Again, the elements of uncertainty, intuition, and indifference are present. The strong intuitive feeling in this case is hope and the lack of concern is related to distant risks and social effects.

In the beginning of this section, I suggested that the term 'precautionary principle' might be a misnomer for the idea that uncertainty should lead to bans and moratoria. My reason for suggesting this should now be clear. If *fear* and *hope* are the decisive factors in choosing either the positive or the negative reading of a Pascal-type wager, the corresponding rules could more informatively be called the 'fearful principle' and the 'hopeful principle'. Precautions in situations of uncertainty could be taken to make sure that neither trepidation nor enthusiasm reaches unwise proportions (whatever they are) in technological decision making.

8.9 Therapeutic rationalities

The assessment of genetic interventions in terms of their consequences seems like a reasonable idea. Distinctions between somatic and germ-line treatments as well as between therapies and enhancements can have some value, but it would still be useful to know what follows if we permit or ban specific medical advances in this area. The problem is that opinions and attitudes seem to steer estimates of outcomes more effectively than empirical data.

People who are suspicious of technological change tend to emphasise the bad effects of new developments. They admit that gene treatments can have desirable aims, but they remain concerned about 'slippery slopes', which would lead from good, intended results to bad, unintended ones. Curing diseases such as X-SCID would in and of itself be desirable, but allowing gene therapies for them could gradually lead to other, more dubious genetic interventions and eventually to plainly unacceptable practices like germ-line enhancements. Moral values, according to the advocates of this view, are more important than physical and mental wellbeing, and in an assessment of harms they should be taken fully into account.

People who are more expectant concerning technology's contribution are inclined to focus on its potential future benefits to humanity. They concede that current treatments can be slightly risky, but they are convinced that the 'automatic escalators' of good progress will in time move us from sketchy experiments to routine procedures for saving lives and improving life quality.[70] Curing diseases by infesting patients with cancer is not an ideal solution, but permitting the X-SCID trials will lead to an accumulation of knowledge and, eventually, to better and safer treatments to presently incurable diseases. If moral values stand in the way of good development, proponents of this view say, they should be ignored, because human freedom and happiness are the only valid ethical considerations.

Different ways of seeing technological change is not the only factor that prevents us from calculating outcomes in a neutral and detached manner. The variation is rooted in the basic notion of assessing consequences. We cannot keep track of all the things that may or may not occur as distant or indirect results of our actions, and this is why we concentrate on how our deeds influence entities that matter. Since we do not, however, agree on which entities genuinely matter, we do not agree on the unit of measurement – and this means that our outcome calculations cannot be helpfully compared or combined. Negotiations between people can decide how different values should be weighed, but this is going beyond the analysis of consequences that was the aim of the present chapter. Besides, negotiations can lead to results more directly: people can go right ahead and decide to allow or to prohibit gene therapies, instead of involving themselves in philosophical discussions on values and their significance.

[70] The expression 'automatic escalator' was introduced by Holm and Takala, 2007, p. 3.

Considerable life extension and the meaning of life

In this chapter, I describe attempts to extend the human lifespan and examine the main ethical responses to these attempts. Factual and theoretical accounts of mortality and life extension are followed by analyses of the moral notions that have been used to reject or to defend induced considerable longevity.

9.1   Mortality and ageing

Human life begins at conception, or during pregnancy, or at birth; but it ends at death. Attempts at life extension are always also efforts to postpone death, although other things, such as the health and happiness of individuals and groups while they are still alive, can be independently valued in the planning and execution of these attempts. It is a conceptual truth that if death could be overcome, we could live forever.

Three factors contribute to human mortality, namely, *trauma*, *disease*, and *ageing*. The prevention and treatment of trauma and disease are time-honoured methods of postponing death and improving life quality; and as long as we are subject to biological vulnerability, these will be needed in life extension. But the ultimate challenge to considerable longevity is ageing. If human beings as biological organisms have a set expiry date, say, of a little over a hundred years from birth, then all we can do is to avoid accidents and illnesses and live as well as we can until the date is reached and our time is up. The question is, is this the case or can ageing be halted or reversed?

Most organisms, but not necessarily all of them, are mortal. Bacteria colonies seem to be immune at least to rapid ageing; hydras and corals do not seem to age at all; the jelly fish *Turritopsis nutricula* can oscillate between being an adult of the species and being a polyp; and the oldest living bristlecone pine is estimated to be over 4800 years old.[1] However, human beings, like most other organisms, undergo one-way, irreversible

[1] D. E. Martinez, 1998, 'Mortality patterns suggest lack of senescence in hydra', *Experimental Gerontology* 33: 217–25; S. Piraino, F. Boero, B. Aeschbach, and V. Schmid,

ageing and subsequent death. Suggested explanations for this phenomenon include that complex systems are just doomed to fail at some point; that an accumulation of chemical damage will clog the system sooner or later; and that something in our genetic constitution renders us vulnerable to eventual physical demise however well we take care of our bodies.[2]

One rationale for the existence of mortality in individual living beings is based on evolutionary biology. Organisms and species need to adapt to their environment in order to survive; and adaptation in the changing circumstances of our biosphere requires virility and diversity. Inbreeding within a species increases genetic similarity, decreases variety, and can therefore pose a threat to species diversity and survival in the long run. Mortality can be seen as a solution to this problem: when individuals die after they have reproduced, they clear space for new generations.[3]

Species with different qualities have achieved mortality in different ways. In small and prey animals 'extrinsic mortality' is often sufficient – other animals and the rest of the environment take care of the generational cleansing. Bigger and predatory animals would in many cases live longer without 'intrinsic mortality', which can be effected by, for instance, lethal mutations. This could be the evolutionary reason why humanity – a species of relatively sizeable, social, and intelligent predators – needs cancer and certain age-related conditions in order to avert excessive and collectively fatal longevity.

It would not do, however, to die of cancer before passing on one's genes to the next generation. This is where, according to one idea, telomeres and their gradual shortening come into the picture. Every time a cell divides, a part of the replicated genetic information is lost from the end of a DNA strand. When this information is meaningful, the incomplete replication leads to mutation, which can be detrimental to the vitality of the organism. Telomeres seem to be helpful here. They are the repetitive, genetically meaningless 'tails' at both ends of the DNA strands in linear chromosomes. As long as the part of the DNA strand that is lost in a dividing cell belongs to the telomere, the essential DNA remains intact and the

1996, 'Reversing the life cycle: Medusae transforming into polyps and cell transdifferentiation in *Turritopsis nutricula* (Cnidaria, Hydrozoa)', *The Biological Bulletin* 190: 302; D. M. Richardson (ed.), 1998, *Ecology and Biogeography of Pinus* (Cambridge: Cambridge University Press).

[2] E.g. Vladimir V. Frolkis, 1982, *Ageing and Life-Prolonging Processes* (Vienna: Springer-Verlag); A. H. Bittles and K. J. Collins (eds), 1986, *The Biology of Human Ageing* (Cambridge: Cambridge University Press).

[3] Peter B. Medawar, 1952, *An Unsolved Problem of Biology* (London: H. K. Lewis).

organism is not put at risk during replication. But telomeres gradually shorten with age; and when they can no longer protect duplicating cells, lethal mutations and cell failure can follow. From the evolutionary point of view, the individual organism has completed its task and has to die to make room for its progeny.[4]

According to a more general idea – the notion of *antagonistic pleiotropy* – biological mechanisms can also work in other ways to favour youth and adulthood over old age. The same gene could control different processes at different stages of life. It is, for instance, good to have a way of gathering calcium into the bones early on, so a gene instructing our body to do so would be beneficial when we are young. The same gene could, however, also instruct the body to gather calcium in the arteries later on, and so become harmful to us at an older age. In evolutionary terms, genes with a combination of functions like these would probably be more viable than genetic arrangements that cause grave childhood diseases but improve the quality of life later on.[5]

Some words of caution and explanation are needed here. Evolutionary and biological matters are difficult to describe without unintended allusions to agency: ageing kills, telomeres safeguard genetic information, and jellyfish jump between adulthood and infancy. All this must, of course, be taken metaphorically and without postulating any intentional action on the part of natural entities. Another matter is that mortality and ageing are not well understood. Although new knowledge is emerging all the time, no one really knows why we die and whether it is genuinely inevitable. What I have said in this section should, therefore, be taken as one medley of possible stories that can be told about the role of mortality and senescence in natural history. The place of the stories in my narrative is to set the background for some popular ethical critiques that will be presented in the later sections of this chapter.

9.2   Towards considerable longevity

Evolutionary explanations of mortality aside, history does not necessarily dictate our present or future. Although it is possible that multifunctional genes or shortening telomeres have contributed to the survival of humanity as we know it, it is also possible that with the help

---

[4] W. R. Clark, 1999, *A Means to an End: The Biological Basis of Aging and Death* (New York, NY: Oxford University Press).
[5] G. C. Williams, 1957, 'Pleiotropy, natural selection and the evolution of senescence', *Evolution* 11: 398–411.

of medical interventions and technological advances we can now enjoy their historical benefits without succumbing to their current adverse impacts. Advocates of considerable life extension deny the inevitability of death caused by old age and argue that ageing is a disease among other diseases, incurable so far but defeatable in theory and in practice. 'Biomedical gerontologists' believe that science is not too far from this goal now, and that every effort should be made to gather more knowledge and to transform it into life-extending medical action. One of the most visible proponents of this view is Aubrey de Grey.

In his 1999 study of mitochondrial free radicals, de Grey characterised the essential features of ageing by commenting that it 'is bad for us', that it 'is not an extension of development, but a decay', and that although it 'doesn't kill us' as such, it 'makes us steadily more killable'. But towards the end of his study he also stated, on a more optimistic note, that 'we have a realistic chance of achieving, in only a few decades, a degree of control over the rate of human aging which far exceeds anything that has hitherto seemed feasible'.[6] During the following years, de Grey developed his own model for understanding age-related deterioration and combating it, called 'Strategies for Engineered Negligible Senescence' (SENS).[7] Central to de Grey's proposal is that there are only seven primary types of structural damage to the body that must be counteracted by medical means as a matter of urgency; and that when these have been overcome, secondary damages will be, by and large, repaired by the body's own mechanisms.

The seven essential flaws, and the tools by which de Grey thinks that they could be set right, are the following.[8] *Cell loss* is the trend that as we get older, some cells in the vital parts of our bodies are replaced too slowly or not at all, allowing, dangerously, some of the original cells to grow larger, or other cells to take their place, or the tissue to shrink. Cures for this include physical exercise, the introduction of growth factors into our bodies, gene therapy, and stem cell treatments. *Nuclear mutations and epimutations* leading to cancer are potentially lethal. According to de Grey, however, cancerous cells replicate themselves so fast that they could die of telomere shortening if their supply

---

[6] Aubrey de Grey, 1999, *The Mitochondrial Free Radical Theory of Aging* (Austin, TX: R. G. Landes Company).

[7] Aubrey de Grey and Michael Rae, 2007, *Ending Aging: The Rejuvenation Breakthroughs that Could Reverse Human Aging in Our Lifetime* (New York, NY: St Martin's Press).

[8] These are all explained in lay terms in SENS Foundation, 2009, 'Seven deadly things' – www.sens.org/index.php?pagename=mj_sens_repairing. For a more detailed description, see de Grey and Rae, 2007.

of telomerase (an enzyme renewing telomeres) is cut off by replacing some or all of our important cells at regular intervals. *Mitochondrial mutations* can cause many kinds of serious disease, as mitochondria are indirectly responsible for the conversion of oxygen and nutrients into energy in our cells. The suggested solution to this is gene therapy, by which mitochondrial DNA is made more resilient against the attacks of free radicals, the toxic residues of the cellular metabolic process. *Death-resistant cells* (visceral fat cells, senescent cells, and immune cells) increase with ageing and they are prone to damage the healthy tissues in their environment. Since they refuse to die spontaneously, gene therapies should be designed to encourage them to commit suicide or to encourage our immune system to kill them. *Tissue stiffening* occurs when proteins in the extracellular spaces become chemically linked, thereby preventing their free movement and making important tissues such as the walls of the arteries rigid and inflexible. This, according to de Grey, can be solved by developing medicinal molecules, enzymes, and proteins that break the detrimental links without breaking anything else in our bodies. *Extracellular junk* that has no function accumulates gradually in the body causing or contributing to Alzheimer's disease and age-related diseases resembling it. Proper responses to this could include vaccines that prompt the immune system to get rid of the unwanted material. *Intracellular junk* consists of chemical residues that the cell's garbage disposal system cannot destroy or discard, and which therefore stay in the cell and, with time, become harmful in tissues that are renewed slowly or not at all. To prevent the damage, de Grey believes, we should identify enzymes, possibly in the micro-organisms of soil, which can break down the harmful stuff, and develop gene therapies to insert them into the body.

It is equally easy to be enthusiastic or sceptical about de Grey's programme. He lists many important constituents of our mortality and suggests seemingly sensible strategies for eliminating them or reducing their effects. On the one hand, if his ideas are even partially true, it is possible that funding the types of research that he champions could prolong numerous human lives in good health in the foreseeable future.[9] On the other hand, de Grey's proposals are not all that well received in the scientific community of biogerontologists – a fact that he himself attributes

[9] Aubrey de Grey, 2007, 'Life span extension research and public debate: societal considerations', *Studies in Ethics, Law, and Technology* 1 – www.bepress.com/selt/vol1/iss1/art5; cf. Matti Häyry, 2007b, 'Generous funding for interventive aging research now?', *Studies in Ethics, Law, and Technology* 1 – www.bepress.com/selt/vol1/iss1/art13.

to professional protectionism and fixed opinions.[10] However, that can also be a reasonable reflection of his relative inexperience in biology and his outstanding confidence in future developments.[11] In many cases, for instance, he offers gene therapies as an answer to the questions of ageing, although he should know as well as anybody that the techniques are at their very early stages.

The value of de Grey's model for the discussion of this chapter is that he presents a clear plan which is designed to halt and reverse ageing, thereby enabling human beings to live considerably longer in their rejuvenated and reinvigorated bodies. Many other proponents of moderate to indefinite life extension have more modest expectations concerning *biological* immortality. Some of them confine their proposals to general risk reduction, healthy lifestyle choices, nutrition supplements, calorie restriction, and the like, anticipating an increase in the average rather than the maximum lifespan. Others look forward to an everlasting life, but without the burden of our bodies, at least in the form in which we now experience them. For de Grey, the target is more focused: we should invest in biomedical gerontology now to make sure that some already living individuals can live at least a thousand years.[12] The realism of this plan is, for the purposes of my ethical discourse, largely a side issue.

9.3   Identity beyond considerable longevity

Advances that partly complement de Grey's line of thinking and partly exceed it include stem cell treatments, body part cultivation, medical nanorobotics, human–machine interfaces, cyborgs, mind uploading, spiritual immortality, bodily resurrection, and teleportation. A theme that needs to be considered with most of these developments and ideas is personal identity. In de Grey's model, medical interventions are geared towards helping our current bodies and minds to live for a very long time. In some of the other methods, it is far less obvious who or what will survive the challenges of disease and ageing.

Stem cells can, in theory at least, be used in the rejuvenation of the decaying adult body. When ageing cells do not renew themselves efficiently any more, stem cells inserted into the system can resume the original functions. One alternative is to harvest some of our own cells,

---

[10] de Grey, 2007.

[11] For a debate on his thoughts, see Jason Pontin, 2006, 'Is defeating aging only a dream?' – www.technologyreview.com/sens/.

[12] de Grey, 2007.

engineer them, and put them back in. But if our own tissue is not usable, other people's cells are needed, and this may cause problems. Although few of us think that cell donation would change who we are, the use of human materials can evoke other off-putting images. Historically, eating the flesh of enemies has been experienced as invigorating; drinking human blood has been seen as a method of regaining youth and possibly obtaining immortality; and sexual and other relations with young people or virgins have been sought after as ways of becoming young again. Stem cell infusions can, particularly when the cells come from very young human beings and 'only' rejuvenation is the goal, be mentally associated with taboos like cannibalism, vampirism, and child sacrifice.

Organs for transplantation are scarce and often rejected by the recipient's immune system. A potential solution to this would be the in vitro cultivation of tissues for therapeutic use. We could all have a stock of compatible spare parts, grown out of our own cells, which could be utilised in threatening medical situations.[13] Although transplant patients sometimes feel that other people's organs can change them in subtle ways, this would not necessarily happen with organs that are biologically our own. The kind of engineering proposed here would provoke other objections, though. Could it be done safely? Who could afford to maintain a stash of body parts? Would it not be weird to have complete organs growing in laboratories? Would this lead to affluent people having entire, perhaps brainless, spare bodies in their closets in anticipation of accidents or sudden health emergencies?

Medical nanorobots could in the future clean and maintain cells and other parts of the body in the way required in de Grey's model. Nanorobots would be very small mechanical devices with instructions and tools to repair intra- and extracellular damage without interfering with healthy organic functions. In some visions, these tiny mending machines would permanently wander around in our bodies locating tissues in need of healing or disposal;[14] in less ambitious but for the time being equally speculative plans the devices would be inserted directly into areas where problems would have been identified by external measurements.

Nanorobots left inside our bodies would constitute a human–machine interface and transform us into cyborgs – by definition, entities that are a combination of natural and artificial elements. The concept can sound

[13] E.g. John Harris, 1998, *Clones, Genes, and Immortality: Ethics and the Genetic Revolution* (Oxford: Oxford University Press), p. 128.

[14] Robert A. Freitas Jr, 2001, *Microbivores: Artificial Mechanical Phagocytes Using Digest and Discharge Protocol* – www.rfreitas.com/Nano/Microbivores.htm.

exotic, but in fact human–machine interfaces are already a medical reality. Heart pacemakers, insulin pumps for people with diabetes, and cochlear implants for those with hearing impairments are everyday examples of machines working within human organisms to control damage or to enhance performance. We may or may not want to assign the name 'cyborg' to people donning these devices; or to Olympic athletes with prosthetic limbs; or to airplane pilots who are hooked up to navigation systems. With advances in technology, however, it seems that many human beings will eventually have more and more pronounced cyborg features.

Although science-fiction cyborgs often have identity problems ('Am I a human being or a machine?'), this would not have to be the case with actual individuals with a few gadgets attached to them, or even with theoretical future people with only artificial parts, provided that they started their lives as biological organisms. As long as I have my memories *and* my body bears at least a family resemblance to what it was originally, I could convince myself that I am still the same person.[15]

Mind uploading would mean going a step further. The idea is to prepare a transcript of our mental life at a particular moment and transport it from our own body, natural or artificial, to another body; or to some other suitable place, for use or for safekeeping. The assumptions of this proposal include that all our mental life is brain activity; that all our brain activity can be captured on a computer; and that this activity, placed in a virtual environment or in another brain, would reproduce the existence and experience of our minds before the upload. All these postulations are rather bold and it would be fair to ask, what exactly would be uploaded, where, and for what purpose. In addition, though, even if a mind were to emerge at the far end of the process, whose mind would it be? Would it be self-evident that the mental life now floating in some sort of virtual space would be the mental life of the embodied person who existed before in the physical realm?

The critical questions of mind uploading are similar to the challenges posed by spiritual afterlife and bodily resurrection. If our immortal souls live on when our bodies die, what form will their existence take? Religious teachings talk about eternal bliss, sometimes individual and

---

[15] 'Family resemblance' here means that although I may have begun my life with features A, B, and C, and now have features D, E, and F, the similarity is rescued by the chronological process from the combination of ABC first to BCD, then to CDE, and only after that the current DEF. Each step has something in common with the previous one, even if none of the original features are present in the end.

sometimes collective, but in either case the experience would presumably be so different from our current awareness of ourselves that we could well query whether our identities as we know and cherish them can survive the transformation. And if in resurrection, having been cremated or buried for years, we are suddenly endowed with new bodies, what would be the basis of our identity?[16] We could feel very different and we would, of necessity, be made of different materials – as many people would have 'worn' the same atoms and molecules since our time. How close would the resurrected future beings, with different minds and different bodies, be to us; and how much should we in the end care about their survival?

Derek Parfit has maintained that as long as our memories are more or less intact, we should indeed value the continuation of our mental lives almost regardless of what happens to our bodies.[17] The logical possibility of teleportation[18] serves to illustrate his view. In teleportation, a machine would prepare a detailed record of all the particles of our bodies and send this record to another machine, which would then produce an exact copy of the original based on the information received but using different materials.[19] The end result would not be identical to us – if the original is preserved in the process, it is still the original and the copy is a copy. But Parfit argues that if the original is destroyed, we should be almost as pleased to see that at least the copy can go on living. Our personal survival depends more on psychological connectedness than on physical permanence, so the continued life of the copy with our memories should be nearly as valuable to us as our own continued life.

In a sense, it is easy to see that Parfit is on to something here. When I woke up this morning, I did not start agonising about my bodily continuity. I had my memories, so the hypothetical possibility that someone may have teleported these memories, or their physical counterparts, into another body did not worry me at all. From my viewpoint, as today's version of me, it is as pleasing to be alive and aware of myself as it would be for any other version of 'me' from their viewpoint. But once the questions have been raised, they are difficult to elude. Would I really be me, the original me, if 'I' had been teleported from another body last night? In what

---

[16] Similar questions could be asked about 'waking up' after a long time of cryopreservation, but in that case at least the body would be roughly the same.

[17] Derek Parfit, 1984, *Reasons and Persons* (Oxford: Clarendon Press).

[18] Parfit uses the term 'teletransportation', but the meaning is the same.

[19] If the Heisenberg uncertainty principle is valid, teleportation may not be possible even in principle. If the position and momentum of our smallest particles cannot be measured simultaneously, it seems that making exact copies of any complex material entity remains beyond our reach.

204 RATIONALITY AND THE GENETIC CHALLENGE

sense would my yesterday's version have survived? How interested should *he* have been in the possibility of someone else – today's me – taking over his mental life?

I will not try to answer the complex questions of identity and indefinite longevity in this section. The chapter's main focus is on considerable life extension as advocated by de Grey, and in that model the relative permanence of the human self is a more straightforward matter. However, since discussions on longer lives and immortality tend to conflate the many dimensions of physical, mental, and spiritual survival, I have briefly outlined the competing proposals so that their influence on the genuinely ethical issues of the case can be more readily detected. Let me start the treatment of these ethical considerations by describing a spirited and influential rejection of making human lives longer.

9.4 How mortality benefits individuals

Leon Kass sees biogerontological attempts to conquer mortality, realistic or unrealistic as they may be, merely as symptoms of a wider scientific ethos that has held humanity increasingly in its grip during the past few centuries.[20] He notes that regardless 'of the imminence of anti-aging remedies, it is most worthwhile to reexamine the assumption upon which we have been operating: that everything should be done to preserve health and prolong life as much as possible, and that all other values must bow before the biomedical gods of better health, greater vigor and longer life'.[21] Life is good and death is bad, but Kass believes that there are limits to be observed in endeavours to create new lives and to extend existing ones.

Even when the things that we pursue are desirable in themselves, we must assess how efficiently they can be reached and how equitably they can be distributed. It is not clear that an assessment of these matters would favour life extension, which presumably aims at making people's lives better. If individuals gradually become longer lived, then what will happen to 'work opportunities, retirement plans, hiring and promotion, cultural attitudes and beliefs, the structure of family life, relations between the generations, or the locus of rule and authority in government, business and the professions'?[22] Proponents of longevity believe that these issues can be settled in due course, but Kass opines that lengthening people's lives could actually make them permanently worse through these social

---

[20] Leon R. Kass, 2002, *Life, Liberty, and the Defense of Dignity: The Challenge for Bioethics* (San Francisco, CA: Encounter Books), pp. 257–74.
[21] Kass, 2002, p. 261.   [22] Kass, 2002, p. 261.

problems. To evade this outcome, longevity could be granted only to some individuals. But although the consequences would then be more contained, questions of justice would emerge. Why should some people get to enjoy immortality while others are doomed to their limited lifespans? How would these people be selected? And so on.[23]

The core criticism that Kass presents, however, is levelled at the assumption that life extension is desirable to begin with. His announced intention is to defend mortality and to argue, in the first instance,[24] that 'the finitude of human life is a blessing for every human individual, whether he knows it or not'.[25] To support his claim, he introduces what he sees as the four main benefits of having a limited lifespan: interest and engagement in life; seriousness and aspiration in actions; appreciation of beauty and ability to love; and the possibility of nobility, virtue, and moral excellence.[26] Let us see what he means by these.

The first point made by Kass is that our interest and engagement in life is not likely to survive a much longer life, whoever we are and whatever we do. People who have already achieved a lot could be in the best position to enjoy a few added years, but what would be on offer even for them in the long run? Kass translates his suspicion into a series of more specific questions. 'Would professional tennis players really enjoy playing 25 percent more games of tennis? Would the Don Juans of our world feel better for having seduced 1,250 women rather than 1,000?' Would parents like to raise their children for another ten years? Would the executives of Microsoft or the presidents of Harvard like to continue their careers for another 15 years?[27] And the doubts are even more pronounced in the case of individuals who have led more ordinary lives. What would they have to live for after 40-odd years in the office? As Paul Barrow has asked in this context, 'is the likelihood of several hundred years more driving on motorways in drizzle a more attractive prospect than the certainty of a shorter life on earth, and the possibility of Christian heaven?'[28] The point Kass is making is that we can all stay focused on our lives as long as we know that they will one day come to an end; but that we would inevitably lose interest in whatever it is that we are doing if we had to face the threat of doing it indefinitely.

[23] Kass, 2002, pp. 261–2.
[24] The social undesirability of indefinite lives is his other theme, and I return to it in Section 9.6.
[25] Kass, 2002, p. 264.   [26] Kass, 2002, pp. 266–8.   [27] Kass, 2002, p. 266.
[28] Paul Barrow, 2003, 'Autonomy: overworked and under-valued', Matti Häyry and Tuija Takala (eds), *Scratching the Surface of Bioethics* (Amsterdam: Rodopi): 133–40, p. 139.

The second observation that Kass makes is that mortality gives seriousness and aspiration to our actions. 'To number our days is the condition for making them count,' he writes.[29] The immortal gods depicted by Homer, for instance, live shallow and frivolous lives, mainly observing mortals whose lives are passionate and meaningful. In most matters, people need to have the deadline in sight, lest they lose the sense of urgency that makes goals worth pursuing. Kass recognises that there are a few exceptions to this rule, notably friendship and the desire for understanding. But for most activities, he thinks, 'it is crucial that we recognize and feel the force of not having world enough and time'.[30]

The third blessing of mortality that Kass evokes is the boost that it gives to our appreciation of beauty and our ability to love. According to him, it is possible that only mortal beings can have an inclination to create art which, unlike them, will never grow old or decay. He also believes that the appreciation of natural beauty can be based on the opposite idea, the awareness of its temporality. And he believes that love can be strongly connected with the impermanence of our objects of desire. 'How deeply', he asks, 'could one deathless "human" being love another?'[31]

The fourth benefit of mortality for Kass is its positive impact on virtue and moral excellence. When we give our lives on the field of battle, the sacrifice we make is the sacrifice of a mortal being – immortals cannot die so they cannot show this kind of devotion. Kass cites the example of Odysseus, who was tempted by the nymph Calypso to join her in blissful immortality, but who chose to suffer and eventually die to be with his loved ones and to fulfil his obligations. In the words of Kass, to 'suffer, to endure, to trouble oneself for the sake of home, family, community and genuine friendship, is truly to live, and is the clear choice of this exemplary mortal'.[32]

9.5   How freedom to choose benefits individuals

The views presented by Kass do not enjoy universal acceptance. Not surprisingly, John Harris is among those who have found the four points

---

[29] Kass, 2002, p. 266.   [30] Kass, 2002, p. 267.

[31] Kass, 2002, p. 267. The passage paraphrased here is not easy to interpret, let alone to present in academic prose. Kass himself employs a series of poetic images and asks more questions than he answers, but I hope that I have captured the gist of his meaning.

[32] Kass, 2002, pp. 267–8.

about the alleged benefits of mortality lacking. He gives his blow-by-blow objections to them in a paper called 'Intimations of immortality'.[33]

To the question of interest and engagement Harris responds that different things might hold different attractions to people over longer periods of time. Having more games of tennis or more sexual relations could appeal to some people, while others could be more interested in developing software companies or leading institutes of academic excellence. The bottom line, however, is that if people do not enjoy doing the same things over and over again, they can always try to do something new and thereby have their interest and engagement revived. They can, if they so wish, also choose to die – due to human vulnerability to trauma, life extension does not amount to irreversible immortality.[34]

As for seriousness and aspiration, Harris rebuffs as ridiculous and void of argumentative power the appeals that Kass makes to imaginary gods and their activities in ancient poems. In this part of Kass's account, according to Harris, 'we get treated to the biography of some nonexistent beings Zeus, Hera, Apollo and Athena who apparently lead frivolous lives on account of their fictional immortality'.[35] The attitude reflected in this passage marks clearly the difference between the approaches of these two thinkers. Kass believes in the value of culturally embedded tales, whereas Harris sees them as nonsensical. It is interesting that the divergence becomes visible in this particular context, though: Harris could have countered Kass simply by referring to the worth of friendship and learning, named by Kass himself as potentially eternal sources of seriousness and aspiration.

Beauty and love get similar treatments from Harris, who refuses to see what relevance Kass's ruminations on art and natural beauty could have on endeavours to extend human lives. However, one of the rhetorical questions posed receives a more direct response. When Kass asks how 'deeply could one deathless "human" being love another?',[36] Harris answers, 'as deeply as any mortal but with the distinctly romantic advantage that they could be lovers for eternity'.[37] I am aware that this oratorical competition is in no need of academic judges, but it seems to me that both authors have with this exchange proceeded beyond the issue of considerable longevity into the realms of literal immortality. Even human beings who live a

---

[33] John Harris, 2003a, 'Intimations of immortality: The ethics and justice of life-extending therapies', M. D. A. Freeman (ed.), *Current Legal Problems 2002* (Oxford: Oxford University Press): 65–95.

[34] Harris, 2003a, p. 88.   [35] Harris, 2003a, p. 88.

[36] Kass, 2002, p. 267.   [37] Harris, 2003a, p. 89.

very long time would have a time limit moderating the duration of their feelings, which means that the intricacies of truly everlasting love would not have to be solved in their case.

Harris divides Kass's call for virtue and moral excellence into two parts: a prompt to do virtuous deeds and an ability to sacrifice one's life for one's family or compatriots. Both, he submits, can actually be accomplished better – with greater efficiency and nobility – by human beings who live for hundreds or thousands of years. Longer-lived people have more time to perform good acts; and, so long as they are not invulnerable, they can also give their lives for others. As for the latter, Harris adds that arguably the sacrifice of immortals 'would be more noble since [they] would be giving up infinite rather than simply finite possibilities'.[38]

Harris himself believes that all forms of life extension and research into them should be allowed and encouraged, because every rational and reasonable person would, according to him, welcome the *opportunity* to stay alive and to experience more good things.[39] This attitude is, Harris contends, evidenced by humanity's near-universal avoidance of death and acceptance of case-by-case life prolongation. Likening acts of life extension by new scientific advances to acts of postponing death by more regular medical means, he writes in his *Enhancing Evolution* that 'life-extending therapies are, and always must be, lifesaving therapies and must share whatever priority lifesaving has in our morality and in our social values'.[40] In other words, since we think that freely chosen life-saving treatments are good, then, because these and other comparable developments will in the end result in moderate, considerable, or indefinite longevity in any case, we would be inconsistent and irrational to restrict the direct development of extension technologies by biomedical gerontologists.

Harris recognises that, in principle, there is a gap between what reasonable people want for themselves and what they can be granted. Legitimate restrictions could be based on considerations of safety, efficiency, and

---

[38] Harris, 2003a, p. 89. Strictly speaking, Harris seems to contradict himself here by saying that his 'immortals' could both die (implying that their lives and opportunities are finite) *and* lose infinite possibilities (implying that their lives and opportunities are not finite). But his message is clear: if sacrificing a few decades is good, then sacrificing centuries should be even better.

[39] 'Opportunity' is in italics to indicate that not everyone needs to prefer a longer life. There are cases in which people can, according to Harris, reasonably want to die. But whatever people want, Harris thinks that it is rationally valuable for them that the choice is theirs.

[40] John Harris, 2007, *Enhancing Evolution: The Ethical Case for Making Better People* (Princeton, NJ: Princeton University Press), p. 61.

justice. In the case of induced longevity, however, he does not see the need to curtail people's liberty to safeguard these.

The safety issues of greatly prolonging human lives include the social problems of overpopulation and the medical dangers of tampering with our genetic constitution. Harris's answer to the first question is to formulate procedures that would reduce the number of future people. He tentatively suggests a sizeable tax for those who opt for indefinite longevity; a rule forbidding their reproduction or restricting it; and an upper limit for the years allowed for any individual.[41] Since all these are morally as well as practically dubious, Harris prefers unlimited longevity to anyone who chooses it and holds that the possible difficulties caused by this arrangement can be contained if and when they ever become tangible.[42] As for the health risks, Walter Glannon has called for caution in our attempts to prolong life through altering our basic biological features. His concern is founded on the idea of antagonistic pleiotropy,[43] and especially on the possibility that making generations of human beings longer-lived in the near future could change their genetics so that their much later descendants would turn out to be shorter-lived than people currently are. If this is possible, he writes, 'then there are biological and moral reasons to assess carefully how the lives of distant future people could be affected by this intervention before thinking about developing it on a broad scale'.[44] Harris, however, is not impressed by this objection, because he believes that precautionary measures driven by mere possibilities of harm are irrational and that these are what Glannon advocates. As Harris comments, in a contribution with Søren Holm, '[in] order to make the caution Glannon urges rational, we need far clearer evidence of the balance of harms and benefits than is at present available'.[45] Theoretical speculations about far-away risks are not enough to justify prohibitions on activities with almost instant positive impacts.

Among the focal questions of efficiency are rising healthcare costs and dwindling advantages to individuals who are not connected to what happened to 'them' hundreds of years ago. Life-extending therapies would be expensive to develop and to dispense, and people living

---

[41] Harris, 2003a, pp. 75–7.

[42] See the exchange in Michael Phillips, Hermogenes Rojas, Patrick Frank, and John Harris, 2000, 'Immortality, anyone?', *Science* 288: 1345.

[43] See Section 9.1.

[44] Walter Glannon, 2002a, 'Extending the human life span', *Journal of Medicine and Philosophy* 27: 339–54, p. 352.

[45] John Harris and Søren Holm, 2002, 'Extending human lifespan and the precautionary paradox', *Journal of Medicine and Philosophy* 27: 355–68, p. 366.

multiply longer would, other things being equal, need multiple health services. Harris responds to the latter worry with two remarks.[46] Since the ideal is to keep people in good physical shape throughout their extended lives, we cannot be sure that longer-lived individuals would actually need more care. And since postponed end-of-life expenses would, in conditions of economic growth, be gradually reduced in real terms, it could be cheaper to cover these costs in a thousand years than it is now. As regards diminishing benefits, Harris takes a Parfitian stance. Even if we could not feel one with all our later selves, and thereby not be the ones who can personally enjoy a millennial life, 'it would not be irrational to wish to be the first and possibly the second in such a series of selves and to wish the subsequent, successive selves long and happy continuance'.[47] Harris also offers the view that it would be economically and ecologically sounder to have several subsequent people inhabiting the same body instead of having to grow new bodies and raise new members of society from scratch.[48]

The final objection that Harris considers is the question of justice. When life-extending treatments become available to existing and prospective people, they will, at least in the beginning, be expensive. This means that citizens of poorer countries would only dream of the treatments, while even in richer countries only the wealthy would be able to afford them for themselves and for their children.[49] 'How are we to understand the demands of justice here?'[50] Harris asks. His own answer is utilitarian and libertarian. By 'utilitarian' I mean that he is primarily focused on the net benefits of the arrangement. If life extension is good, then more of it is better than less or none at all. By 'libertarian' I mean that Harris is not confined by solidaristic notions. It is of no consequence that the advantages would be reaped by those who are already in the best position: since they are the only ones who could enjoy longer lives, it would serve no purpose not to let them do so. No one is harmed by someone else having an opportunity to live a thousand years.[51] The conclusion is that appeals to

---

[46] Harris, 2003a, pp. 85, 92; Harris 2007, pp. 61, 70. He postpones the treatment of the former issue to the discussion on justice.

[47] Harris, 2003a, p. 86.

[48] Harris, 2007, pp. 66–7. It is not always clear to me how seriously Harris intends his ideas to be taken. His own conclusion here (p. 67) is: 'Indeed, multiplication of selves in the same body is so ecologically sound, environmentally friendly, and population efficient that it might well become the preferred method of procreation for all except the most unregenerated eco-wastrels or sex-obsessed chauvinists.'

[49] Harris, 2003a, p. 71; Harris, 2007, p. 62.   [50] Harris, 2003a, p. 71; Harris, 2007, p. 62.

[51] Harris, 2003a, pp. 71–2; Harris, 2007, pp. 62–3.

justice as equal access for all should not be allowed to stand in the way of considerable longevity for some.

9.6   From individual immortality to social transcendence

The discussion so far has centred on individual harms and benefits. Moving on to the realm of spiritual aspirations and community ties, Kass argues that medical life extension does not in the end deliver what it promises. People want to transcend themselves in some sense, and this is what motivates their attempts to overcome ageing, but even the longest lives do not satisfy the original desire. Individual survival can only offer more of the same, and our only chances of reaching beyond our own boundaries are to achieve personal completeness or to participate in the 'immortality' of our family line and community life.

Kass concedes that most cultures are obsessed with immortality, but he claims that the primary reason for this is not that people want to go on performing their daily chores forever. In his view, 'the human soul yearns for, longs for, aspires to some condition, some state, some goal toward which our earthly activities are directed but which cannot be attained in earthly life'.[52] For Kass, the quest for immortality could on the individual level be a quest for completeness, which cannot be reached by living on indefinitely. If it can be reached at all, this will be through the love of another person; the pursuit of ultimate wisdom; or the redemption of the soul in the presence of God.[53] So the 'human taste for … the imperishable and eternal [is] not a taste that the biomedical conquest of death could satisfy', as this conquest would take us no closer to the wholeness of love, wisdom, or divine bliss.[54] On the contrary, our preoccupation with medical life extension can be detrimental in that it diverts our attention from our true goal. We can forget to take care of the wellbeing of the soul if we focus solely on keeping it alive and embodied for perpetuity.[55]

For those who do not believe in souls and their completion, Kass offers a biologically based social justification for dying willingly and before too long. As he notes, procreation, 'the bearing of and caring for offspring', is a goal for 'which many animals risk and even sacrifice their lives'. 'Indeed', he continues, 'in all higher animals, reproduction *as such* implies both the acceptance of the death of self and participation in its transcendence.'[56] In human beings, Kass believes that this is further intensified by social

---

[52] Kass, 2002, p. 269.   [53] Kass, 2002, pp. 269–70.   [54] Kass, 2002, p. 270.
[55] Kass, 2002, p. 270.   [56] Kass, 2002, p. 271.

interaction and cultural activities, especially by the creation of beliefs and traditions and their transmission to children. Families and communities teach the young their ideals, opinions, and rituals; including their views on the proper succession of generations. This is how the old prepare to pass on the torch to new people who have more vitality and a fresher take on life. Those who wish to live forever conspire, albeit unintentionally, to prevent this progression and thereby deny the value not only of procreation but also of culture, tradition, and all other higher ends of life.[57]

Two details in Kass's account need some specification. First, what does he mean by saying that reproduction implies the acceptance of death? When the claim is stripped of its connotations of animal intentions and human sex-related suicidality, the answer will probably be found in the recognition of functions and roles. Biologically, animals have fulfilled their function once they have completed their procreative tasks; and socially, human beings have performed their role once they have produced offspring and brought them up. Metaphorically speaking, then, having children is approving one's dispensability in a greater scheme of things.[58] Secondly, what about aspiring immortals who value having progeny, only do not want to die quite yet?[59] In what way are they hindering procreation and all the good stuff flowing from it? Kass's idea seems to be that in the history of cultures and traditions, children are supposed to be the ones who take the place of their parents. If parents never die, there will be no places to be taken and hence no role for the members of the new generation in community and society. Since this means that, communally and socially, the new people might as well not exist at all, parents' wishes of immortality make, in this sense, their own children's lives void of meaning.

9.7 Natural morality and the meaning of life

With his biological and social justification of mortality, Kass comes close to the thirteenth-century natural law doctrine of Thomas Aquinas. In the Aquinian theory, based on Aristotle and Plato, all creatures seek their own highest good by moving towards the essential goals of their species. For human beings – vulnerable, social, and intelligent animals – these goals are survival, procreation, and the search for truth, especially

---

[57] Kass, 2002, pp. 271–2.
[58] Kass, 2002, p. 271.
[59] See, e.g. Harris, 2003a, p. 90, n. 43.

regarding God.[60] In many cases, the higher aims further down the list override the preceding lower ones; as in the liberation of holy women and men from reproduction, or in the licence of parents to risk their lives to protect their children. The views advocated by Kass seem to conform to these rules rather seamlessly. Truth lies in religious and moral tradition, which cannot live and thrive without the revitalising effect of successive generations. Successive generations, in their turn, cannot assume their positions and enliven the community tradition without the death of older people. Hence human beings cannot reach their goals nor fulfil their purpose in life if they live on indefinitely. The meaning of life itself demands that we allow ourselves to be mortal.[61]

Harris can easily accept all the separate goals listed by Aquinas, if they are given appropriate interpretations. It is important to seek truth, particularly by the use of scientific methods.[62] It is also important to have children and to raise them.[63] And it is acutely important to survive – this is why the efforts of biomedical gerontologists are so laudable.[64] But Harris cannot and does not accept the way in which Kass, following Aquinas, concocts the hierarchical order of these values. Truth, for Harris, does *not* reside in religious and moral traditions, most decidedly not in a tradition that requires people to die once they have reproduced. He is alert to the reverse connection between indeterminate longevity and religion, though. 'One possible consequence of writing immortality into the genes of the human race', he notes, 'might be the final extinction of religion.'[65] Since so many religious creeds rely on the punishments and rewards that allegedly meet us in an afterlife, the postponement of such sanctions indefinitely could erode people's motivation to act on them. Harris hypothetically mentions the idea that angry deities could send us calamities if we cease to worship them, but this is clearly not meant as a serious consideration. He seems to think, contra Aquinas and Kass, that the overall effect of dethroning gods would be 'comforting' and 'liberating'.[66]

The idea that gods should play no role in our moral decision making has, since Greek antiquity, been a part of the Western school of

---

[60] Thomas Aquinas, 1988, *On Law, Morality and Politics* [1265–1272], edited by W. P. Baumgarth and R. J. Regan (Indianapolis, IN: Hackett Publishing Company), pp. 47–8.

[61] This inference is my interpretation rather than anything written by Kass. Its role is to draw attention to the different ways in which moral theorists have pictured the meaning of human life.

[62] John Harris, 2005, 'Scientific research is a moral duty', *Journal of Medical Ethics* 31: 242–8.

[63] Harris, 2003a, p. 90, n. 43.   [64] Harris, 2003a, pp. 80–2; Harris, 2007, p. 61.

[65] Harris, 2003a, p. 94.   [66] Harris, 2003a, p. 95.

Epicureanism.[67] Epicurus taught philosophy in Athens after Plato and Aristotle; and held that the foundation of ethics is hedonism, properly understood. The only goals worth pursuing are pleasure and the absence of pain, and the best way to achieve these goals is to lead a quiet life, enjoying the little good things and cultivating relations with one's friends. The confinement to passive gratification – peace of mind – is justified in this model by the dangers of more direct strategies of seeking happiness. If we try to maximise our enjoyment by chasing active pleasures in excess, we will probably end up paying the price in reduced satisfaction or suffering later on.

Despite their relative modesty, the tenets of Epicureanism have not always been hailed by people who hold more traditional views. Epicurus himself attributed this to people's fears: the fear of gods, the fear of death, and the fear of dying. All these are, in Epicurus's view, unwarranted. Gods, according to him, belong to another level of existence altogether, and they lead blessed lives untouched by human affairs, with no inclination to interfere with our doings. Gods will not punish us if we are wicked or reward us if we are good. Likewise, death belongs to a realm that has no connection with our current being: where we are, death is not; and where death is, we are not. Death is sensory nonexistence, so we do not have to worry that we will be tormented in an afterlife. Dying, too, is a natural event and not to be dreaded. A premature or agonising end to our lives would, of course, be undesirable in many ways, but the mere fact that we are going to die sometime during the next few decades should not cause us undue anxiety.

Harris could accept most Epicurean credos, but the view that we should not be afraid of dying would be lost on him. For Harris, the point of our existence – its 'meaning' – is to lead worthwhile lives; and anything that interrupts this against our own wishes is bad. An Epicurean could, lining up with Kass, argue that any considerable life extension would carry with it a diminishing marginal utility, so that in the end continued existence would be more trouble than it is worth. But although some things decrease in value with quantity (the first glass of water satisfies more than the tenth), not all do (two concert tickets might be more useful than one), and all Harris has to say here is that, for him, more life is better than less. Longevity may have a diminishing marginal utility for Kass and his allies, but as long as it has an increasing marginal utility for Harris, the objection to life extension fails.

---

[67] See, e.g. James Warren, 2004, *Facing Death: Epicurus and His Critics* (Oxford: Clarendon Press).

Green considers in his *Babies by Design*[79] the objections to life extension presented by the President's Council of Bioethics chaired by Kass.[80] He finds, however, that these objections are based on fear of change rather than on concrete facts about future harms. New generations *could* become blocked behind old ones and people's motivation to reproduce *might* be curbed, but none of this happens inevitably or inexorably.[81] People did spontaneously find ways of living together during the twentieth century, in spite of lifespans being prolonged by decades in many countries.[82] And regulations could be put in place to make sure that the worst scenarios were not realised. Green asks those who remain sceptical to reflect on the matter in terms of the 'reversal test'.[83] If they think that a ten-year life extension would be bad, what about a ten-year *reduction* to average life expectations? If this sounds equally bad, resistance to change is probably just an indication of 'status quo bias', the desire that things would forever remain the same.[84] Green seems to find more meaning for human lives in progress moderated by reasonable decency.

Habermas appears to have two partly different views on considerable life extension in *The Future of Human Nature*.[85] In his conclusions on assisted procreation, gene therapy, and reproductive cloning he attributes the wrongness of genetic selection and manipulation firmly to the decisions that others make without the future individual's consent.[86] If we make fundamental biological life choices for the unborn, even to secure their health and wellbeing, we violate their right to be heard in the moral discourse. This is why we should, among other things, refrain from trying to produce germ-line genetic changes that would extend our children's lifespan. But since this particular prohibition applies only to decisions made for others, it leaves open the option that competent adult individuals could choose longevity treatments for themselves without doing anything wrong.

[79] Ronald M. Green, 2007, *Babies by Design: The Ethics of Genetic Choice* (New Haven, CT: Yale University Press).

[80] President's Council on Bioethics, 2003, *Beyond Therapy: Biotechnology and the Pursuit of Happiness* (Washington, DC: President's Council on Bioethics) – www.bioethics.gov/reports/beyondtherapy/.

[81] Green, 2007, pp. 101–2.   [82] Green, 2007, pp. 103–4.   [83] See Section 2.4.

[84] Green 2007, pp. 104–6; citing Nick Bostrom and Toby Ord, 2006, 'The reversal test: Eliminating status quo bias in applied ethics', *Ethics* 116: 656–79.

[85] Jürgen Habermas, 2003, *The Future of Human Nature*, translated by William Rehg, Max Pensky, and Hella Beister (Cambridge: Polity Press).

[86] Habermas, 2003, pp. 51–2.

In an earlier section of his book, however, Habermas drifts towards a more stringent view, at least against clearly mechanical methods of extending human lives.[87] He discusses nanorobotics and mind upload-ing; and argues that by creating a 'fusion of the organically grown with the technologically made' these tools 'dissolve boundaries and break connections that in our everyday actions have up to now seemed to be of an almost transcendental necessity'.[88] Our ethical self-understanding requires that we know what is naturally grown and what is human-made in us,[89] and this knowledge is not possible if tiny self-replicating medical robots circulate in our bodies, or if the contents of our minds have been transferred into computer files. Habermas appears to suggest that people's own choices for longevity should in these cases be restricted, because the choices could be harmful to the individuals themselves or to society as a whole. This view makes moral equality based on untampered-with biol-ogy the core of human life.[90]

Sandel's publicised views on life extension also go in two directions. In the introduction of *The Case Against Perfection*,[91] he illuminatingly contrasts two uses of genetic engineering as follows: 'Everyone would welcome a gene therapy to alleviate muscular dystrophy and to reverse the debilitating muscle loss that comes with old age. But what if the same therapy were used to produce genetically altered athletes?'[92] He then goes on in the rest of the book to condemn the latter kind of prac-tice on the grounds that it would blur the distinction between what is given and what is made in our lives, and eventually erode the basis of solidarity.[93] The two interpretations to be drawn from this are, on the one hand, that case-by-case age retardation is acceptable even if it can lead to life extension; and, on the other hand, that human-made lon-gevity could be seen as a part of the 'project of mastery' which threat-ens our view of the human life as a gift.[94] Answering questions in the President's Council on Bioethics chaired by Kass, Sandel stated: 'I am

---

[87] Habermas, 2003, pp. 41–2.   [88] Habermas, 2003, p. 41.

[89] Habermas, 2003, pp. 29, 41–2, 56–8. See Section 2.4.

[90] Most of de Grey's strategies for engineered negligible senescence do not involve human–machine interfaces, so a series of questions remains. Does Habermas condone the 'nonmechanical' strategies? If not, does he condone regular life-saving treatments? If yes, what is the difference? Habermas does not provide answers to these questions in his book.

[91] Michael J. Sandel, 2007, *The Case Against Perfection: Ethics in the Age of Genetic Engineering* (Cambridge, MA: The Belknap Press of Harvard University Press).

[92] Sandel, 2007, p. 10.   [93] Sandel, 2007, pp. 86, 89–92, 96, 97–100. See Section 2.3.

[94] Sandel, 2007, pp. 97 ff.

not saying that we should never fix things. Often we will come to the conclusion that what has been given is something that is in need of fixing it, of repairing.'[95] The implication is that the impact of different types of age retardation and life extension should be examined separately and in their own right. The meaning that Sandel finds for human life, though, remains steadily on the side of 'giftedness' and mutual solidarity based on its recognition.

[95] The discussion followed Sandel's presentation 'What's wrong with enhancement' as a member of the Council on 12 December 2002 – www.bioethics.gov/transcripts/dec02/session4.html.

10

Taking the genetic challenge rationally

In this chapter, I summarise the assumptions and arguments employed in the ethical analysis of the genetic challenge; present complete versions of the three main approaches to the issue; and conclude that my findings call for changes in the work of philosophers in the field of genethics.

10.1 From challenges to solutions

In the previous chapters, I have presented seven challenges that advances in genetics and related fields pose to humanity; three philosophical ways of tackling these challenges; and the main arguments that have been used in ethical debates concerning them. In this chapter, I will summarise my findings and eventually suggest directions into which philosophical studies in this field could be usefully taken. Before formulating this conclusion, however, I must sum up the arguments introduced in the preceding chapters (Sections 10.2, 10.3, and 10.4) and the cases that can be made for and against genetic practices from the viewpoints of the three philosophical approaches (Sections 10.5, 10.6, 10.7, 10.8, and 10.9).

The main arguments presented in the context of the genetic challenge can be divided into six categories: (i) general tenets accepted by all in theory but interpreted in different ways in practice; (ii) more specific arguments that can be used by both sides of the debate; (iii) arguments for advances; (iv) arguments for restrictions; (v) arguments against restrictions; and (vi) arguments against advances. The ensuing layers of counterarguments and counter-counterarguments are infinite, but these six levels should enable me to pin down the main points.

10.2 Basic tenets and their interpretations

(i) The *general tenets accepted by all* are that:
  - it is good and right to create good lives;
  - it is good and right to preserve, restore, and improve health and life quality;

- it is good and right to save and to extend lives;
- it is good and right to empower people as decision makers; and
- it is good and right to improve humanity.

All the conflicting views outlined in the preceding chapters can be derived from these principles, given that they are read in convenient manners.

It is good and right to create good lives, but which lives are good and what are acceptable methods of producing them? One view says that any life is a good life as long as it has not been brought about by using technology or by sacrificing other human lives, and as long as it has a role and a place in its community. Another view states that while this is almost true, technical means are not always undesirable and lives of undue suffering should not be deliberately instigated. And some maintain that only the most alert physical and mental lives are really worth bringing into existence, and that prenatal selection does not involve any considerable loss of value.

It is good and right to preserve, restore, and improve health and life quality, but are there limits to the means that can be used for these tasks? Some argue that sacrificing human beings, unborn, newborn, or adult, is wrong and should not be done when medical treatments are developed or administered. An alternative line is to talk about wrongful use and instrumentalisation and allow only practices that treat people and their bodies with proper respect. Against both restrictions, proponents of advances claim that saviour sibling, stem cell, and gene therapies do not involve unacceptable degrees of instrumental use provided that embryos are the only ones used without their consent, and that other donors and research subjects have volunteered for the role or are adequately compensated for their services.

It is good and right to save and to extend lives, but not everyone believes that this should be done indefinitely or at any cost. There are those who think that considerable increases in maximum lifespan would be bad both for individuals and societies, and should therefore be banned. There are also those who admit that problems might emerge but recommend regulations rather than prohibitions as a cure. Champions of technological progress, in contrast, like to point out that since saving lives extends them anyway, it would not make much logical sense to oppose extensions for their own sake.

It is good and right to empower people as decision makers, but what exactly does this mean and against what do we need protection? The situation is illustrated in Figure 10.1.

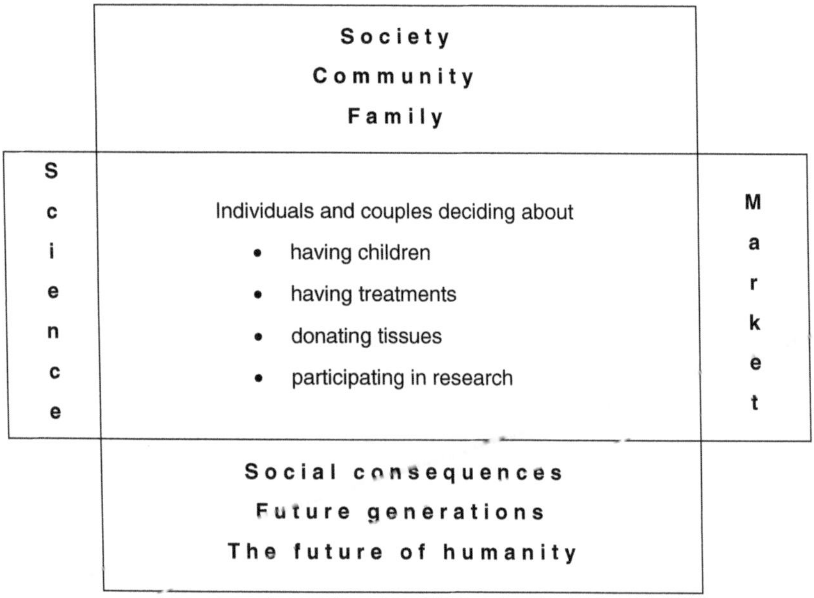

Figure 10.1   From what do we need protection?

Our decisions are influenced in significant ways by the values that our societies, communities, and families have bestowed on us; by our understanding of science; by our reliance on the market; and by considerations of social impacts, future generations, and humanity's survival. Ethicists like Jürgen Habermas, Michael Sandel, and Leon Kass want to protect us mainly against pressures created by advances in the life sciences and by their commercialisation (left and right in Figure 10.1), and are less concerned about the 'moral' inducements given by communal beliefs and precautionary reflections. Ethicists like Jonathan Glover, John Harris, and Ronald Green, on the other hand, have more faith in scientific innovations and market exchanges, and endeavour to safeguard our choices against the 'irrational' pressures of tradition and trepidation (top and bottom of Figure 10.1).

Finally, it is good and right to improve humanity, but in what sense? Genetic and medical advances are designed to make people healthier, stronger, and longer-lived, and this is what most proponents of selection, stem cell research, and gene treatments advocate. Arguably, however, these developments come with a moral price, and this is why some commentators oppose new technologies in the name of ethical self-understanding, solidarity, and traditional ways of life. Those who see some truth in each warring claim can try to find a middle way and aim at both physical *and* moral improvements through suitable regulations.

10.3   Arguments that cut both ways

(ii) In addition to the general tenets, there are also *more specific arguments that can be used by both sides of the debate.* These address concerns that include:
  • loss of life;
  • risk assessment, benefit assessment, and precaution;
  • slippery slopes;
  • status quo bias;
  • parity of reasoning;
  • reproductive freedom and parental autonomy;
  • nondirectiveness;
  • social pressures;
  • parental responsibility; and
  • the assumption that parental love almost always prevails.
  As in the above, variation is produced by different attitudes, which can, for philosophical purposes, be presented as conceptual and normative distinctions.

Lives are lost if embryos are used for research; and lives are lost if embryos are not used for research. In the first case, the loss of life is direct and active; in the second case it is indirect and passive. Assuming that embryonic human life matters, ethical judgements here turn on the distinction between killing and letting die: those who believe that these are morally different can argue that killing embryos for research is wrong but letting people die in the absence of stem cell therapies is acceptable; whereas those who believe that the two practices are morally equivalent can claim that both aspects of losing lives should be taken fully into account in moral calculations.

Risk assessment, benefit assessment, and precaution are all dependent on our choice of values, strategy of risk taking, and degree of boldness or timidity. If our primary value is the continuation of healthy human lives now, we can easily gamble on traditions and future developments. If, on the other hand, our morality is based on communal beliefs and conventions, we are more likely to make light of lives potentially saved by high technology. In both instances, our opponents can criticise us for reckless risk taking and erroneous benefit appraisal, and we can accuse them of excessive caution.

Slippery slope arguments are often directed against scientific advances. In their causal form, they warn that if certain safe and beneficial techniques are developed and implemented, the development and implementation of certain unsafe or harmful techniques becomes more probable, which is why the progress in question should be halted already at its early stages. Nothing, however, prevents proponents of science from applying the same logic to restrictions of research and treatments. They can argue that the prohibition of unpredictable scientific practices (such as cloning) now can, through the reinforcement of a compulsive regulative mentality, lead to the prohibition of perfectly innocent research in the future.

The idea that opponents of science suffer from *status quo bias* works for ethicists who concentrate on the measurable changes that can be brought about by scientific innovations. If a person does not want to make human lives longer, they ask whether the same person would like to make them shorter, and conclude that since adjustments into both directions are opposed, the person's views must be attributed to fear of change. In another sense, however, science enthusiasts can be made to taste their own medicine by focusing on the evolution of moral ideas. Proponents of advances take the pace at which new technologies become accepted and traditional ethical ideals go extinct for granted and would not like to slow down the process. But would they want to double the speed of the development from what it is currently? Since this would probably have dire social consequences, the answer must be no, which means that champions of science can be diagnosed as having a severe case of 'dynamic status quo' bias. (It is, in fact, improbable that advocates of science would be alarmed by accelerated moral evolution. But their opponents would not necessarily shun the idea of shortening average lifespans, either, if they could exchange lived years for added moral fibre. Fundamental values and ideologies influence strongly the way such ideas are applied.)

Arguments appealing to *parity of reasoning* make claims about the consistency and coherence of our views. The debate on somatic and germ-line gene therapies provides an example of the essential neutrality of this form of argument. Harris and Kass agree that the two types of intervention are essentially similar. From this, Harris goes on to say that since somatic treatments are ethical, so are germ-line alterations. Kass, on the contrary, argues that since germ-line interventions are wrong, the same goes for somatic therapies. Parity of reasoning arguments polish the rails leading from one normative position to another, but where the train ends up depends on the direction in which our moral intuitions steer it.

Reproductive freedom and parental autonomy are mostly advocated by champions of genetic selection, as a justification for prospective mothers and fathers to be allowed to choose their children's qualities and conditions. Opponents of selection have, however, claimed that healthcare professionals and genetic counsellors guide their clients towards 'medically approved' decisions, persuading people to terminate pregnancies on account of impending diseases and disabilities. This tendency could be counterbalanced by *nondirectiveness* in genetic and related consultation, although *social pressures* can also prompt people to choose what is seen as normal. As long as the selected features are related to health and ability, freedom is favoured by proponents of new technologies and directiveness and pressures are defied by their competitors. But as the case of deaf embryos shows, the arguments can also work reversely: parental autonomy would legitimise the choice of having babies who cannot hear, and culturally sensitive medical advice and communal peer support could favour the decision to create deaf individuals.

Parental responsibility is linked with reproductive freedom and it requires progenitors to assume proper attitudes and to take proper actions towards their offspring. What these attitudes and actions are, however, is a matter of dispute. One group of ethicists states that producing anything short of the best possible child, in genetic and medical terms, is foolish. Another group asserts that wanting anything but the child that is given by nature is evil. And middle groups say that while givenness has its advantages, we are not obliged to undertake great sacrifices or permitted to allow grave suffering just to receive nature's procreative 'gifts'.

The assumption introduced by Green, according to which *parental love almost always prevails*, is yet another example of principles that can be used to support conflicting views. It is originally intended to alleviate fears concerning designer babies and saviour siblings. Even if the manufactured children cannot deliver what is expected of them – genius or medicine – they will be loved and cared for by their parents. But similar observations can be made about children with disabilities. It does not matter what parents expect or hope for; in the end they will embrace the babies that nature gives them, so why select for 'normality'?

10.4   Arguments for and against

Although many instruments in the philosopher's toolbox can be used in favour of contradictory views, there are more specific notions that can be employed only as reasons for *or* against advances or restrictions.

(iii) The specific *arguments for advances* presented in the foregoing chapters state a goal for all human action and make a claim about how it can be reached. The goal is the creation and continuation of lives worth living: in reproduction, we should bring into existence the healthiest and most intelligent children that we can; and in medicine and healthcare, we should try to keep alive and in the best possible condition every individual who wants it, for as long as they want it. The claim concerning means is that science in general and life sciences in particular provide the most efficient way of achieving the stated goal. Scientific development eliminates diseases and discovers cures, and although other practices can also contribute to human wellbeing, science takes precedence due to its greatest potential to improve humanity's condition.

(iv) The *arguments for restrictions* identify certain social goods that need protection from uncontrolled changes and stipulate a set of rules that are believed to offer the best protection. The social goods are tradition, solidarity, and ethical self-understanding; and their survival is understood to depend on a good grasp of the distinction between what is 'given' and what is 'made' in our lives. Advances in bioscience need restrictions, because they are prone to confuse the division. Some of the main entities and principles that need to be safeguarded in order to retain the distinction are the sanctity and dignity of human life; justice as equality among all human beings, including the unborn; immunity from being treated instrumentally, wrongfully, or as a thing; respect for organically developed communities; and cautiousness against drastic changes.

(v) The *arguments against restrictions* include a positive case for freedom and a string of reactions to prohibitions and regulations. The positive case is that liberty is a value worth cherishing, either because it is a fundamental value in itself or because it promotes the long-term wellbeing of individuals and communities. Even if a proposed set of changes is seen as threatening, it can be experimented with to find out its actual effects and side effects. The reactions to restrictive views are more varied, but they are mostly based on charges of sloppiness or inconsistency. Only confusion can be created by calling embryos children, disabilities cultures, market exchanges wrongful instrumentalisation, and irrational resistance to change higher wisdom. Talking about consistency, how can people relish most medical advances but draw the line arbitrarily at genetics? By not developing this field they unethically prevent, as omissions are morally equivalent to acts, thousands of people from having life-saving treatments in the near future. And why are people concerned about discarded embryos? At least as long as healthier embryos are implanted in their stead, the principle of replaceability guarantees that nothing of value is lost.

(vi) The *arguments against advances* deny the unquestioned value of medical life sciences and evoke issues of consent, distribution, and equal treatment. Science enthusiasts believe that genetics and related disciplines produce unequivocally good results, and do this in a way that contributes maximally to our health and happiness. Opponents argue that indefinite longevity and the manufacture of people by design are undesirable developments, and should not be pursued in the first place. The more modest aims of genetic advances, such as cures for lethal childhood conditions, could be more worthy, but in this area the success rate is not very promising. In any case, ethical considerations overshadow all effects that can be expected. Children, embryos, and future generations cannot consent to the procedures, which makes the practices suspect. Since not everyone can, in a long time, enjoy all the benefits of novel interventions, questions of justice loom large. Who should have the scarce treatments? And when the solution has been found, there will still be those who have not benefited from new developments and who can be seen to form an inferior class in society. The demand for equality warns us against allowing this.

10.5   What is required of a complete case?

Complete ethical cases in the context of the genetic challenge have two main requirements. They have to define their background rationality, for instance, in the terms indicated in Table 2.1 (Section 2.6). And they have to cover all the relevant arguments and counterarguments presented in the debate (summarised in Sections 10.2, 10.3, and 10.4 above).

The questions that define approaches in the sense of my 'nonconfrontational notion of rationality' (see Section 2.6) are:

- What level of coherence is required?
- How are things in the world?
- How should impacts be optimised?
- What entities matter?
- What makes decisions moral?

These queries are intended to tease out the main variations on the themes of what makes sense and what is ethically acceptable.

All the views that I have surveyed require a *high level of coherence*, although not all of them sing the praises of logical analysis and arithmetical precision. When philosophers say, for instance, that A has a moral duty to do X in situation P, they cannot say that B does *not* have a duty to do X in situation Q, unless they can show that either agents A and B or situations P and Q differ from each other in a morally significant sense. This type of observation is the basis of parity of reasoning arguments and it is, as such, accepted by all. But since there is considerable disagreement on what counts as a morally significant difference, philosophers can reasonably disagree on the applications of the principle.

According to the nonconfrontational notion, our beliefs should be *consistent with how things are in the world*. People who in ethical discussions unmistakably refer to products of their own imagination instead of shared realities step outside the bounds of rationality. Beyond such cases, however, it is not clear how things in fact are in the world. Some say that only material beings exist, others believe that spiritual ideas also have a place in moral considerations, and still others argue that our lives together create social entities including rules and norms that need to be taken into account. Theorists with different worldviews tend to have different rationalities in this respect, and charges of making things up are frequently launched against competitors by proponents of all major schools.

Rational agents *optimise the immediate and long-term impacts* of their decisions on *entities that matter*. The preceding chapters have revealed at least three distinct ways in which ethical theorists believe that this optimising can be done. Put in simple terms, these are *measuring, sensing,* and *negotiating*. Advocates of the first option think that once we have defined the entities that matter to us, ethical assessments can be reduced to a reckoning of concrete consequences. Harms should be minimised and benefits should be maximised; and as long as the basic values have been determined correctly, no other considerations should interfere with the calculation. Champions of the second tactic see a more intimate link between values and norms; and hold that sustained community traditions and ways of life are more important than the quantifiable physical and mental wellbeing of individuals. The impacts of our choices are optimised by resisting trends and practices that threaten social ties and human existence as we know and cherish them. Proponents of the third approach focus on procedures of decision making rather than on the individual outcomes or the collective symbolism of our choices. The entities that matter for them are rules and principles; and they see negotiations on the content and applications of these rules and principles as the optimal way to respect them.

Views on *what makes decisions moral* also come in at least three packages. In liberal consequentialist doctrines, actions that concern only or mainly agents themselves are considered prudential and nonmoral; whereas actions that also concern others are subject to moral evaluation. In communitarian and natural law theories, actions aimed at maximising the material good of individuals are regarded as nonmoral or even immoral; while moral assessment and praise belong to practices that aim at collective or spiritual wellbeing. In purely deontological creeds, both individual and collective goals are, as far as the criterion of morality goes, secondary; the moral character of actions depends on the (universal or reasonable) acceptability of the rules on which they are based, and on their conformity to those rules.

Relevant arguments and counterarguments (surveyed in Sections 10.2, 10.3, and 10.4) start from the basic tenets that we all hold but interpret differently. A complete ethical case has to take a stand on the issues of acceptable life quality, use of human beings in research and treatments, meaning attached to extended lives, autonomy's friends and foes, and humanity's future. These fundamental choices will in most instances automatically define the sides to be taken with more specific arguments, for instance, the ones dealing with loss of life, parity of reasoning, and parental responsibility. And once these basic elements are put together, the cases for or against restrictions should be as complete as they can be.

10.6   Measuring the challenge

The allegiances between ethical theories and normative views on scientific advances have become clear in the preceding chapters on the dimensions of the genetic challenge. It would be logically possible to mix tradition and progress, for instance, by arguing that our best accustomed ways of living can be preserved only by selection and cloning. It would also be possible to combine the no-harm ethos of liberal consequentialism with restrictions by insisting that present and future individuals will suffer physically and mentally from the use of novel technologies. In real-life discussions, however, these views are seldom expressed. Tradition is linked with restrictions, while choice and wellbeing are paired with permissive policies. The other two logical alternatives are used, if at all, only in counterarguments and in inadequately developed forms.

The most straightforward way to defend genetic and related advances proceeds from the 'rational tangibility' approach of Glover and Harris. The only entities that ultimately matter are persons (that is, beings who are aware of themselves and of the value of their existence) and their lives when they are worth living. Persons as decision makers are allowed to do anything that is either safe or involves only individuals who partake in the endeavour voluntarily. Persons have no moral obligations to themselves, so if they freely and informedly decide to harm themselves, nothing unethical happens unless others are also harmed against their will. Persons do have moral obligations to others, though, and they have a duty to promote the creation, preservation, improvement, and extension of human lives worth living. The most effective method for doing this is to encourage scientific work, make sure that it is not hindered, and participate in it as a research subject if required to do so. Proponents of this view have to decide, of course, how far the duty to promote other people's wellbeing can be extended, and how well they think that science can assist in its performance. Helping all others could be too demanding, and there are alternative ways of helping humankind besides volunteering as a human guinea pig. But these considerations do not undermine the main point, which is that, according to the view, scientific progress should not be held back by bans or prohibitions.

When it comes to the interpretation of the 'general tenets', the view produces the following results. A life that is not worth living is not worth creating; a life that is worth living is worth creating; and the more a life is worth living, the more it is worth creating. A longer worthwhile life is better than a shorter one, and humanity should be improved in terms of health, strength, intelligence, and other concrete and measurable qualities. Embryos can always be used in research and treatments (with their parents' permission), because they are not persons and thereby not entities that matter; and persons can also be used if the procedures are safe *or* voluntarily undertaken. (Both conditions are sufficient without the other, since people cannot complain if they are not harmed and since their own volition justifies anything that happens to them.) The only choice-related empowerment that we need is intellectual prowess against emotions, traditions, and conventional rules, which hinder our rational decision making.

As for the more specific arguments, proponents of the 'rational tangibility' view ask us to side with them against time-honoured but tenuous distinctions and attitudes. Letting people die is, according to them, essentially as bad as killing them, and this is why we have a strict obligation to advance science that promises to save lives in the future. Precautionary and slippery slope scares are irrational and paralyse all reasonable decision making, as does commitment to how things currently are. The best use of parity of reasoning arguments is to show similarities between allowed and disallowed practices and then deduce that the latter should, like the former, be permitted in the name of consistency. Parents have a responsibility to produce physically and mentally the best children that they can, and their freedom and entitlement to use genetic tests in order to achieve this should be recognised. This also means that parents who want to opt for conditions like deafness in their offspring are within their legal rights to do so, although morally they can be criticised for their choice.

The practical norms that emanate from this view are legally permissive but morally demanding. People should be free to select their children in any way they see fit; but it is their moral duty to create the best children they can, both in terms of the new individuals' lives *and* (in saviour sibling cases) in terms of their medical usefulness. Similarly, scientists should be legally free to conduct research on embryos (because they are not entities that matter), and all others should be legally free to become voluntary research subjects (because the willing cannot be harmed); but women have a moral duty to provide eggs for work on embryos, everybody is morally obliged to offer experimental services to life scientists, and life scientists themselves are morally required to conduct useful research. As a special instance, human reproductive cloning is *not* allowed as long as it is unsafe for the (nonconsenting) individuals produced in the process.

Here, then, we have the first complete case for advances, and against restrictions, in genetics and related fields. The rightness and wrongness of choices and policies can be defined by measuring their impacts on persons and their lives worth living. All other considerations are intrinsically superfluous and unnecessary for ethical assessments.

10.7   Sensing the challenge

The 'moral transcendence' approach favoured by Kass and Sandel provides an equally straightforward case for restrictions and against advances. The comparison of the two opposite views is, on the surface, difficult, because they expressly disagree on the value of analysis and logical consistency. Glover and Harris swear by these hallmarks of reason and enlightenment, while Kass and Sandel see them as sources of shallowness and moral decay in contemporary ethics. This does not, however, mean that either side would be willing to abandon coherence, or the lack of it, as an element of criticism against opponents. Kass exemplifies this well by arguing that considerable longevity is self-defeating, as people's desire for immortality cannot be fulfilled by added life years. Both schools appreciate consistency and coherence, and both use them in attempts to trip their opponents.

The underlying rationality of the 'moral transcendence' view is less scientific, less calculating, and less individualistic than that of its consequence-driven competitor. Although Kass and Sandel do not deny the importance of modern science in our lives, they are not willing to give it a decisive role in the normative evaluation of practices and policies. Especially when it comes to moulding human beings, they want to retain a traditional or spiritual 'given' or 'gift' element that transcends anything life scientists can accomplish. This element, incorporated in ways of collective thinking and communal living, is the entity that matters morally to Kass and Sandel, and its preservation as intact as possible would for them be the best outcome of regulations and restrictions. The loss of unconstrained freedom and material wellbeing of individuals is, according to this strand of thought, a small price to pay for the true morality of human dignity and social solidarity.

In the dispute over the 'general tenets', the interpretations given by Kass and Sandel are diametrically opposed to the ones preferred by Glover and Harris. Human lives are not made better by selection; on the contrary, the best babies are the babies that are naturally given to their parents. Medical means can and must be used to keep people healthy once they have been born; but there are limits to this, which should not be overstepped. The use of human embryos for research or treatments is, potentially, one such limit, and very good reasons would be needed for its acceptance. Since the design and manufacture of children would go against the 'given' aspect of reproduction, the creation of saviour siblings should also be carefully considered. People should be kept alive and well for a decent lifetime, but dignity and solidarity dictate that not too much effort should be made to extend and improve individual lives at the expense of higher values. These higher values, derived from community traditions and considerations of humanity's future, are constantly under attack from scientific advances and commercial marketing efforts; and people should be empowered to resist these attacks and concentrate on what is genuinely desirable.

Kass and Sandel defend traditional ideals, and it stands to reason that they support distinctions and ideals which are consistent with these. Killing people is one thing and letting them die is another, and although we should not stand idly by when we can effortlessly save lives, we should not take on excessive social obligations, either. The total obliteration of the division would mean either that killing is all right in principle or that we are always required to save and extend lives, whatever the moral and social consequences. Both alternatives are unacceptable. As regards precaution, slippery slopes, and the status quo, Kass and Sandel prefer being safe to sorry and remain unmoved by accusations of irrational timidity. Parity of reasoning for them means, predominantly, that when two dubious practices are morally similar, they should both be banned. Reproductive freedom in the sense of a licence to select one's offspring at will is not authorised by the 'moral transcendence' view; but parental autonomy construed in another way is encouraged and even promoted. Good, directive counselling and solid peer pressure can persuade potential mothers and fathers to do what they ought to do, namely, to forgo the use of genetic technologies and to receive the children given to them as nature's gifts. This would be an expression of their autonomy, or integrity, against the all-pervading powers of the bioscientific industry and uncontrolled market economy.

The practical norms that can be derived from this view are legally restrictive and morally conservative. People considering procreation should not test or select their children; and legislators and regulators should not give them the opportunity to begin with. Kass and Sandel are not very specific about selecting for disability or saviour siblings, but as instances of design and manufacture these practices should not be looked upon favourably. The effects of stem cell research can be beneficial, but since the routine use of human embryos is deeply disrespectful, alternative sources of stem cells should be explored, and permitted embryonic research should be confined to cases in which the advantages are morally and socially commensurate to the cost. Cloning as the ultimate form of design should be clearly prohibited. Somatic gene therapies are seemingly innocuous medical procedures, and as such they would not raise objections. But the continuum they form with germ-line changes and genetic enhancements makes them vulnerable to charges of 'design' and 'mastery'. The same logic applies to age retardation and life extension. It is, of course, good to improve people's life quality and their chances of moderate longevity, but the (hubristic) pursuit of bodily immortality is so closely linked with these that caution is needed.

The views advocated by Kass and Sandel, unlike those held by Glover and Harris, deviate at times considerably from each other. Sandel is generally more lenient than Kass when it comes to stem cell research, somatic gene therapies, and life extension. The foundations of their views are, nonetheless, similar. Both rely on traditional ideals and both emphasise the notion of life as a gift, as opposed to something that can be chosen, made, or tampered with.

10.8   Negotiating the challenge

The remaining, 'everybody's acceptance' view does not provide patent answers to the normative questions raised by the genetic challenge. Habermas and Green take the essentially Kantian idea of universal norms in two diverse directions and come, as a result, to two different sets of conclusions. Habermas argues that moral rules cannot be acknowledged as right unless everyone, including every future individual, can consent to their bindingness. Green contends that the voluntary participation of reasonable persons in moral legislation will guarantee its universal validity.

The entities that matter are, within this doctrine, ethical rules and their acceptability. Morality is not primarily concerned with material consequences or spiritual traditions; but with alternative procedures by which decisions are made, and the implications of employing these procedures. Habermas underlines strict universality as a distinctly moral dimension in decisions concerning scientific progress and its regulation. Green is more interested in the commonsense aptness of scientific activities from a pragmatic point of view. Both put equal weight on the requirements of analytic clarity and conceptual coherence.

What, then, about the 'general tenets' and their shifting interpretations in this model? Habermas stresses that children should be cherished as gifts; and that parents should not engage in activities which can confuse the distinction between what is originally given in their offspring and what is the result of the children's own choices and other people's actions. This gives him grounds for opposing selection, as he believes that babies chosen for their genetic qualities would become more or less their parents' projects. Green, interestingly, does not have to reject the idea of a gift to reach a competing conclusion. Since, according to him, parental love almost always prevails, mothers and fathers will see their children as wondrous gifts regardless of the way in which they are produced. Even after selection there will be something surprising in the new individuals, parents will appreciate this unexpected feature, and the children will retain their 'given' identity in this element of surprise.

Green condones in principle all current and projected methods of making human lives better and longer, including saviour sibling, stem cell, and gene treatments – therapies and enhancements alike. Reasonable people would, according to him, find these agreeable, even if sometimes in need of regulation. For Habermas, saviour siblings and germ-line interventions are problematic, because we cannot ask in advance for the consent of the targeted individuals, and we cannot take it for granted that they would sanction our actions. Stem cell research and therapies, in their turn, can be criticised for their undignified treatment of early human beings; but since opinions on the use of embryos can reasonably vary, Habermas stops short of drawing (universal) moral conclusions in this case. On the matters of empowering people's decisions and improving humanity, Green sides with Glover and Harris against restrictive opinions and precautionary concerns; whereas Habermas comes close to Kass and Sandel in his condemnation of biological engineering and in his uneasiness in the face of decaying ethical ideals.

The arguments that cut both ways elicit partly similar and partly dissimilar readings from Habermas and Green. Both believe that rules and their observance are paramount to morality. As action by rules requires intentionality and as the intentions behind killing people and letting them die are for the most part different, the distinction can be made by both; and so can the division into parents who do or do not want the best lives for their children. But the views are drawn apart by conflicting notions of life's goodness: Green finds this in the healthy and continued existence of living individuals; Habermas locates it in the preservation of our ethical self-understanding. As a result, Green hails controlled advances and scorns resistance to change; Habermas recommends caution and demands respect for all human beings, including those who have not been born yet.

Green's practical conclusions are permissive, and they state that as long as safety and fairness are not an issue, anything useful is worth developing, be it testing, experimenting, cloning, engineering, or extending human lives. Habermas could allow gene therapies aimed at restoring the health of existing individuals and age retardation treatments that are not likely to mix up the 'given' and 'made' elements of human beings. Selection in any shape or form, cloning, and germ-line interventions would, however, encounter his firm rejection as ways of moulding people without their knowledge and consent.

Since the 'everybody's acceptance' view requires, at least hypothetically, negotiations on the norms that we should assume, it has the theoretical potential of incorporating insights and intuitions from both the lenient 'rational tangibility' and the strict 'moral transcendence' stances. The doctrine cannot, however, be seen merely as an intermediate position reconciling the extreme ends of the debate. It is an approach in its own right, defining its own method, based on the idea of universality, of making sense of the genetic challenge. As evidenced by the disagreement between Green and Habermas, the practical conclusions can vary depending on the content given to the central concepts of 'universality' and 'everybody'.

10.9   The methods of genethics

Henry Sidgwick defined in *The Methods of Ethics* in 1874 three main lines of thought in the moral philosophy of his time. In a similar vein, I suggest that the rationalities summarised in Sections 10.6, 10.7, and 10.8 define three major approaches in the current ethics of genetics, or genethics. Other ways of thinking exist in this field, just as other ways of moral thinking existed in Sidgwick's era, but most opinions expressed in academic debates on the genetic challenge and ways of improving humanity can be traced back to these views and their variations.

The methods that Sidgwick distinguished were 'dogmatic intuitionism', 'ethical egoism', and 'universalistic hedonism'. The first equated the rightness of choices and actions with conformity to prevailing moral intuitions that can be expressed in terms of traditional virtues, universal duties, absolute rights, and the like. The second decreed that all moral agents have an obligation to pursue their own good; and the third stipulated that all moral agents have an obligation to pursue everybody's good. Many ideals and notions presented by Green, Habermas, Kass, and Sandel would probably in Sidgwick's analysis have ended up in the first category, while Glover and Harris would have found their place in the third class.

Sidgwick's background theory enabled him to critically assess and rank the 'methods' that he named. He thought that ethical theories should be internally *coherent* and conform to the higher principles of *justice* (what is right for one person in certain circumstances is also right for another in a similar situation), *prudence* (future benefits and harms are as weighty as immediate ones), and the *universality of goodness* (from the viewpoint of the universe, one person's good is no better than another's; also, if compared, the good of the many always outweighs the good of the few). Armed with these criteria, Sidgwick concluded that dogmatic intuitionism can be rejected, because it produces conflicting norms for practical situations and does not therefore abide by the requirement of coherence. He was, however, unable to make a decisive judgement between ethical egoism and universalistic hedonism, since they both meet the conditions of justice and prudence, and since it is a matter of reasonable dispute whether individuals should regards things from their own angle (the one) or from the viewpoint of the universe (the many).

Even if we were to follow Sidgwick in his selection of background principles, it would not be easy to make similar critical distinctions among the 'rational tangibility', 'moral transcendence', and 'everybody's agreement' approaches to genethics. On the one hand, due to Sidgwick's utilitarian framework, the views advocated by Glover and Harris should fit his model nicely; and as far as justice (what is right for one is right for another) and the universality of goodness (everybody counts as one and only as one) go, they do. But prudence could pose difficulties, if our consequentialists insist on immediate impacts at the expense of future harms, as they seem to do in debates on indirect risks, cumulative damage, and precaution. The lack of coherence found by Sidgwick in dogmatic everyday intuitionism, on the other hand, evaporates when appeals to virtues, duties, and rights are separated into their own doctrines and not randomly mixed together. Justice and prudence in the Sidgwickian sense should not present problems to the creeds of Green, Habermas, Kass, or Sandel, as they do not, presumably, advocate double standards, and as they all explicitly stress the future of humanity as opposed to the instant desire fulfilment of the present generations. The essentially utilitarian idea of the good of the many trumping the good of the few could create difficulties, although at least Kass and Sandel seem to be happy with the possibly related notion of collective community good outweighing individual satisfaction. Questions of coherence can be raised from all camps, but their resolution depends on basic attitudes and fundamental values rather than pure logic.

10.10   Taking the genetic challenge nonconfrontationally

My nonconfrontational notion of rationality provides even fewer grounds for ranking the contradictory approaches to genethics than Sidgwick's principles do. None of the three views is grossly incoherent, and the rest of the variation can be seen as just that – variation. But what does this mean in terms of my findings?

If different approaches (or rationalities or methods of genethics) cannot be universally graded and put into order, as I am saying, then conflicting normative views cannot be put into one rational order, either, and we have no philosophical way of telling once and for all whether we should or should not engage in procreative selection, reproductive or therapeutic cloning, genetic engineering, or considerable life extension. This raises two pertinent questions. Nonphilosophers can justifiably ask, 'What is the point of this book, then?' And philosophers can enquire, 'Do we have any role in genethics, if all this is to be believed?'

The answer to the lay question is twofold. First, the book provides all the normative guidance that books on philosophical ethics can. It presents the main arguments for and against genetic and related techniques and practices, with commentaries on their strengths and weaknesses. Intelligent readers can, in the light of these, articulate their own views on the activities involved and make their own moral judgements concerning them. Secondly, the book refuses to claim absolute validity for particular norms on philosophical grounds. Philosophical considerations can show that some arguments are flawed and others open to discussion, but they cannot prove to everybody's satisfaction the rightness or wrongness of selection, cloning, or new treatments. The practical point of the book, then, is to empower readers to make up their own minds on genetic and related technologies and not to lull themselves into thinking that they can find ready-made answers of universal validity in philosophical writings.

The answer to the philosophers' question is that the nonconfrontational approach actually defines *more* tasks for them than the prescriptive style that currently prevails in genethics. Contributions in the field typically describe two competing positions on a practice, aim to show that one of them is conceptually unsound or emotionally unacceptable, and conclude that the other position must be chosen. This strategy is by no means intrinsically faulty, but it underuses the potential of philosophical analysis and reflection. If the described positions are the only choices available, if one of them is undeniably incoherent or intolerable, and if the other one fares better in an impartial analysis, the conclusion indeed has some support. Many questions remain unanswered, though. Are these the only possible stances on the matter or can useful alternatives be found in other kinds of thinking? Are the assessments of conceptual coherence and emotional acceptability based on ideas that are agreeable to everyone or do they proceed from a predetermined ethical outlook?

When all the variety in background theories, normative views, and real-life practices is taken into account, the number of stances and cases in need of scrutiny becomes considerable. I have in this book described three main methods of ethical thinking and observed that even authors within one approach – Glover and Harris, Kass and Sandel, Habermas and Green – have their differences. Although I have accepted, in the main, the received wisdom that outcome-based doctrines advocate freedom, virtue-based models support prohibitions, and rule-based theories promote regulations, I have also noted that other combinations of ideology and attitude are logically possible. A prominent feature of the preceding chapters is that I have examined in detail only one ethical idea and one genetic or medical practice at a time – parental responsibility and selection, legality and deafness, instrumental use and saviour siblings, design and cloning, vulnerability and stem cells, consequences and gene therapies, and life's meaning and longevity. But as I have indicated, the majority of the ethical considerations can be applied to most of the other practices, as well.

A quick calculation shows that if there are three viable methods of ethics (outcomes, virtues, and rules), three normative stands (permissive, restrictive, and regulative), and eight topics (the themes of Chapters 3, 4, 5, 6, 7, 8, and 9 and the genetic challenge in general), there are at least 72 stances that could be critically examined by philosophers. I have covered ten of these in this book. Some of the remaining ones could be theoretical nonstarters, but the range widens again when other potential approaches (say, based on gender, culture, ethnicity, or religion), normative views (there is considerable variation within the regulative view, for instance), and topics (the number of advances in technology is ever-increasing) are taken into account. Philosophers in the ethics of genetics have their work cut out for them.

Practical philosophers can do their work reactively or proactively, and both schemes can produce helpful results. In the first model, ethicists learn about a new development in science, medicine, ethics, or legislation; lay out their conceptual tools; and produce an analysis of the logical and emotional aspects of the case, complete with a normative conclusion derived from their background assumptions and the facts of the case. Glover, Harris, Kass, Sandel, Habermas, Green, and others have done a thorough job in this area, and as a consequence books and journals in the field contain a fairly comprehensive archive of outcome-driven defences of freedom in genetics, virtue-inspired justifications of bans and prohibitions, and rule-inclined arguments for regulations. In the second model, philosophers create alternative ways of thinking about ethically contested issues such as the genetic challenge. These can be based on traditional philosophical ideas; as in the revival of libertarian and communitarian doctrines in political philosophy at the end of last century. But they can also be small-scale test attempts to bring together elements that are usually seen as incompatible; say, in a critique of genetic advances on consequentialist grounds. The genetic challenge has many aspects, and a systematic exploration of all the rationalities surrounding it that fulfil the requirements of coherence and consistency will keep proactive philosophers occupied for quite some time. I, for one, intend to turn my attention to the rationalities of justice, often alluded to in genethical discussion but rarely pursued in any real depth.

BIBLIOGRAPHY

All the websites cited in this bibliography were accessed on 15 May 2009.

Agar, Nicholas, 2004, *Liberal Eugenics: In Defence of Human Enhancement* (Oxford: Blackwell).

Annas, George J., 1989, 'A French homunculus in a Tennessee court', *Hastings Center Report* **19**: 20-2.

Anscombe, Elizabeth, 1970, 'War and murder', Richard A. Wasserstrom (ed.), *War and Morality* (Belmont, CA: Wadsworth Publishing): 42-53.

Anstey, Kyle W., 2002, 'Are attempts to have impaired children justifiable?', *Journal of Medical Ethics* **28**: 286-8.

Apfel, Roberta J. and Fisher, Susan M., 1984, *To Do No Harm: DES and the Dilemmas of Modern Medicine* (New Haven, CT: Yale University Press).

Aquinas, Thomas, 1988, *On Law, Morality and Politics* [1265-1272], edited by W. P. Baumgarth and R. J. Regan (Indianapolis, IN: Hackett Publishing Company).

Archard, David (ed.), 1996, *Philosophy and Pluralism* (Cambridge: Cambridge University Press).

Aristotle, 1981, *The Politics*, translated by T. A. Sinclair (Harmondsworth: Penguin Books).

1982, *Nichomachean Ethics*, translated by H. Rackman (Cambridge, MA: Harvard University Press).

1991, *History of Animals* Volumes VII-X, translated by D. M. Balme (Cambridge: Loeb Classical Library).

Atwood, Margaret, 1985, *The Handmaid's Tale* (Toronto: McClelland and Stewart).

Australian Stem Cell Centre, 2009, 'What are stem cells?' – www.stemcellcentre. edu.au/public-education_what-cells_cord.aspx.

Baron, Jonathan, 2007, *Against Bioethics* (Cambridge, MA: MIT Press).

Barrow, Paul, 2003, 'Autonomy: overworked and under-valued', Matti Häyry and Tuija Takala (eds), *Scratching the Surface of Bioethics* (Amsterdam: Rodopi): 133-40.

Bartlett, Thomas, 2005, 'The man who would murder death: A rogue researcher challenges scientists to reverse human aging', *The Chronicle of Higher Education* **52**, Issue 10 (28 October): A14.

Baruch, S., Kaufman, D. and Hudson, K. L., 2008, 'Genetic testing of embryos: practices and perspectives of US in vitro fertilization clinics', *Fertility and Sterility* **89**: 1053-8.

Baylis, Françoise and McLeod, Caroline, 2007, 'The stem cell debate continues: the buying and selling of eggs for research', *Journal of Medical Ethics* **33**: 726–31.

BBC News, 2001, 'Europe rejects human cloning ban', 29 November – news.bbc. co.uk/1/hi/sci/tech/1682591.stm.

BBC News, 2008, 'MPs reject "saviour sibling" ban'. 19 May – news.bbc.co.uk/2/hi/ uk_news/politics/7409264.stm.

Beeson, Diane and Lippman, Abby, 2006, 'Egg harvesting for stem cell research: medical risks and ethical problems', *Reproductive Biomedicine Online* **13**: 573–9.

Benatar, David, 2006, *Better Never to Have Been: The Harm of Coming into Existence* (Oxford: Clarendon Press).

Bentham, Jeremy, 1931, *The Theory of Legislation*, edited by C. K. Ogden (London: Kegan Paul).

    1982, *An Introduction to the Principles of Morals and Legislation* [1789], edited by J. H. Burns and H. L. A. Hart (London: Methuen).

Berry, Caroline and Engel, Jacky, 2005, 'Saviour siblings', *Christian Medical Fellowship Files* Nr 28 – www.cmf.org.uk/literature/content.asp?context= article&id=1317.

Beyleveld, Deryck and Brownsword, Roger, 2001, *Human Dignity and Biolaw* (Oxford: Oxford University Press).

Bittles, A. H. and Collins, K. J. (eds), 1986, *The Biology of Human Ageing* (Cambridge: Cambridge University Press).

Bostrom, Nick, 2005, 'In defence of posthuman dignity', *Bioethics* **19**: 202–14.

Bostrom, Nick and Ord, Toby, 2006, 'The reversal test: Eliminating status quo bias in applied ethics', *Ethics* **116**: 656–79.

Boyce, Nell, 2001, 'Trial halted after gene shows up in semen', *Nature* **414**: 677.

Brandt, Richard B., 1979, *A Theory of the Good and the Right* (Oxford: Clarendon Press).

Brazier, Margaret R., 2006, 'Human(s) (as) medicine(s)', Sheila MacLean (ed.), *First Do No Harm: Law, Ethics and Healthcare* (Aldershot: Ashgate): 187–202.

Brazier, Margaret and Cave, Emma, 2007, *Medicine, Patients and the Law*, fourth edition (London: Penguin Books).

Brock, Dan W., 2006, 'Is a consensus possible on stem cell research? Moral and political obstacles', *Journal of Medical Ethics* **32**: 36–42.

Brown, Eric, 2004, 'The dilemmas of German bioethics', *The New Atlantis* **Nr 5**, pp. 37–53 – www.thenewatlantis.com/publications/the-dilemmas-of-german-bioethics.

Brown, Mark T., 2000, 'The morality of abortion and the deprivation of futures', *Journal of Medical Ethics* **26**: 103–7.

    2002a, 'A future like ours revisited', *Journal of Medical Ethics* **28**: 192–5.

    2002b, 'Abortion and the value of the future: A reply to a defence of the potential future of value theory', *Journal of Medical Ethics* **28**: 202.

Buchanan, Allen, Brock, Dan W., Daniels, Norman and Wikler, Daniel, 2000, *From Chance to Choice: Genetics and Justice* (Cambridge: Cambridge University Press).

Burt, Richard K., Loh, Yvonne, Pearce, William, Beohar, Nirat, Barr, Walter G., Craig, Robert, Wen, Yanting, Rapp, Jonathan A. and Kessler, John, 2008, 'Clinical applications of blood-derived and marrow-derived stem cells for nonmalignant diseases', *Journal of the American Medical Association* **299**: 925–36.

Byrne, James A. and Gurdon, John B., 2002, 'Commentary on human cloning', *Differentiation* **69**: 154–7.

Cao, Antonio, Rosatelli, Maria Cristina, Monni, Giovanni and Galanello, Renzo, 2002, 'Screening for thalassemia: A model of success', *Obstetrics and Gynecology Clinics of North America* **29**: 305–28.

Chadwick, Ruth, 1982, 'Cloning', *Philosophy* **57**: 201–9.

Check, Erika, 2003, 'Second cancer case halts gene-therapy trials', *Nature* **421**: 305.

2005a, 'Gene therapy put on hold as third child develops cancer', *Nature* **433**: 561.

2005b, 'Gene-therapy trials to restart following cancer risk review', *Nature* **434**: 127.

Chung, Young, Klimanskaya, Irina, Becker, Sandy, Li, Tong, Maserati, Marc, Lu, Shi-Jiang, Zdravkovic, Tamara, Ilic, Dusko, Genbacev, Olga, Fisher, Susan, Krtolica, Ana, and Lanza, Robert, 2008, 'Human embryonic stem cell lines generated without embryo destruction', *Cell Stem Cell* **2**: 113–17.

Clark, W. R., 1999, *A Means to an End: The Biological Basis of Aging and Death* (New York, NY: Oxford University Press).

CNN World News, 1998, '19 European nations sign ban on human cloning', 12 January – edition.cnn.com/WORLD/9801/12/cloning.ban/video.html.

Coghlan, Andy, 2004, '"Saviour sibling" babies get green light', *New Scientist*, 22 July – www.newscientist.com/article/dn6195-saviour-sibling-babies-get-green-light.html.

Columbia Pictures, 1997, *Gattaca*.

Condorcet, Marie-Jean-Antoine-Nicholas de Caritat, Marquis de, 1955, *Sketch for a Historical Picture of the Progress of the Human Mind* [1795], translated by June Barraclough (New York, NY: Noonday Press).

Conrad, Sabine, Renninger, Markus, Hennenlotter, Jörg, Wiesner, Tina, Just, Lothar, Bonin, Michael, Aicher, Wilhelm, Bühring, Hans-Jörg, Mattheus, Ulrich, Mack, Andreas, Wagner, Hans-Joachim, Minger, Stephen, Matzkies, Matthias, Reppel, Michael, Hescheler, Jürgen, Sievert, Karl-Dietrich, Stenzl, Arnulf and Skutella, Thomas, 2008, 'Generation of pluripotent stem cells from adult human testis', *Nature* **456**: 344–9.

Corveleyn, Anniek, Zika, Eleni, Morris, Michael, Dequeker, Elisabeth, Lawford
    Davies, James, Sermon, Karen, Antiñolo, Guillermo, Schmutzler, Andreas,
    Vanecek, Jiri, Palau, Fransesc and Ibarreta, Dolores, 2007, *Preimplantation
    Genetic Diagnosis in Europe* (Executive Summary), EUR22764 EN – ftp://
    ftp.jrc.es/pub/C&S/?.
Council of Ethical and Judicial Affairs, 1994, *Pre-Embryo Splitting*, American
    Medical Association.
Crockin, Susan L., 2001, 'Embryo "adoption": A limited option', *Reproductive
    BioMedicine Online* 3: 162–3.
de Grey, Aubrey, 1999, *The Mitochondrial Free Radical Theory of Aging* (Austin,
    TX: R. G. Landes Company).
    2007, 'Life span extension research and public debate: societal considerations',
    Studies in Ethics, Law, and Technology 1 – www.bepress.com/selt/vol1/iss1/
    art5.
de Grey, Aubrey and Rae, Michael, 2007, *Ending Aging: The Rejuvenation
    Breakthroughs that Could Reverse Human Aging in Our Lifetime* (New York,
    NY: St Martin's Press).
de Grey, Aubrey, Ames, Bruce N., Andersen, Julie K., Bartke, Andrzej, Campisi,
    Judith, Heward, Christopher B., McCarter, Roger J. M. and Stock, Gregory,
    2002, 'Time to talk SENS: Critiquing the immutability of human aging',
    Annals of the New York Academy of Sciences 959: 452–62.
Delmonico, Francis L. and Harmon, William E., 2002, 'The use of a minor as a live
    kidney donor', *American Journal of Transplantation* 2: 333–6.
Department of Health, 2005, 'UK to vote against UN human cloning decision',
    News Releases, 7 February – www.dh.gov.uk/en/Publicationsandstatistics/
    Pressreleases/DH_4105348.
Derrida, Jacques, 1995, *The Gift of Death*, translated by David Wills (Chicago,
    IL: Chicago University Press).
Devolder, Katrien and Savulescu, Julian, 2006, 'The moral imperative to conduct
    embryonic stem cell research', *Cambridge Quarterly of Healthcare Ethics*
    15: 7–21.
Dickenson, Donna and Alkorta Idiakez, Itziar, 2008, 'Ova donation for stem cell
    research: An international perspective', *International Journal of Feminist
    Approaches to Bioethics* 1: 125–44.
Dudley, William (ed.), 2001, *The Ethics of Human Cloning* (San Diego,
    CA: Greenhaven Press).
Durkheim, Émile, 1997, *The Division of Labor in Society* [1893], translated by
    George Simpson (New York, NY: The Free Press).
Dworkin, Ronald, 1989, 'The original position', Norman Daniels (ed.), *Reading
    Rawls: Critical Studies on Rawls' 'A Theory of Justice'* [1975] (Stanford,
    CA: Stanford University Press).
Edgar, Gail, 2008, 'The saviour sibling', *Belfast Telegraph*, 18 May – www.sunday-
    life.co.uk/news/article3714984.ece.

Ehrich, Kathryn, Farsides, Bobbie, Williams, Clare and Scott, Rosamund, 2007, 'Testing the embryo, testing the fetus', *Clinical Ethics* 2: 181–6.

Eisenberg, Leon, 2003, 'Life, liberty, and the defense of dignity: The challenge for bioethics' (book review), *The New England Journal of Medicine* 348: 766–8.

Ekberg, Merryn, 2007, 'The old eugenics and the new genetics compared', *Social History of Medicine* 20: 581–93.

Elwyn, Glyn, Gray, Jonathon and Clarke, Angus, 2000, 'Shared decision making and non-directiveness in genetic counselling', *Journal of Medical Genetics* 37: 135–8.

Examination of Witnesses (Questions 805–819) before the Joint Committee of the Human Tissue and Embryos (draft) Bill, 2007, 26 June – www.publications. parliament.uk/pa/jt200607/jtselect/jtembryos/169/7062608.htm.

Feinberg, Joel, 1967, 'The forms and limits of utilitarianism', *Philosophical Review* 76: 368–81.

1984–88, *The Moral Limits of the Criminal Law* Volumes I-IV (Oxford: Oxford University Press).

Finger, Reginald, 'Embryo adoption: A life-affirming parenthood choice' – www. cmdahome.org/AM/Template.cfm?Section=Home&TEMPLATE=/CM/ ContentDisplay.cfm&CONTENTID=11075.

Foot, Philippa, 1978, *Virtues and Vices and Other Essays in Moral Philosophy* (Berkeley, CA: University of California Press).

2001, *Natural Goodness* (Oxford: Clarendon Press).

2002, *Moral Dilemmas: And Other Topics in Moral Philosophy* (Oxford: Clarendon Press).

Ford, Norman, 2001, 'The human embryo as person in Catholic teaching', *The National Bioethics Quarterly* 1: 155–60.

Freedman, B., 1987, 'Equipoise and the ethics of clinical research', *The New England Journal of Medicine* 317: 141–5.

Freeman, Michael, 1997, *The Moral Status of Children: Essays on the Rights of Children* (The Hague: Kluwer Law International).

Freitas, Robert A. Jr, 2001, *Microbivores: Artificial Mechanical Phagocytes Using Digest and Discharge Protocol* – www.rfreitas.com/Nano/Microbivores.htm.

Frew, Sarah E., Sammut, Stephen M., Shore, Alysha F., Ramjist, Joshua K., Al-Bader, Sara, Rezaie, Rahim, Daar, Abdallah S. and Singer, Peter A., 2008, 'Chinese health biotech and the billion-patient market', *Nature Biotechnology* 26: 37–53.

Frolkis, Vladimir V., 1982, *Ageing and Life-Prolonging Processes* (Vienna: Springer-Verlag).

Fukuyama, Francis, 2002, *Our Posthuman Future: Consequences of the Biotechnology Revolution* (London: Profile Books).

Gelfand, Scott and Shook, John R. (eds), 2006, *Ectogenesis: Artificial Womb Technology and the Future of Human Reproduction* (Amsterdam: Rodopi).

Gelsinger v. *Trustees of the University of Pennsylvania*, 2000 – www.sskrplaw. com/links/healthcare2.html.

Giles, Jim and Knight, Jonathan, 2003, 'Dolly's death leaves researchers woolly on clone ageing issue', *Nature* **421**: 776.

Gillon, Raanan, 1985, *Philosophical Medical Ethics* (Chichester: John Wiley & Sons).

Glannon, Walter, 2002a, 'Extending the human life span', *Journal of Medicine and Philosophy* **27**: 339–54.

    2002b, 'Identity, prudential concern, and extended lives', *Bioethics* **16**: 266–83.

    2002c, 'Reply to Harris', *Bioethics* **16**: 292–7.

Global Lawyers and Physicians, 2005, 'Database of global policies on human cloning and germ-line engineering' – www.glphr.org/genetic/genetic. htm.

Glover, Jonathan, 1977, *Causing Death and Saving Lives* (Harmondsworth: Penguin Books).

    1984, *What Sort of People Should There Be? Genetic Engineering, Brain Control, and Their Impact on Our Future World* (New York, NY: Penguin Books).

    1999, *Humanity: A Moral History of the Twentieth Century* (London: Jonathan Cape).

    2006, *Choosing Children: Genes, Disability, and Design* (Oxford: Clarendon Press).

Godwin, William, 1985, *Enquiry Concerning Political Justice and its Influence on Modern Morals and Happiness* [1793], edited by I. Kramnick (Harmondsworth: Penguin Books).

Goldman, Bruce, 2007, 'Reproductive medicine: The first cut', *Nature* **445**: 479–80.

Goodman, Nelson, 1955, *Fact, Fiction, and Forecast* (Cambridge, MA: Harvard University Press).

Green, Ronald M., 1991, 'The first formulation of the categorical imperative as literally a "legislative" metaphor', *History of Philosophy Quarterly* **8**: 163–79.

    2001a, 'What does it mean to use someone "as a means only": Rereading Kant', *Kennedy Institute of Ethics Journal* **11**: 247–61.

    2001b, *The Human Embryo Research Debates: Bioethics in the Vortex of Controversy* (New York, NY: Oxford University Press).

    2005, 'New challenges of genetics and ethics' – www.dartmouth.edu/~ethics/ resources/elsi2005.html.

    2007, *Babies by Design: The Ethics of Genetic Choice* (New Haven, CT: Yale University Press).

Griffin, James, 1986, *Well-Being: Its Meaning, Measurement, and Moral Importance* (Oxford: Clarendon Press).

    2008, *On Human Rights* (Oxford: Oxford University Press).

Guerra, Marc D., 2003, 'Life, liberty, and the defense of human dignity: The challenge for bioethics' (book review), *First Things* – www.firstthings.com/article.php3?id_article=429.

Gurnham, David, 2005, 'The mysteries of human dignity and the brave new world of human cloning', *Social and Legal Studies* **14**: 197–214.

Habermas, Jürgen, 1984–87, *The Theory of Communicative Action* Volumes I-II, translated by Thomas McCarthy (Cambridge: Polity Press).

  1990, *Moral Consciousness and Communicative Action*, translated by Christian Lenhardt and Shierry Weber Nicholsen (Cambridge, MA: MIT Press).

  1993, *Justification and Application: Remarks on Discourse Ethics*, translated by Ciaran Cronin (Cambridge: Polity Press).

  2003, *The Future of Human Nature*, translated by William Rehg, Max Pensky, and Hella Beister (Cambridge: Polity Press).

Hardcastle, Rohan, 2007, *Law and the Human Body: Property Rights, Ownership and Control* (Oxford: Hart Publishing).

Hare, Richard M., 1975, 'Abortion and the Golden Rule', *Philosophy & Public Affairs* **4**: 201–22.

  1976, 'Survival of the weakest', Samuel Gorovitz (ed.), *Moral Problems in Medicine* (Englewood Cliffs, NJ: Prentice-Hall): 364–9.

  1981, *Moral Thinking: Its Levels, Method and Point* (Oxford: Clarendon Press).

Harris, John, 1975, 'The survival lottery', *Philosophy* **50**: 81–7.

  1980, *Violence and Responsibility* (London: Routledge & Kegan Paul).

  1985, *The Value of Life: An Introduction to Medical Ethics* (London: Routledge and Kegan Paul).

  1992, *Wonderwoman and Superman: The Ethics of Human Biotechnology* (Oxford: Oxford University Press).

  1998, *Clones, Genes, and Immortality: Ethics and the Genetic Revolution* (Oxford: Oxford University Press).

  1999a, 'Justice and equal opportunities in health care', *Bioethics* **13**: 392–404.

  1999b, 'The concept of the person and the value of life', *Kennedy Institute of Ethics Journal* **9**: 293–308.

  2000, 'Is there a coherent social conception of disability?', *Journal of Medical Ethics* **26**: 95–100.

  2001, 'One principle and three fallacies of disability studies', *Journal of Medical Ethics* **27**: 383–7.

  2003a, 'Intimations of immortality: The ethics and justice of life-extending therapies', M. D. A. Freeman (ed.), *Current Legal Problems 2002* (Oxford: Oxford University Press): 65–95.

  2003b, 'Stem cells, sex, and procreation', *Cambridge Quarterly of Healthcare Ethics* **12**: 353–71.

  2004, *On Cloning* (London: Routledge).

  2005, 'Scientific research is a moral duty', *Journal of Medical Ethics* **31**: 242–8.

2007, *Enhancing Evolution: The Ethical Case for Making Better People* (Princeton: Princeton University Press).

Harris, John and Cutas, Daniela, 2007, 'The ethics of ageing, immortality and genetics', Richard E. Ashcroft, Angus Dawson, Heather Draper, and John R. McMillan (eds), *Principles of Health Care Ethics*, second edition (Chichester: John Wiley & Sons): 797–801.

Harris, John and Holm, Søren, 2002, 'Extending human lifespan and the precautionary paradox', *Journal of Medicine and Philosophy* 27: 355–68.

Harsanyi, John C., 1978, 'Bayesian decision theory and utilitarian ethics', *The American Economic Review* 68: 223–8.

Hartley, David, 1834, *Observations on Man, His Frame, His Duty and His Expectations* [1749], sixth edition (London: Thomas Tegg and Son).

Hawking, Stephen, 1993, *Black Holes and Baby Universes* (New York, NY: Bantam Books).

Häyry, Heta, 1991, *The Limits of Medical Paternalism* (London: Routledge).

1994, 'How to assess the consequences of genetic engineering?' Anthony Dyson and John Harris (eds), *Ethics and Biotechnology* (London: Routledge): 144–56.

Häyry, Matti, 1994a, 'Categorical objections to genetic engineering – A critique', Anthony Dyson and John Harris (eds), *Ethics and Biotechnology* (London: Routledge): 202–15.

1994b, *Liberal Utilitarianism and Applied Ethics* (London: Routledge).

1999, 'What the fox would have said, had he been a hedgehog: On the methodology and normative approach of John Harris's Wonderwoman and Superman', Veikko Launis, Juhani Pietarinen and Juha Räikkä (eds), *Genes and Morality: New Essays* (Amsterdam: Rodopi): 11–19.

2001a, *Playing God: Essays on Bioethics* (Helsinki: Helsinki University Press).

2001b, 'Abortion, disability, assent and consent', *Cambridge Quarterly of Healthcare Ethics* 10: 79–87.

2001c, 'But what if we *feel* that cloning is wrong?' *Cambridge Quarterly of Healthcare Ethics* 10: 205–8.

2003a, 'European values in bioethics: why, what, and how to be used?', *Theoretical Medicine and Bioethics* 24: 199–214.

2003b, 'Deeply felt disgust – a Devlinian objection to cloning humans', B. Almond and M. Parker (eds), *Ethical Issues in the New Genetics: Are Genes Us?* (Aldershot: Ashgate): 55–67.

2003c, 'Philosophical arguments for and against human reproductive cloning', *Bioethics* 17: 447–59.

2004a, 'If you must make babies, then at least make the best babies you can?', *Human Fertility* 7: 105–12.

2004b, 'Another look at dignity', *Cambridge Quarterly of Healthcare Ethics* 13: 7–14.

2004c, 'A rational cure for pre-reproductive stress syndrome', *Journal of Medical Ethics* **30**: 377–8.

2004d, 'There is a difference between selecting a deaf embryo and deafening a hearing child', *Journal of Medical Ethics* **30**: 510–12.

2005a, 'The tension between self-governance and absolute inner worth in Kant's moral philosophy', *Journal of Medical Ethics* **31**: 645–7.

2005b, 'Precaution and solidarity', *Cambridge Quarterly of Healthcare Ethics* **14**: 199–206.

2005c, 'The rational cure for prereproductive stress syndrome revisited', *Journal of Medical Ethics* **31**: 606–7.

2006, 'Three questions about the Principle of Acceptable Outlook', *Journal of Medical Ethics Online*, 8 march – jme.bmj.com/cgi/eletters/32/3/166.

2007a, 'Utilitarianism and bioethics', Richard E. Ashcroft, Angus Dawson, Heather Draper, and John R. McMillan (eds), *Principles of Health Care Ethics*, second edition (Chichester: John Wiley & Sons): 57–64.

2007b, 'Generous funding for interventive aging research now?' *Studies in Ethics, Law, and Technology* **1** – www.bepress.com/selt/vol1/iss1/art13.

2007c, *Cloning, Selection, and Values: Essays on Bioethical Intuitions* (Helsinki: Societas Philosophica Fennica).

2008, 'The historical idea of a better race', *Studies in Ethics, Law, and Technology* **2** – www.bepress.com/selt/vol2/iss1/art11.

2009a, 'The moral contestedness of selecting "deaf embryos"', Kristjana Kristiansen, Simo Vehmas, and Tom Shakespeare (eds), *Arguing About Disability: Philosophical Perspectives* (London: Routledge): 154–68.

2009b, 'An analysis of some arguments for and against human reproduction', Matti Häyry, Tuija Takala, Peter Herissone-Kelly, and Gardar Árnason (eds), *Arguments and Analysis in Bioethics* (Amsterdam: Rodopi): 147–54.

2009c, 'Is transferred parental responsibility legitimately enforceable?', in Frida Simonstein (ed.), *Reprogen-Ethics and the Future of Gender* (Dordrecht: Springer): 135–49.

Häyry, Matti and Häyry, Heta, 1998, 'Genetic engineering', Ruth Chadwick (ed.), *Encyclopedia of Applied Ethics* Volume II (San Diego, CA: Academic Press): 407–17.

Häyry, Matti and Takala, Tuija, 1998, 'Genetic engineering and the risk of harm', *Medicine, Health Care and Philosophy* **1**: 61–4.

2001, 'Cloning, naturalness and personhood', D. C. Thomasma, D. N. Weisstub, and C. Hervé (eds), *Personhood and Health Care* (Dordrecht: Kluwer Academic Publishers): 281–98.

2007, 'American principles, European values, and the mezzanine rules of ethical genetic data banking', Matti Häyry, Ruth Chadwick, Vilhjálmur Árnason, and Gardar Árnason (eds), *The Ethics and Governance of Human Genetic Databases: European Perspectives* (Cambridge: Cambridge University Press).

Hedgecoe, Adam M., 1998, 'Gene therapy', Ruth Chadwick (ed.), *Encyclopedia of Applied Ethics* Volume II (San Diego, CA: Academic Press): 383–90.

Hegel, Georg Wilhelm Friedrich, 1857, *Philosophy of History*, translated from the third German edition by J. Sibree (London: Henry G. Bohn).

Heilbronn, Leonie K. and Ravussin, Eric, 2003, 'Calorie restriction and aging: review of the literature and implications for studies in humans', *The American Journal of Clinical Nutrition* **78**: 361–9.

Hensley, Samuel, 2004, 'Designer babies: One step closer', *The Center for Bioethics and Humanity*, 1 July – www.cbhd.org/resources/genetics/hensley_2004-07-01.htm.

Herder, Johan Gottfried von, 1966, *Outlines of a Philosophy of the History of Man* [1784–1791], translated by T. Churchill (New York, NY: Bergman).

Herissone-Kelly, Peter, 2006a, 'Procreative beneficence and the prospective parent', *Journal of Medical Ethics* **32**: 166–9.

2006b, 'Häyry's three questions', *Journal of Medical Ethics Online*, 23 March – jme.bmj.com/cgi/eletters/32/3/166.

Hinkley, Charles C. II, 2005, *Moral Conflicts of Organ Retrieval: A Case for Constructive Pluralism* (Amsterdam: Rodopi).

Hoedemaekers, Rogeer and ten Have, Henk, 1998, 'Geneticization: The Cyprus paradigm', *The Journal of Medicine and Philosophy* **23**: 274–87.

Holm, Søren, 1993, 'The spare embryo – A red herring in the embryo experimentation debate', *Health Care Analysis* **1**: 63–6.

1996, 'The moral status of the pre-personal human being: The argument from potential reconsidered', Donald Evans (ed.), *Conceiving the Embryo: Ethics, Law, and Practice in Human Embryology* (Dordrecht: Kluwer): 193–220.

1998, 'A life in the shadow: One reason why we should not clone humans', *Cambridge Quarterly of Healthcare Ethics* **7**: 160–2.

2002, 'Going to the roots of the stem cell controversy', *Bioethics* **16**: 493–507.

2003a, 'The ethical case against stem cell research', *Cambridge Quarterly of Healthcare Ethics* **12**: 372–83.

2003b, '"Parity of reasoning" argument in bioethics – some methodological considerations', Matti Häyry and Tuija Takala (eds), *Scratching the Surface of Bioethics* (Amsterdam: Rodopi): 47–56.

2008, 'Time to reconsider stem cell ethics – the importance of induced pluripotent cells', *Journal of Medical Ethics* **34**: 63–4.

Holm, Søren and Takala, Tuija, 2007, 'High hopes and automatic escalators: A critique of some new arguments in bioethics', *Journal of Medical Ethics* **33**: 1–4.

Horsey, Kirsty, 2005, '"Saviour sibling" born to Fletcher family', *IVF News*, 23 July 2005 – www.ivf.net/ivf/saviour_sibling_born_to_fletcher_family-o1555-en.html.

Human Fertilisation and Embryology Authority, 2004, *Embryo Splitting & Cloning Statement*, 15 January – www.hfea.gov.uk/hfea/rss/791.html.

Human Reproductive Cloning Act, 2001 – www.opsi.gov.uk/ACTS/acts2001/ukpga_20010023_en_1.

Huxley, Aldous, 1932, *Brave New World* (London: Chatto & Windus).

Isasi, Rosario M. and Annas, George J., 2003, 'Arbitrage, bioethics, and cloning: The ABCs of gestating a United Nations cloning convention', *Cape Western Reserve Journal of International Law* **35**: 397–414.

Jackson, Jennifer, 2006, *Ethics in Medicine* (Cambridge: Polity Press).

Johnson, Robert, 2004 [substantive revision 2008], 'Kant's moral philosophy', *Stanford Encyclopedia of Philosophy* – http://plato.stanford.edu/entries/kant-moral/.

Jonas, Hans, 1984, *The Imperative of Responsibility: In Search of Ethics for the Technological Age* [1979], translated by Hans Jonas and David Herr (Chicago, IL: University of Chicago Press).

Josefson, Deborah, 2000, 'Couple select healthy embryo to provide stem cells for sister', *British Medical Journal* **321**: 917.

Journal of Gene Medicine, 2009 [updated March], 'Gene Therapy Clinical Trials Worldwide' – www.wiley.co.uk/genetherapy/clinical/.

Juengst, Eric T. and Grankvist, Hannah, 2007, 'Ethical issues in human gene transfer: A historical overview', Richard E. Ashcroft, Angus Dawson, Heather Draper, and John R. McMillan (eds), *Principles of Health Care Ethics*, second edition (Chichester: John Wiley & Sons): 789–96.

Kant, Immanuel, 1887, *The Philosophy of Law: An Exposition of the Fundamental Principles of Jurisprudence as the Science of Right* [1796], translated by W. Hastie (Edinburgh: T. and T. Clark, 1887) – oll.libertyfund.org/?option=com_staticxt&staticfile=show.php%3Ftitle=359&chapter=55777&layout=html&Itemid=27.

  1959, *Foundations of the Metaphysics of Morals* [1785b], translated by Lewis White Beck (Indianapolis, IN: Bobbs-Merril).

  1994, *Grounding for the Metaphysics of Morals* [*Grundlegung zur Metaphysik der Sitten* 1785a], in Immanuel Kant, *Ethical Philosophy*, translated by James W. Ellington, second edition (Indianapolis, IN: Hackett Publishing Company).

  1994, *Ethical Philosophy* [*Metaphysische Anfangsgründe der Tugendlehre* 1797a], translated by J. W. Ellington, second edition (Indianapolis, IN: Hackett Publishing Company).

  1999, *Metaphysical Elements of Justice* [*Metaphysische Anfangsgründe der Rechtslehre* 1797b], translated by J. Ladd, second edition (Indianapolis, IN: Hackett Publishing Company).

Kass, Leon R., 1985, *Toward a More Natural Science: Biology and Human Affairs* (New York, NY: The Free Press).

1994, *The Hungry Soul: Eating and the Perfecting of Our Nature* (New York, NY: The Free Press).

2002, *Life, Liberty, and the Defense of Dignity: The Challenge for Bioethics* (San Francisco, CA: Encounter Books).

2003, *The Beginning of Wisdom: Reading Genesis* (New York, NY: Free Press).

Kass, Leon R. and Kass, Amy A., 2000, *Wing to Wing, Oar to Oar: Readings on Courting and Marrying* (Notre Dame, IN: University of Notre Dame Press).

Kass, Leon R. and Wilson, James Q., 1998, *The Ethics of Human Cloning* (Washington, DC: The AEI Press).

Koch, Tom, 2000, 'Life quality vs the "quality of life": assumptions underlying prospective quality of life instruments in health care planning', *Social Science & Medicine* **51**: 419–28.

2001, 'Disability and difference: balancing social and physical constructions', *Journal of Medical Ethics* **27**: 370–6.

2005, 'The ideology of normalcy – the ethics of difference', *Journal of Disability Policy Studies* **16**: 123–9.

Korcz, Keith Allen, 2002, 'Two moral strategies regarding abortion', *Journal of Social Philosophy* **33**: 581–605.

Kuflik, Arthur, 2008, 'The "future like ours" argument and human embryonic stem cell research', *Journal of Medical Ethics* **34**: 417–21.

Kuhse, Helga and Singer, Peter, 1985, *Should the Baby Live? The Problem of Handicapped Infants* (Oxford: Oxford University Press).

Kuliev, A., Rechitsky, S., Tur-Kaspa, I., and Verlinsky, Y., 2005, 'Preimplantation genetics: Improving access to stem cell therapy', *Annals of the New York Academy of Sciences* **1054**: 223–7.

Laurie, Graeme T., 2002, *Genetic Privacy: A Challenge to Medico-Legal Norms* (Cambridge: Cambridge University Press).

Lee, Patrick, 1996, *Abortion and Unborn Human Life* (Washington, DC: Catholic University of America Press).

2004, 'The pro-life argument from substantial identity: A defence', *Bioethics* **18**: 249–63.

Levy, N., 2002, 'Deafness, culture, and choice', *Journal of Medical Ethics* **28**: 284–5.

Lukes, Steven, 1973, *Émile Durkheim: His Life and Work – A Historical and Critical Study* (London: Allen Lane/The Penguin Press).

Maclean, Anne, 1993, *The Elimination of Morality: Reflections on Utilitarianism and Bioethics* (London: Routledge).

Marquis, Don, 1989, 'Why abortion is immoral', *The Journal of Philosophy* **86**: 183–202.

2001, 'Deprivations, futures and the wrongness of killing', *Journal of Medical Ethics* **27**: 363–9.

2002, 'A defence of the potential future of value theory', *Journal of Medical Ethics* **28**: 198–201.

2004, 'Korcz's objections to the future-of-value argument', *Journal of Social Philosophy* **35**: 56–65.

2005, 'Savulescu's objections to the future of value argument', *Journal of Medical Ethics* **31**: 119–22.

Martinez, D. E., 1998, 'Mortality patterns suggest lack of senescence in hydra', *Experimental Gerontology* **33**: 217–25.

Matthews, Kirstin, 2007a, 'Overview of world human cloning policies', *The Connexions Project*, 3 August – http://cnx.org/content/m14834/latest/.

2007b, 'World cloning policies', *The Connexions Project*, 3 August – http://cnx.org/content/m14836/latest/.

2007c, 'Stem cells: A science and policy overview' – http://cnx.org/content/col10445/1.1.

McGleenan, Tony, 1998, 'The jurisprudence of genetic privacy', *Medicine, Health Care and Philosophy* **1**: 225–33.

McIntyre, Alison, 2004 [substantive revision 2009], 'Doctrine of double effect', *Stanford Encyclopedia of Philosophy* – plato.stanford.edu/entries/double-effect/.

Medawar, Peter B., 1952, *An Unsolved Problem of Biology* (London: H. K. Lewis).

Mendieta, Eduardo, 2004, 'Habermas on human cloning: The debate on the future of the species', *Philosophy & Social Criticism* **30**: 721–43.

Meyer, John R., 2006, 'Embryonic personhood, human nature, and rational ensoulment', *The Heythrop Journal* **47**: 206–25.

Milkov, Nikolay, 2005, 'The meaning of life: A topological approach', A.-T. Tymieniecka (ed.), *Analecta Husserliana* **84**: 217–34.

Mill, John Stuart, 1869, *On Liberty* [1859], fourth edition (London: Longman, Roberts & Green) – www.bartleby.com/130/5.html.

1987, *Utilitarianism* [1861], Jeremy Bentham and John Stuart Mill, *Utilitarianism and Other Essays*, edited by Alan Ryan (Harmondsworth: Penguin Books).

Muasher, Suheil, Garcia, Jairo, and Jones, Howard, 1984, 'Experience with diethylstilbestrol-exposed infertile women in a program of in vitro fertilisation', *Fertility and Sterility* **42**: 20–4.

Mundy, Liza, 2002, 'A world of their own', *Washington Post*, 31 March 2002, p. W22.

Munthe, Christian, 1999, *Pure Selection: The Ethics of Preimplantation Genetic Diagnosis and Choosing Children without Abortion* (Gothenburgh: Acta Universitatis Gothoburgensis).

National Conference of State Legislatures, 2008, 'State human cloning laws', January – www.ncsl.org/programs/health/Genetics/rt-shcl.htm.

National Institute of Health, 1998, *NIH Policy and Guidelines on the Inclusion of Children as Participants in Research involving Human Subjects* – http://grants.nih.gov/grants/guide/notice-files/not98-024.html.

Newson, Ainsley and Smajdor, Anna C., 2005, 'Artificial gametes: new paths to parenthood?', *Journal of Medical Ethics* **31**: 184–6.

Norsigian, Judy, 2004, 'Stem cell research and embryo cloning: Involving laypersons in the public debates', *New England Law Review* **39**: 527–34.

2005, 'Egg donation for IVF and stem cell research: Time to weigh the risks to women's health', *Different Takes*– 33 – popdev.hampshire.edu/projects/dt/33.

Nozick, Robert, 1974, *Anarchy, State, and Utopia* (Oxford: Blackwell).

Nuffield Council on Bioethics, *Critical Care Decisions in Fetal and Neonatal Medicine: Ethical Issues* – www.nuffieldbioethics.org/go/ourwork/neonatal/publication_406.html.

Nussbaum, Martha C., 2001, *Upheavals of Thought: The Intelligence of Emotions* (Cambridge: Cambridge University Press).

Oduncu, Fuat S., 2002, 'The role of non-directiveness in genetic counseling', *Medicine, Health Care and Philosophy* **5**: 53–63.

O'Neill, Onora, 2002, *Autonomy and Trust in Bioethics* (Cambridge: Cambridge University Press).

Orwell, George, 1949, *Nineteen Eighty-Four* (London: Secker and Warburg).

Papadimos, Thomas J. and Papadimos, Alexa T., 2004, 'The student and the ovum: The lack of autonomy and informed consent in trading genes for tuition', *Reproductive Biology and Endocrinology* **2**: 56 – www.pubmedcentral.nih.gov/articlerender.fcgi?artid=479702.

Parfit, Derek, 1984, *Reasons and Persons* (Oxford: Clarendon Press).

1986, 'Comments', *Ethics* **96**: 832–72.

Parker, Michael, 2007, 'The best possible child', *Journal of Medical Ethics* **33**: 279–83.

Parsons, Simon J., 2002, 'Present self-represented futures of value are a reason for the wrongness of killing', *Journal of Medical Ethics* **28**: 196–7.

Pascal, Blaise, 1995, *Pensées and Other Writings*, translated by Honor Levi (Oxford: Oxford University Press).

Pearson, Helen, 2006, 'Health effects of egg donation may take decades to emerge', *Nature* **442**: 607–8.

Pearson, Sue, Jia, Hepeng, and Kandachi, Keiko, 2004, 'China approves first gene therapy', *Nature Biotechnology* **22**: 3–4.

Pence, Gregory E. (ed.), 1998, *Flesh of My Flesh: The Ethics of Cloning Humans, A Reader* (Lanham, MD: Rowman & Littlefield).

Peng, Zhaohui, 2005, 'Current status of Gendicine in China: Recombinant human ad-p53 agent for treatment of cancers', *Human Gene Therapy* **16**: 1016–27.

Pennings, Guido and Steirteghem, André Van, 2004, 'The subsidiarity principle in the context of human embryonic stem cell research', *Human Reproduction* **19**: 1060–4.

Phillips, Michael, Rojas, Hermogenes, Frank, Patrick, and Harris, John, 2000, 'Immortality, anyone?', *Science* **288**: 1345.

Piraino, S., Boero, F., Aeschbach, B., and Schmid, V., 1996, 'Reversing the life cycle: Medusae transforming into polyps and cell transdifferentiation in *Turritopsis nutricula* (Cnidaria, Hydrozoa)', *The Biological Bulletin* **190**: 302.

Plato, 2007, *The Republic*, translated by Desmond Lee (Harmondsworth: Penguin Books).

Plessner, Helmut, 1981, *Die Stufen des Organischen* [1927], *Gesammelte Schriften* Volume IV (Frankfurt am Main: Suhrkamp).

Pontin, Jason, 2006, 'Is defeating aging only a dream?'– www.technologyreview.com/sens/.

Prainsack, Barbara and Seagal, Gil, 2006, 'The rise of genetic couplehood? A comparative view of premarital genetic testing', *BioSocieties* **1**: 17–36.

Prentice, David A. and Tarne, Gene, 2007, 'Treating diseases with adult stem cells', *Science* **315**: 328.

President's Council on Bioethics, 2002, *Human Cloning and Human Dignity: An Ethical Inquiry*, (Washington DC), July – bioethicsprint.bioethics.gov/reports/cloningreport/fullreport.html.

2003, *Beyond Therapy: Biotechnology and the Pursuit of Happiness* (Washington, DC) – www.bioethics.gov/reports/beyondtherapy/.

Purdy, Laura, 1995, 'Loving future people', Joan Callahan (ed.), *Reproduction, Ethics and the Law* (Bloomington, IN: Indiana University Press): 300–27.

Putnam, Hilary, 1999, 'Cloning people', Justine Burley (ed.), *The Genetic Revolution and Human Rights: The Oxford Amnesty Lectures* 1998 (Oxford: Oxford University Press): 1–13.

Qureshi, Naveen, Foote, Drucilla, Walters, Mark C., Singer, Sylvia T., Quirolo, Keith and Vichinsky, Elliott P., 2005, 'Outcomes of preimplantation genetic diagnosis therapy in treatment of β-thalassemia: A retrospective analysis', *Annals of the New York Academy of Sciences* **1054**: 500–3.

Rawls, John, 1972, *A Theory of Justice* (Oxford: Oxford University Press).

Reindal, Solveig Magnus, 2000, 'Disability, gene therapy and eugenics – a challenge to John Harris', *Journal of Medical Ethics* **26**: 89–94.

Rhodes, Rosamond, 1999, 'Abortion and assent', *Cambridge Quarterly of Healthcare Ethics* **8**: 416–27.

Richardson, D. M. (ed.), 1998, *Ecology and Biogeography of Pinus* (Cambridge: Cambridge University Press).

Robertson, John A., 2003, 'Extending preimplantation genetic diagnosis: the ethical debate', *Human Reproduction* **18**: 465–71.

Rowland, Robyn, 1987, 'Making women visible in the embryo experimentation debate', *Bioethics* **1**: 179–88.

Sandel, Michael J., 1982, *Liberalism and the Limits of Justice* (Cambridge: Cambridge University Press).

1996, *Democracy's Discontent: America in Search of a Public Philosophy* (Cambridge, MA: Harvard University Press).

2002, 'What's wrong with enhancement' – http://www.bioethics.gov/transcripts/dec02/session4.html.

2005a, *Public Philosophy: Essays on Morality in Politics* (Cambridge, MA: Harvard University Press).

2005b, 'The ethical implications of human cloning', *Perspectives in Biology and Medicine* **48**: 241–7.

2007, *The Case Against Perfection: Ethics in the Age of Genetic Engineering* (Cambridge, MA: The Belknap Press of Harvard University Press).

Saunders, Rhodri and Savulescu, Julian, 2008, 'Research ethics and lessons from Hwanggate: what can we learn from the Korean cloning fraud?', *Journal of Medical Ethics* **34**: 214–21.

Savulescu, Julian, 1998a, 'Consequentialism, reasons, value and justice', *Bioethics* **12**: 212–35.

1998b, 'The present-aim theory: a submaximizing theory of reasons', *Australasian Journal of Philosophy* **76**: 229–43.

1999, 'Desire-based and value-based normative reasons', *Bioethics* **13**: 405–13.

2001, 'Procreative beneficence: why we should select the best children', *Bioethics* **15**: 413–26.

2002a, 'Abortion, embryo destruction and the future of value argument', *Journal of Medical Ethics* **28**: 133–5.

2002b, 'Deaf lesbians, "designer disability", and the future of medicine', *British Medical Journal* **325**: 771–3.

2005, 'New breeds of humans: the moral obligation to enhance', *Ethics, Law and Moral Philosophy of Reproductive Biomedicine* **1**: 36–9.

SENS Foundation, 2009, 'Seven deadly things' – www.sens.org/index.php?pagename=mj_sens_repairing.

Shapshay, Sandra and Pimple, Kenneth D., 2007, 'Participation in biomedical research is an imperfect moral duty: A response to John Harris', *Journal of Medical Ethics* **33**: 414–17.

Sheldon, Sally, 2005, 'Saviour siblings and the discretionary power of the HFEA', *Medical Law Review* **13**: 403–11.

Sheldon, Sally and Wilkinson, Stephen, 2004, 'Should selecting saviour siblings be banned?', *Journal of Medical Ethics* **30**: 533–7.

2005, '"Saviour siblings": Hashmi and Whitaker – An unjustifiable and misguided distinction', *Pro-Choice Forum* – www.prochoiceforum.org.uk/irl_rep_tech_2.asp.

Sidgwick, Henry, 1907, *The Methods of Ethics* [1874], seventh edition (London: Macmillan).

Singer, Peter, 1979, *Practical Ethics* (Cambridge: Cambridge University Press).

2005, 'Ethics and disability: A response to Koch', *Journal of Disability Policy Studies* **16**: 130–3.

Smart, J. J. C., 1973, 'An outline of a system of utilitarian ethics' [1961], J. J. C. Smart and Bernard Williams (eds), *Utilitarianism: For and Against* (Cambridge: Cambridge University Press).

Smith, Adam, 1982, *The Wealth of Nations* [1776], edited by Andrew Skinner (Harmondsworth: Penguin Books).

Smith, Lynn and Fowler Byers, Jacqueline, 2002, 'Gene therapy in the post-Gelsinger era', *JONA's Healthcare Law, Ethics, & Regulation* 4: 104–10.

Snyder, Evan Y. and Loring, Jeanne F., 2006, 'Beyond fraud – stem cell research continues', *The New England Journal of Medicine* 354: 321–4.

Spar, Debora, 2007, 'The egg trade – Making sense of the market for human oocytes', *The New England Journal of Medicine* 356: 1289–91.

Sparrow, Robert, 2005, 'Defending Deaf culture – the case of cochlear implants', *The Journal of Political Philosophy* 13: 135–52.

Specter, Michael and Kolata, Gina, 1997, 'After decades of missteps, how cloning succeeded', *The New York Times*, 3 March – http://query.nytimes.com/gst/fullpage.html?res=9A04E0D71F31F930A35750C0A961958260.

Spriggs, Merle, 2002, 'Lesbian couple create a child who is deaf like them', *Journal of Medical Ethics* 28: 283.

Spriggs, Merle and Savulescu, Julian, 2002, 'Saviour siblings', *Journal of Medical Ethics* 28: 289.

Stanković, Bratislav, 2005, '"It's a designer baby": Opinions on regulation of preimplantation genetic diagnosis', *UCLA Journal of Law and Technology* 3– www.lawtechjournal.com/articles/2005/03_050713_stankovic.php

Stark, Andrew, 2006, *The Limits of Medicine: Cure or Enhancement* (Cambridge: Cambridge University Press).

Steinbrook, Robert, 2006, 'Egg donation and human embryonic stem-cell research', *The New England Journal of Medicine* 354: 324–6.

Stich, Stephen P., 1978, 'The recombinant DNA debate: A difficulty for Pascalian-style wagering', *Philosophy & Public Affairs* 7: 187–205.

Stretton, Dean, 2000, 'The argument from intrinsic value: A critique', *Bioethics* 14: 228–39.

Strong, Carson, 2005, 'Lost in translation: Religious arguments made secular', *American Journal of Bioethics* 5: 29–31.

Sullivan, Roger J., 1994, *An Introduction to Kant's Ethics* (Cambridge: Cambridge University Press).

Suter, Sonia M., 1998, 'Value neutrality and nondirectiveness: Comments on "Future directions in genetic counseling"', *Kennedy Institute of Ethics Journal* 8: 161–3.

Takahashi, K., Tanabe, K., Ohnuki, M., Narita, M., Ichisaka, T., Tomoda, K., and Yamanaka, S., 2007, 'Induction of pluripotent stem cells from adult human fibroblasts by defined factors', *Cell* 131: 861–72.

Takala, Tuija, 2003, 'Utilitarianism shot down by its own men?', *Cambridge Quarterly of Healthcare Ethics* **12**: 447–54.

2005, 'The many wrongs of human reproductive cloning', Matti Häyry, Tuija Takala, and Peter Herissone-Kelly (eds), *Bioethics and Social Reality* (Amsterdam: Rodopi): 53–66.

2007, 'Acts and omissions', R. E. Ashcroft, A. Dawson, H. Draper, and J. R. McMillan (eds), *Principles of Health Care Ethics*, second edition (Chichester: John Wiley & Sons): 273–6.

Takala, Tuija and Häyry, Matti, 2007, 'Benefiting from past wrongdoing, human embryonic stem cell lines, and the fragility of the German legal position', *Bioethics* **21**: 150–9.

Tännsjö, Torbjörn, 1998, *Hedonistic Utilitarianism* (Edinburgh: Edinburgh University Press).

Thomas, Cordelia, 2004, 'Pre-implantation testing and the protection of the "saviour sibling"', *Deakin Law Review* **9** – www.austlii.edu.au/au/journals/DeakinLRev/2004/5.html.

Thomson, James A., Itskovitz-Eldor, Joseph, Shapiro, Sander S., Waknitz, Michelle A., Swiergiel, Jennifer J., Marshall, Vivienne S. and Jones, Jeffrey M., 1998, 'Embryonic stem cell lines derived from human blastocysts', *Science* **282**: 1145–7.

Tooley, Michael, 1972, 'Abortion and infanticide', *Philosophy and Public Affairs* **2**: 37–65.

1985, *Abortion and Infanticide* (New York: Oxford University Press).

1998, 'Personhood', Helga Kuhse and Peter Singer (eds), *Companion to Bioethics* (Oxford: Blackwell): 117–26.

Torres-Padilla, Maria-Elena, Parfitt, David-Emlyn, Kouzarides, Tony, and Zernicka-Goetz, Magdalena, 2007, 'Histone arginine methylation regulates pluripotency in the early mouse embryo', *Nature* **445**: 214–18.

Turing, Alan, 1950, 'Computing machinery and intelligence', *Mind* **59**: 433–60.

UCL Institute of Child Health, 2007, 'Gene therapy for X-SCID; additional briefing', 18 December – www.ich.ucl.ac.uk/pressoffice/pressrelease_00592.

United Nations Educational, Scientific and Cultural Organization, 2004, *National Legislation Concerning Human Reproductive and Therapeutic Cloning* (Paris: Division of Ethics of Science and Technology).

United Nations, 2005, Press Release GA/10333 – www.un.org/News/Press/docs/2005/ga10333.doc.htm.

Universal Declaration on the Human Genome and Human Rights, 1997, adopted by the General Conference of UNESCO at its 29th session on 11 November 1997.

Vehmas, Simo, 2001, 'Assent and selective abortion: A response to Rhodes and Häyry', *Cambridge Quarterly of Healthcare Ethics* **10**: 433–40.

2002, 'Is it wrong to deliberately conceive or give birth to a child with mental retardation?', *Journal of Medicine and Philosophy* **27**: 47–63.

2004, 'Ethical analysis of the concept of disability', *Mental Retardation* **42**: 209–22.

Vehmas, Simo and Mäkelä, Pekka, 2008, 'A realist account of the ontology of impairment', *Journal of Medical Ethics* **34**: 93–5.

Verlinsky, Y., Rechitsky, S., Schoolcraft, W., Strom, C. and Kuliev, A., 2001, 'Preimplantation diagnosis for Fanconi anemia combined with HLA matching', *Journal of the American Medical Association* **285**: 3130–3.

Verlinsky, Y., Rechitsky, S., Cieslak, J., Tur-Kaspa, I., Morris, R. and Kuliev, A., 2005, 'Accuracy and outcomes of 3631 preimplantation genetic diagnosis (PGD) cycles performed in one center', *Fertility and Sterility* **84**: S98.

Vernon, McCay, 2005, 'Fifty years of research on the intelligence of deaf and hard-of-hearing children: A review of literature and discussion of implications', *Journal of Deaf Studies and Deaf Education* **10**: 225–31.

Warnock, Mary, 2002, *Making Babies: Is There a Right to Have Children?* (Oxford: Oxford University Press).

Warren, James, 2004, *Facing Death: Epicurus and His Critics* (Oxford: Clarendon Press).

Watson, James and Crick, Francis, 1953, 'Molecular structure of nucleic acids – A structure for deoxyribose nucleic acid', *Nature* **171**: 737–8.

Weber, Max, 1978, *Economy and Society* [1921], edited by Guenther Roth and Claus Wittich (Berkeley, CA: University of California Press).

Weikart, Richard, 2004, *From Darwin to Hitler: Evolutionary Ethics, Eugenics, and Racism in Germany* (New York, NY: Palgrave Macmillan).

Wells, H. G., 2005, *The Time Machine* [1895] (London: Penguin Books).

Wilkinson, Stephen, 2003, *Bodies for Sale: Ethics and Exploitation in the Human Body Trade* (London: Routledge).

Williams, Bernard, 1973a, 'A critique of utilitarianism', J. J. C. Smart and Bernard Williams (eds), *Utilitarianism: For and Against* (Cambridge: Cambridge University Press).

1973b, 'The Makropoulos case: Reflections on the tedium of immortality', Bernard Williams, *Problems of the Self: Philosophical Papers 1956–1972* (Cambridge: Cambridge University Press): 81–100.

Williams, G. C., 1957, 'Pleiotropy, natural selection and the evolution of senescence', *Evolution* **11**: 398–411.

Wilmut, I., Schnieke, A. E., McWhir, J., Kind, A. J., and Campbell, K. H. S., 1997, 'Viable offspring derived from fetal and adult mammalian cells', *Nature* **385**: 810–13.

Wilson, James M., 2005, 'Gendicine: The first commercial gene therapy product', *Human Gene Therapy* **16**: 1014.

Wu, D. C., Boyd, A. S., and Wood, K. J., 2007, 'Embryonic stem cell transplantation: potential applicability in cell replacement therapy and regenerative medicine', *Frontiers in Bioscience* **12**: 4525–35.

Yu, Junying, Vodyanik, Maxim A., Smuga-Otto, Kim, Antosiewicz-Bourget, Jessica, Frane, Jennifer L., Tian, Shulan, Nie, Jeff, Jonsdottir, Gudrun A., Ruotti, Victor, Stewart, Ron, Slukvin, Igor I., and Thomson, James A., 2007, 'Induced pluripotent stem cell lines derived from human somatic cells', *Science* **318**: 1917–20.

INDEX

abortion
  arguments against, 164–7
  harm resulting from, 82
  mother's assent to pregnancy, 62–3
  prenatal selection, 53
  rational tangibility, 30, 31
  reason vs. rationality, 68, 69
acceptance, 26, 35–40, 42–3
actual consent, 103
adult stem cells, 151
afterlife, 202–3
ageing, 20, 195–7
  see also considerable life extension
aids, genetic, 19
antagonistic pleiotropy, 197, 209
Aquinas, Thomas, 212–13, 215
Argentina, 125
Aristotle, 27, 52, 55–6, 57–8, 165
asexual reproduction, 134–6, 137
aspiration, 206, 207
assisted insemination, 33
assumed consent, 103
Australia, 100
Austria, 125
autonomy, 163–4

Babies by Design (Green) 217
Barrow, Paul, 205
beauty, 206, 207–8
Beeson, Diane, 155–6
beliefs, 44–5
beneficence, 156–60
benefits, 182–4, 223–4
Bentham, Jeremy, 27, 53, 184–5
best babies, the
  arguments against, 232, 233
  arguments for, 4, 231

considerations, 3–6, 22
everybody's acceptance, 234–5
genetic challenge, 225
moderate approach, 61–4, 70–2, 75
moral transcendence, 34–5
options, 52–5
parental duty, 4–6, 153
permissive approach, 64, 75
rational tangibility, 30
rationality of parental choices,
  75–7
restrictive approach, 58–61, 72
Western philosophical view, 55–8
biogerontology *see* considerable life
  extension
bodies, 165–6
bodily resurrection, 202–3
Bostrom, Nick, 39, 143–4
Brazil, 125
Brock, Dan, 155
'bubble boy' syndrome, 18, 176,
  182
Bush, George W., 149

capacity, 162
Case Against Perfection, The (Sandel)
  218
Causing Death and Saving Lives
  (Glover) 216
cells, 129, 198
change, resistance to, 39, 142–4, 217,
  224
  see also technological change
children, 63–4, 136–8
China, 175
Choosing Children (Glover), 216
Christianity, 116

circumcision, 105
cloning, reproductive
   arguments against, 12–13, 127–9,
     130–42, 153, 233
   arguments for, 13, 127–9, 231
   considerations, 11–13, 22
   designing humans, 131–42
   Dolly the sheep, 11–12, 124, 129
   meaning of, 126
   moral transcendence, 33
   prohibition, 130–1
   rationalities, 144–5
   regulation, 124–5
   vs. therapeutic cloning, 126, 146
   transhuman world, 142–4
coercion, 111–12
coherence, 44–5, 46, 228, 236–7
commodification, 121, 164
communitarianism, 229
communities
   deaf embryos, 90, 97
   genetic challenge, 226
   gradual human development,
     170–1
   reproductive cloning, 136–8
   see also societies
Condorcet, Antoine de, 188
consent, 103–4, 111–2, 161–4
consequentialism
   deaf embryos, 7, 8, 83–4, 86–7, 88–9,
     95–6
   embryonic stem cell research,
     152–3
   vs. moral transcendence, 32
   morality, 229
   rational tangibility as, 27, 30–1
   values, definition of, 184–7
considerable life extension
   arguments against, 21, 204–6,
     232–3, 234
   arguments for, 21, 206–11
   considerations, 19–22, 23
   everybody's acceptance, 235–6
   genetic challenge, 221
   identity, effects upon, 200–4
   life, meaning of, 212–15
   meaning of, 20
   moral transcendence, 33
   mortality, explanations for, 195–7

rational tangibility, 30
rationalities, 215–19
   social transcendence, 211–12
   somatic cell nuclear transfer, 129
   techniques, 197–200
consistency, 45, 46, 228
cryonics, 21
culture, 90, 97, 117
cyborgs, 21, 201–2

danger, 190–3
De Grey, Aubrey, 198–200
deaf embryos
   arguments against, 7, 8, 153, 233
   arguments for, 7–8
   considerations, 22
   legal neutrality argument, 86–7
   meaning of, 6–8
   medical view, 81–4, 88–9, 92–6
   nondirective compromise, 92–5,
     97–8
   parental autonomy, 225
   polarisation of views, 78–9
   rational tangibility, 30
   rationalities, 95–8
   social view, 81, 84–6, 90–5, 97
   techniques, 79–80
death, 20, 195–7
death-resistant cells, 199
decisions, rationality of, 44, 190–3
defective individuals, 131–4
democracy, and reproductive cloning,
   139
Denmark, 125
deontology, 7, 8, 27, 229
deoxyribonucleic acid (DNA), 2, 174,
   176, 196–7, 199
Derrida, Jacques, 138–9
designing humans, 131–42
determinism, technological, 189–90
development, technological, 187–9
Devolder, Katrien, 155
Diamond Blackfan anaemia (DBA),
   99–100
diethylstilbestrol (DES), 158–9
difference principle, 113
dignity
   arguments against scientific
     advances, 232–3

embryonic stem cell research, 15–16
gene therapies, 180
genetic challenge, 226
Kant's view, 117
parental responsibility, 59–60, 72–3
reproductive cloning, 12, 138–40
violation of, 5–6
disabilities, 85–6
disclosure of risks, 162
discrimination, 107–8
'do no harm' principle, 82, 88–9,
    93–4
Dolly the sheep (clone) 11–12, 124, 129
double effect, doctrine of, 110n.38
Down's syndrome, 5
Duchesneau, Sharon, 84, 85, 87, 91
duty, 157–8
dwarfism, 68–9

egg retrieval in embryo creation,
    153–64
embryo selection (ES), 79–80
embryo transfer (ET), 79–80
embryonic stem cell research
    adult stem cells, 151
    arguments against, 233
    arguments for, 231
    considerations, 14–16, 22
    creation of stem cells, 126–7
    destruction of embryos, 164–72
    everybody's acceptance, 235
    genetic challenge, 152–3, 172–3, 221
    and life extension, 200–1
    moral transcendence, 173
    rational tangibility, 30, 31,
        172–3
    rationalities, 172–3
    regulation, 147–8
    risks, 158–9, 173
    single cell removal, 151–2
    sources of stem cells, 148–52
    techniques, 146–7
    women, use of, 16, 22, 153–64,
        172–3, 231
embryos
    arguments against scientific
        advances, 232
    arguments for scientific advances,
        231

destruction of, 164–72
egg retrieval from women, 153–64
splitting, 126
status of, 148–52, 172
value of, 150, 152
ends, and means, 119–22
engagement, 205, 207
enhancements, 18–19, 180–2
Enlightenment, 187–8
entities that matter, 46, 228–9
Epicureanism, 213–14, 215
equality, 226
equipoise, 49–50
ethics
    complete ethical case, 227–9
    embryonic stem cell research, 152–3,
        172–3
    ethical rationalities, 46
    gene therapies, 193–4
    genethics, 236–7
    genetic challenge, 227
    humanity as category of, 132–4
    resolving differences of opinion,
        87–8
    self-understanding, 226
eugenics, 52, 54, 55, 94
    see also reproductive testing
Europe, 100, 127, 148
everybody's acceptance
    evaluation of, 42–3, 237
    genetic challenge, 234–6
    as rational approach, 26, 35–40
evolution, 196
exploitation, 111–12, 161–4
extracellular junk, 199
extrinsic mortality, 196

fairness, 107, 156–60
families, 134–6, 137, 138–40,
    170–1
Fanconi's anaemia, 99–100
fear, in decision making, 190–3
feasibility, 159–60
financial incentives, 160–4
Fletcher family (saviour sibling case)
    100, 111–12
France, 148, 176
freedom, 208, 226–7
function, 18–19

future of human beings, 90–1, 97, 166,
   167–8, 171
Future of Human Nature, The
   (Habermas) 140, 217–18

Gelsinger, Jesse, 175–6, 182
Gendicine, 175
gene therapies
   arguments against, 17–18, 233–4
   benefits vs. harms, 182–4
   considerations, 16–19, 22
   enhancement vs. therapy, 180–2
   everybody's acceptance,
      235–6
   genetic challenge, 221
   germ-line gene therapies, 17, 177–80,
      224–5, 233–4, 235–6
   precautionary principle, 190–3
   rational tangibility, 30
   rationalities, 193–4
   somatic gene therapies, 17, 177–80,
      224–5, 233–4
   technological determinism, 189–90
   technological optimism, 187–8
   technological pessimism, 187,
      188–9
   technological voluntarism, 189–90
   trials, 174–7
   values, definition of, 184–7
genethics, 236–7, 239–40
genetic challenge
   alternative approaches, 24–7
   arguments against scientific
      advances, 220, 223–7, 232
   arguments for scientific advances,
      220, 223–7, 229–31, 234
   basic tenets, 220–3
   considerations, 22–3
   everybody's acceptance argument,
      234–6
   genethics, 236–7
   meaning of, 1
   moral transcendence, 232–4
   nonconfrontational notion of
      rationality, 227–9, 237–40
   rational tangibility, 230–1
genetic privacy, 109
genetic selection

arguments against, 7, 8, 153, 233
arguments for, 7–8
considerations, 22
deaf embryos, 6–8
legal neutrality argument, 86–7
medical view of deaf embryos, 81–4,
   88–9, 92–6
nondirective compromise, 92–5,
   97–8
parental autonomy, 225
polarisation of views, 78–9
rational tangibility, 30
rationalities, 95–8
social view of deaf embryos, 81,
   84–6, 90–5, 97
techniques, 79–80
genetic testing
   arguments for, 4
   considerations, 3–6
   parental duty, 4–6
   saviour siblings, 99–101
Georgia, 125
Germany, 125, 127, 148–9
germ-line gene therapies, 17, 177–80,
   224–5, 233–4, 235–6
   see also gene therapies
giftedness, 34–5
Glannon, Walter, 209
Glover, Jonathan
   considerable life extension, 216
   embryonic stem cell research, 172
   ethical approach, 25, 27,
      42, 46
   gene therapies, 178–9, 181
   genethics work, 239–40
   genetic challenge, 222, 236–7
   means, individuals as, 112–13, 115
   rational tangibility, 28–31, 40–1,
      230, 232
   rationality of, 46
   saviour siblings, 122–3
   technological change, 190
   values, definition of, 185
God
   existence of (Pascal's wager) 191–2
   and immortality, 211, 212–13
   'playing' (acting as) 129, 130, 131–2,
      177

gods, and immortality, 206, 207,
213–14
gradual human development, 169
Green, Ronald
considerable life extension, 217
embryonic stem cell research, 172
ethical approach, 25, 26, 27, 46
everybody's acceptance, 37–40,
42–3
gene therapies, 179, 180–1
genethics work, 239–40
genetic challenge, 222, 234–7
means, individuals as, 116–18
rationality of, 46
saviour siblings, 123
technological change, 190
Gurnham, David, 138–40

Habermas, Jürgen
considerable life extension, 217–18
embryonic stem cell research, 172
ethical approach, 25, 26, 27, 46
everybody's acceptance, 35–8, 39,
42–3
gene therapies, 179, 181–2
genethics work, 239–40
genetic challenge, 222, 234–7
means, individuals as, 114–15
precaution, 61, 74–5
rationality of, 46
reproductive cloning, 140–2
saviour siblings, 123
technological change, 190
harm
vs. benefit, 182–4
gene therapies, 178–9, 182–4
gradual human development,
171–2
physical harm, 10
psychological harm, 10, 106–7
women in embryonic stem cell
research, 157–8, 163–4
harmed condition, 83–5, 93–4
Harris, John
considerable life extension, 206–11,
213, 214, 215
deaf embryos, 83–4, 86, 88–9,
95–6

embryonic stem cell research, 154–5,
156–9, 172–3
ethical approach, 25, 27, 42, 46
gene therapies, 178, 180, 181, 182
genethics work, 239–40
genetic challenge, 222, 236–7
means, individuals as, 110–12, 115
organ donors, 105–6
parity of reasoning, 224–5
rational tangibility, 28–31, 40–1,
230, 232
saviour siblings, 122–3
technological change, 190
values, definition of, 185
Hartley, David, 186
Hashmi family (saviour sibling case)
100
Hawking, Stephen, 85
Hegel, Georg Wilhelm Friedrich, 188
Herder, Johann Gottfried von, 188–9
Herissone-Kelly, Peter, 63–4, 70–1, 76
Holm, Søren, 169–72, 192–3, 209
hope, in decision making, 190–3
human body, 121–2
Human Fertilisation and Embryology
Authority (HFEA) 100–1, 111–12,
147–8
human leucocyte antigen (HLA) 99
human reproductive cloning
arguments against, 12–13, 127–9,
130–42, 153, 233
arguments for, 13, 127–9, 231
designing humans, 131–42
meaning of, 126
moral transcendence, 33
prohibition, 130–1
rationalities, 144–5
regulation, 124–5
vs. therapeutic cloning, 126, 146
transhuman world, 142–4
humanity
end, treatment as an, 119–22
as ethical category, 132–4
and reproductive cloning, 140–2
science, argument for, 226
self-understanding, 36–7, 140–2,
226
social transcendence, 211–12

human–machine interfaces, 201–2
Hwang Woo Suk, 155

Iceland, 125
identity, 200–4
immortality (considerable life
    extension)
  arguments against, 21, 204–6,
    232–3, 234
  arguments for, 21, 206–11
  considerations, 19–22, 23
  everybody's acceptance, 235–6
  genetic challenge, 221
  identity, effects upon, 200–4
  life, meaning of, 212–15
  meaning of, 20
  moral transcendence, 33
  mortality, explanations for, 195–7
  rational tangibility, 30
  rationalities, 215–19
  social transcendence, 211–12
  somatic cell nuclear transfer, 129
  techniques, 197–200
  see also mortality
impartial co-legislation, 117–18
in vitro fertilisation (IVF)
  deaf embryo selection, 79–80
  embryonic stem cell research, 146,
    149–50, 159–60
  saviour siblings, 99
  sex and reproduction, 33
indefinite life extension, 21
induced pluripotent cells (iPCs) 151
infanticide, 52–3
information, 162
insofar as, 44
instrumental use of people, 109–18,
    119–22, 226
  see also means, individuals as
integrity, 117, 140–2
interest (personal) 205, 207
intracellular junk, 199
intrinsic mortality, 196
invasive procedures, 103–6

justice
  considerable life extension, 210–11
  evaluation of genethics, 236–7

genetic challenge, 226
women in embryonic stem cell
    research, 156–60

Kant, Immanuel
  ends and means, 119–22
  everybody's acceptance, 27
  infanticide, 52
  means, individuals as, 113, 116–18
  parental responsibility, 56–8
  saviour siblings, 123
Kass, Leon
  considerable life extension, 211–12,
    213, 215
  embryonic stem cell research, 172
  ethical approach, 25, 26, 27, 42, 46
  gene therapies, 180, 181
  genethics work, 239–40
  genetic challenge, 222, 236–7
  moral transcendence, 31–3, 35, 41,
    232–4
  mortality, benefits of, 204–6
  parity of reasoning, 224–5
  rationality of, 46
  reproductive cloning, 134–6
  saviour siblings, 123
  technological change, 190
killing, 28–30, 164–7, 169–72
Koch, Tom, 87

Lee, Patrick, 165–6
legality, 78–9, 80–1, 86–7, 92–5
leukaemia virus, 176
liberty, 160–4, 226–7
life
  choice of longer life, 208
  gradual human development, 169
  loss of, 195–7, 223
  meaning of, 31–5, 41, 212–15
  moral transcendence, 31–5, 41
  right to, 62–3
  sanctity of, 164–7, 172, 226
  social transcendence, 211–12
  'worth living' categories, 29–31
life extension
  arguments against, 21, 204–6,
    232–3, 234
  arguments for, 21, 206–11

considerations, 19–22, 23
everybody's acceptance, 235–6
genetic challenge, 221
identity, effects upon, 200–4
life, meaning of, 212–15
moderate life extension, 20
moral transcendence, 33
mortality, explanations for, 195–7
rational tangibility, 30
rationalities, 215–19
social transcendence, 211–12
somatic cell nuclear transfer, 129
stem cell research, 200–1
techniques, 197–200
Lippman, Abby, 155–6
longevity *see* considerable life
    extension
long-term impacts, 45–6, 228–9
Loring, Jeanne, 156
love, 206, 207–8

male circumcision, 105
Marquis, Don, 166, 168, 172
McCullough, Candace, 84, 85,
    87, 91
means, individuals as
    considerations, 22
    ends and means, 119–22
    genetic challenge, 221, 226
    saviour siblings, 9–11, 109–18,
      119–22, 153
    techniques, 99–100
    women in embryonic stem cell
      research, 164
measuring, in ethical assessment,
    228–9
medical nanorobots, 201
Methods of Ethics, The (Sidgwick), 51,
    236
Mexico, 125
Mill, John Stuart, 57–8, 86–7, 185
mind, role of the, 32
mind uploads, 21, 202–3
mitochondrial mutations, 199
moral transcendence
    evaluation of, 41, 237
    genetic challenge, 232–4
    as rational approach, 26, 31–5, 173

morality
    arguments against scientific
      advances, 233–4
    arguments for scientific advances,
      231
    deaf embryos, 82–6, 88–9, 90–5
    embryos, status of, 172
    embryos, value of, 150, 152
    ethical rationalities, 46
    everybody's acceptance, 234–6
    gene therapies, 193–4
    and legality, 78–9, 80–1
    moral norms, 37–40
    and mortality, 206
    mortality, benefits of, 208
    natural morality, 212–15
    nonconfrontational notion of
      rationality, 43–8, 229
    saviour siblings, 101–3
mortality
    benefits of, 204–6, 208
    life, meaning of, 212–15
    possible explanations, 195–7
    social transcendence, 211–12
    see also immortality (considerable
      life extension)
multipotent stem cells, 14
mystery, loss of, 138–40

nanorobots, 201
Nash family (saviour sibling case),
    100–1
natural law, 229
natural morality, 212–15
necessity, as argument, 153–6
negotiation, in ethical assessment, 229
nonconfrontational notion of
    rationality
    beliefs, 44–5
    coherence, 44–5, 228
    complete ethical case, 227–9
    consistency, 45, 228
    decisions, 44
    entities that matter, 46, 228–9
    genetic challenge, 227–9, 237–40
    insofar as, 44
    long-term impacts, 45–6, 228–9
    morality, 43–8, 229

nonconfrontational notion of
    rationality (*cont.*)
  optimisation, 45–6, 228–9
  purpose of, 237–40
nondirective compromise for deaf
    embryos, 92–5, 97–8
noninvasive procedures, 106–8
nonviable embryos, 149–50
Norsigian, Judy, 155–6
Norway, 125
Nozick, Robert, 113–14
nuclear mutations, 198–9
nuclear transfer, 124, 125–6, 146

Odysseus, 206
optimisation, 45, 228–9
optimism, technological, 187–8
Ord, Toby, 39, 143–4
organ donors, 105, 201
ornithine transcarbamylase deficiency
    (OTCD) 175–6
ova harvesting, 153–64

pain, 171–2
Papadimos, Alexa, 161–3
Papadimos, Thomas, 161–3
parental autonomy, 225, 233
parental control, 136–8
parental duty, 4–6, 22, 112, 153, 231
parental love, 38, 225
parental responsibility
  arguments against, 232, 233
  arguments for scientific advances,
    4, 231
  considerable life extension, 211–12
  gene therapies, 179–80, 181–2
  genetic challenge, 225
  legal permissiveness, 94
  moderate approach, 61–4, 70–2, 75
  options, 52–5
  permissive approach, 64, 75
  rationalities, 70–2, 75–7
  restrictive approach, 58–61, 72
  Western philosophical view, 55–8
Parfit, Derek, 203–4
parity of reasoning arguments, 44–5,
    224–5, 228, 231, 233
Pascal, Blaise (Pascal's wager), 191–3

Pennings, Guido, 154
personhood
  arguments for embryo destruction,
    167–9
  gradual human development,
    169–72
  rationalities, 172
Peru, 125
pessimism, technological, 187, 188–9
physical harm, 10
Pimple, Kenneth, 157–8
Plato, 52, 54, 55, 57–8
pluripotent stem cells, 14, 147
polite bystander's view, 50
potential, 171
precaution
  gene therapies, 190–3
  parental responsibility, 60–1,
    74–5
  precautionary principle, 190–3
  and risk, 6, 223–4
preimplantation genetic diagnosis
    (PGD)
  best babies, the, 53–4
  deaf embryo selection, 79–80
  nonviable embryo identification, 149
  saviour siblings, 99, 103, 104, 106
prenatal selection, 53
privacy, genetic, 109
procreation *see* reproduction
procreative beneficence, 64–7, 70
proxy consent, 104
prudence, in ethical theory, 236–7
psychological harm, 10, 106–7
Putnam, Hilary, 138–9

rational consent, 103–4, 108–9
rational tangibility
  evaluation of, 40–1, 237
  genetic challenge, 230–1
  as rational approach, 25, 28–31,
    172–3
rationalities
  arguments against scientific
    advances, 232–4
  arguments for scientific advances,
    229–31
  arithmetical rationality, 67–70

complete ethical case, 227–9
considerable life extension, 215–19
deaf embryos, 95–8
embryonic stem cell research, 172–3
gene therapies, 193–4
immortality (considerable life
    extension) 215–19
moral norms, 37–40
parental responsibility, 70–2, 75–7
personhood, 172
reflective equilibrium, 48–9
reproductive cloning, 144–5
saviour siblings, 108–9, 122–3
technological change, 193–4
see also everybody's acceptance;
    moral transcendence;
    nonconfrontational notion of
    rationality; rational tangibility
Rawls, John, 113, 114, 115
reasoned willing, 116
reflective equilibrium, 48–9
reflective equipoise, 49–50
regulation
    control of risks, 39
    embryonic stem cell research,
        147–8
    human reproductive cloning,
        124–5
    saviour siblings, 100–1
reproduction
    asexual reproduction, 134–6, 137
    freedom of, 225, 233
    moral transcendence, 32–3, 41
    procreative beneficence, 64–7, 70
    social transcendence, 211–12
reproductive cloning
    arguments against, 12–13, 127–9,
        130–42, 153, 233
    arguments for, 13, 127–9, 231
    considerations, 11–13, 22
    designing humans, 131–42
    Dolly the sheep, 11–12, 124
    meaning of, 126
    moral transcendence, 33
    prohibition, 130–1
    rationalities, 144–5
    regulation, 124–5
    vs. therapeutic cloning, 126, 146

transhuman world, 142–4
reproductive selection ('best babies')
    arguments against, 232, 233
    arguments for, 4, 231
    considerations, 3–6, 22
    everybody's acceptance, 234–5
    genetic challenge, 225
    moderate approach, 61–4, 70–2, 75
    moral transcendence, 34–5
    options, 52–5
    parental duty, 4–6, 153
    permissive approach, 64, 75
    rational tangibility, 30
    rationality of parental choices,
        75–7
    restrictive approach, 58–61, 72
    Western philosophical view, 55–8
reproductive testing, 3–6
resource allocation, 91–2, 97, 182–4
resurrection of the body, 202–3
reversal test, 39, 143–4, 217
Rhodes, Rosamond, 62–3, 71–2
risks
    assessment of, 223–4
    disclosure, 162
    embryonic stem cell research, 158–9,
        173
    precaution, 6, 190–3, 223–4
    regulation, 39
Romanticism, 187, 188–9
Rowland, Robyn, 158–9

Sandel, Michael
    considerable life extension, 218–19
    embryonic stem cell research, 172
    ethical approach, 25, 26, 27,
        42, 46
    gene therapies, 179–80, 181–2
    genethics work, 239–40
    genetic challenge, 222, 236–7
    means, individuals as, 114–15
    moral transcendence, 31–2, 33–5, 41,
        232–4
    rationality of, 46
    reproductive cloning, 136–8
    saviour siblings, 123
    solidarity, 60, 74
    technological change, 190

saviour siblings
    arguments against, 9–11, 122, 153,
        232, 233
    arguments for, 9
    considerations, 9–11, 22
    ends and means, 119–22
    everybody's acceptance, 235
    genetic challenge, 221
    invasive procedures, 103–6
    as means, 9–11, 109–18, 119–22, 153
    morality, 101–3
    noninvasive procedures, 106–8
    privacy, genetic, 109
    rational tangibility, 30
    rationalities, 108–9, 122–3
    techniques, 99–100
Savulescu, Julian, 64, 76, 77, 86–7, 155
science, argument for, 226
selection, consequences of, 6
self-preservation, 32
self-understanding, 36–7, 140–2, 226
sensing, 229
seriousness, 206, 207
sex, 134–6, 137
    see also reproduction
Shapshay, Sandra, 157–8
Sidgwick, Henry, 51, 236–7
slippery slope, 10, 61, 193, 224, 231
Slovakia, 125
Smith, Adam, 188
Snyder, Evan, 156
social goods, 226
social perception, 170–1
social transcendence, 211–12
societies
    considerable life extension, 208–10
    mortality, benefits of, 204–5
    parental responsibility, 67
    and reproductive cloning, 138–40
    social perception, 170–1
    social transcendence, 211–12
    see also communities
solidarity
    arguments against scientific
        advances, 232–3
    embryonic stem cell research,
        15–16
    genetic challenge, 226

    meaning of, 6
    moral transcendence, 34–5
    parental responsibility, 60, 74
    reproductive cloning, 137–8
somatic cell nuclear transfer, 124,
    125–6, 129, 146
somatic gene therapies, 17, 177–80,
    224–5, 233–4
    see also gene therapies
souls, 165
South Africa, 125
Spain, 125
spiritual afterlife, 202–3
sports, 34
state role, 67
status quo bias, 143–4, 217, 224
Steirteghem, André Van, 154
stem cell lines, 147
stem cell research
    adult stem cells, 151
    arguments against, 233
    arguments for, 231
    considerations, 14–16, 22
    creation of stem cells, 126–7
    destruction of embryos,
        164–72
    everybody's acceptance, 235
    genetic challenge, 152–3, 221
    and life extension, 200–1
    moral transcendence, 173
    rational tangibility, 30, 31,
        172–3
    rationalities, 172–3
    regulation, 147–8
    risks, 158–9, 173
    single cell removal, 151–2
    sources of stem cells, 148–52
    techniques, 146–7
    women, use of, 16, 22, 153–64,
        172–3, 231
Strategies for Engineered Negligible
    Senescence (SENS) 198
supernumerary embryos, 149–50

Takala, Tuija, 192–3
technological change
    determinism, 189–90
    optimism, 187–8

pessimism, 187, 188–9
rationalities, 193–4
voluntarism, 189–90
teleology, 27
teleportation, 203–4
telomeres, 196–7
thalassaemia, 54, 99–100
therapeutic cloning, 126, 146
therapies, 18–19, 180–2
Thomas, Aquinas *see* Aquinas, Thomas
tissue stiffening, 199
totipotent stem cells, 14, 146–7
tradition, 226
transcendence, 211–12
transhuman world, 142–4
transplantation of organs, 201
Turing, Alan, 133

uncertainty, 190–3
understanding, in financial arrangements, 162
unipotent stem cells, 14
uniqueness, loss of, 13, 140–2
United Kingdom, 100–1, 125, 126–7, 147–8, 160, 176
United Nations, 124–5, 126–7
United Nations Educational, Scientific and Cultural Organization (UNESCO) 12, 124–5

United States
cloning regulation, 127
embryonic stem cell research, 148–9, 160
gene therapy trials, 174–6, 176
saviour siblings, 100–1
universality of moral rules, 35–8, 236–7
utilitarianism, 32

values, definition of, 184–7
virtue, 206, 208
virtue theory, 7
voluntariness, 161
voluntarism, technological, 189–90
vulnerability, 15–16

Weber, Max, 76
Whitaker family (saviour sibling case), 100
Wilmut, Ian, 124
Wilson, James, 135–6
women, in embryonic stem cell research, 16, 22, 153–64, 172–3, 231

X-linked severe combined immunodeficiency (X-SCID) 18, 176